Traditions and Transitions in Israel Studies

SUNY Series in Israeli Studies
Russell Stone, editor

TRADITIONS AND TRANSITIONS
IN ISRAEL STUDIES

Books on Israel, Volume VI

Edited by
Laura Z. Eisenberg
Neil Caplan
Naomi B. Sokoloff, and
Mohammed Abu-Nimer

State University of New York Press

Published by
State University of New York Press, Albany

Printed in the United States of America

For information, address State University of New York Press,
90 State Street, Suite 700, Albany, NY 12207

Production by Christine L. Hamel
Marketing by Jennifer Giovani

Library of Congress Cataloging in Publication Data

Traditions and transitions in Israel studies / edited by Laura Zittrain Eisenberg . . . [et al.].
p. cm. (Books on Israel ; v. 6) (SUNY series in Israeli studies)
Includes bibliographical references.
ISBN 0-7914-5585-8 (alk. paper) — ISBN 0-7914-5586-6 (pbk.)
1. Israel—Social conditions—20th century. 2. Palestinian Arabs—Israel—Social conditions—20th century. 3. Israel—Politics and government—20th century. 4. Arab-Israeli conflict—1993—Peace. 5. Israel—Foreign public opinion. 6. Israel—Ethnic relations. 7. Israel—Book reviews. I. Eisenberg, Laura Zittrain. II. Association for Israel Studies. III. Series. IV. Series: SUNY series in Israeli studies

DS102.95.B66 1988 vol. 6
[DS126.5]
956.9405—dc21 2002026679

10 9 8 7 6 5 4 3 2 1

Contents

Whither Post-Zionism?

Peace Process

Israel Studies Around the World

Introduction

The relatively young field of "Israel Studies" continues to thrive. The essays gathered in this volume showcase sixty-five recent books (more than half of them published in languages other than English) on a wide range of topics relating to Israel. In the tradition of the preceding five volumes in the *Books on Israel* series, this collection is interdisciplinary in nature, encompassing contributions from social science and the humanities. Each chapter goes beyond the limits of the standard review "essay" to use selected works as starting-points for original examinations of the state of scholarship within various fields dealing with Israel. At the same time, the contributors explore recent changes in Israeli society and politics as revealed through their respective fields of expertise.

Volume 6 includes several distinctive features, reflecting the changing interests among Israel Studies researchers and writers. One is the scholarly "trialogue" that opens the volume. A reassessment of Israel's policies leading to the 1956 Sinai/Suez War, this tripartite exchange takes the debates involving the "new historians" onto new ground. A second innovation is the inclusion of essays specifically devoted to recent publications dealing with political, social, and educational changes among Arab citizens of Israel. Another novel feature is the closing series of essays offering perspectives on Israel Studies from around the world.

Many of the essays in volume 6 are themselves explicitly interdisciplinary, and readers will note that the volume is not divided, as in the past, into sections on literature, politics, history, or other traditional disciplines. Rather, many essays offer multiple approaches to pressing issues in both academia and in Israeli society in general. So, for instance, Rachel Feldhay Brenner's essay on the Holocaust and the post-Holocaust generation encompasses history, literature, and psychology, while Ruth Amir and Leah Rosen's essay on multiculturalism deals with law, anthropology, sociology, history and philosophy. In similar fashion, David Newman discusses space and territory by combining questions of geography, sociology, and political science. These are but a few examples. The multifaceted essays collected in this volume offer not only interdisciplinary breadth but also reflect, and contribute to, an exciting integration of scholarly approaches in the field of Israel Studies.

Scholarship about Israel is no stranger to controversy, criticism, and self-criticism, and this volume explores and fully reflects many current issues of contention in Israeli academic circles and society at large. Volume 6 of *Books on Israel* grapples, inter alia, with the complex problems of multiculturalism in the Jewish State, inequalities in the political and economic status of Arab and Jewish citizens, the relationship between the state and Jewish religious identity, the best path to peace, and the impact of newly available archival material on the treatment of Israeli history. Thanks to the variety of perspectives adopted by the volume's contributors, readers will not find dull dogma or predictable uniformity, but will rather get an authentic taste of the lively clash of ideas and visions that increasingly characterizes the field. Whether this is a sign of the robust state of Israel Studies or an unhealthy penchant for self-excoriation is itself a question in dispute. The persistence of a post-Zionist perspective among many of the essays reflects the domination of Israel Studies in the 1990s by a wave of scholars questioning the ideological and cultural foundations of Zionism. Evidence of a scholarly backlash had already begun as this collection was being prepared for publication. The editors of the next volume of *Books on Israel* will no doubt want to explore the emergent stream of work that challenges the current dominant school of "post-Zionist" analysis. Whatever the merits of the post-Zionist and anti-post-Zionist arguments, the essays in this volume reflect the fact that some of the sharpest criticism of Israeli society and politics comes from within Israel—at the very time, paradoxically, when writers in Germany, Italy, and China seem to be abandoning many inherited anti-Israel positions in favor of a more nuanced and sympathetic understanding of the country and its people.

Since the preparation of this book, Israel and the Palestinians have become locked in another round of sustained violence, with the "Madrid/Oslo" peace process in tatters. Clearly, these new events have significant social, political, economic and cultural implications that no academic writing can safely prophesy; yet, our understanding of Israel in both calm and troubled times is enhanced with the benefit of the background provided by the academic contributions gathered together here.

We, the editors, have endeavored to produce a volume that conveys an accurate overview of the issues and the scholarship in the arena of Israel Studies at the end of the 1990s and at the beginning of the twenty-first century. In editing individual submissions, we have sought to help each author articulate his or her own views, regardless of our personal visions of how we would like to see the field or Israeli society develop. The opinions of the contributors are their own. Our mandate, as editors, has been to accurately convey the vigorous discussions that mark, and contribute to, the evolving field of Israel Studies.

Part 1

History and Memory

1. Reassessing Israel's Road to Sinai/Suez, 1956: A "Trialogue"

During the late 1980s and early 1990s, one of Israel's most popular academic controversies involved the "new historians" and their treatment of the 1948 war. Advancing the historiographical debate to new ground and to a new generation of historians, Haifa University historian Motti Golani published in 1997 (with Israel's Ministry of Defense publishing house) an important two-volume study entitled, "There Will Be War this Summer": Israel on the Road to the Sinai War, 1955–56. *The book, along with Golani's lectures and articles, that reassessed the leadership roles of Minister of Defense David Ben-Gurion and Chief of Staff Moshe Dayan, generated considerable discussion and controversy among academics as well as among military and political personalities who were active during that period.*

This essay features translated adaptations of reviews of "There Will Be War this Summer" *originally published in Hebrew in 1998 and 1999 by two prominent Israeli scholars, Mordechai Bar-On and Benny Morris, followed by a rejoinder written specially for* Books on Israel *by Golani.*

Motti Golani, *"There Will Be War this Summer": Israel on the Road to the Sinai War, 1955–56,* 2 vols., Tel Aviv: Ministry of Defense Press/ Ma'arachot, 1997 (in Hebrew: *Tihiyeh Milhama ba-Kayitz: Yisra'el ba-Derekh le-Milhemet Sinai, 1955–56*).

Mordechai Bar-On,
Yad-Yitzhak Ben-Zvi

Seeking a War?[1]

The title of Golani's important new book, *There Will Be War Next Summer,* refers to an Egyptian-Israeli war that strategic experts in Israel, as well as in the British Middle East listening posts (erroneously) predicted might break out sometime during the summer of 1956. The book adds an important new dimension to the scholarly research of the events that led to the Suez War that did erupt in late October of that year. The first generation of serious research on the subject worked primarily in the diplomatic archives that were opened to historians in the late 1980s. Golani has also had access to much of the relevant documentary material stored in the archives of the Israel Defense Forces (IDF), closed to researchers hitherto. He has made ample use of documents produced in the different departments of the IDF General Staff, notably the Departments of Operation, Strategic Planning, and Intelligence. This enabled him to present a more in-depth picture of the military aspects of the war.

Of special pertinence is the detailed treatment of the changes in the strategic doctrine of the IDF, which from the end of 1953 focused on the preemption of offensive war plans contemplated by the Arab armies through a first-strike initiative. Golani also describes in great detail how, during 1955, the Israeli military elite came to the conclusion that the 1949 Armistice Agreements had ceased to serve Israel's security requirements and how many began to look for an opportunity to change these arrangements and the territorial boundaries delineated by them. These changes led General Dayan (IDF chief of staff from the end of 1953 until the start of 1958) to seek a military confrontation that would enable the Israelis to strike first and to bring about a basic change in Israel's security parameters.

Unlike previous periodization that started the countdown to the Sinai campaign in the fall of 1955, with Egypt's President Gamal Abdel-Nasser's announcement of the large arms deal he had concluded with the Soviets, Golani prefers to begin his story in the spring of 1955. At that time Ben-Gurion had recently returned from a year's absence in Sde Boqer to become once again minister of defense. In Golani's perception, sometime during April or May 1955, under the strong encouragement of Dayan, Ben-Gurion adopted an offensive posture and looked for an early opportunity to strike at Egyptian forces in the Sinai and to conquer the Gaza Strip, the area around the Straits of Tiran and perhaps a strip of land connecting the two areas. According to Golani, all the smaller operations initiated by Israel against the Egyptian army during the summer and fall of that year were not meant merely to redress local grievances, but primarily to trigger a major conflagration.

The notion that a war with Egypt might break out sometime in the summer of 1956 was often mentioned among the military elite of Israel during the final months of 1955. Golani does not see this as a mere appreciation of the situation, but rather as a declaration of intention, or at least a "self-fulfilling prophecy." The exact timing of the war eventually became contingent upon the requirements of the French and British in their struggle against Nasser, but, according to Golani, the decision to launch an attack in the Sinai had already been taken more than a year before the nationalization of the Suez Canal in late July 1956, which brought about a general international crisis.

Another thesis that Golani presents throughout his book is that the prime mover of the events was not the aging Ben-Gurion, but rather the young Dayan, whose mind was totally fixated on the need to confront the Egyptian army. Despite his decision, taken in principle, to look for an opportunity to change the nature of Israel's relations with Egypt, Ben-Gurion was full of hesitations, stemming primarily from his fears of negative international repercussions. But Dayan, assisted by Shimon Peres, director-general of the Ministry of Defense at the time, kept prodding the government to initiate a war that he deemed vital to Israel's security.

Golani tries to create the impression that it was Dayan who led Ben-Gurion to the decision to launch the war. Thus, for example, he tells us that the strategic planning that developed among members of the General Staff in 1954 "may help us to understand how Dayan succeeded in bringing about a new security policy in 1955" (p. 50). He also adds a psychological explanation: "Dayan provided the seventy-year-old leader (Ben-Gurion), whose physical stamina and political authority were on the wane, with the energies which he no longer had in him" (p. 614). According to Golani, Ben-Gurion "needed help to come to a decision" (p. 616).

On the whole, Golani's book is well researched and his arguments are convincing in most of his assertions. Indeed, during 1955 and more so during 1956, Israel's security establishment was living under the shadow of deep anxiety. The fear was that the Arab armies would launch an attack once they achieved military superiority. This anxiety was fortified by the conviction that any war that began with a first strike by the enemy would give the Arabs important initial advantages and make the defense of Israel much more difficult and costly. In one of his lectures to the General Staff, Dayan expressed this anxiety succinctly: "The lack of strategic depth with which we have to live when the Gaza Strip is only seventy kilometers from Tel Aviv confronts us with serious danger, since the first fifty kilometers which the enemy may gain as a result of his initial surprise attack are fifty out of the seventy kilometers on the way to Tel Aviv."[2]

Moreover, during 1955 the Israel military was preoccupied with far-reaching disappointments in the 1949 Armistice Agreements. A desire to annul these agreements and to make some changes in their demarcation lines became well entrenched in Israel's strategic thinking. Ben-Gurion was also well aware of these considerations, but it was General Dayan's responsibility to suggest measures that he deemed appropriate in preparation for what he believed to be an unavoidable confrontation with the enemy.

My criticism of the way in which Golani presents his case has mainly to do with the rationale he believes underlay Dayan's approach. Unlike some writers, Golani does not associate Dayan with simple and crude "Zionist expansionism"; yet he connects Dayan's drive with his image of eventually improved borders of the State of Israel. At one point Golani writes,

> Dayan wanted to address Israel's requirements under conditions which would prevail in times of permanent peace. . . . He and Ben-Gurion considered peace within the 1949 boundaries—without control of water resources, without freedom of navigation in the Straits of Eilat [Tiran]—to be not a good enough peace for Israel. Therefore they considered war as a way to impose a proper peace with the Arab states. (p. 613)

Dayan, however, did not believe that peace was really possible at the time. He was not interested in the eventuality of peace, which seemed to him totally hypothetical. He was fully preoccupied with preparing Israel for another military confrontation with an Arab war coalition led by Gamal Abdel-Nasser. Dayan was deeply convinced that "without a helmet and the muzzle of a gun we will not be able to plant a tree or build a house."[3] His concern for Israel's water resources and maritime lanes were linked with the prospects of war, not of peace.

Golani's description of the attitudes that prevailed during those years among the key leaders of Israel's security establishment is too simplistic, and sometimes complexities and nuances are lost in his narrative. Even as Dayan and his staff seriously considered the advantages of initiating a war, they were fully aware of the dangers and international complications involved in such an initiative. Therefore, Golani is wrong in stating that a concrete decision was taken as early as April 1955. Only when the international situation changed radically as a result of Nasser's nationalization of the Suez Canal Company (at the end of July 1956) did the conditions that made possible a decision of such moment begin to ripen. Even then, the final decision was taken only during the secret tripartite talks in Sèvres, only five days before the beginning of the actual fighting.

Israel was never confronted with simple and easy decisions, and Ben-Gurion's political behavior during these months was characterized by agonizing hesitations and procrastination. Since the documentation does not yield any clear substantiation for Golani's main assertion (i.e., that the decision to go to war was made in the spring of 1955), he must rely on the fallacious logic known as *post hoc, propter hoc* (after this, therefore because of this). He often deduces earlier intentions from later events. Golani claims that "we can learn about Dayan's opinions with regard to the changes needed in the strategic doctrine from his actions better than from his own articulations" (p. 48). Why? Actions taken by the Israeli military may have totally different interpretations. And since Dayan revealed his opinions quite clearly and amply at the time,[4] why not rely on his own explicit words?

Both Dayan and Ben-Gurion were fully aware of the fact that, under the prevailing international conditions, Israel could not simply go to war. Under the May 1950 Tripartite Declaration, the Western powers were committed to preventing any changes in the armistice demarcation lines by force. Documents declassified recently in British and American archives reveal detailed military plans prepared in London and Washington for operations to be launched against Israel in the event of an act of aggression perpetrated against her neighbors. Even without knowing this secret information, Ben-Gurion suspected as much and feared a clash between the IDF and British forces, which he wanted to prevent at any cost. Only when such a danger was clearly averted by the secret agreement in Sèvres was the way cleared for an Israeli operation in the Sinai. Until then, Ben-Gurion kept vetoing all suggestions raised from different quarters to launch a "preventive war."

In April 1955 Ben-Gurion submitted to the Cabinet (headed at the time by Moshe Sharett) a proposal to "throw the Egyptians out of the Gaza Strip." He understood well that such an operation might escalate into an all-out war, but his proposal came in reaction to several atrocious terror attacks against Jewish civilians in the vicinity of Gaza. Against this backdrop, he believed that by internationally accepted moral standards an Israeli countermeasure would not result in outside intervention. "Throwing the Egyptians out of Gaza" did not amount, in his mind, to a "war initiated by Israel," but rather an action aimed at the defense of its citizens. This may sound like self-righteous and pious hairsplitting, but there is a difference between, on the one hand, an attack on Gaza aimed at intentionally bringing about an all-out war, and, on the other hand, an action taken to alleviate current security problems, —even if the results of both actions could turn out to be the same.[5]

The precautions taken by the IDF for the contingency of the spread of hostilities, which Golani quotes from the IDF's operational orders, can in this case be explained simply as normal "contingency planning" that every military planner must undertake. Documents in the IDF archives reveal that, during the summer of 1955, preparations for an all-out war were part of the plans for every local operation, including the contingency of capturing the entire Gaza Strip. From this, Golani concluded that, "from now on, every retaliation operation would be examined in terms of the possibility of dragging Egypt into war" (p. 51). This indeed applied to the situation later that year, during October and November, as a result of the Egyptian-"Czech" arms deal. In October 1955 Ben-Gurion (who, in addition to keeping the defense portfolio, soon became prime minister over a new government announced on 2 November 1955) ordered Dayan specifically to try and draw the Egyptians into war.[6] But, up to this point, all military initiatives undertaken by the IDF were still bound up in the logic of the traditional "retaliation strategy," which was aimed at ensuring the Arabs' full compliance with their commitments under the 1949 Armistice Agreements—not at undoing those very arrangements. Golani's interpretation also fails to explain why Ben-Gurion and Dayan did not exploit the large-scale guerrilla attacks the Egyptians unleashed at the end of August 1955 as an opportunity to conquer the Gaza area and start an all-out war.

Moreover, Ben-Gurion, and even Dayan, had grave doubts as to the wisdom of conquering the Gaza Strip. Both were fully aware of the problems that would result from the need to control and feed the three hundred thousand Palestinian refugees who huddled in the Gaza zone since 1948. Only a few weeks before the start of the Sinai Campaign, Dayan told senior officers, "I am afraid that if we now conquer the strip, the next generation will ask us: 'why were you so stupid to exchange a boundary which could be controlled by two infantry companies for that can of worms?'"[7]

Similar complications were connected with the closure of the Straits of Tiran to Israeli shipping. Ben-Gurion was well aware of the fact that the capture of the area around the southernmost tip of the Sinai could escalate into a full-scale war with Egypt. Yet he realized that such an operation could be seen as an act of legitimate defense of intrinsic rights in terms of the international law governing navigation in international waterways. As such it would gain Israel at least some world sympathy.[8] Only in this way is it possible to explain the strange contradiction between Ben-Gurion's total negation of the idea of "preventive war" and his support for Operation "Omer," aimed at the conquest of Sharm el-Sheikh.

The distinction between a "preventive war" and a "preemptive strike" was not yet in use in Israel's military discourse in the mid-1950s.[9] Therefore Golani uses the less differentiated term, *milhama yezuma*—an "initiated war." But in so doing he fails to note that Ben-Gurion was already acutely aware of the difference at the time. The Israeli leader understood well that the difference was not merely over terminology, but rather lay at the heart of Israel's ability to justify its policy in the international arena. Ever since the formation of the United Nations in 1945, an international ethos branded as aggression any preventive action that could not be proven to have been needed to avert a real and imminent danger or threat. In the fall of 1955, Ben-Gurion knew very well that an arms deal for Egypt, as large and threatening as it might be, was not a good enough justification for Israel to launch a "preventive war." Golani fails to notice that these considerations were central in Ben-Gurion's decision making and they go a long way toward explaining many of his fluctuating reactions. Only when he was able to disregard international legality by aligning himself with the two major powers at Sèvres could he rid himself of his hesitations. As we now know, he was wrong even then.

There was, understandably, a difference in approach between Ben-Gurion, who as prime minister had to take all parameters (military, domestic political, diplomatic, and even psychological) into consideration, and Dayan, who as commander in chief had to concentrate on strategic and military aspects only. In November 1955, Dayan came to the conclusion that "a major confrontation between our forces and the Egyptian army must be brought about."[10] But even Dayan was aware of the international implications, and Golani quotes him as having told Ben-Gurion a year earlier, "I am not advocating an initiated war. But I oppose conceding to the Arabs any of our rights even if such insistence may trigger war. An Arab threat of war should not prevent any action which may be needed to defend our interests" (p. 42). Golani interprets Dayan's formula as "cautious talk" and claims that Dayan did not reveal to his boss what he was really thinking.

But this is mere conjecture. Even after the Egyptian arms deal, Dayan understood well that a "preventive strike" was out of the question. He agreed with Ben-Gurion that Nasser had to be provoked into taking the blame for turning their low-level conflict into an all-out conflagration. Dayan wanted a total confrontation, but he recommended only a gradual escalation of that low-level warfare that had become routine along Israel's borders since 1953.

For a few weeks during November 1955, it appeared as though Ben-Gurion's policy coincided with Dayan's strategy. By the middle of December, though, to Dayan's dismay, Ben-Gurion accepted his foreign minister's approach. Sharett persuaded the government to reject, in principle, not only the idea of a "preventive war," but even Dayan's proposed "escalated war." From mid-December onward, primacy was given to different efforts aimed at obtaining military equipment in an effort to correct the balance that had been upset by the Czech arms deal. Dayan was certainly unhappy, but as a soldier and totally loyal to Ben-Gurion, he accepted the government's decision. For the next six months, he dedicated most of his energies to the preparation of his forces for a defensive posture—the offensive option being closed for the time being.

As just mentioned, throughout his book Golani gives the impression that Dayan and Shimon Peres advocated a policy that was different from, and more radical than, Ben-Gurion's. Moreover, in some places Golani hints that the two took liberties and acted contrary to the explicit decisions of the government. One section of the book is entitled "The Independent Policy of the IDF." It is my firm belief that, throughout this period, both Dayan and Peres never overstepped the legitimate authority vested in them in their functions as IDF chief of staff and director-general of the Ministry of Defense, respectively. Their activities in advising Ben-Gurion and advocating the policies they deemed necessary for Israel's security were an integral part of their duties. They actively and vigorously performed their duty to express their views to their superiors, without breaking the rules of discipline and obedience. Even when disappointed with his decisions, they accepted Ben-Gurion's leadership with a deep sense of loyalty and admiration.[11]

The different cases that Golani brings up as examples of excessive pressure or as acts of insubordination on the part of Dayan do not show, in my opinion, that he overstepped his lawful rights and duties. Thus, for example, in discussing Operation "Olive Leaves," in which Israeli paratroops smashed Syrian positions along the entire northeastern shores of Lake Kinneret in early December 1955, Golani claims—but does not bring any proof—that Dayan "went beyond the limits imposed on him [by Ben-Gurion]" (p. 104). Such criticism was also flung at Dayan at the time, but Ben-Gurion gave his chief of staff full backing. Both Dayan and Ben-Gurion had been hoping that Nasser would stand by his new treaty commitment to the defense of Syria and thereby trigger a large-scale confrontation. As prime minister and minister of defense, Ben-Gurion had fully endorsed this strategy. It is not true that he was ignorant of the scope of Operation "Olive Leaves"; he had approved it in its full scale.[12]

The accusation that Dayan unduly pressured the government merits a few additional comments. Dayan, as much as Ben-Gurion and many others in the policy-making elite at the time, was convinced that an Arab coalition led by Nasser, unable to accept the results of the 1948 war as an irreversible verdict of history, were doing their utmost to prepare their nations for the first opportunity to liquidate the hated Zionist state. He was also convinced that the 1949 armistice demarcation lines put Israel at a dangerous disadvantage in case of a war initiated by the Arabs, and he recommended certain measures to correct this situation. These were, strictly speaking, "military considerations." Who, if not the commander in chief of the armed forces, should present these considerations and concerns to the decision makers? Dayan would have been guilty of negligence if he had not done his utmost to explain his strategic calculations in clear and unequivocal terms. The fact that Ben-Gurion never discouraged him from presenting his opinions, even in the many cases where he disagreed with them, shows that he did not accept Sharett's complaints that Dayan was "politicizing the military."

Golani has made good use of the secret files of Shimon Peres and of the Israeli intelligence officers who were in charge of clandestine relations with the French defense establishment during 1955–1956. He describes in full detail the negotiations that climaxed in the secret conference convened in a château near Vermars in late June 1956. At this conference, Israel and France forged what amounted to an informal alliance.[13] I have, nevertheless, some reservations regarding Golani's interpretations. He attributes Peres's and Dayan's efforts to obtain large quantities of armaments from France in the winter of 1956 to the following motives: "Only the redress of the balance of power could help Ben-Gurion recover his self-confidence and move the prime minister to support an initiated war *[le-tzaded be-milhama yezuma]*" (p.123). Following this rationale, Golani adds that, right after the Vermars Conference, when French arms began to pour into the country, Israel "returned . . . to concentrate on the idea of initiating a war *[hazra . . . la-asok be-ra'ayon ha-milhama ha-yezuma]*" (p. 601).

These interpretations are not very convincing. I have seen no document produced at the time that reflects the assumption that Dayan and Peres looked for ways to help Ben-Gurion "recover his self-confidence." As a matter-of-fact, they did not need any such reason to pursue their efforts, beyond the ardent desire felt by every Israeli at the time to redress the balance of power that was so shockingly tilted in favor of Egypt by the Czech arms deal. This was, after all, the main policy line of the government, endorsed by everyone at the end of 1955. Moreover, as a result of the June 1956 conference, Israel needed many months to absorb the large quantity of new arms promised at Vermars. The attentions of Dayan and the entire high command would have been devoted at this point to the reorganization of the forces—not to initiating a war. The prospect of getting involved in all-out war became a real possibility only in late September 1956, and even then it was considered by the IDF as premature in terms of ideal battle-readiness.

Golani also gives an incorrect and inflated interpretation of the military aspects of the Vermars accord. In exchange for substantial arms-procurement, Israel agreed to far-reaching intelligence cooperation with French agencies, including a plan for joint sabotage operations (which never materialized) against Egyptian and Syrian installations suspected of supporting the Algerian rebellion. Golani's conclusion—that "the [Suez] crisis found Israel and France in the middle of building an infrastructure for a military operation against Egypt" (p. 602)—is far-fetched. In this respect, the late-July nationalization of the Suez Canal was a major watershed in Franco-Israeli relations, more important than the meeting in Vermars. When the French appealed to Israel to join their planned operation in the Canal Zone in late September, they never referred to any of the understandings reached at Vermars. This was a totally new situation in which the small-scale operations envisaged at Vermars were shelved.

Hermeneutics and interpretation are the necessary tools in the historian's craft. Suspiciousness is a vital instinct of historians. They must always inquire why the documents they find were written, and what lies behind the bare text. They must interpret not only what the words expose, but also what they may be hiding.

Yet constructive suspiciousness has its limits. It cannot be sustained and utilized without eventually finding some hard evidence to confirm one's initial suspicions. Golani is blessed with a healthy measure of such suspiciousness, but he is not always careful to substantiate a suspicion or to discard it if he is unable to produce corroborating evidence. Thus, for example, Golani refers to many memorandums circulated during 1955 and 1956 by Gen. Yehoshafat Harkabi, in which the chief of military intelligence offered repeated assessments to the effect that Egypt might initiate a war in the foreseeable future—adding his own evaluation that "[o]nly a thin intelligence base stood behind these assessments. Behind them stood sincere concerns of growing Egyptian military potential, but also a wish to spread alarm which would facilitate the return to the policy of the initiated war *[ha-milhama ha-yezuma]*" (p.119). This is the sort of judgment in which Golani goes far beyond what the documents themselves can substantiate.

Benny Morris,
Ben-Gurion University of the Negev

"Kadesh": Israel's First War of Choice[14]

Golani begins this important study with the Gaza Raid—the devastating IDF operation against an Egyptian army base on the outskirts of Gaza City on the night of 28 February / 1 March 1955. This unleashed a chain reaction of attacks and reprisals, beginning with a series of Egyptian raids that included a grenade attack on a wedding party in Moshav Pattish on 25 March. The latter attack so angered Ben-Gurion that, from that point on, according to Golani (p. 48), Israel sought a war with Egypt and initiated an escalatory process *(tahalich dirdur)* which in the end resulted in a major war in the sands of Sinai at the end of October and early November 1956.

Dating the Start of the Process

Golani is aware of the problem of dating the start of the process—a question which is of central importance in any discussion of the Sinai War because it is vitally linked to the question of the reasons that prompted Israel to go to war. Was it a defensive war, or was it a "war of choice" that in retrospect raises serious questions regarding the wisdom and morality of the Israeli leadership in its decision making?

Golani's position on this question of dating is a type of compromise between two viewpoints. The first—which dominates Israel's collective memory and appears in Mordechai Bar-On's books[15]—holds that Israel's political and military leadership, save for Sharett (prime minister from the end of 1953 until early November 1955 and foreign minister from May 1948 until June 1956), decided to go to war against Egypt following the conclusion of the Czech arms deal (in fact, a Soviet-Egyptian arms deal) announced by President Gamal Abdel Nasser of Egypt at the end of September 1955. From that moment on it was understood that Egypt was embarking on a giant military expansion program, and Ben-Gurion and Dayan saw this as an existential threat to Israel. They therefore decided on a preemptive or "preventive war" *(milhemet mena)*, in which the IDF would destroy the Egyptian army before it became too strong and possibly also topple Nasser, and thereby win for Israel a lengthy period of tranquillity.

The second approach, exemplified in my own book, *Israel's Border Wars, 1949–1956,*[16] holds that it was the "current security" *(bitahon shotef)* problems of 1949–1956 that fueled the mutual antagonism and the continuous thinking, since 1948, about a "second round"—no less in Israel than in the Arab states. It was the pattern of Arab infiltration into Israeli territory, the terrorist attacks that were part and parcel of it, the IDF's retaliatory operations, and the skirmishes and battles between the IDF and the Arab armies along the borders and in and around the demilitarized zones which, in the end, propelled Egypt to turn east in an effort to obtain arms and to send *fedayeen* (guerilla) squads into Israel. Israel, for its part, was pushed into massively arming itself (with French equipment) and in the end into going to war. According to this approach, were it not for the continuous violence along the borders and the psychological preparation that it constituted for the Israeli leadership and public, it is quite possible that the Sinai War would not have been launched. Seen from this perspective, the "basic security" *(bitahon besisi)* considerations (grand strategy, geopolitical realities and borders, etc.) that were expressed in Israel's decision to go to war were, in large measure, a product of this series of "current security" incidents and calculations of the previous eight years. "Operation Kadesh" was but the natural conclusion of the previous chain of reprisals, of which it was the last and largest.

Golani takes a middle course but, when all is said and done, is closer to the first approach. He too argues that the geopolitical realities and calculations linked to "basic security"—Israel's sense of isolation as a beleaguered island in a sea of enemies bent on its destruction, her desire to neutralize her enemies' ability to do this, and her quest for a "big brother" who would underwrite her security—these are what motivated Israel to unleash her offensive in Sinai on 29 October 1956. Golani modifies and "corrects" this approach, arguing that Dayan and, in more restrained fashion, Ben-Gurion, as early as 1953–1954 and in line with "basic security" considerations, sought a "second round," with the focus usually on Jordan and on the conquest of the West Bank.

Starting in March–April 1955, Golani writes, this desire was expressed in attempts to propel the region into war through an escalatory cycle. According to Golani, the decision in 1955 to force open the Straits of Tiran, which had been blocked by the Egyptians, was "a direct consequence of the changes that had occurred in [Israel's] defense policy in spring 1955. . . . The decision was not connected to the Czech-Egyptian arms deal. . . . On the contrary, the Czech deal was what stymied the escalation toward war" (p. 73). By contrast, Bar-On and traditional Zionist historiography normally date the process leading to the Sinai War as starting in late September 1955.

Golani bases his views on a series of documents from 1953 to 1954, when talk began "in the IDF about an initiated war not merely as a possibility, but as the preferred plan from Israel's perspective" (p. 80). In April 1955 the IDF began "to prepare . . . for the possibility of an initiated war" (p. 88) and in the spring and summer of 1955 "Dayan linked [considerations of] current security with [those of] basic security" (p. 90). The conquest of Gaza and the Red Sea straits—as Dayan and others expected—would drag Egypt into a general war.

"Activists" versus "Moderates"

Golani goes even further and argues that Moshe Sharett joined those advocating the policy of escalation *(medinyut ha-dirdur)*, as Bar-On called it, and in 1955 backed war with Egypt. More accurately, Golani argues that Sharett supported Operation *Tsefa* (viper), the first plan, from the summer of 1955, for the takeover of the Straits of Tiran and for the opening of the Gulf of Eilat (Aqaba) to Israeli shipping. I think Golani is mistaken on this point, and is wrong in the spin he gives to Sharett's quoted words in the matter. Sharett, Dayan, and Ben-Gurion all understood that such an operation would necessarily lead to a general war with Egypt, and Sharett opposed such a war. That is why Dayan asserted that the operation would have to take place "when there is another government"—in other words, a government not headed by Sharett. Nonetheless, Golani tries to "mobilize" Sharett for the "activist" (i.e., Ben-Gurion-Dayan) camp. "The plan in general was acceptable to Sharett," he writes (p. 71), and refers as evidence to passages from Sharett's *Personal Diary.*[17] But from these cited passages it is not at all clear that Sharett supported the operation, while it is extremely clear from what he consistently said and wrote during those months that he was decidedly opposed to a large-scale military operation and preferred to continue to explore political-diplomatic options for opening the Straits.

The main flaw in Golani's description of the period lies in his treatment of Sharett. Throughout 1954–1955, the Israeli Cabinet consistently rejected—usually with Sharett setting the tone, and usually with a large majority—proposals to conquer this or that patch of Egyptian territory. In other words, the Israeli government rejected Dayan's and Ben-Gurion's "activist" policy, and it was usually Dayan, as Golani tellingly illustrates, who egged Ben-Gurion on toward ever more "activist" positions to embark on this or that military initiative. The escalatory policy, though propounded in late 1955, never became Israeli *government* policy, but rather remained the preserve and aspiration of Ben-Gurion and his supporters among the IDF brass; these people failed to bring the Cabinet majority round to their view. Therefore, Golani's contention that Israel's defense outlook changed during those years is a logical fallacy. True, Dayan's and Ben-Gurion's views changed during 1953–1955. However, it was only in the summer and autumn of 1956, after Ben-Gurion dismissed Sharett from the Foreign Ministry (and from the Cabinet), that the two managed to mobilize majority support in the Cabinet and to translate their will into government policy and actions.

At the same time, Golani's portrayal of the two competing "schools of thinking" in the Israeli hierarchy in the years 1949–1956 is simplistic. Ben-Gurion and Dayan certainly put into operation an "activist"-warlike line, while Sharett did indeed often speak of "moderation." But the truth is that, during the first few years of Israeli statehood, the two principal leaders, Ben-Gurion and Sharett, were in agreement on most of the main, fateful ideological and political issues—the establishment of the state, the transfer or expulsion of the Arabs, reprisals as a correct response to infiltration and to the constant threat posed by the Arab states, and so forth. To try to portray the Ben-Gurion/Sharett dichotomy as a deep, permanent, all-encompassing ideological-political rift is to paint history in black and white—whereas the difference between the two men was most often in that gray area that envelops most of history. But, true enough, by the spring of 1956 the expanding gap between the two men's positions was such that Ben-Gurion felt he had to get rid of Sharett if he was going to have a free hand in preparing Israel for an initiated war.

Military History

Golani's book is written with admirable objectivity. Occasionally his prose is even infiltrated by a refreshing criticality, though his phraseology is almost always cautious in the extreme. Golani's objectivity can be seen particularly in the full one third of his book devoted to military aspects of the Sinai War. For example, with respect to the balance of forces between Egypt and Israel Golani does not inundate us with descriptions of "poor David" versus the "Egyptian Goliath." According to Golani, "the IDF had quantitative superiority in Sinai" (p. 440). Dayan, in fact, phrased it even more emphatically: "We fought the battle for Sinai with a 3-to-1 advantage" (p. 567). Unlike the traditional Israeli portrayals of the Sinai War, which describe only the Israeli and Egyptian forces, Golani also describes other actions as major contributions to the IDF victory. These include the Anglo-French air strikes, beginning on 31 October, against the Egyptian airfields, plus the aerial umbrella supplied by the French air force over Israel's cities beginning on 29 October, and the general retreat order issued by the Egyptian high command that reached the Egyptian units in Sinai on 31 October and on 1 November. Golani concludes, "[In truth], the main problems faced by the IDF were the difficult terrain and the limited amount of time at its disposal until the UN intervened," and not the might of the Egyptian army (p. 441).

But Golani's main contribution to the historiography of 1956 is the amassing and presentation of a great amount of new information. For the first time (pp.239, 136–138), the Franco-Israeli discussions and agreements about launching commando attacks in the summer of 1956 to destroy Cairo's and Damascus' radio stations are described. In the end, the attacks were never launched, but, according to Golani, the demolition of the Egyptian station by Israel almost took place. Golani also adds to our knowledge with regard to the Israel Air Force's (IAF) mistaken attacks on IDF ground forces. Another revelation concerns the French naval bombardment of Egyptian army camps around Rafah on 31 October and on 1 November, and the French contribution to the capture of the Egyptian destroyer, the *Ibrahim al-Awal,* on 31 October.

While these are interesting military details, *en large*, Golani's main innovations lie in his extensive descriptions of the forging of the Israeli-French relationship during 1956, and of the interconnection between the IDF's moves in Sinai and the diktats and exigencies stemming from the political planning of the tripartite alliance. Golani thus sheds fresh and persuasive light on what transpired on the main battlefields between 29 October and 2 November, by which time it was essentially all over. Yet, in a book of such size—appearing in Hebrew in two volumes—which is critical of the traditional Israel-centric take on the Sinai War, I would have expected a more in-depth description of the Anglo-French war moves of 31 October–6 November, for which the IDF assault in Sinai served as a prelude and pretext.

Israel's War Aims

But why did Israel attack? Golani quotes at length Ben-Gurion's official government declaration of 28 October about Egypt's "renewal of the fedayeen operations"; the establishment of the Egyptian-Syrian-Jordanian military alliance; "the mobilization [i.e., deployment] of the Iraqi Army along Jordan's borders"; and forestalling a future Arab offensive against Israel (p. 400). Golani writes, cautiously, that "this was true, but not the whole truth"—but then proceeds to demonstrate that Ben-Gurion was in effect lying:

> Contrary to the government's official declarations on the eve of the war, there was no significant fedayeen activity along the Egyptian border on the eve of the war . . . [and] there was no threatening military deployment on Egypt's part. Indeed, the Egyptian Army in Sinai [in July 1956] was [substantially] reduced in favor of a deployment along the Suez Canal [to confront a potential Anglo-French offensive]. Moreover, the Iraqi Army had no intention of entering Jordan [and deploying along the Israeli border], and Israel knew it. (p. 401)

According to Golani, Israel's "main war aims" were three: opening the Straits of Tiran; "reducing the Arab military threat to Israel," although that threat was not seen as immediate; and toppling the Nasser regime. The last two were "the more basic and long-range" goals of the war, meaning "changing the face of the Middle East" in a way that would assure Israel's position and security in the region. Ben-Gurion believed that a "second round" was ineluctable and necessary, and that it would be better for Israel to initiate it at a time and in circumstances of her own choosing. He believed that destroying the Kingdom of Jordan, taking over the West Bank (where Israel would institute limited "autonomy"), and conquering and annexing southern Lebanon up to the Litani River and parts of eastern Sinai would enhance Israel's security. In addition, it would give it more territory on which to absorb and settle future Jewish waves of immigration (pp. 402–5).

Golani reinforces the arguments of those—like myself—who see the Sinai War as an expansionist war, in which Dayan and Ben-Gurion aimed to expand Israel's territory. The two did not only covet the eastern marches of Sinai, from Rafah or el-Arish down to Ras Muhammad. Both (but perhaps Dayan more than Ben-Gurion) believed and hoped that Jordan would be drawn into an Israeli-Egyptian war and would provide the excuse or provocation to, *enfin*, "conquer" the West Bank. Golani makes clear that Israel's deployment of troops along the Jordanian frontier, and its minatory declarations vis-à-vis Jordan on the eve of the war, were not just efforts to camouflage the intended assault on Sinai. They were not merely a deception, but evidence of a genuine desire and expectation that Jordan would also join the fray and that the IDF would then be able to conquer the West Bank. As Dayan wrote in his diary on 26 October, "I assume that Jordan will initiate action against us . . . [and,] in accordance, we have laid our plans for the Jordanian front" (quoted in Golani, p. 426). And when Ben-Gurion was asked that day if there was a "danger" that Jordan would attack Israel as the IDF assaulted Sinai, he replied, "If she attacks—that is no danger, perhaps it is even the opposite" (p. 426). At Sèvres, as we know from Bar-On and others, Ben-Gurion repeated his "grand design" that included an Israeli takeover of the West Bank and southern Lebanon, and annexation of eastern Sinai.

On the eve of the departure for Sèvres, Dayan and Peres agreed to persuade Ben-Gurion that "there must be agreement in advance between the parties [i.e., Israel, France, and Britain] regarding the sharing of the fruits of the victory. Israel would insist on annexing areas up to the Rafah-Abu Awgeila-at-Tur line, and perhaps also up to the Canal itself [i.e., about half of Sinai or all of Sinai]" (p. 365). The plan to conquer and annex the Gaza Strip included a provision that related to the fate of the inhabitants. Various documents spoke of transferring *(ha'avara)* many of the Strip's inhabitants, most of whom were refugees from 1948, to Egypt proper or to the West

Bank. Dayan, for example, wrote, during the war itself that "[i]mmediately upon conquest, the Strip should be surrounded to isolate it from the rest of the country. Refugees can be transferred to the Hebron Hills" (quoted on p. 473). As it turned out, Jordan did not give Israel cause or excuse to conquer the West Bank, and the powers—spearheaded by the United States—did not allow Ben-Gurion to continue to occupy the eastern half of Sinai or the Gaza Strip. But these were certainly among his aspirations and aims in going to war against Egypt in 1956.

These three principal war aims, Golani notes, were joined by two others: "strengthening the alliance with France, and neutralizing the British threat" (p. 404). This phraseology is somewhat curious, for two reasons: First, there was no British "threat" to Israel—though Ben-Gurion periodically and obsessively, since 1948, believed there was—so long as Israel refrained from attacking the Kingdom of Jordan. Second, encapsulated or camouflaged in the phrase "alliance with France" is France's assistance in the development of Israel's nuclear capability—but Golani refrains from explaining or expanding on the subject.

Privileged Access to Sources

Golani wrote his book for the IDF's History Department, which provided financing. Had the book remained a classified "internal" study, with limited distribution within the defense establishment, there would be no cause for criticism. But it was published by Ma'arachot, the Israel Ministry of Defense Press, and is distributed and sold like any other book about the first decade of Israel's existence. Thus, this book can be said to be in competition with other academic studies of the period, and this raises a number of problems on both the ethical and practical levels.

Principally, many documents seen and used by Golani in preparing this book were not open to researchers who were not working for the defense establishment, and so Golani—who is a university lecturer, not a Defense Ministry employee—enjoyed a major advantage over his competitors in the academic marketplace. In effect, he thus violated norms of fair play.

Secondly, given the fact that some of the documents used by Golani are still closed to other researchers, readers and critics are prevented from verifying his use of source-materials. How can one know whether Golani has made appropriate and balanced use of his documents, whether he has (inadvertently or otherwise) misquoted from them, or whether he has chosen marginal sentences and paragraphs at the cost of ignoring the major point or argument in a given document? And, among the files that he was given access to, perhaps he has selected documents that corroborated his theses while ignoring those that undermined his conclusions? There is no way of knowing, and other scholars will have great difficulty in assessing the overall quality of Golani's work in this respect.

Third, Golani's contractual bonds to the Israel Defense Ministry engender other problems. For one thing, most of the references in Golani's book direct the reader to "the IDF Archive" but do not provide the necessary group or file number. Thus (and this applies even to declassified documents, which are available to all researchers), scholars and critics will have major difficulties in tracing Golani's spadework.

Censorship or Self-censorship?

Moreover, the book was subjected to censorship and deletions above and beyond those that apply to books about defense matters written by "outsiders" to the defense establishment. The IDF History Department or Ma'arachot (or Golani himself, because he knew what was expected of him) excised complete subjects from the manuscript. For example, four years ago Golani's Ph.D. thesis—of which this book is an expanded version—triggered a public controversy after a journalist quoted from it a passage relating to the IDF massacre of about forty Egyptian prisoners of war (POWs). Golani's published book makes no mention of this episode or, more generally, of the IDF slaughter of Egyptian POWs elsewhere during the war.

The defense establishment certainly had a point in trying to avoid publication of such unpleasant facts. The press revelations about the massacre at the Parker Monument had, indeed, led to a diplomatic tiff with Egypt, which protested and demanded an official inquiry and the prosecution of those responsible. But there were no prosecutions, and only a lukewarm inquiry, whose findings were never published, causing Israel some embarrassment. But once the horse had bolted, once the story had been published on the basis of Golani's Ph.D. thesis, what was the point, three or four years later, of shutting the barn doors and preventing republication of the matter in Golani's book?

Nor is the censorial damage to the book limited to the IDF-image-related subject of massacres. It would appear that censorship (external or self-inflicted) prevented Golani from disclosing the nature of the intelligence material that Israel passed on to France in 1955 and 1956 relating to the Algerian rebellion, material that was a substantial part of the Israeli dowry in the forging of the alliance with France on the eve of the Sinai collusion. What harm would have been caused to Israel in 1997 had Golani recounted that the IDF Intelligence Division, through signals interception, had penetrated the logistic infrastructure of the rebellion and traced Nasser's help to its leaders?

Similarly, as stated eralier, the book almost completely ignores France's nuclear assistance to Israel (the matter was apparently concluded, in principle, on the last day of the talks at Sèvres), which was an important part of the French dowry. Golani makes do with the following pithy remark: "The alliance with France was greatly deepened, above and beyond cooperation in the joint war against Egypt. Thus, the nuclear reactor in Dimona was built in 1958 with French assistance" (p. 617). But the book leaves us wondering about the exact place, and importance, of the nuclear component in the forging of the alliance. Surely Golani, with the rich material he was privy to, could have ventured a little beyond these banalities.

Again, the long arm of censors (or self-censorship) is evident in Golani's treatment of Israel's engineered eve-of-war lies and deceptions, which were designed to give Israel the excuse needed to launch its strike. Among them was the presentation to a group of journalists of a number of captured fedayeen, who in fact were Israeli soldiers,[18] and the demolition with explosives of one or two disused water-pumping stations by IDF sappers on the Israeli side of the Israel-Gaza border, made to look as if it had been the handiwork of Arab saboteurs. Golani only offers hints (p. 433) of this skulduggery. One would have expected an historian who had access to all the relevant IDF documents to at least reproduce in his book what has already been published on these matters, if not to enlighten us further.

Conclusion

Golani has reconstructed an historical narrative, crammed with data, which is generally accurate, but mistakes have slipped in here and there. For example, he claims that the dispatch of the fedayeen squads into Israel in August 1955 was "the first organized infiltration operation of terrorist squads" (p. 54) by the Egyptian authorities in Gaza—but this is incorrect. Egyptian Military Intelligence in Gaza had already activated terrorist squads in April and in the summer of 1954, in retaliation for attacks by the IDF against targets in the Strip. And Gen. Sir John Bagot Glubb ("Glubb Pasha") was not "the founder of the Arab Legion and its commander for the previous 25 years" (p. 182)—its founder and first commander was, in fact, Col. F. G. Peake. As to Glubb, Golani claims that in January 1956 he proposed attacking Israel to force it to agree to a cease-fire if it attacked Egypt (p. 328). It is difficult to believe that Glubb could really have made such a proposal. He knew, at the time, exactly what the balance of forces was, and well understood that a Jordanian attack on Israel would have resulted in the fall of the West Bank to the IDF. In addition, Glubb detested and feared Nasser's Egypt, and would not have suggested anything that might endanger Jordan in order to aid Nasser or Egypt.

Golani's bibliography leaves something to be desired. It contains completely irrelevant books by Shlomo Avineri on prestate Zionist ideologues and by Yehiam Weitz on Israel Kastner—but fails to include, among others, Meir Har-Zion's diary, Rami Ginat's book on Soviet-Egyptian relations, and P. J. Vatikiotis's books on Jordan and Egypt.[19] The index needs some editing; occasionally there is no correlation between index entries and actual page numbers.

But in summation, these defects are minor in relation to the breadth and depth of this well-written study. This is a major and crucial contribution to the historiography of the origins and course of the Sinai War, and will no doubt be in use among scholars and students for many years.

Motti Golani,
University of Haifa

The Limits of Interpretation and the Permissible in Historical Research Dealing with Israel's Security: A Reply to Bar-On and Morris

It is not a common occurrence for an author to be asked to reply to reviews of his book. It does me great honor that among those who reviewed my study of Israel's road to the Sinai War and the war itself are two of the leading Israeli historians of that period. Each of them has published his own study of the events that are the subject of my book, and both of them used some of the same archives. Unlike some other critics who attacked my work in a less dignified way, the critical reviews of Prof. Benny Morris and Dr. Mordechai Bar-On are those of experts well acquainted with all details of the matter under discussion. The inclusion of our "trialogue" in this current volume is perhaps an omen that Israelis will be able in the not-too-distant future to debate their past history without making accusations of "disloyalty" and without hurling pejorative epithets at anyone who dares to question the Ben-Gurion-oriented narrative that still holds sway in the Israeli collective consciousness.[20]

Although there is much in their reviews that could be rebutted, my comments will be devoted to replying to two important, broad, issues arising from these reviews. The first, raised primarily by Bar-On, concentrates on the manner in which the historian deals with the materials at his disposal. The second, brought up by Morris, concerns how the Israeli historian relates to the defense establishment of his own country, and how he or she deals with the sensitive issues of security and war.

Between Text and Context

While Bar-On and Morris draw conclusions from the historical study of 1956 that are in some ways poles apart, they review my book from a common historiographical perspective. Bar-On, who lived through the events and was intimately involved with the small group of players that led Israel to a preemptive campaign in the fall of 1956[21] is bent upon preserving something of the "innocence" of the episode. The objective of Morris, a leading figure among Israel's "new historians," is, by contrast, to bring to light additional information that remains suppressed or concealed from Israel's collective memory. Despite the difference between them, both criticize my study as positivist historians who do not like to deviate from the documentary evidence. Both of them are devotees of interpretation that sticks closely to the text. Bar-On accuses me of being overly sharp (almost of being overly delighted) in my analysis of Israel's activist road to war, while Morris castigates me for my "self-censorship" and for being "cautious in the extreme."

Bar-On's review ends with a sentence that sums up his attitude: "Golani goes far beyond what the documents themselves can substantiate." His objection is composed of two interrelated elements. First, he asks why a historian cannot sometimes accept things at face value without having recourse to more complex explanations; second, he claims that my interpretation of certain issues is not sufficiently substantiated by the documentation available. Bar-On claims that the efforts of Dayan and Peres in 1955–1956 to push Ben-Gurion to the brink of war were no more than the legitimate actions of senior military advisors, doing their duty. But his assertion is based—exactly like my conclusion that Dayan and Peres led Ben-Gurion into war in the fall of 1956—on what Bar-On calls the "spirit of things" *(ne'imat d'varim)*.[22] His contention that the steps taken by Dayan and Peres lacked any hidden intentions is based, in the final analysis, on the way in which he today remembers that period, on the manner in which he interprets the documentation, and on that very same elusive "spirit of things."

Bar-On, in his arguments in favor of relying as much as possible on documentary evidence, does not seem to recognize the legitimacy of historians having recourse to "the spirit of things" to buttress their analysis. And yet, as we can see, he himself resorts to this "spirit" as an element in his own interpretation of the events of the period. I would argue that the "spirit of the events" is sometimes no less important that their content. Relying on a combination of documentation and this "spirit," for example, I stand firm by my conclusion that, on the whole, Dayan never really put aside his intentions for a preemptive war—even when his government instructed him otherwise.

In criticizing my interpretation, Bar-On accuses me of adopting "the fallacious logic known as *post hoc, propter hoc*" (after this, therefore because of this). He is absolutely right—for that, I believe, is the essence of the historian's task. Without such an approach, historiography would be no more than a chronicle of events. At the same time, I agree that the historian must also accept the fact that there is a certain dynamic of unguided developments. It is the responsibility of the historian to exercise historical judgment, to distinguish carefully between causal links and random coincidences.

There is a generation gap that separates me from Bar-On, and this is most naturally expressed in his basic assumption that the motives of the Israeli leadership on the eve of the Sinai Campaign were primarily defensive. My interpretation of the period is different. I see a pattern of Israeli activism based on choices and initiatives, rather than on leaders assuming a mainly defensive and reactive posture.

Textual Detail and Historical "Truth"

Morris's review highlights a methodological gap between us. Time and again he dwells upon details, for in them, he believes, lies historical "truth." While I fully share his insistence on historical accuracy, a plethora of detail is not always a guarantee of a thesis or a generalization that enlightens and convinces the reader. There is surely an important difference between, on the one hand, a "journalistic" account, whose prime motive is sensationalism (leading to the incorporation of more and more piquant historical facts, sometimes quite esoteric), and, on the other hand, an analysis that tries to understand a historical process and its results. While the historian should encourage public discussion of the past (even if it is painful), he or she should be wary of stirring up blind anger. This, in the end, prevents serious discussion and usually causes a backlash that reinforces, in the public mind, the patriotic historiography that both Morris and I reject.

Morris's excessive positivism causes him to leave no fact unturned. For him, the documentary evidence is more important than the spirit of the times. But my differences with Morris are not over details; nor do they stem from the gap between the IDF documentation that I was able to consult and that he did not see (see the next section). Rather, we have diametrically opposed interpretations of the events of that period. In his important study of Israel's security problems during the fifties,[23] Morris concludes that the Sinai War was just one more "operation," a large-scale retaliatory raid in direct continuation of similar ones mounted by the IDF since 1953 in its efforts to put a stop to Palestinian infiltration of Israeli territory. My interpretation of these years leads me to believe that Morris is wrong, and that he completely overlooks the major reasons and circumstances that led to Suez/Sinai:

- the desire to introduce changes in Israel's borders in anticipation of a possible future permanent settlement with the Arabs
- the desperate need to lean on a Western power for both arms supplies and political support
- the assumption that Egypt had to be dealt a blow so that it would relinquish its warlike aspirations and that, at the same time, something had to be done to try to overthrow the Nasser regime
- the need to solve the problem of Israeli passage through the Straits of Tiran, and, finally,
- the officially-declared goal of assuring peace and quiet along Israel's borders.

It is not surprising that Morris prefers to use the term *Operation Kadesh* when referring to the Sinai War. Such terminology blends in well with the tripartite Franco-British-Israeli collusion that tried to conceal the fact that they were heading into a full-scale war. The three allies presented their action deceptively as a Franco-British action designed ostensibly to "separate the combatants," Israel and Egypt, and to restore order in the Suez Canal zone. It was convenient for Israel to present its action as just another retaliatory "operation" that was so characteristic of the times. Unfortunately, Morris fell for that ruse.

Morris is partly correct in his discussion of the questions of dating and timing. It is true that Bar-On and I differ fundamentally over the historical role played by the "Czech"-Egyptian arms deal, which became public knowledge late in September 1955. For Bar-

On, this was the beginning of the road to war, while I see it as an element that delayed the war. We understand the historical documentation in different ways. But I also disagree with Morris, for whom the Gaza raid at the end of February 1955 was the beginning of the road to war. For me, it all started when Ben-Gurion rejoined the Cabinet in February 1955, serving as a channel through which Dayan could implement his war policy.

Bar-On claims that my conclusions are exaggerated, while Morris complains that (despite my "admirable objectivity" and "refreshing criticality") my "phraseology is almost always cautious in the extreme." Nonetheless, I hold to my opinion that what is called for is a combination of a critical attitude that does not accept anything at face value, together with a responsible approach that attempts to understand, rather than antagonize or create headlines.

The Historian and the Israeli Defense Establishment

Morris devotes his strongest criticism to the fact that I had privileged access to many documents in the IDF Archives before they were declassified and made available to the public. If Morris had bothered to check with me, I would have gladly explained to him the details of my employment by the defense establishment. I would also have informed him that my Ph.D. thesis was available for all to consult in the libraries of the University of Haifa and Yad Yizhak Ben-Zvi in Jerusalem. He might then have written his review in *ha-Aretz* without casting aspersions upon my professional integrity.

Having said that, I must admit that in other respects his complaint is well founded, and the remainder of my comments will attempt to elucidate several murky issues of crucial importance to historical research into Israel's wars. As Morris rightly notes, my study was financed by the Israeli defense establishment. This meant that, in addition to the salary that allowed me to devote myself entirely to research (something very rare in Israel and abroad), I was given access to documents that had been classified until then. While some of these papers had been closed for good reason, others had been held back for reasons that I found hard to fathom.

I had made one condition with my employers: they must not interfere with my professional considerations and with the manner in which I interpreted the material at my disposal. They lived up to that condition, more or less—while making it clear that they were authorized to prevent publication of anything that might be detrimental to Israeli security. In retrospect, in contrast to Morris's suspicions, the censors' impact on my work was only marginal.

As a doctoral student, I was well aware of the standard requirement of disclosing my sources, so that others may critically examine the same evidence and argue with the theses presented. But my employers in the defense establishment could not understand why I obstinately and repeatedly asked them whether I could make exact citations to the classified material, and if—as a result—other scholars would be allowed to consult that material. People in the defense establishment did not know what to make of my requests to declassify the material quickly and to make it accessible to all. They did not comprehend why I wanted to share my "great prize" with others, nor could they grasp that disclosure of the source material was a basic precept of academic research. I soon understood that, as far as they were concerned, my motives were fraught with danger; without proper supervision, they felt, I might make public my sources, and then the defense establishment would not be able to refuse to make anything it placed at my disposal available to all other interested parties.[24]

My sense that not all was well was heightened when I worked at the Israel Defense Forces and Defense Establishment Archives in the Tel Aviv suburb of Givatayim—the "mecca" for any historian dealing with the military history of Israel. There, in the archives, my freedom of action was limited even though I was labeled (to my great embarrassment) "an institutional user" on behalf of the Military History Unit of the IDF.[25] No one bothered to inform me of the criteria of censorship, concealment, or unavailability of the material I wished to see. As I progressed, I found that certain files that I had just ordered suddenly disappeared. In most cases the staff denied that there were any limitations on my access—everything was fine, I was told; it was a simple case of not being able to locate the requested files. Things like that happen. . . .[26]

My only consolation was the formal decision of the incumbent minister of defense, Yitzhak Rabin, to declassify all military material dealing with the years 1948–1956 on the first of January 1990. While it was obvious that this process would take a long time because of the understandable need to screen the material being declassified, I believe that this verification process was used as a sweeping pretext to prevent consultation of new material by the general public, and even by someone, such as myself, who supposedly enjoyed institutional clearance. I appealed to my employers in the Military History Unit, but they were powerless to help, even though they were sympathetic to my complaint.

Security, Image, and Self-image

Israelis engaged in studying the history of their country frequently run up against efforts to prevent them from using certain archival materials. This is almost always done in the name of "security"—a concept that for most Israelis is still above dispute, but whose scope and nature have never been openly and impartially debated and defined. In the realities of Israeli life, freedom of expression is often sacrificed to the Moloch of "Security."

There is no denying that Israel is faced with real and difficult security problems. Yet it seems that there is a glaring gap between the dictates of national and personal security, on the one hand, and other, more dubious, considerations that lead to concealment of documentation, on the other hand. What lies behind the latter are too often, in my view, questions not of security, but rather of national pride or personal self-image, this or that political inclination, or—perhaps—simply irrational fear.

In any society, professional historians who wish to research a chapter in contemporary history must pay a certain price if their evidence leads them to challenge the prevailing consensus. It is always a delicate matter to contend directly with the memory of "those who were there," or, more importantly, with the still-fresh collective memory. Historians who write the history of a war in which their own society was one of the combatant parties naturally expose themselves to harsh recrimination if they do not defend the policies and actions of their country. Those who order others into battle, those who are sent to fight, and their families and descendants—everyone expects that historical research will provide definitive proof that the sacrifices were necessary and that the wars were justified.

Since the establishment of the state, Israelis have been living in an ongoing state of siege, if not of war. Under such circumstances, how can an historian convincingly report on finding evidence that shows that there was a clear dimension of *choice* in a war, or that they or their loved ones were not sent to fight because of *ein-*

breira—because there was "no alternative"? That, after all, is the major conclusion of my volume—a blunt statement that threatens the self-image, assumptions, worldview, and perhaps even the psychological well-being of many citizens of my country.

Dayan and Ben-Gurion: Who Led Whom?

The uproar first came from the direction of veteran members of the defense establishment. In April 1995, I was invited by the Ben-Gurion Research Center to give one of a series of lectures devoted to leaders and leadership in Israel. I chose to discuss the Dayan-Ben-Gurion relationship on the eve of the Sinai War. I gave my lecture a title intended to express the gist of the message I wanted to get across: "Ben-Gurion and Dayan—A Disciple Who Led His Mentor."[27]

At the appointed hour, I arrived at Ben-Gurion House in Tel Aviv. The former prime minister and minister of defense had, of course, been dead since 1973, but his spirit still reigned supreme. The audience was composed mainly of those who had worked alongside "the Old Man," especially in the IDF and in the Ministry of Defense. The title of my lecture was enough to set them off: to say of the "founding father" that someone had "led" him along was sacrilege of the first degree. To claim that Dayan, then chief of staff, had maneuvered Ben-Gurion so that he opted for war was evidently a sin—although I was by no means the first to propagate such heresy.[28] The audience found my presentation unconvincing and a hostile atmosphere pervaded the room. The most outspoken was Gen. (Res.) Meir Amit, who had been chief of operations during the Sinai War and was later to be chief of intelligence (Aman) and director of the Mossad (until 1968). For many months thereafter he conducted an all-out campaign against my claim—as he put it—"that Dayan led Ben-Gurion by the nose."[29]

For the first time, I came face-to-face with the problem of "image" in its most acute form. It made no difference what I said; what was important was what my listeners heard. Any statement that did not fit in with the way they have chosen to remember their past aroused opposition. I found myself up against a group of people who had left the best years of their lives back in the first decade of Israel's existence. This was a group still vigorous and ready to fight to shape the image of the past as it saw fit. For members of this informal group, any historical interpretation that they did not like was seen not only as a personal blow, but also as one that damaged the very State of Israel.

"OK, So They Murdered POWs—But Why Talk About It?"

Though the veterans of the defense establishment considered banning the publication of my book,[30] my confrontation with them was nothing compared to the public uproar that broke out in the summer of 1995. At that time I was accused of creating a diplomatic crisis with Egypt. In his review, Morris refers to the commotion raised by my disclosure—made before the book was published—about thirty-five Egyptian POWs who were murdered during the Sinai War near the Mitla Pass, and he criticizes me for omitting this episode from the published volume.

No doubt, the uproar that ensued was indicative of a widespread hostile attitude of Israelis toward the efforts of historians who deal with contemporary history, especially with issues that touch public and personal sensitivity. How I handled the episode of the murder of the POWs—intricately bound up with the way in which the book was written, published, and attacked—is a story too complex to recount in full here. You can be sure that it has all the elements of crass media sensationalism, and has helped me to shed some of my earlier academic "naïveté."[31] But a brief summary of part of that saga is appropriate here, because it suggests a different complexion to Morris's complaint.

What is good for the journalist is not necessarily suitable for the historian. In late July 1995, *Davar* published its "scoop" about the murdered POWs based on research reports I had made available for internal IDF use. Until the POW affair was leaked to journalists, no one in the Military History Unit had even bothered to read my study. Had responsible people done so, they would surely have wanted to suppress this information and to delete other sections as well—those dealing, for example, with widespread looting, or my evidence arguing that Israel had chosen to initiate this war. The latter point was, after all, the heart of my research, rather than the more "newsworthy" side episodes of murder and looting, ugly as they may be.

I have no intention to call journalists to account for what they did with my findings, just as I have no quarrel with the defense establishment. Each party was only doing its job. But there is a difference between their approach and that of the academic researcher who has his or her own task to fulfill. During the course of this episode, I came to realize that the historian engaged in studying the history of his or her own times and society cannot treat with equanimity the reactions that his or her revelations might engender. I realized that if I wanted to continue with historical research, I had to do my best not to become embroiled in the contemporary controversy over the murdered Egyptian POWs. Unfortunately, my supposedly academic historical discussion of what had transpired in 1956 could not be separated from a highly emotional public debate on contemporary Israel and Israelis, a sort of collective look in the mirror. I, who was bent upon analyzing a historical episode from as clear-eyed a perspective as possible, now began to receive fascinating letters and phone calls, all dealing with ghastly deeds committed by IDF soldiers over the years. (I overcame the impulse to publicize the shocking new disclosures that had been brought to my attention.)

The apprehensions of Israeli society, the realization that "we are like all the nations" and that "war is war," no matter how you look at it, produced sharp reactions. There were some who, to clear themselves and their society of guilt, demanded that those who participated in the murder of the POWs be tried for war crimes. But the most widespread reaction came as no surprise, though its intensity was unexpected: "All this is the product," people would say, "of the sick minds of the historians—'new' historians, of course—who at all costs want to innovate, to surprise, to anger and, above all, to destroy myths."[32]

Of course, no one denied what had happened. The argument did not center around the text, but rather the context. The most common reaction was: "OK, so they murdered POWs—but why talk about it?" or: "Sure, it happened, but this was an exception that proves the rule." What really seemed to bother most Israelis was expressed in the form of self-righteous rhetorical questions: "How could something like this happen to *us*—*we*, of all people, who were indoctrinated to use our arms only for legitimate purposes, *we* who have engaged only in defensive wars, the most moral of wars?"[33]

Establishment Reaction

What especially interested me was how the defense establishment, in general, and the IDF's Military History Unit, in particular, reacted. I am convinced that had it been up to senior defense officials, my study would have been buried forever. They call this policy "letting it rest": they won't ban publication outright, but simply tell you that the matter of clearance is still "under consideration," or is "being discussed." Anyone who has confronted a bureaucracy—any bureaucracy—knows what I am talking about.

Following the public uproar, my manuscript was returned to the Military and to the Civil Censors, as well as to the Cabinet Committee on Publications, for a very careful second round of checking. The criticism of these three bodies focused almost exclusively on one aspect: how the book would affect the *"image"* of Israel, the IDF, and Israeli society. One of the documents produced by the Cabinet Committee asked me to delete a phrase intimating that Israel sought to create more convenient borders. What was the committee's reasoning? It was that the author should abstain from such an interpretation

> so as to make his text more compatible with the geo-political realities of the Middle East and prevent the creation of an image of Israel as an expansionist and exceptional state in the region, whose borders are still volatile. . . . Ever since [Israel's] establishment, no Arab state can match it in its search for peace. This search [for peace] has contributed to its domestic sturdiness and to a balanced foreign policy.[34]

Here we have a committee not only dictating what should be deleted, but also instructing the historian what to think and how to interpret the facts! It was difficult for me to believe that this was the Israel of 1997.

For me, as an academic, this intervention was unacceptable. If the security of the state was at stake, then I could have no grounds for objection. But why should I submit to a censorship of historical assessments, images, and interpretations? In my negotiations with the Military Censor, who was involved more than others, I sensed that his office was willing to meet me halfway. It is to their credit that in most cases where I showed that certain issues had already been published, they withdrew their objections. But this was not true in all cases, especially where "image" was involved. Difficult as it was, I had to reconcile myself to the restrictions, for I had conducted the research within the defense establishment and had to abide by its rules.

There is no doubt that most of the people I dealt with were sincerely concerned about Israel's image. That's fine; they were just doing their duty. The system that is entrusted with the security of Israel, with conducting its wars and, above all, with training its soldiers must, by its very nature, adopt a subjective attitude toward past wars. It is the task of the defense establishment to train highly motivated fighters and to ensure the high morale of combat units and of all others who support the fighting forces. Israeli society is perhaps unique in its exceptionally high expectations of the defense establishment, in general, and its armed forces, in particular. The unceasing attention paid in Israel to issues such as "purity of arms" (i.e., legitimate use of weapons), "defensive wars," and "just wars," expresses a sincere aspiration to deal with, and refine, harsh realities. State institutions, like the defense establishment, have no alternative but to adopt the axiomatic assumption that we are dealing with an indisputably just cause that determines the very existence of the state that its soldiers are called upon to defend.

A critical historical approach is foreign to the very nature of such a framework; I cannot imagine how a professional historian can reconcile himself or herself to working within such a mind-set. The reality that historians encounter is rather one in which the use of arms is not always irreproachable, in which wars are not always strictly defensive in the accepted interpretation of that term, and in which there is an incessant uncertainty over the weighty moral issues that wars inevitably raise.

Who Will Write the History of Israel's Wars?

As the case of *There Will Be War this Summer* amply demonstrates, some of the questions raised in an academic framework are incompatible with the objectives of the defense establishment, which is not capable of dealing with them. The situation I have described resulted, above all, from a premature and awkward clash of two different value-systems: that of the world of scholarship, and that of the defense establishment. It is not a question of deciding which is right. Security should be left to the defense establishment, and the writing of history left to those who have made it their profession. The academic world must be aware of the fact that cooperation with the defense establishment in such an undertaking is problematic, and carries a price tag. Only one who is willing to pay that price should embark upon such a venture.

I believe that Israeli society needs to clarify the difference between education, socialization, and the inculcation of its "military heritage," on the one hand, and historical research, on the other hand. The focus on "new historians," at least as far as the general public is concerned, is a red herring that stirs up needless panic—as though their critical approach might undermine the very foundations of Israel's existence. Historians in general, and particularly those in Israel, do not speak with one voice. They are individuals who, even if they are part of the same intellectual milieu, generally do not coordinate the spirit of their studies or their conclusions. That is the very essence of academia. It is superfluous to note that there does not exist a group of historians who meet secretly to plot evil against Israel.

There are, in my view, no "new historians" or "old historians," only differing approaches and schools of thought. When their research leads to tricky issues of image and security, as we have seen, Israeli historians may be faced with restrictions, whether voluntarily or involuntarily, living and working as they do within a society that is always apprehensive, sometimes with good reason, at other times without. With regard to documentation, the defense establishment must continue to carry out the professional processes of collecting, reviewing, and arranging archival material for future research, leaving to both in-house and external, academic researchers the challenge of adducing, and debating, the lessons of the past.

Perhaps it was a mistake for me to conduct a historical study within the framework of the defense establishment. It seems impossible for an historian—whose modus operandi, at least in principle, recognizes no limits on what documents should be seen and what questions should be raised about the past—to operate comfortably as an employee within such an environment. But since, in the real world, there will always be some forms of cooperation between the defense establishment and professional historians in Israel, the rules and restrictions must be better defined for both sides: those who write the history, and those who commission it.

There is some justification, therefore, in Morris's argument. But, while Morris has based his critique solely on the "rules of fair competition" in the academic marketplace, we can see that there are far deeper and trickier issues involved.

Notes

1. Translated and condensed by the author from a review that appeared originally in Hebrew as "An Initiated War?" *Cathedra* 90 (December 1998/January 1999): 150–66.

2. Lecture delivered to senior officers, 15 January 1956 (copy in author's possession—MBO).

3. From Moshe Dayan's eulogy at the grave of Ro'i Rothberg, 30 April 1956, quoted in Dayan, *Avnei Derekh: Autobiografia* (Jerusalem: Edanim & Tel Aviv: Dvir/Yediot Aharonot, 1976), 191. Translated extract in Mordechai Bar-On, *The Gates of Gaza: Israel's Road to Suez and Back 1955–1957* (New York: St Martin's, 1994), 126–27.

4. Precisely during that period, Dayan formulated his perceptions publicly. See Dayan, "Military Activities in Time of Peace," *Ba-Mahane* 14, 21 (September 1955).

5. David Ben-Gurion's biographer explains the proposal as "a fruit of [Ben-Gurion's] pain and rage at the murder of a girl in Pattish," perpetrated a few days earlier. See Michael Bar-Zohar, *Ben-Gurion* (Tel-Aviv: Am Oved, 1978), III: 1137.

6. For full details, see Bar-On, *Gates of Gaza*, chapter 4.

7. Quoted in the chief of staff's office diary, 17 September 1956.

8. The Soviets never supported the Egyptians' claim for unlimited sovereignty over the Straits of Tiran. See Bar-On, "The USSR and the Straits of Tiran, 1954–1967," *Iyyunim be-Tkumat Israel* 1 (1991): 276–307.

9. These differentiations began to appear in Hebrew only in the late fifties. See, for instance, Yigal Allon, *A Curtain of Sand* (Tel Aviv: ha-Kibbutz ha-Meuhad, 1959).

10. Dayan to Ben-Gurion, 14 November 1955, quoted in chief of staff's office diary of the same date.

11. There was, however, at least one interesting exception, which had to do with an act of disloyalty of Dayan toward Prime Minister Sharett: namely, the resignation that Dayan submitted in protest against the last-minute cancellation of a planned reprisal operation in the Gaza Strip in late August 1955. The resignation was clearly an attempt to press the hand of the prime minister and force the government to adopt an operation the latter had chosen not to endorse. One and a half years later, Dayan unwittingly give himself a negative verdict. In March 1957, when asked why he did not resign in protest against the government's decision to order a total withdrawal from the Sinai and Gaza, Dayan answered piously,: "As a citizen and soldier, I consider it extremely improper for the Commander-in-

Chief to try to throw his personal weight into forcing the government's decisions." See Dayan, *Avnei Derekh*, 341–42.

12. For details, see Bar-On, *Gates of Gaza*, chapter 5; Bar-On, "Olive Leaves: The Excursion on the Shores of Lake Kinneret, 12 December 1955," *Iyyunim be-Tkumat Israel* 9 (1999): 87–127; Benny Morris, *Israel's Border Wars, 1949–1956: Arab Infiltration, Israeli Retaliation, and the Countdown to the Suez War* (Oxford: Clarendon Press, 1993; rev. ed. 1997), 364–69; Neil Caplan, *Futile Diplomacy,* vol. 4; *Operation Alpha and the Failure of Anglo-American Coercive Diplomacy in the Arab-Israeli Conflict, 1954–1956* (London: Frank Cass, 1997), 205–9.

13. For an earlier treatment of these developments, see Bar-On, *Challenge and Quarrel: The Road to Sinai—1956* (Sde Boqer: Ben-Gurion Research Center, 1991), 99–166 (in Hebrew).

14. Translated by the author and condensed by the editors, from a review that appeared originally in Hebrew in *ha-Aretz (Sefarim)*, 27 April 1998, pp. 4, 14.

15. Bar-On, *Challenge and Quarrel;* Bar-On, *Gates of Gaza.*

16. Morris, *Israel's Border Wars, 1949–1956.*

17. Moshe Sharett, *Personal Diary [1953–1957]*, ed. Yaakov Sharett (Tel Aviv: Sifriyat Maariv, 1978), IV: 995–97 (16 May 1955) and IV:1171 (26 September 1955).

18. See, for example, Eyal Kafkafi's treatment of the episode in *An Optional War: To Sinai and Back, 1956–1957* (Tel Aviv: Yad Tabenkin, in association with the Society to Commemorate Moshe Sharett, 1994), 99–101 (in Hebrew).

19. Rami Ginat, *The Soviet Union and Egypt, 1944–55* (London: Frank Cass, 1993); P. J. Vatikiotis, *The Egyptian Army in Politics; Pattern for New Nations?* (Bloomington: Indiana University Press, 1961); *The History of Modern Egypt: from Muhammad Ali to Mubarak*, 4th ed. (Baltimore: Johns Hopkins university Press, 1991); *Politics and the Military in Jordan, A Study of the Arab Legion, 1921–1957* (London: Frank Cass, 1967); Meir Har Zion, *Chapters of a Diary* (Tel Aviv: Lewin-Epstein, n.d.) (in Hebrew).

20. Some of the more vicious attacks emanated from circles associated with Ariel Sharon, commander of the 202d Brigade during the Sinai Campaign, whose unit became entangled in a needless, bloody battle at the Mitla Pass in western Sinai. See Uri Dan, "How I Discovered at Last that I Am a Murderer," *Ma'ariv,* 4 August 1995, pp.16–17 (in Hebrew).

21. During 1956–1957, Bar-On was adjutant to chief of the general staff Dayan. It was he who kept the daily record of events and wrote the summary of the campaign that was printed in four copies only in 1958, and

subsequently published, with omissions demanded by Israeli military censorship, as *Challenge and Quarrel.*

22. Bar-On, "An Initiated War?" 153 (in Hebrew).

23. Morris, *Israel's Border Wars 1949–1956.*

24. In the end, all the sources were cited in full in my Ph.D. thesis, which was deposited in major libraries in Israel. In the published volume, I was forced to agree to omit file numbers of documentation held by the defense establishment. This "compromise"—based on the fallacy that there is a difference between a commercial publication and an academic thesis to which access is ostensibly limited only to academics—proves that trepidation is generally not a guarantee of a logical solutions.

25. The exact relationship between the Military History Unit of the IDF and the defense establishment is not clear—certainly not with what pertains to ongoing research. Each institution does as it pleases and the guidelines of one do not seem to obligate the other.

26. A proper discussion of the difficulties that this important archive places before scholars engaged in studying the history of the State of Israel lies beyond the scope of this essay. Let me only state that, in my opinion, a suitably inspired directorate of the IDF Archives could find a way to supply the information needs of a progressive and democratic society without impairing Israel's security.

27. The basis for the essay was an article that had been published somewhat earlier. See Motti Golani, "Dayan Leads to War: The Role of the Chief of Staff in the Israeli Government Decision to Go to War in October 1956," *Iyyunim Bi-Tkumat Israel* 4 (1994): 117–35 (in Hebrew). I provided further elaboration in the book under review here.

28. In eulogizing Dayan over twenty years ago, the respected journalist Amos Elon wrote that in 1956, as army chief of staff, he had "pushed Ben-Gurion into the military adventure of the Suez war." See his "End of an Affair," *ha-Aretz*, 6 August 1981, translated in *A Blood-Dimmed Tide: Dispatches from the Middle East* (New York: Columbia University Press, 1997), 61.

29. Meir Amit, "David Ben-Gurion and Moshe Dayan," lecture at Ben-Gurion University, Beersheva, April 1995 (stenographic record). See also M. Kafra, "One of the Boys," *Ma'ariv Weekend Supplement*, 28 April 1995, pp. 6–10. Amit recently published a book in which he takes issue with my views in a manner no less "violent" than he did orally or in the press in 1995. See Amit, *Head On: A Personal View of Great Events and Unknown Episodes* (Or Yehuda: Hed Arzi,1999), chapters 4–6 (all citations in Hebrew).

30. Amit's campaign against me included turning to Haim Israeli, assistant to the minister of defense and for the past fifty years the person unofficially responsible for the history of Israel's defense establishment in general and the heritage of Ben-Gurion in particular. Amit requested that he prevent my study from being published on the grounds that I was defaming the image of Ben-Gurion. Israeli's function as "state guardian of the collective memory" is a subject worthy of a study of its own.

31. A. Oren, "The Reflection of the October War," *Davar*, 21 July 1995, p. 5; "Raful Involved in Murder of 35 Egyptian POWs," *Yediot Aharonot*, 21 July 1995, p.2; Sh. Segal, "Golani Mounts a Charge at the Myth," *Arei Hamifratz* (Haifa), 28 July 1995, pp. 38–40; R. Fisher, "Massacre in Sinai," *Ma'ariv,* 4 August 1995, Weekend Supplement, pp. 4–8, 10, 12. Coordinated and prearranged interviews with, and news stories about, Brig. Gen. (Res.) Aryeh Biro were published that very same day in *Yerushalayim, Koteret* and *Yediot Aharonot* (all articles in Hebrew).

32. Such reactions are primarily characteristic of those who are generally unaware of the intensive internal debate that has been conducted during the past few years about all facets of Israeli historiography, including its relationship to the Israeli, Zionist, and Jewish identities. These debates, on the whole, also include members of the defense establishment. See, for instance, P. Ginossar and A. Bareli, eds., *Zionism—A Contemporary Controversy: Research Trends and Ideological Approaches* (Sde Boqer: Ben-Gurion Research Center, 1996); Y. Weitz, ed., *From Vision to Revision: A Hundred Years of Historiography of Zionism* (Jerusalem: Zalman Shazar Center, 1997) (both anthologies in Hebrew).

33. I was fascinated to learn that there is nothing new in this respect. In the early 1950s Lt. Gen. Netanel Lorch had a run-in with the defense establishment in his efforts to publish the study he had prepared on the 1948 war in his capacity as head of the Historical Section of the IDF. Lorch brought to his IDF job what he had been taught at the Hebrew University, and soon clashed with senior military and political officials. "[C]ertain factual statements," he recalled in a recent memoir, "were not to the liking of the distinguished committee members"—a committee headed by former chief of staff, Ya'akov Dori, commissioned with "improving" the study. "The line its deliberations took can be summed up as: 'Why do you need to . . .', i.e., 'Why do you need to tell about abandoned property, about the handling of prisoners and about operations that were a failure'?" Lorch, *Late Afternoon: My First Seventy Years* (Tel Aviv: Ministry of Defense, 1997), 199 (in Hebrew).

34. Arie Zohar, deputy government secretary, to the director of the IDF publisher, Ma'arachot, 23 June 1997.

2. The Holocaust and Its Fifty-Year-Old Commemoration: Have We Reached the Limit?

Rachel Feldhay Brenner,
University of Wisconsin-Madison

Recent Holocaust Studies have become increasingly reflexive and retrospective. Historical, psychological, and literary approaches now focus less on the events of the Holocaust and more on the ways in which the Holocaust has been commemorated and represented over the past half century. New works in this area generally follow two trajectories: some collect, sum up, categorize, and group past findings, while others attempt a critical revision of accepted historical interpretations. This essay provides a broad survey of these developments in connection with Israeli society, including the transmission of memory from one generation to the next. The author concludes by examining several works of fiction in light of the questions raised here.

Appelfeld, Aharon, *The Story of a Life,* Jerusalem: Keter, 1999 (in Hebrew: *Sippur Hayim*).

Doron, Lizi, *Why Didn't You Come Before the War?*, Tel Aviv: Halonot, 1998 (in Hebrew: *Lama Lo Bat lifney ha-Milhama?*).

Friling, Tuvia, *An Arrow in the Fog: David Ben-Gurion, the Yishuv Leadership and Rescue Attempts during the Holocaust*, Sde Boker: Ben

Gurion Research Center, 1998 (in Hebrew: *Hets ba-Arafel: David Ben-Gurion, Hanhagat ha-Yishuv ve-Nisyonot Hatsala ba-Sho'ah*).

Govrin, Michal, *The Name*, New York: Riverhead Books, 1998.

Peled, Oded, ed., *My Yellow Robe: The Holocaust in Poetry of the Second Generation—An Anthology,* Tel Aviv: Agudat ha-Sofrim ha-Ivrim b'Israel, 1997 (in Hebrew: *Kutonti ha-Tsehuba: ha-Sho'ah be-Shirat ha-Dor ha-Sheni—Antologya*).

Rappel, Yo'el, ed., *Memory and Awareness of the Holocaust in Israel*, Tel Aviv: Masua, 1998 (in Hebrew: *Zikaron Samui, Zikaron Galui : Toda`at ha-Sho'ah bi-Medinat Yisra'el).*

Rosenthal, Gabriele, ed., *The Holocaust in Three Generations: Families and Victims and Perpetrators of the Nazi Regime*, London: Cassel, 1998.

Sicher, Efraim, ed., *Breaking Crystal: Writing and Memory after Auschwitz*, Urbana: University of Chicago Press, 1998.

Zertal, Idith, *From Catastrophe to Power: Holocaust Survivors and the Emergence of Israel,* Berkeley: University of California Press, 1998.

To set the parameters for this discussion, I resort to two eminently qualified writers on the Holocaust. In his "Afterword: The Shoah between Memory and History" in Efraim Sicher's *Breaking Crystal: Writing and Memory after Auschwitz,* Saul Friedländer claims that "on the one hand, the memory of [the] victims [of the Holocaust] is more present than ever in our historical consciousness; on the other hand, both the representation of the events and their interpretation approach the limits that may well be inherent in the very nature of this crime" (p. 355).[1] In his recently published autobiography, *The Story of a Life,* Aharon Appelfeld confesses,

> I can feel that time in my . . . body. Whenever it rains, or it's cold, or a hard wind blows, I go back to the ghetto, to the camp, to the forests. Memory has deep roots in the body . . . though I have not yet found words for these powerful shadows of memory. . . . All I could come up with was gibberish . . . wrong words, discordant rhythm, weak or exaggerated images. Even now I will not touch this fire. Not about the camp shall I tell. . . . (p. 49)

The teller of Holocaust experience corroborates the observation of the Holocaust historian: the means and ways of transmitting the event have reached their limits, exposing the writer's limitations. Though it has branded our consciousness, the "fire" of the event has erected linguistically impenetrable boundaries around its memory.

The biographies of these writers invest their perceptions with particular authority. As children-survivors, both Friedländer and Appelfeld witnessed the Holocaust; as bona fide Israelis, they became participants in Israel's efforts to deal with the catastrophic legacy. Their perspectives, which contrast the power of memory with the limited extent to which this memory can be artistically and scientifically explored and communicated, raise important questions. Do recent responses to the Holocaust signal future approaches beyond the kinds of limitations noted by both survivors? Or, do they rather reconfirm the notion that the search for the meaning of the Holocaust has reached its final stage? Though there are of course no clear-cut answers to these questions, this essay suggests that, with some exceptions, recent studies of the Holocaust for the most part no longer ponder the event itself but rather dwell on its effects.

At this historical juncture that marks over a half-century since the end of the war, the jubilee of the State of Israel, and the new millennium, studies of the Holocaust signal a compulsive preoccupation with Holocaust memory in both personal and communal spheres. In other words, rather than continuing the discussion initiated by Theodor Adorno, George Steiner, and Elie Wiesel about the im/possibility of Holocaust representation, or suggesting new approaches to the Holocaust thematic, these recent studies sum up, classify, and historicize the impact of the Holocaust on the arts, literature, psychosociological attitudes, and ideological orientations. The volumes before us in this review—collected essays, reexamined histories, an anthology and post-Holocaust life stories—provide surveys of more than fifty years. These books demonstrate very clearly that the preoccupation with the memory of the Holocaust now has a history of its own. The prevailing mode of writing is retrospective, that is, this literature takes stock of what has been done in the area of Holocaust representation.

My discussion will focus first on matters of history, ideology, and public rhetoric. I then turn to psychological, sociological, and literary approaches to the second generation and to intergenerational patterns of Holocaust consciousness. Finally, I conclude with a discussion of recent fiction that suggests a new perspective and a concern with a question of faith.

History, Ideology, and Rhetoric

The tendency to reevaluate the impact of the Holocaust on Israeli life and culture in the 1990s must be considered in the context of the 1980s, which saw a transformation of Israel's *Weltanschauung*. At that time, Israel's self-image as a collective of "new" Jews collapsed—due to the post-1967 War of Attrition, the catastrophe of the October 1973 war, the unjustified (according to many) Lebanon war of 1982, and the Intifada (uprising) that began in late 1987. In view of problematic victories and questionable military operations, it was no longer possible to claim Israel's invincibility; in view of the prolonged Intifada and the cause of its fighters, it was no longer possible to claim that the occupation had a humanistic nature. Recent history, which exposed the military weakness of the "new" Jews and collapsed their sense of moral superiority, ushered in a process of critical self-revision in Israeli society. Having entered a stage of collective reckoning, Israel could no longer maintain its ideological dissociation from the Diaspora. The events that called in question the Zionist vision of a powerful and righteous nation diminished what had seemed, in the first decades of the state, a nonnegotiable distance from the history of the Diaspora—and especially from the victimization that Jews had experienced during the Holocaust. Indeed, in the 1980s, identification with the Holocaust permeated Israel's public life.

Popularized, some would say trivialized and exploited, the historical legacy of the Holocaust indelibly affected Israel's politics, culture, education, and perhaps, most importantly, an ongoing reevaluation of Zionist ideology. In fact, the Holocaust became an extremely powerful rhetorical tool in Israel's public life. It has often been enlisted for Israel's new discourse of cultural and historical revision and change. In a very real sense, Holocaust memory became a norm against which Zionist politics was judged. In other words, the revisionist evaluation of the Zionist establishment was, to a remarkable extent, determined by what was perceived as manipulation of Holocaust memory to promote the Zionist project.

Israel's evolving perceptions of the Holocaust have been thoroughly covered in two recently published edited volumes. Yo'el Rappel's *Memory and Awareness of the Holocaust in Israel* complements the section of Israeli responses to the Holocaust in Sicher's volume, *Breaking Crystal*. The two books present a comprehensive and well-researched multidisciplinary review of pre-state and state responses to the Holocaust. (Sicher's volume also includes essays on responses to the Holocaust in the Diaspora that are not under the purview of this essay).

Rappel's volume opens with a recent interview with Aharon Appelfeld. Appelfeld's view of the Zionist response to the Holocaust marks the negative pole on the revisionist spectrum. Like his memoir, *The Story of a Life,* this interview reflects his bitterness not only about cynical Zionist attitudes toward Holocaust victims in the past, but also about neglect of the issue at present. He accuses Zionism of having assumed a triumphalist position vis-à-vis the victims. "The Zionist approach in Israel," he claims, "can be summed up in the actually never uttered words—we were right. This is the ultimate point of view which says that the Zionist prognosis was correct. . . . The assumption that Zionism will create a 'new' Jew saw in the Holocaust an event that happened to a Jew from an old and bad stock." As Appelfeld sees it, even today there is no sensitivity or recognition of the importance of the Holocaust: "I am the only writer who writes obsessively on the Holocaust. . . . My books are not for everybody. I write for an elite which is sensitive to what happened to Jews there and to what has been happening to Jews here" ("Personal and Public Memory: A Conversation with Aharon Appelfeld," in Rappel, pp. 13, 17, 15, 16).

Whereas Appelfeld notes no redeeming features in today's attitudes toward the Holocaust and the world of the Diaspora, others see some signs of change. In contrast with the attitude of triumphalism that led Israelis to emphasize stories of heroic ghetto uprisings and courageous resistance on the part of the partisans, increasing attention has now been paid to the story of suffering and loss. In her overview of the history of Holocaust monuments in Israel, Judith Tydor Baumel notes a recent shift in the culture of official commemoration that intended to reinforce the Zionist ethos of Jewish self-sufficiency and to glorify the concept of the "new" Jew. Baumel notes a growing inclination to include the story of annihilated communities, and thereby to pay more attention to the history of suffering and victimization. She reaches the conclusion that "there has been a conceptual transformation in Israeli society in recent years, namely the willingness to legitimize European immigrant culture, [and] recognize its vitality by integrating some of it in the official patterns of commemoration." Among the reasons for this increased attention to the destroyed world of the Diaspora, Baumel singles out the Israeli youth journeys to Poland. She notes that recent educational emphasis on the history of the Jewish culture, coupled with less intense promotion of the national ethos of triumphalism, might have contributed to the changing patterns of commemoration ("'For Eternal Remembrance:' Commemoration of the Holocaust by the Individual and the Community in the State of Israel," in Rappel, p. 38).

The enterprise of youth journeys to Poland is taken to task, however, in Nili Keren's incisively critical essay. Keren denounces the educational failure of these tours and recommends a serious rethinking of the project. According to Keren the excursions to the "killing fields" in Poland were intended as a quick and simplistic remedy, meant to strengthen disintegrating values, such as "nationality," "Zionism," and "Jewish consciousness." Tours to death camps have become "a corrective experience" intended to revalidate these no longer meaningful concepts through superficial identification with the Holocaust. Ironically, by placing the Holocaust in the center of Jewish-Israeli identity, the journeys continue to reinforce the Zionist ethos of triumphalism, that is, the indispensability of a "strong Israel." Like Baumel, Keren points to attempts to transform the excursions into meaningful, educational experiences. Nonetheless, Keren has found that the students seem to be compulsively drawn to the death camp experience while remaining disinterested in the cultural heritage of the Diaspora. Therefore, the attempts to draw attention to issues such as pre-Holocaust Jewish history, the past and the present of the hosting countries, and the ethics of response to brutality and dehumanization have ultimately failed ("Students' Excursion to Poland—A Journey for Shaping Memory," in Rappel, pp. 98, 99).

Invariably, these reevaluations of Israel's sociological (Appelfeld), cultural (Baumel), and educational (Keren) responses to the Holocaust entail a critical evaluation of Zionist ideology and especially the triumphalist construct of the "new" Jew. Criticism of a similar nature emerges also in the examination of the relationship between gender and the Holocaust story. Ronit Lantin's essay explores the connection between the politics of silence toward the Holocaust story and the male dominant culture of the "new" Jews. She associates Israel's chauvinist orientations with its derogatory attitude to the "weak" and therefore "feminine" Diaspora Jew. According to Lantin, recently emerged personal stories of second-generation women writers and filmmakers about their encounters with Holocaust memory is an important sociological phenomenon. As she sees it, "breaking the silence imposed on the Holocaust story amounts to breaking the male hegemony over Israeli identity" ("To Conquer Again the Territory of Silence—Women Writers and Film Makers as Daughters of Holocaust Survivors," in Rappel, p. 171). Nonetheless, Lantin notes that the reluctant reception of these stories communicates that "most Israelis either cannot or will not apologize for their silence toward the survivors from 'over there'" and that "the myth of the male Sabra in contradistinction to the feminine victim of the Holocaust still exists" (pp. 181, 182).

The evolution toward this new phase in Israel's attitude, which recognizes the Diaspora and acknowledges Holocaust memory in Israeli life, came after periods of almost complete silencing of the survivor's personal experience. The suppression of personal suffering was combined with exploitation of the Holocaust for national and political gains. In her essay on the early formation of Holocaust consciousness in Israel, Hanna Yablonka points out that while the left-wing Mapai party oriented itself toward "building the future, almost without looking back," the right-wing Herut party "looked almost entirely to the past," constructing the rhetoric of Holocaust mythification. According to Yablonka, the survivors rejected the Herut rhetoric altogether, since they wished to forget the past to rebuild their lives and to "rehabilitate themselves as an integral part of Israeli society." The historian points to the survivors' introjection of the negative image of "sheep to the slaughter," which imposed silence upon their experience of annihilation "over there," in the Diaspora ("The Formation of Holocaust Consciousness in Israel," in Sicher, p. 133).

The image of the Diaspora Jews who let themselves be exterminated "like sheep to the slaughter," became a focal point in reevaluations of the prestate Yishuv and its responses to the European tragedy. Controversy about the efforts to save European Jewry is still raging on. In the center of the controversy looms the figure of David Ben-Gurion and the question of his dedication to the rescue of European Jews. The dispute began with Tom Segev's 1991 *Seventh Million: The Israelis and the Holocaust,* which presented Ben-Gurion as a cold and petty politician who exploited the suffering of the Holocaust victims to promote the idea of statism, that is, the establishment of the Jewish State.[2] Shabtai Teveth, Ben-Gurion's biographer and unwavering admirer, offered a vehement refutation of Segev's condemnation. In his 1996 *Ben-Gurion and the Holocaust,* Teveth maintains that "Ben-Gurion's thinking was quite the opposite of what his critics allege: If he could have rescued all the Jews of Europe by sacrificing the state, he would have done it." Teveth goes on to claim that Ben-Gurion's seeming indifference to the fate of Holocaust victims in Europe was by no means rooted in an ideological bias against the Diaspora. His focus on strengthening the Yishuv, with a view to the future state, revealed a remarkable measure of redeeming pragmatism. Teveth conjectures that early on Ben-Gurion realized that nothing could be done for the Jews trapped in Nazi Europe. "[A] case can be made," he argues, "that in focusing his energy on preparing for the postwar revival of the Jewish people in Palestine, Ben-Gurion showed unprecedented courage and determination. Where others resorted to tears and wailing, he took up the tools of the mason to rebuild the ruins."[3]

In a recent essay, Anita Shapira attempts to defuse the conflicted appreciations of Ben-Gurion's response to the Holocaust. She maintains that one-sided characterizations of Ben-Gurion serve revisionist purposes, but by no means do they reflect the two facets of his attitude to the Diaspora. While "on the one hand, he did not like the concept of the 'Diaspora Jew' and what it represented, . . . on the other hand, he identified with the real Jewish people, and considered himself responsible for its fate." Shapira claims that his towering stature made Ben-Gurion the visible target of the controversy. However, she refutes the argument that ideological condemnation of Diaspora Jews who did not recognize the Zionist cause caused Ben-Gurion and his colleagues to abandon European Jewry. Curiously, Shapira fends off this accusation by minimizing the power of ideology in personal and collective decision making. In what seems quite a puzzling proposition in a century both shaped and governed by ideologies, Shapira claims that even though Ben-Gurion and others did not, for some undisclosed reason, reveal their emotions, their attitude toward European Jewry was shaped by feelings rather than by ideological considerations. The mistakes that they made, Shapira concludes, "were not rooted in some immanent moral deficiency of the Zionist movement, but rather in a particular and coincidental convergence of people and circumstances, which is the essence of any historical event."[4]

Other recent studies of the Yishuv and its responses to the Holocaust are far from subscribing to the notion of historical arbitrariness. Nor are they ready to dismiss the centrality of the role Ben-Gurion played in shaping the collective attitude toward the Holocaust. Idith Zertal's historical study, *From Catastrophe to Power: Holocaust Survivors and the Emergence of Israel,* demonstrates that the revisionist debate over the Holocaust is by no means over. Zertal tells the history of the clandestine immigration (*ha'apalah*) of Holocaust survivors from Europe to Palestine in the interim years between the end of the war in Europe and the establishment of the State of Israel. It is the story of the so-called illegal immigration launched despite the British White Paper that barred Jews from entering Palestine. The main episodes, especially the famous story of the *Exodus,* are vividly presented. The stories of the Mossad agents who organized the immigration and accompanied the survivors in the old boats to face the British navy are often moving narratives of acts of self-sacrifice and civil courage for the sake of the survivors.

The representation of this dramatic chapter in post-Holocaust Jewish history, however, is not the main objective of Zertal's study. The author rather uses the story in order to undermine the heroic legend of the *ha'apalah,* that is, the image of the "new" and dauntless Jews from Eretz Israel rescuing the pitiful weak Diaspora Jews. The underlying claim is that the plight of the immigrants was often cynically exacerbated for the purposes of publicity that would gain the world's support for the future Jewish State. The study especially targets Ben-Gurion, who had no sympathy for the Diaspora Jews, infamously calling them "human dust," and who, according to Zertal, ruthlessly exploited the misery of the survivors for the sake of the political interests of the Yishuv. Zertal thus perceives the story of the clandestine immigration as a test of the ethical integrity of the Zionist establishment at large. As she sees it, the establishment failed the test on all counts.

Zertal concludes her study with an indictment of opportunistic Zionist manipulation of the victims. She claims that "[i]n order to realize the ultimate, complete Zionist redemption . . . to forge from the catastrophe of millions a redemption and power for millions, in Ben-Gurion's words, the Zionist collective had to sanctify the victims of the catastrophe and tarnish them at the same time. . . . Thus the Holocaust, its victims, and its survivors all played their crucial historical roles according to the Zionist script." To explain this less than noble attitude toward the survivors, Zertal quite unexpectedly, and one might claim incongruously, turns in the last pages of this long study to the psychoanalytic concept of the uncanny. The survivors represented to the Zionist establishment "the coming to light of what should remain concealed, the unearthing of the unconscious. The 'otherness' of the horror, severed from the very logic of life [defied] any attempt of being directly looked at, of being understood, represented, and memorized. . . ." That is why, according to the author, the Zionists chose not to see the victims and their suffering, but rather only "what was supposed to be seen, what served the Zionist project" (pp. 273, 274).

The revisionist claim, that for the sake of "complete Zionist redemption" irredeemable ethical transgressions were committed, has evoked dialectical responses aimed at clearing the name of the Zionist establishment. Tuvia Friling's study of Zionist responses to the Holocaust, which runs to over a thousand pages, is a recent example of an establishment counterattack directed at the so-called post-Zionists. Ironically, the underlying intention of this enormous undertaking demonstrates some interesting similarities with Zertal's revisionist study. Ostensibly objective historical research, Friling's *Arrow in the Fog: David Ben-Gurion, the Yishuv Leadership and Rescue Attempts during the Holocaust* reveals in its impassioned tone a desire to defend Zionist conduct as intense as his revisionist opponents' wish to condemn it. It seems that on both the dissident and the conservative sides, it is, to a large extent, the prevailing need to either attack or protect the Zionist enterprise at large that has informed the investigations into the Yishuv's responses to the Holocaust. Even more significant is the ironic consensus revealed in both Friling's line of defense and that of his ideological opponents. Friling and Zertal concur in condemning the exploitation of the Holocaust and its victims for the political interests of the Yishuv. Neither of them seeks to rationalize such behavior by, for instance, claiming extenuating historical circumstances. And so, whereas Zertal, a revisionist critic, desires to expose and condemn Zionist opportunism, Friling, a defender of the Zionist project, passionately denies the accusation altogether and claims that it is historically false.

The overarching intention of Friling's study is to disprove the well-known argument that the "Palestinocentric" Yishuv neither cared nor did enough about the fate of European Jewry. According to Friling, and we recall Shapira's similar argument, this opinion was formed due to the Zionist tenet of the "negation of the Diaspora," which posited the superiority of the "new" Jew and insisted on complete estrangement from the Diaspora. Friling cannot deny the politics of Diaspora negation cultivated by the Zionist establishment under Ben-Gurion. He therefore constructs a strategy of defense according to which negation did not amount to abandonment. He claims that even though they disapproved of Jewish life in the Diaspora, the Yishuv and especially Ben-Gurion tried every possible way to rescue the Jews in Europe. Consequently, the question that Friling is desirous to settle is why, despite the persistent rescue efforts, "the image of Ben-Gurion as a cold and pedantic, dry and down-to-earth man, and as a cruel revolutionary dedicated exclusively to promoting his objective [of the Jewish State] became associated with his position vis-à-vis the European Jews in the Holocaust"?

According to Friling the reason lies, first of all, in the fact that Ben-Gurion's attempts to save Jews have remained for the most part unknown until now. The most obvious reason for this obscurity was the complete failure of the rescue efforts. The other reason was the clandestine nature of these efforts. The "Parallel System" established by Ben-Gurion for the rescue operations included only two other members beside him. As Friling sees it, Ben-Gurion did not consider the Yishuv mature or unified enough to handle the seriousness of the matter, and the plans were kept secret. That is why, Friling claims, "the documentation is scarce, encoded . . . it was kept away from the historians as well as the public" (p. 939).

Then, in an attempt that reveals an intense desire to exonerate Ben-Gurion at all cost, in the very last paragraphs of the long historical study, Friling, unexpectedly and as incongruously as Zertal, resorts to a psychoanalytic explanation. This line of defense allows him to place the blame on Ben-Gurion's accusers among whom he includes the Holocaust survivors. Friling claims that the revisionist accusations derive from a psychological need for a scapegoat. The Israelis, he maintains, were burdened with unbearable feelings of guilt toward annihilated European Jewry and so they projected their guilt on the "founding father" (p. 947) whom they chose as the "sacrifice of atonement" (p. 946). The survivors also needed a scapegoat. They sought to relieve their pain and rage incurred by the difficulties of emigration from Europe after the terror of the Holocaust, followed by the hardships of the war of Independence. They attempted to ease their disaffection by "sacrificing the 'king,' who, sacrificed, as it were, his brothers in Europe for the state" (pp. 951).

It is of interest to note how both the "post-Zionist" dissident and the "establishment Zionist" enlist Sigmund Freud to defend their ideologic positions. I would suggest that these psychoanalytic speculations are by no means substantiated by the research that precedes them and are therefore hardly convincing. At the same time, the recourse to psychoanalytic speculations reinforces my initial notion of the reflexive and retrospective nature of recent Holocaust studies.

The Second Generation

Since this literature spans a period of fifty years, the issue of intergenerational patterns of Holocaust consciousness is at the center of its attention. In *The Holocaust in Three Generations: Families and Victims and Perpetrators of the Nazi Regime,* Gabriele Rosenthal presents us with an interesting study of memory transmission from one generation to the next, examining Israeli families of the victims and East German families of the perpetrators. Rosenthal has conducted a courageous, thoughtful, and thorough study, which has led to interesting, though not entirely unexpected conclusions. Generally, she claims, "in survivor families, the construction of and identification with [family myths] focus on the themes of 'strength' and resistance. . . . In families with a Nazi past, this takes the form of emphasizing the victimhood of the family members" (p. 31). This is an interesting categorization that points to the psychological defenses that the descendants on both sides erected to protect themselves against parental and grandparental legacies. It also points to the often latent sense of guilt embedded in both responses. Since the fascinating research on the East German families lies outside the purview of this essay, I turn to Rosenthal's findings on Israeli families.

Of particular interest for this discussion is the distinction that Rosenthal draws between the families of the survivors and the families of Youth Aliyah "forced emigrants," who came to Palestine as children having left their families behind. In the survivor families, the victims, determined to rebuild their lives and therefore motivated to comply with Israel's ideological expectations, were reluctant to tell the story. Not surprisingly, the children and grandchildren were unwilling for the longest time to acknowledge the indignities and the helplessness of the survivors. At the same time, they also experienced a sense of guilt for not having been "over there." According to the researcher, while the survivors often find it very difficult to tell the story to their own children, the consciousness of their losses promotes extremely close family ties. The children often wish to compensate for their parents' suffering by protecting and taking care of them.

In the case of families of "forced emigrants," the sense of guilt for having abandoned their families and for not having done more to help them translated into a lifelong devotion to the Zionist idea and to the State of Israel. The children of these ardent Zionists have continued to glorify the parental pioneering history, disregarding their European past and heritage, identifying with "Zionism as a collective duty," while "their image of being Sabras . . . became a crucial part of their identity" (pp. 151, 150). However, in terms of the third generation, Rosenthal, like the other scholars discussed here, notes a considerable change of attitude in the 1980s marked by empathic responses to the Holocaust and even identification with the Holocaust victims. Let me reiterate that this transformed attitude toward Jewish victimization in the Holocaust resulted from the traumatic historical events of the Yom Kippur War in 1973, the controversy concerning the Lebanon War in 1982, the national split over the Intifada, and the shocking reality of the Gulf War in 1991. The ritual of journeys of young people to concentration camps in Poland has also contributed significantly to a new outlook on the Holocaust. According to Rosenthal's findings, even though they continue to emphasize the building of the country and underplay their family history in Europe, the members of the third-generation Sabras reveal interest in their grandparents' past.

The merit of Rosenthal's study lies in its sociological reconfirmation of the patterns of Israeli responses to the Holocaust, which have been researched through other disciplines. As we have seen, the sociological findings of changing attitudes in the 1980s complement, to a large extent, the conclusions of research in areas such as history, cinema, fiction, and poetry. The traumatic events of this period in the history of the state mark the transformation of Israel's collective self-image and cultural norms that resulted in a new consciousness of the Diaspora at large and of the Holocaust in particular.

The psychoanalytic dimension in Israel's response to the Holocaust is emphasized in Ilan Avisar's survey of the phenomenon that he names "the Holocaust complex in Israeli cinema" ("Personal Fears and National Nightmares: The Holocaust Complex in Israeli Cinema," in Sicher, p. 137). According to this Israeli film scholar, Israeli cinema has reflected the changing social responses from "suppression and rejection" of Holocaust memory to "fixation and obsession" on the event. Avisar's observations of the cinematic promotion of ideological and political purposes confirms Yablonka's historical research. As Avisar sees it, films produced in the first decades of the state "conveyed a patronizing view toward the victims and a triumphalist attitude regarding their harsh circumstances." Even the Eichmann trial in 1961 did not remove the stigma from the survivor's past. On the contrary, the dramatic capturing of Eichmann and his trial in the Israeli court reinforced the concept of the "new" Jew, the triumphant avenger of the "old" Diaspora Jew.

Like Rosenthal, Avisar notes the importance of the 1980s in terms of Israel's changing attitudes. He sees the changes in Israeli cinema during that period as a reflection of the reconsidered views of the Diaspora and the Holocaust. Avisar makes an important differentiation between two categories in the revisionist response of Israeli cinema. The cinema of the Holocaust, produced by the children of the survivors, took a revisionist stand toward the suppression of parental Holocaust experience. This position focuses on the psychological predicament of both parents and children. These documentaries demonstrate the unresolved issues of parental experience transmitted to the generation of the children. Avisar singles out the documentary *Because of That War,* in particular, for its insightful and sensitive treatment of "the lingering traumas of the survivors, and the psychological wounds inherited by their children" (p. 154).

The documentary film is, of course, only one of the media that the "second generation" has used to approach parental experience of the Holocaust. In her discussions of Holocaust literature, Hanna Yaoz distinguishes between the "historical" trend of literary expression of the Holocaust, which is mimetic, and the "transhistorical" expression, which avoids the realistic and moves to the realms of the absurd and the fantastic. According to Yaoz, the latter typifies the second-generation expression of parental legacy.

Yaoz situates this generation in a larger historical scheme of Israeli literary responses to the Holocaust. This literature starts with poets, such as Natan Alterman, Avraham Shlonsky, and Uri Zvi Greenberg, who responded to the catastrophe from the distance of the Yishuv in the forties. These poets adopted the tradition of lamentation, mourning, and protest. The following was the generation of survivors-witnesses, such as Dan Pagis, Itamar Yaoz-Kest, Ya'akov Besser, Ben-Zion Tomer, and Ka-Tzetnik joined by the younger Aharon Appelfeld, Shamai Golan, and Uri Orlev. These writers' search for an adequate representation of their experiences oscillated between the genres of the realistic and the mythical, that is, between concrete depictions of the horror and idealized recollections of life before the Holocaust. The subsequent response of the next generation, of the children of survivors, has moved to the fantastic that conflates the realistic and the absurd. The genre of the fantastic demonstrates the reality of the absurd in the world of the Holocaust. Among prose writers Yaoz mentions David Grossman, Savyon Liebrecht, and Nava Semel. According to Yaoz, they "write about concerns that are very familiar to them, such as the conspiracy of silence, guilt feelings, traumatic anxieties and fears, the burden of immortalizing memory, and the legacy of suffering" ("Inherited Fear: Second Generation Poets and Novelists in Israel," in Sicher, p.161). The post-Holocaust writers both resist, and are drawn to, parental history. Not having been "over there," they attempt to come to terms with the burden of history by creating their own images of the unimaginable world of parental Holocaust experience.

From the second generation of novelistic writing, it was especially David Grossman's *See Under Love* that was singled out by critics for its innovative perception of the Holocaust.[5] Of particular biographical interest is the fact that Grossman is not a child of Holocaust survivors; he therefore has no personal attachment to Holocaust memory. The recognition of Grossman's imagined representation of the Holocaust marks the extensiveness of Holocaust collective consciousness. The memory of the Holocaust has extended beyond the domain of the survivors and their families. In his reading of Grossman, Leon Yudkin claims that "autobiography is not a relevant criterion here. What matters is a depiction of the world of the child of survivors. . . . Transmission of the experience and its aftermath remains a constant reality as long as there is a psychic genetic link between the generations" ("Holocaust and Trauma in the Second Generation: The Hebrew Fiction of David Grossman and Savyon Liebrecht," in Sicher, p. 171). As Yudkin sees it, Grossman demonstrates that the experience can be represented through an imaginative effort that creates art. The art of storytelling snatches the final victory away from the Nazis and acknowledges the moral victory of the storyteller. Yudkin refers here to the controversial segment in Grossman's novel where Wasserman, a Jew whose family was murdered in a death camp, is compelled to tell stories to the Nazi commandant of the concentration camp.

Controversy about the fictional construction of the concentration camp constitutes the focus of Gilead Morahg's essay, "Breaking Silence: Israel's Fantastic Fiction of the Holocaust" that appeared in a recent volume on Israeli fiction in the 1980s.[6] Morahg refines Yaoz's perception of second-generation fiction by identifying the genre of the fantastic in a limited number of novels, namely, Grossman's *See Under Love,* Yitzhak Ben-Ner's *The Angels Are Coming,* Dorit Peleg's *Una,* and Itamar Levy's *The Legend of the Sad Lakes,* all published in the later 1980s.[7] He classifies the other novels of the period as mainly descriptive; they offer realistic representations of the damaging effects of the Holocaust. In contrast, the fantastic novels, "characterized by iconoclastic postmodern structures,"[8] herald a new attitude to the Holocaust in Israeli culture.

Morahg's reading of the novels adopts a psychoanalytic orientation. The underlying intention of the postmodern fantastic novels, he asserts, is to liberate the second generation from an unhealthy relationship to the world, whereby denial of the Holocaust experience resulted in an anxiety of survival. In other words, the refusal to acknowledge the horror of the parental past results in haunting uncertainties about the present. The solution to this psychological conundrum in the four novels is predicated upon "an unflinching encounter with the agonies of the concentrationary universe," (p. 145) that is, a fictional reconstruction of the death camp experience. In all four novels, the Holocaust horror is revisited and reexperienced through the genre of the fantastic. Morahg is aware that this approach defies the convention that has excluded the concentration camp from the realm of fictional representation. However, he approvingly notes that the transgression marks "the need to advance the work of healing [which] outweighs all ethical and cultural aversions to recuperating the traumas and losses of the victim" (p. 162)

In contrast to this interpretation, Avner Holzman's reading emphasizes that representation of the Holocaust in this fiction is unacceptable.[9] Holzman contends that this literature, by no means healing, is psychologically damaging and ethically untenable. Like Morahg, he categorizes second-generation literature into the descriptive-testimonial and the fantastic. However, in contrast with Morahg's endorsement, Holzman sees no positive values in the "postmodern direction" in Holocaust literature. Holzman proposes that this literature cynically exploits the reality of the Holocaust, precisely "because of its horrific nature, as building blocks for complex literary experimentations." Thus these works of fiction "transgress aesthetic borderlines and break ethical codes" (p. 144).

Focusing especially on Grossman and Levy, he finds their fiction unequivocally damaging and dangerous on two accounts. One negative aspect consists of the "direct, uninhibited description of the horror" (p. 148). The fictional descriptions of gas chambers and tortured Jewish victims that aspire to realism trivialize and therefore diminish the Holocaust experience. The other, even more dangerous aspect lies in the intentional "blurring of the distinctions between the victim and the victimizer" (p. 149). The universality suggested in Grossman's concept of "the little Nazi inside you," namely, the notion that everybody has the potential for inhuman behavior, creates a problematic symbiosis of the Nazi and the Jew, a conflation that degrades all ethical values. As Holzman sees it, the postmodern tendency to privilege all sides signals loss of parameters for moral behavior.

The phenomenon of the "little Nazi inside you" that Holzman considers so dangerous is by no means limited to fiction. Avisar remarks on films that connect the suffering of the Jews in the Holocaust with the Palestinian situation under Israeli rule, thus implying the Nazi-like qualities of the Israeli soldier. The motif emerges in poetry as well. In Oded Peled's *My Yellow Robe,* an anthology of second-generation poetry, the children of the survivors resort to the imagery of the Holocaust to protest Israel's cruelty toward the Palestinian population. Thus for instance, in an unmistakable reference to the Eichmann trial, Giora Segal writes, "Let there be nobody to collapse on the witness stand / Let there be no soldier to slap my father's face / Let us not be represented by a learned attorney." Drawing upon Shlonsky, one of the poets of the forties mentioned, and his famous line on the Holocaust atrocities committed against the children, "Even Satan has not created proper revenge for a little child," Tzvi Atzmon writes about Arab children who were mercilessly, with impunity shot during the Intifada. Assuming collective responsibility for Israel, the oppressor, the poet admits, "I stand accused" (in Peled, pp. 78, 33).

It is important to note that the condemnation of Israel as occupier by no means signals a new confident outlook that transcends the insecurities inherited from parents-survivors. Even as they show empathy for the subjugated Palestinians, the poets do not hide their own legacy of anxiety and insecurity instilled by the memory of the horrific parental experience. Indeed, Peled, a poet and the editor of *My Yellow Robe,* admits that he conceived the idea of the anthology in an epiphany that confronted him with his indelible, instinctual connection with the Holocaust. Peled recounts how at the time of the Gulf War, having left his sealed room to walk his dog, he rushed to the forest; after awhile he realized that his body had reconstructed the old path of escape: from the gas chamber to the forest. As Peled sees it, the poetry presented in the anthology attests to the fact that "fifty years later . . . the event of the Holocaust *still* constitutes the central experience in our collective memory and consciousness." Indeed, Peled insists that the embedded sense of empathic identification with the victims of the Holocaust is expressed in poetry written not only by the children of the survivors, but also by those whose life story was not connected directly to the memory of the Holocaust (p. 5, emphasis in original).

The extensiveness of the phenomenon of second-generation literary responses to the Holocaust reaffirms the emerging changes of Israel's *Weltanschauung* in the past two decades. An uninhibited affinity with Jewish suffering has counteracted earlier glorification of Jewish heroism and contempt for the victim. Focus on *Sho'ah* rather than on *gevurah*, "destruction" rather than "heroism," communicates a doublefold transformation of national identity. The collective claim to the memory of the Holocaust has removed the stigma of the *sheep to the slaughter* label that was attached to the victims in the first decades of the state; and, at the same time, it has undermined the perception of the Sabra as the "new" Jew. Clearly, memory of the Holocaust has grown as an integral element of Israeli identity, and stands in opposition to the Zionist construct of the "new" Jew, which was predicated upon conscious disassociation from the Diaspora past and deliberate suppression of its history.

Recent Fiction

Liberating the Holocaust story of victimization from silence constitutes a far-reaching and significant outcome of Israel's historical transformation in the 1980s. In one sense, this liberation expressed itself in the children's attempt to address the issue of their parents' horrific experience. This desire conflated with their need to examine their own lives in the shadow of that past. From this perspective, the ideological transformation in the 1980s engendered the inclination for an introspective search for roots "over there," a search that greatly furthered recognition of the Diaspora's presence in Israeli consciousness. This introspective trend has been noted in surveys of documentary films, fiction, and poetry, as well as in the sociological studies of Israeli families.

As I have suggested at the opening of this discussion, over half a century after the catastrophe, the literature on the Holocaust reassesses its own history of the often conflicted and controversial responses to the survivors and their legacy. This literature sums up, categorizes, and psychoanalyzes the ways in which the trauma of the European tragedy has affected Israel on both collective and individual levels. Do these acts of reckoning communicate, to recall Friedländer and Appelfeld, the limits of Holocaust representation? Does this mean that henceforth the memory will be merely reinterpreted in literature and the arts and reevaluated in literary, historical, and ideological debates? Is it possible that while the memory of the catastrophe will haunt us forever, our search for new understanding and meaning has run its course?

Recently published fiction indicates that the struggle for understanding is not over yet. Three literary pieces before us posit the question of spiritual survival in the aftermath of the tragedy. Lizi Doron's *Why Didn't You Come Before the War?* is a series of biographical vignettes of Helena, a survivor, narrated by her daughter, Elizabeth. The episodes focus on the survivor's excruciating experience of adjusting to the reality of Israel. Savyon Liebrecht's short story, "Ruchale's Perfect Groom," about the survivors, Shelomo and Staszek, reveals the fragility of seemingly achieved adjustment when an uncanny incident unleashes memories of the past. Michal Govrin's novel, *The Name,* is narrated by Amalia, a young woman whose parents are survivors. She tells how the haunting parental past has stunted her social and emotional adjustment, sending her on a tormenting quest for the meaning of her legacy. The quest to adjust is a common denominator in these narratives, despite considerable differences in narration, genre, content, and the intent of the texts.

The question underlying all three is how one deals in a post-Holocaust world with memory that *will not* be suppressed. A dangerous precariousness characterizes the storylines; the past constantly threatens to invade and destroy the present. For instance, an old valise in Helena's closet, containing "worms, a striped camp garb, a yellow star, sandals, and the smell of the dead" (Doron, p. 90), is a reminder of the past, always on the verge of taking over the present. Similarly, in the consciousness of Shelomo and Staszek a horrific vision emerges when it turns out that Ruchale, Shelomo's daughter, is marrying the nephew of a kapo they knew in the camp: "as if in a film projected backwards," they see Feldman, the kapo they killed on the day of liberation, arise from the dead and assume the identity of Ruchale's husband-to-be.[10] Amalia—named after Mala, her father's first wife, who died a heroic death in Auschwitz—carries memory in her name; in vain does she attempt "to flee, to cut off connections, to change the name, *Amalia, Amy, Emily,* to change place. . . ." (Govrin, p. 55, emphasis in original). The past is always there, interfering with the present, shaping her perception of the world.

In these narratives, the confrontation with the memory does not promise emotional healing. In contrast with psychoanalytic assumptions, the reencounter with the past is by no means conducive to social readjustment. On the contrary, the memories that transfer the protagonists back into the terrible past of the concentration camps bring forth fear, self-loathing, and disorientation. Thus, rather than seeking the meaning of the past, the protagonists are compelled, each in his or her own way, to explore the signification of the present. It is not the consciousness of what has been lost that they seek, as the awful reality faces them constantly. Rather, the protagonists are preoccupied with what has remained besides the overriding feeling of loss and terror. They struggle to rediscover among the ruins a measure of hopefulness that would restore some meaning in post-Holocaust existence. Against disheartening odds they engage in an inner struggle, trying to maintain enough faith to protect themselves against nihilism and despair. In the three texts, this quest for spiritual fortitude follows the theological path of questioning God.

The distinction between questioning God and questioning the existence of God is of the essence. In none of the narratives is the existence of God in doubt. In doubt, rather, is God's dependability, intentions, and potency. Questioning God, therefore, attests to continuing faith in the existence of providential God and, at the same time it attests to a collapse of trust in his judgment. In all three narratives the protagonists reach the understanding that to fend off despair, their faith must not dissipate; however, the nature of their faith must change. In the post-Holocaust world, faith in God is maintained through an impossible confluence of doubt and belief: paradoxically, while I believe in God, I find his acts terrifying and untrustworthy; therefore the responsibility to maintain and preserve faith has become mine.

The three texts point to the complexity of affirmation of faith in the aftermath of the Holocaust. The particularity of this affirmation does not lie in innovation; after all, the question of theodicy has preoccupied humanity for ages. It is rather the desperation of the search and the terrible intensity that impels revision and redefinition of the divine that point to the particular nature of this struggle. Holocaust remembrance confronts us with the precariousness of post-Holocaust human/e existence. While we may have possibly reached the limits of Holocaust representation, this fiction signals that the struggle against nihilism and despair in a world imbued with Holocaust consciousness has hardly begun.

Notes

All translations of extracts from the Hebrew are the author's—RFB.

1. Even though the essay was first delivered as an address at the opening ceremony of the Tenth World Congress of Jewish Studies in 1989, I assume, on the basis of Saul Friedländer's permission to reprint it here, that the author's opinion has not changed.

2. Tom Segev, *The Seventh Million: The Israelis and the Holocaust* (New York: Hill & Wang, 1993) (in Hebrew, Jerusalem: Keter, Domino, 1991).

3. Shabtai Teveth, *Ben-Gurion and the Holocaust* (New York: Harcourt, 1996), xxi, lii. See also, Zeev Sternhell, *The Founding Myths of Israel* [discussed in chapter 7 by Deborah Wheeler], trans. David Maisel (Princeton: Princeton University Press, 1998), 387–89.

4. Anita Shapira, "The History of Mythology—Outlining the Historiography of Ben-Gurion and the Holocaust," *Alpayim* 18 (1999): 48, 51 (in Hebrew). Cf. Teveth's response, "Un-Historiographical 'Historiography'," *Alpayim* 19 (2000): 224–35 (in Hebrew).

5. David Grossman, *See Under Love* (Jerusalem: ha-Kibbutz ha-Meuhad, 1986) (in Hebrew). In English translated by Betsy Rosenberg (N.Y.: Farrar, Straus Giroux, 1989).

6. Gilead Morahg, "Breaking Silence: Israel's Fantastic Fiction of the Holocaust," in *The Boom in Contemporary Israeli Fiction,* ed. Alan Mintz (Hanover, New Hampshire: Brandeis University Press, 1997).

7. Itamar Levy, *The Legend of the Sad Lakes* (Jerusalem: Keter, 1989); Yitzhak Ben Ner, *The Angels Are Coming* (Jerusalem: Keter, 1987); Dorit Peleg, *Una* (Tel Aviv: Siman Kri'ah/ha-Kibbutz ha-Meuhad, 1987) (all three in Hebrew).

8. Morahg, p. 147.

9. Avner Holzman, “The Theme of the Holocaust in Israeli Fiction: A New Wave,” *Dapim le-Mehkar ba-Sifrut* 10 (1996) (in Hebrew).

10. Savyon Liebrecht, *On Love Stories and Other Endings* (Jerusalem: Keter, 1995), 204–5 (in Hebrew).

Part 2

Israeli Society: The Jewish Community

3. Controlling Territory: Spatial Dimensions of Social and Political Change in Israel

David Newman,
Ben-Gurion University of the Negev

This essay examines the roles of territory, space, and place within Israeli society as reflected by several important new studies. These works herald a new appreciation for spatial elements, both territorial and symbolic, which have always been crucial to the relations among different population groups in Israel and how each relates to the hierarchy of spaces in which they all reside, work, and interact. The author analyzes four dimensions of territory covered by the books under review: (a) tangible territorial division (demarcated boundaries); (b) the symbolic and mythical dimensions of territory and the use of places in the formation of a Zionist national identity; (c) the geographic differentiation among Jews and between Jews and Arabs, as reflected by the distribution of resources; and (d) the central role of territory in the ultranationalist and irredentist political discourse, versus its marginalization in an emerging postnationalist, post-Zionist, discourse.

Ben-Ari, Eyal, and Yoram Bilu, eds., *Grasping Land: Space and Place in Contemporary Israeli Discourse and Experience*, Albany: State University of New York Press, 1997.

Benvenisti, Meron, *Sacred Landscape: The Buried History of the Holy Land since 1948*, Berkeley: University of California Press, 2000.

Gonen, Amiram, *Between City and Suburb: Urban Residential Patterns and Processes in Israel*, Aldershot, England: Avebury Press, 1995.

Portugali, Juval, *Implicate Relations: Society and Space in the Israeli-Palestinian Conflict*, Dordrecht, Netherlands: Kluwer Academic Publishers, 1993.

Schnell, Izhak, *Perceptions of Israeli Arabs: Territoriality and Identity*, Aldershot, England: Avebury Press, 1994.

Yiftachel, Oren, and Avinoam Meir, eds., *Ethnic Frontiers and Peripheries: Landscapes of Development and Inequality in Israel*, Boulder, CO: Westview Press, 1997.

The role of territory and space is central to any understanding of Israeli society in general, and to the Arab-Israel conflict in particular. Yet, with the exception of geographers, most social scientists have ignored this dimension in their studies during the first forty years of scholarship. A notable exception to this was the study, *Zionism and Territory: The Socio-Territorial Dimensions of Zionist Politics,* by Israeli sociologist Baruch Kimmerling, published in 1983.[1] During the past decade, space has figured more prominently in the writings of Israeli social scientists, not only with respect to the hard-core territorial dimensions of the Arab-Israel conflict (borders, settlements, state territories, etc.) but also in terms of the multidimensionality of spatial analysis that views space in both concrete and symbolic terms, and that perceives territory as a changing, dynamic phenomenon, both in terms of its physical configuration as well as the way in which space is perceived by those residing within its limits.[2]

The renewed focus on the spatial dimensions of Israeli society is partly a response to the general rediscovery of space by the social sciences in general. What was traditionally seen as an exclusive construct of the geographic discipline has now been reformulated by many other disciplines, most notably sociologists, political scientists, and economists. This is part of a postmodern social science discourse that has begun to cross the traditional lines separating the compartmentalized social scientific categories and that has come to understand the importance of the territorial dimension to any analysis of changing social processes—the inherent relationship between society and space.[3] For their part, geographers have become more aware of the multidimensionality of spatial analysis, not simply as a bounded physical construct, but also as a metaphor for social relations, both real and perceived. This is also reflected in the changing nature of much geographic work on Israel itself, drawing on wider theoretical constructs and frameworks in their respective analyses of territorial change, as contrasted with the largely descriptive geographic studies of the past.

This essay reviews the spatial theme within Israeli society as it is reflected in a number of recent studies by geographers and other social scientists. For some of them, space is the explicit focus for their analysis, while for others it is implicit in the subtexts of their narratives. For some, territory is a concrete construct that undergoes change as a result of political decisions and their implementation, while for others it is a perceived and metaphysical construct that cannot be defined in rigid geographic terms, but that is central to the way in which people—Israelis and Palestinians, religious and secular, Ashkenazim and Mizrahim (Sephardim)—understand, and react to, the hierarchy of spaces within which they reside, work, and interact.

Society, Space, and the Control of Territory

The discourse on territory is two-dimensional, dealing with the concrete and tangible characteristics of territoriality on the one hand, and its symbolic or abstract dimensions on the other hand.[4] Political geographers have, until recently, tended to focus on the concrete dimensions of territoriality, such as boundaries, state configuration, resources (especially water), and settlements,[5] while psychologists, anthropologists, and sociologists have focused on many of the symbolic dimensions associated with space, notably the perceptions of place and space at both local and national levels, the meaning of "homeland" for Israelis and Palestinians, respectively, and the way in which space is imbued with meaning (and, in some cases, sanctity) by various population groups.[6]

The symbolic and abstract dimensions of space have been introduced into the territorial debate only during the past ten years, and this has added an important complementary dimension to the wider discourse over land and territory. The concrete dimensions of territory, particularly the way in which territory is used as an agent of spatial change and control under conditions of conflict, were highlighted in groundbreaking studies published in the early 1990s by Oren Yiftachel, Anthony Coon, and Aaron Kellerman.[7] Territory is contested between Israelis and Palestinians, not only in the most tangible way inside Israel and throughout the Occupied Territories, but also as a social construct that contains mythical places associated with such notions as "homeland,"[8] holy sites, and places of pilgrimage.

The use of planning legislation and zoning as a means of limiting settlement expansion for one community while consolidating the settlement network for another is a theme that has been developed in other studies, particularly in the controversial work of Palestinian geographer, Ghazi Falah.[9] In a number of debates that have appeared in the literature during the past fifteen years, Falah has challenged Israeli academic interpretations of Beduin sedentarization, the Judaization of the Galilee, as well as a general critique of the Israeli geographic establishment for having, in his words, assisted in the "Israelization of the Palestinian human landscapes" and therefore directly contributed to the way in which the academic community has helped implement the territorial policies of the state. These accusations have been contested and rebutted by a host of Israeli geographers,[10] with much of the debate focusing around the selective interpretations by the respective authors of the spatial and geographic data and by the raising of important questions concerning the extent to which the academic debate is being used by geographers to promote the political agendas of the Israeli government and the Palestinians, respectively.[11]

Spatial Control: Recent Research

The theme of spatial control as a general process affecting both the Israeli Jewish community and Israeli-Palestinian communities is highlighted in the collection of essays edited by Oren Yiftachel and Avinoam Meir. *Ethnic Frontiers and Peripheries: Landscapes of Development and Inequality in Israel* explores the "evolution of ethnic spaces and interactions within a modern 'nation state'" by focusing on the notions of frontier and periphery through an examination of the country's "main ethnic and national cleavages and margins" (p. 1). As such, the agents of control are not limited to the national conflict between Jews and Arabs, but also apply to the development of peripheral areas and populations within Israeli-Jewish society, notably the Mizrahi and Ethiopian Jews, women, and Beduin populations within the Negev. A number of the authors undertake comparative studies that include both Jewish and Palestinian marginalized populations, such as Hanna Herzog's essay on Oriental and Arab women, or the contribution by Yoav Peled that examines exclusionary policies affecting both Mizrahi Jews and Palestinian Arabs.

The populations, like some of the locations, are in the periphery. Agencies of control, be they public- or private-sector, are central to the way in which social and spatial cores and peripheries are constructed and maintained. Where the existence of a marginalized population coincides with a peripheral location (e.g., Mizrahi unemployed in a Negev development town, or Beduin in an unrecognized village lacking basic municipal services), they suffer conditions of "double peripherality,"[12] where low social and political status is exacerbated by a remote and inaccessible geographic location. The chances of breaking out of the cycle of economic marginality is even more difficult in these locations than it is for marginalized populations who reside within the geographic core (e.g., in the poverty neighborhoods of Tel Aviv) and, despite the attempts at some useful comparisons in this collection of essays, much more difficult for Palestinian populations who suffer national marginalization in addition to socioeconomic and geographic peripheralization. Thus, the true frontiers of Israeli society are to be found in those locations where the social and spatial dimensions of marginalization coincide.[13]

The essays in this book touch upon what Yiftachel and Meir describe as different types of frontier that exist in Israeli society. The changing perception of just what constitutes the frontier is dealt with by both Shlomo Hasson and Amiram Gonen. Hasson discusses the frontier narrative and shows how the concept has changed, over time, from being the frontier where pioneers go to the frontier that has become the location of peripheral and marginalized segments of society, in particular, the development towns of the Negev and the Galilee. Gonen develops this theme further, discussing the policies that bring about the settling of the frontier regions in periods of mass immigration. In these cases, many of the immigrants have no choice but to go to the places they are sent by the government authorities because they lack the resources and/or the information necessary to choose other, more central, locations, rather than because the frontier is a location that attracts the economic and social elites out of a constructed sense of national mission—following the model promoted by David Ben-Gurion in retiring to kibbutz Sede Boqer in the heart of the Negev desert.

This critical and multidisciplinary study (with essays by geographers, sociologists, and political scientists) contrasts with Amiram Gonen's study of changing residential patterns in Israel. While *Between City and Suburb: Urban Residential Patterns and Processes in Israel* also touches upon Palestinian and ethnic residential marginality as middle-class Jews move out of the inner cities and into the suburbs, it is more of a descriptive presentation of the changing spatial patterns that have occurred during the more than fifty years of Israel's history. Drawing on some of the classic urban geography literature relating to suburbanization, the land market, and patterns of residential segregation, Gonen shows how Israeli urban centers have expanded and become spatially differentiated in much the same way as urban centers elsewhere in the world, with the affluent moving on and the poor being left behind in inner-city neighborhoods. In addition to the Palestinian and Mizrahi populations, Gonen also discusses the residential patterns of Israel's ultra-Orthodox populations, opting for urban concentration in voluntary self-imposed ghettos. Gonen only hints at the processes—both public and private—which are responsible for this increasingly segregated landscape. The impact of the planners and zoners, and the housing managers and the residential gatekeepers[14]—in the form of private realtors on the one hand and the state and quasi-state agencies such as the Jewish Agency on the other hand—are not sufficiently explored in this text.

Notwithstanding, this study of "city and suburb" is important for two important reasons. In the first place it discusses the city and the processes of urban change, where too many Israeli geographic studies of the past have concentrated on the rural landscapes which, however unique to Israel (e.g., the kibbutz and the moshav) have never encompassed more than a small minority (less than 7 percent at the most) of the Israeli population. Secondly, in moving from the rural to the urban, and from the suburban and the exurban, Gonen places the study of Israeli residential patterns firmly within the wider economic and social processes of residential change that affect all postindustrial societies, rather than remaining within the realm of the unique explanatory factors that have plagued Israel's social scientists in general, and its geographers in particular, for so long.

Thus, the notion of spatial control through processes of urban planning and residential segregation is both explicit and implicit in these studies. But they all demonstrate the importance of the microspatial and local dimension in the study of social and political geography. The macro (national) and micro (local and urban) do not exist in separate spheres. While the public discourse concerning contested space and territory tends to focus around the notion of national and state territory, such as the demarcation of national boundaries or the formulation of security zones, it is at the micro, residential, level of daily activity where the spatial dimensions of the conflict are experienced by most citizens. As such, civilian practices such as town planning and the zoning of residential areas become intertwined within the wider national conflict. They demonstrate the way in which the expansion of territorial control by the state and the collective is just as much an aggregation of the microterritories that are brought under control at the local level, as it is the demarcation of the outer boundaries of the state territorial configurations. Nowhere is this demonstrated as strongly as in the cases of the so-called mixed towns, places where Arabs and Jews reside within the same city, but where the competition for living space, developmental resources and, ultimately, residential separation, have become even stronger during fifty years of statehood (Gonen).[15] Here too, the national conflict is played out at the level of the residential block and, in some cases, within the same apartment building.

Abstract and Symbolic Notions of Space

Territory is not only concrete and visible; it is also perceived. People walk around with diverse mental maps and images of the territories within which they live.[16] A contested territory between groups is often a result of the fact that what is seen by one is not that which is perceived by the other. The historic perception of the "Promised Land" based on the biblical accounts of a perceived "Garden of Eden, flowing with milk and honey" was confronted with a harsh geographic reality by many of the early pioneers when they encountered the arid and semi-arid conditions of the Middle East. Perceptions of just what comprises the "Land of Israel," or "Palestine," or the "West Bank" do not always accord with the bounded realities of past and present political regimes. Of great significance in this respect is (a) the way in which Jews and Arabs, whether pragmatists or territorial irredentists, perceive the spaces within which they live as consisting of Jewish or Arab territories, respectively; (b) the extent to which such territories are perceived as being exclusive to their national group or inclusive of other groups; and (c) the way in which perceived spaces and territories are translated into policy actions on the ground as a means of implementing a specific political agenda (e.g., the establishment of settlements in the West Bank as a means of ensuring political control over the "Promised Land" for the Jewish people).

Izhak Schnell's study *Perceptions of Israeli Arabs: Territoriality and Identity* focuses on the territorial perceptions of Israel's Arab-Palestinian residents. The book deals with the way in which the Palestinian residents of the country delineate their own boundaries, between themselves and Israeli-Jewish citizens, as well as between themselves and the Palestinian residents of the West Bank and Gaza. In effect, the author shows how the "crisis of identity" that is faced by the country's Arab citizens is reflected in their territorial behaviour and awareness. His study goes a long way to demonstrating the interlinkages between concepts of territoriality and identity, and how each feeds on the other in the social construction of national identity and belonging.[17]

Schnell's extensive use of survey material, including the drawing of maps by the respondents, shows how each national group relates to a similar territorial configuration that takes in the whole of mandatory Palestine from the Mediterranean Sea in the West to the Jordan River in the East, the spatial content of which varies greatly in the mental images of the respondents. And yet the content of the map—the geographers' narrative—is vastly different. Each sees its own ethnic and national space, and is blind to—or in many cases consciously ignoring—the neighboring spaces that have been created by "the Other." Landscapes tend to be perceived as being "Arab" or "Jewish," while the Hebrew or Arabic naming of landscapes—an important factor in the social construction of territorial awareness—is not recognized by the other side.[18] It reminds this author of the tour guide who, taking a trip through the Galilee, remarked to the tour participants that when a Jewish traveler passes a particular place he or she immediately see the kibbutz on the hill, while when his or her Arab neighbors pass the same point, they only see the obliterated Arab village that was destroyed over fifty years ago.

This is further highlighted in the chapter in Juval Portugali's book, *Implicate Relations: Society and Space in the Israeli-Palestinian Conflict,* which deals with the respective cognitive maps of Israelis and Palestinians. In response to a survey asking people to mark down the ten nearest settlements and communities to their own, Israelis and Palestinians respectively drew maps that consisted of homogeneous and exclusive ethnic corridors, with little heed for the full spatial ethnic mix in the vicinity of their homes. Despite the fact that they pass neighboring Palestinian or Jewish communities in their daily commute, their spatial awareness blocks the settlements of "the Other" out of their mental maps. This phenomenon has increased in recent years as Israel has constructed bypass roads both in Israel and the West Bank, as a result of which travelers have even less contact with their geographic, but ethnically different, neighbors than ever before.

Years have passed since the publication of Schnell's and Portugali's studies, and even more time has elapsed since their actual field research was carried out. During this period, the 1993 Oslo Accords began to be implemented in stages, and Israelis and Palestinians embarked on negotiating a final-status agreement that would include territorial separation between the two peoples. We may reasonably assume that the identity of these groups, as expressed through these perceived territorial configurations, has strengthened even further during this period. This is particularly the case among the adolescent, better-educated, and more politically aware populations whose Palestinian identity was much more marked in all the surveys than was that of their parents' generation. This is evident in the behavior of Arab members of the Knesset, such as Ahmed Tibi and Azmi Bishara, who emphasize their *Palestinian,* rather than Arab, identity. The former served as an advisor to Palestinian Authority Chairman Yasser Arafat, while the latter is one of the most outspoken proponents of Israel as the "state of all its citizens."

There are a number of unresolved questions concerning the territorial and national links between the Palestinian residents of Israel and the residents of a West Bank-Gaza Palestinian state, when the latter is eventually established. How will this territory be defined? How relevant will the formal boundaries between sovereign entities be, when a sizable proportion of Israel's population sees this as no more than an administrative line running through a single cultural ecumene? After the establishment of a separate Palestinian entity, national identities will have to be reformulated and reconfigured, given the underlying importance of territoriality in the formation of national identity and the fact that, as just noted, such identities are constructed not only at the level of national territories, but also—and more importantly—at the level of the local community. In this respect, Schnell's study is a picture in time, one of many that will have to be compared with past and future snapshots, enabling us to see the way in which perceived territorial identities undergo change as national groups become increasingly self-confident in claiming their independence.

It is the sociologists and anthropologists whose study of space and place have focused more strongly on the metaphysical and the abstract. The collection of essays put together by Eyal Ben-Ari and Yoram Bilu is significant in this respect. The book *Grasping Land: Space and Place in Contemporary Israeli Discourse and Experience* focuses on the way in which Israeli landscapes figure in the creation and the re-creation of identity, presence, and history of the groups living there. Unlike Schnell's discussion of the Arab-Israel equation, this collection touches upon the creation of identities and spatial mythologies among some of the diverse ethnic groups that make up the overall mosaic of Jewish-Israeli society. The essays vary in their scope, but they touch upon the social construction of space and place through such diverse examples as saints' tombs, the design of kibbutz museums, and hiking in the countryside.

While Schnell's book is largely empirical in its presentation of survey material relating to territorial identities, the Ben-Ari/Bilu collection focuses on the qualitative dimensions of mythical and abstract notions of space and place. The essays show how places can be imbued with meanings—new or historical—and how meanings attached to other places can be spatially transported to new locations, around which there develop feelings of attachment and piety. The notion of sacred spaces that are attached to gravesites, battle sites, and national territories are eloquent illustrations of the theoretical literature on human territoriality and the agencies through which humans are prepared to defend their own territory—be it the gravesite of "their" rabbi, or the national territory of "their" state. It is not only the renaming of landscapes after historical or religious associations, but also the transportation of territorial meaning from one place to another. Many of the Hassidic neighborhoods in Israel are named after their original village names in Eastern Europe, while when the cornerstone for the Belz Hassidic synagogue in Jerusalem was laid some years ago, earth was brought from the "holy" village of Belz in Galicia and placed under the building in the newly transposed "holy" site—the city of Jerusalem.

The symbolic notions of space and landscape are strongly brought out in Meron Benvenisti's *Sacred Landscape: The Buried History of the Holy Land since 1948,* in which he discusses the landscape changes that took place as a result of the outflow of Palestinian refugees and the subsequent abandonment of their villages and residences. The process of mapping and naming that took place throughout Israel during the 1950s was a process that was intended to re-create the ancient names of Jewish and Hebrew civilizations, thus cementing the bond between a modern nation and its ancient past, providing an important component in the formation of the new national identity, as well as emphasizing the almost mystical links between the people and their "homeland." Although religion is not a central theme in his book, Benvenisti uses the neutral terms *holy land* and *sacred landscape* that are equally relevant to both Jews and Arabs, rather than the contemporary political and politicized labels *Israel* and *Palestine.*

Benvenisti's use of religious terminology to define the relationship between people and territory is a theme that repeats itself, both directly and indirectly, in many of the studies reviewed in this essay. The metaphor of "sacred" space applies both to the national-religious conceptions of territory, especially among the West Bank settlers (a theme which, while discussed in much of the literature of the past two decades, is not directly addressed in any of the texts reviewed here), as well as to the sacred microspaces around graves and shrines. What is common to both of these is the importance attached to the territory—be it macro or micro—and the inviolability of these territories because of their mythical-divine associations. While not directly mentioned in any of these essays, it is the notion of "geopiety" that springs to mind, a notion that "assumes a sense of belonging to, and ownership of, homeland as an exclusive right emanating from a divine, or supernatural, claim to territory . . . an expression of dutiful devotion and habitual reverence for territory, land or space."[19] Within the Israeli-Jewish context, this contrasts strongly with the theological view, expressed unambiguously by

Abraham Joshua Heschel, that Judaism sanctifies time, not space,[20] and the work of Israeli geographer Yosseph Shilhav, who draws on Jewish source material to argue that, if space is sanctified at all, it occurs through the actions of the people residing in that space, and not because of any inherent "sanctity" in the earth and stones.[21]

The Israel-Palestine Conflict

It goes without saying that territory constitutes one of the core concerns of the Arab-Israel conflict in general, and of the Israel-Palestine conflict in particular. We have already discussed the way in which territory is used as an agent of control, both within Israel itself as well as in the occupied territories. But territory is much more than simply an agent through which practices of control are implemented. It constitutes the construct around which the competing national identities of both Israelis and Palestinians are fought and over which neither is prepared to voluntarily cede control. It provides the raison d'être for the conflicting claims put forward by each side, both with respect to strategic priorities as well as to symbolic attachments to place that constitute the core of these claims. Canadian geographer Andrew Burghardt, in his discussion of the contrasting claims to sovereignty over territory made by groups throughout history, emphasizes the duality of claims based on "priority" and "duration."[22] The applicability of this duality to the respective territorial claims of Israelis and Palestinians is readily apparent. While Israel emphasizes reasons of Jewish and biblical historic priority, the Palestinians have focused their claims more strongly on the long period of uninterrupted residence prior to the period of Zionist immigration and the establishment of the State of Israel.

This ties in with the concept of *moledet* (homeland). While *Moledet* is also the name of one of the most extreme right-wing, anti-Arab political parties in the Israeli Knesset (Parliament), it used to be the term that described the school curriculum concerning the Land of Israel.[23] This curriculum would include the study of geography coupled with school trips to the countryside, where emphasis would be placed upon sites of ancient biblical or historic significance and/or Zionist battle sites, with little—if any—emphasis given to the Arab-Palestinian landscapes that existed in these same areas during the course of history, even up to just fifty years ago. Thus, the landscape becomes exclusive in terms of its exclusive relation to Jewish history, as part of the process in which a *moledet* (homeland) is inculcated into the impressionable thought processes of young schoolchildren.

The use of history, archaeology, and other sciences to strengthen these respective claims, mixing historical reality with constructed myth, is a common practice that emerges from much of the literature discussed here. Geography, not normally known as a profession around which there is heated political debate, has become a subject of much contention within the Israel-Palestine context,[24] as too have conflicting archaeological claims concerning the national significance of ancient artifacts discovered throughout the Israel/Palestine landscape.[25]

This theme is developed strongly in Benvenisti's book, *Sacred Landscape*. Drawing on much of his previous work, Benvenisti has compiled an impressive narrative of the way in which the landscape has been changed as part of the state-formation process. In particular, he focuses on the processes of landscape change that took place after the establishment of the Israeli state and the outflow of Palestinian refugees, and the subsequent obliteration of much that remained from the previous Arab-Palestinian landscape. He shows how the Arabic names of more than nine thousand natural features, villages, and ruins have been replaced by Hebrew-Jewish names, and how the Arab landscape has been transformed into a Jewish homeland. The book, which originally appeared in a Hebrew version, discusses the evolution of the "Hebrew map," (pp. 11–54) the uprooting of Arab settlements, and the planting of Jewish settlements (pp. 193–228). Benvenisti argues that the cultural transformation of the landscape has created a struggle around the "signposts of memory" (pp. 229–69) that remain structurally inherent to the conflict, and that will remain so long after the contemporary conflict has been resolved and managed. By focusing on "holy sites" (be they real or socially constructed), Benvenisti also notes the way in which maps have been used to depict a landscape that is Israeli-Zionist and that has links to the Jewish past. *Sacred Landscape* also discusses, albeit briefly, the struggle for hegemony within the academic community, highlighting the alternative and contested narratives produced by Arab-Palestinian and Israeli-Jewish geographers, respectively (pp. 169–71).

Indeed, all the books reviewed here deal directly or indirectly with aspects of the Palestinian-Israeli conflict. Contextually, only

Portugali develops an analytic framework that attempts to address the wider spatial dimensions of what he terms *implicate relations* that exist between Israelis and Palestinians. His basic thesis is that the actions of one people are a mirror image of the actions of "the Other," and that these are reflected in the nature of the spatial relations. Drawing on detailed empirical field survey material, much of which was carried out during the 1980s and subsequently published as a series of essays that have been assembled in this book, Portugali argues that space and society "enfold each other, exist inside each other, and in this respect coexist in implicate relations. . . . [F]rom this point of view space is not a passive entity, but an active actor in the theatre of social reality" (p. xiii).

This is an important point. Too many nongeographers see geography and territory as being no more than the spatial and territorial, fixed, outcome of complex social and political processes, rather than as a dynamic factor in its own right. As the territorial realities change, so too they become a factor in their own right in the next round of decision making, conflict, or planning. While history and symbolism play an important role in understanding how national identities are formed and why people become so fiercely attached to territory, contemporary social and political decision making takes account of the existing territorial realities, many of which are themselves the outcome of historical—recent and ancient—change. Perhaps the best example of this in the Israel-Palestine conflict, one to which Portugali devotes an entire chapter, is the issue of Israeli settlements in the West Bank. They exist. They contain over 150,000 residents and, while all Palestinians and many Israelis would simply like to remove them in their entirety in an attempt to reach a final territorial agreement, they nevertheless constitute a major impediment to the continuation of this process.[26] The final configuration of territorial boundaries will have to take account of many of these settlements remaining in situ, simply because there is little alternative. In this sense, Portugali's account of the West Bank settlement process is a direct continuation of Kellerman's longer-term analysis of the way in which settlements have created facts throughout the contemporary history of Zionism, and how these facts have, in turn, altered the geographic realities on the ground and have had a major influence in determining the final course of the territorial boundaries.

Portugali's book is of particular interest because its various chapters touch upon a variety of theoretical frames, ranging from a discussion of nationalism as *moloch,* Bohm's notions of the implicate, explicate, and generative, the suburban and commuting dimensions of Jewish settlement in the occupied territories;[27] Palestinian "nomadic" labor through which the spatial diffusion of information was transferred between the West Bank and Gaza,[28] the cognitive and ethnically segregated mental maps and spatial awareness of Israelis and Palestinians; to a localized analysis of the impact of national conflict in the Ajami neighborhood of Tel Aviv. Although disjointed at times, the book highlights the multidimensional nature of examining conflict in general, and the society-space relations in particular.

Many of the chapters in the Yiftachel and Meir collection relate, directly and indirectly, to the Israel-Palestine conflict, not only in terms of the territorial relationship between Israel and the West Bank and Gaza Strip, but also by incorporating the Arab population of the country as an integral part of the conflict. The essays by geographers Oren Yiftachel and Izhak Schnell, sociologists Dan Rabinowitz and Hanna Herzog, and political scientist Yoav Peled all touch upon the marginalization of Israel's Arab-Palestinian population, explicitly linking their status and self-perceived identity with the wider Israel-Palestine conflict. Implicit in these essays is the fact that the grievances of Israel's Arab-Palestinian minority will not, as some politicians and social scientists might wish, mysteriously disappear if and when the wider conflict has reached a final stage of resolution. For minority populations to feel equal, and to participate fully in the life of the state, they must feel less marginalized, not only politically, but also—and perhaps especially—in the wider fields of education, economics, technology, and the provision of public services. This dilemma is highlighted even more strongly in the two essays by Avinoam Meir and Ze'ev Zivan and by Ismael Abu-Saad, who discuss the situation of the bedouin population of the country, a population that is marginalized both territorially and socially and that also finds itself marginalized vis-à-vis the country's Arab population. Together, the books by Portugali, Schnell, Benvenisti, and Yiftachel and Meir all point to the fact that the conflict is not only about territorial sovereignty, but also about the structural conditions of the Palestinian population—both in the West Bank and Israel itself—which have to be improved if the populations are to feel equal and are to relate to each other as part of a peace process that includes such lofty ideas as normalization and cooperation, rather than simply an end to conflict and violence.

Conclusion

Of all the books discussed here, only one contains a contribution by a Palestinian scholar: Ismael Abu-Saad's study of higher education among the Bedouin community (Yiftachel and Meir). Given that reality, one cannot avoid being impressed by the relatively high level of social and political critique displayed by most of the Jewish-Israeli authors and contributors regarding their own society's policies relating to minorities. But one cannot avoid being concerned about the way in which knowledge about Israeli society in general, and space and geography in particular, is being constructed by Israeli academic elites. Geography, in particular, is a profession which, until recently, had no Arab or Palestinian (and very few women) practitioners at all, and even now their number (two out of sixty) is insignificant in terms of making any major impact.[29] It has been suggested to this author by senior practitioners of geography that this profession—which until recently had been a very descriptive profession focusing almost entirely on the "Land of Israel" and rarely breaking into conceptual modes of thought—deals with land-related issues and, as such, was too politically sensitive a subject for Palestinian or Arab practitioners to become involved, especially regarding access to maps, planning archives, and other "security"-related materials. In this sense, Ghazi Falah's critique of the Israeli "geographic guild,"[30] while taken to an extreme of political rhetoric, is something that should concern all those involved in studying Israeli space and territory. The study of "lost Palestinian landscapes" may not be music to the ears of most Israelis, but any attempt to reach a more meaningful understanding of the processes of spatial change, past and present, must be prepared to recognize and deal with alternative spatial and territorial narratives. Here one can see similarities to the better-known struggle over "correct" historical narratives between Israel's "old" and "new" historians during the past decade.

It is perhaps not surprising therefore that—with the notable exceptions of Yiftachel, Portugali and, to a lesser extent, Schnell—the more critical accounts of the ways in which human spaces evolve are to be found among the sociologists and political scientists who have contributed to the volumes reviewed here. But where they are more critical, their understanding of what space and territory is all about is more abstract and often ignores the very real concrete dimensions of the way in which territory is used as a means of spatial compartmentalization and control through the agencies of the state. This may explain why nongeographers tend to ignore space altogether in the more recent discussions of post-nationalism and post-Zionism, simply because once relegated to the tangible level of demarcated territories, they view the territorial issue as being irrelevant in an era of perceived deterritorialization, which is supposed to have been accompanied by the so-called end of the nation-state and by a move toward a "borderless world."[31] This is an error which, if uncorrected, will result in the evolving debate concerning the transition from a national (Zionist) society to a "state of all its citizens" being devoid of one of its essential components, namely, territory and space.[32] These two contradictory trends—the interest in space by sociologists and political scientists, on the one hand, but the exclusion of territory from the debate on post-Zionism, on the other hand—remains to be resolved as the younger generation of Israeli social scientists continues to construct alternative multidisciplinary and more theoretical paradigms for understanding the changes that are being experienced by Israeli society. It is precisely the combination of the sociological, political, and geographic accounts to be found in the texts reviewed here, which makes our understanding of Israeli space and society so much richer and more challenging.

Notes

1. Baruch Kimmerling, *Zionism and Territory: The Socio-Territorial Dimensions of Zionist Politics* (Berkeley: University of California Press, 1983).

2. A survey of contemporary trends within Israeli geography is to be found in Yehuda Gradus and Gabriel Lipschitz, eds., *The Mosaic of Israeli Geography* (Beer Sheva: Negev Center for Regional Development, 1996). This collection of short essays was prepared for the World Congress of the International Geographic Union that was held in the Hague in August 1996.

3. This is reflected in such journals as *Society and Space, Place and Polity, Political Geography,* and *Geopolitics,* all of which are less than twenty years old, and all of which include essays by scholars from a variety of social science disciplines.

4. David Newman, "Real Spaces—Symbolic Spaces: Interrelated Notions of Territory in the Arab-Israel Conflict," in Paul Diehl, ed., *A Road*

Map to War: Territorial Dimensions of International Conflict (Nashville: Vanderbilt University Press, 1999), 3–34.

5. The main themes of political geography as a discipline can be found in Martin Glassner, *Political Geography,* 3rd ed. (New York: Wiley, 1998), or for a more critical approach, see Peter Taylor and Colin Flint, *Political Geography: World Economy, Nation-State and Locality,* 4th ed. (London: Longman: 1999). Within the Israeli context, a strong school of political geography has emerged, with the main practitioners being Oren Yiftachel and David Newman at Ben-Gurion University; Stanley Waterman, Nurit Kliot, and Arnon Soffer at Haifa University; Moshe Brawer at Tel Aviv University; Yosseph Shilhav at Bar-Ilan University; and Shlomo Hasson at the Hebrew University.

6. These themes are highlighted in the book by Eyal Ben-Ari and Yoram Bilu reviewed in this essay. In addition, the recent studies by Adriana Kemp, a political sociologist, Michael Feige, an anthropologist (both at Ben-Gurion University), and Yosseph Shilhav, a geographer (Bar-Ilan University) focus on the abstract and symbolic dimensions of the territorial discourse.

7. Aaron Kellerman, *Society and Settlement: Jewish Land of Israel in the Twentieth Century* (Albany: State University of New York Press, 1993); Oren Yiftachel, *Planning a Mixed Region in Israel: The Political Geography of Arab-Jewish Relations in the Galilee* (Aldershot, England: Avebury Press, 1992); Anthony Coon, *Town Planning Under Military Occupation: An Examination of the Law and Practice of Town Planning in the Occupied West Bank* (Aldershot, England: Dartmouth Publishers, 1992). See also, David Newman, "The Role of Civilian and Military Presence as Strategies of Territorial Control: the Arab-Israel Conflict," *Political Geography Quarterly* 8 (1989): 215–27.

8. Newman, "Metaphysical and Concrete Landscapes: The Geopiety of Homeland Socialization in the Land of Israel," in Harold Brodsky, ed., *Land and Community: Geography in Jewish Studies* (College Park: University of Maryland Press, 1998), 153–84.

9. Ghazi Falah, "The Development of the Planned Bedouin Settlement in Israel, 1964–1982: Evaluation and Characteristics," *Geoforum* 14:3 (1983): 311–23; Falah, "Israeli Judaization Policy in Galilee and its Impact on Local Arab Urbanization," *Political Geography Quarterly* 8:3 (1989): 229–53; Falah, "Israelization of Palestine Human Geography," *Progress in Human Geography* 13 (1989): 535–50; Falah, "The Frontier of Political Criticism in Israeli Geographic Practice," *Area* 26 (1994): 1–12.

10. For the debate on Bedouin settlement, see "Planned Bedouin Settlement in Israel: A Critique," *Geoforum* 16:4 (1985): 423–27; Nurit Kliot

and Arnon Medzini, “Bedouin Settlement Policy in Israel, 1964–1982: Another Perspective,” *Geoforum* 16:4 (1985) 428–39; Falah, “Planned Bedouin Settlement in Israel: The Reply,” *Geoforum* 16:4 (1985): 440–51. For the debate on Judaization of the Galilee, see Arnon Soffer, “Israeli Judaization Policy in Galilee and its Impact on Local Arab Urbanization: A Response,” *Political Geography Quarterly* 10:3 (1991): 282–85; Oren Yiftachel and Dennis Rumley, “On the Impact of Israel’s Judaization Policy in the Galilee,” *Political Geography Quarterly* 10:3 (1991): 286–96; Falah, “The Facts and Fictions of Judaization Policy and its Impact on the Majority Arab Population in the Galilee,” *Political Geography Quarterly* 10:3 (1991): 297–316. For the debate on Israeli geographic practices, see Aaron Kellerman, “On Israeli Geographic Practice: A Brief Response to Falah and Thoughts on Future Prospects,” *Area* 27 (1995): 76–77; Falah, “On Israeli Geographic Practice: A Brief Response to Kellerman and Thoughts on Future Prospects,” *Area* 27 (1995): 225–28.

11. David Newman, “Writing Together Separately: Critical Discourse and the Problems of Cross-ethnic Co-authorship,” *Area* 28 (1996): 1–12.

12. The concept of double peripherality was developed by political geographer John House in “The Frontier Zone: A Conceptual Problem for Policy Makers,” *International Political Science Review* 1:4 (1980): 456–77.

13. On this subject, see also Aziz Haidar, *On the Margins: The Arab Population in the Israeli Economy* (New York: St. Martin’s, 1995), reviewed in this volume by Ilham Nasser in chapter 5.

14. The urban managerialist thesis concerning the manipulation of the housing market as a means of maintaining both ethnic and socioeconomic stratification and residential segregation was originally developed by British sociologist Ray Pahl in “Urban Social Theory and Research,” *Environment and Planning* I (1969):143–53.

15. See also Falah, “Living Together Apart: Residential Segregation in Mixed Arab-Jewish Cities in Israel,” *Urban Studies* 33 (1996): 823–57.

16. Perceptions of territory, mental maps, and the notion of spatial awareness are well-developed themes in human geography. See, for instance, Kevin Lynch, *The Image of the City* (Cambridge: Massachusetts Institute of Technology Press, 1960); Roger Downs and David Stea, *Maps in Mind: Reflections on Cognitive Mapping* (New York: Harper, 1977); Robert Lloyd, *Spatial Cognition: Geographic Environments* (Dordrecht, Netherlands: Kluwer Academic, 1997).

17. The relationship between identity and territory, particularly the way in which such identity is socially constructed, has become an important theme in political geography. See, for example, Anssi Paasi, *Territories, Boundaries and Consciousness* (New York: Wiley, 1996).

18. On the naming of landscapes in Israel/Palestine, see Saul B. Cohen and Nurit Kliot, "Israel's Place Names as Reflection of Continuity and Change in National Building," *Names* 29 (1981): 227–46; Cohen and Kliot, "Place Names in Israel's Ideological Struggle over the Administered Territories," *Annals of the Association of American Geographers* 82 (1992): 653–80; Benvenisti's discussion of the naming and "Hebraization" of landscape in *Sacred Landscape* (2000).

19. See Yi-Fu Tuan, "Geopiety: A Theme in Man's Attachment to Nature and Place," in David Lowenthal and Martyn J. Bowden (with the assistance of Mary Alice Lamberty), eds., *Geographies of the Mind: Essays in Historical Geosophy in Honor of John Kirtland Wright* (New York: Oxford University Press, 1975), 11–39; David Newman, "Metaphysical and Concrete Landscapes."

20. Abraham Joshua Heschel, *The Sabbath* (orig. published 1951), in *The Earth Is the Lord's* and *The Sabbath* (New York: Harper Torchbooks, 1966), 6–10.

21. Yosseph Shilhav, "Interpretation and Misinterpretation of Jewish Territorialism," in Newman, ed., *The Impact of Gush Emunim: Territory and Settlement in the West Bank* (London: Croom Helm, 1985), 111–24.

22. Andrew Burghardt, "The Bases of Territorial Claims," *Geographical Review* 63 (1973): 225–45. By "priority" is meant the claim by members of a group that they were there first, before anybody else. "Duration" relates to the claim that the group has resided continually on a piece of territory for as long as the collective memory cares to go back, regardless of whether there were other groups there previously.

23. For an important study of the content of geography text books used in the Israeli school curriculum, see Yoram Bar-Gal, "Boundaries as a Topic in Geographic Education," *Political Geography Quarterly* 12:5 (1993): 421–35.

24. See sources cited in notes 9–11.

25. See Alexander Glock, "Archaeology as Cultural Survival: The Future of the Palestinian Past," *Journal of Palestine Studies* 23:3 (1994): 70–84; Glock, "Cultural Bias in the Archaeology of Palestine," *Journal of Palestine Studies* 24:2 (1995): 48–59.

26. Falah and Newman, "The Spatial Manifestation of Threat: Israelis and Palestinians Seek a 'Good' Border," *Political Geography* 14:8 (1995): 689–706; Newman, "Creating the Fences of Territorial Separation: The Discourse of Israeli-Palestinian Conflict Resolution," *Geopolitics and International Boundaries* 2:2 (1998): 1–35.

27. This theme is well developed in Shalom Reichman, "Policy Reduces the World to Essentials: A Reflection on the Jewish Settlement Process in the West Bank since 1967," in Aryeh Shachar and David Morley, eds., *Planning in Turbulence* (Jerusalem: Magnes Press, 1986), 83–96; Newman, "The Territorial Politics of Exurbanization: Reflections on 25 Years of Jewish Settlement in the West Bank," *Israel Studies* 3:1 (1996): 61–85.

28. The most thorough study of Palestinian labor in Israel is Noah Lewin-Epstein and Moshe Semyonov, *Hewers of Wood and Drawers of Water: Noncitizen Arabs in the Israeli Labor Market* (Ithaca: Cornell University Press, 1987).

29. The introduction of the Maof Fellowships in recent years, a program aimed at appointing Arab-Palestinian scholars in Israeli universities, is perhaps a first step in the direction of affirmative action in this respect.

30. Falah, "Israelization of Palestine Human Geography."

31. This argument, mostly put forward by economists and information scientists, has little relevance to the world of ethno-territorial conflict. For a critique of the deterritorialization argument, see Newman, "Boundaries, Territory and Postmodernism: Towards Shared or Separate Spaces?" in Martin Pratt and Janet Brown, eds., *Borderlands Under Stress* (London: Kluwer Law Academic, 2000), 17–34.

32. This critique is developed further in David Newman, "From National to Post-national Territorial Identities in Israel/Palestine," in Adriana Kemp, Newman, Oren Yiftachel, and Uri Ram, eds., *Israelis in Conflict: Hegemonies, Identities and Challenges* (Albany: State University of New York Press, forthcoming).

4. "A Nation that Dwelleth Alone": Judaism as an Integrating and Divisive Factor in Israeli Society

Ephraim Tabory,
Bar-Ilan University

Assessing recent surveys of Jewish identity and religious practice in Israel, this essay shows how Judaism acts as a force that both unites and divides Jews in the Jewish State. The author notes a broad spectrum of religious observance in which distinctions between secular and religious are not as clear-cut as often assumed, since many so-called secular Jews incorporate traditional practices into their lives. The author attributes increasing friction between religious and secular groups to rising tensions regarding the role of religion in politics and to dramatic demographic changes—in particular, the growth of the Haredi communities and large waves of immigration from the former Soviet Union. Through a comparative analysis of Jewish religious observance in America and Israel, the author also considers the strained relations between Israelis and American Jews that stem from the disenfranchisement of Conservative and Reform Judaism in Israel.

Dowty, Alan, *The Jewish State: A Century Later*, Berkeley: University of California Press, 1998.

Liebman, Charles S., and Elihu Katz, eds., *The Jewishness of Israelis: Responses to the Guttman Report,* Albany: State University of New York Press, 1997.

Susser, Bernard, and Charles S. Liebman, *Choosing Survival: Strategies for a Jewish Future,* New York and Oxford: Oxford University Press, 1999.

"Together with Pride, Together in Hope" was the motto of Israel's fiftieth anniversary celebration in 1998 (see Plate). Billboards bearing this message depicted Ethiopian, Russian, and (Israeli-born?) Jewish children standing together, smiling. Arabs were not shown together with Jews, nor were Jewish Orthodox children shown with non-Orthodox children (or even religious boys with religious girls).[1] There is a limit to what kinds of "togetherness" can be portrayed without straining credulity or becoming the focus of a parliamentary coalition crisis. Israel is still somewhat of a fragile society, not necessarily because of the physical threat to its security, but because of the multiple identities of its inhabitants that inhibit full social cohesion and integration. Israelis are split, at least to some degree, along ethnic, social, national and, in particular, religious lines.[2] Even as Judaism and Jewish identity serve as the fundamental bases for the unity of non-Arab society, variant interpretations of Judaism and different levels of acceptance of religious precepts lead to friction and factions that undermine Jewish unity. Opinion surveys, as Alan Dowty in *The Jewish State: A Century Later* notes, routinely indicate the public to perceive the relations between religious and nonreligious Jews to be one of the most severe internal social problems in Israeli society (p. 158). Given this situation, the focus of this essay is on the manner in which Judaism serves to bring together diverse groups of Jews in Israel, and at the same time divides them and creates strain and even antagonism.[3]

Together with Pride, Together in Hope.

Israeli Jewish Identity

The question of how to define a Jew has engrossed Israeli society since the establishment of the state in 1948.[4] Is Israel a state of the Jews, defined as such because the majority of its citizens are Jewish, or is it unique because of its particular Jewish character?

Should a religious definition or a nationalist definition be used to determine who is a Jew? Who determines the religious definition—Orthodox law, or Conservative or Reform precepts? What does a nationalist definition mean?[5] For the state, what does a particular Jewish character entail? Can Jewish character be divorced from religious custom? How complicated these issues are for a state that also purports to be democratic, because any incorporation of religious precepts in civil law against the will of the majority seems to contravene a legal system based on individual rights and social consensus. Indeed, one can ask whether the concept of a Jewish-democratic state is an oxymoron.[6]

These issues are all dealt with in the volumes under discussion. Dowty, professor of government and international studies at the University of Notre Dame, first analyzes the factors that shaped Israeli democracy, its structures, and institutions. He then deals with challenges to Israeli democracy and focuses on ethnic factions, Jewish relations with Arabs, and the section to which I will relate, religion and politics. Dowty defines "Jewishness" in a manner that includes religious precepts but does not give them a dominant position in determining Jewish identity. For most observers, he says, Jewishness mean: "a common national or ethnic identity as a historically developed community of people with distinctive cultural, linguistic, and other attributes. This includes a distinctive Judaic religion, which makes Jews unusual, though not unique, among ethnic groups. Jews are a people, a nation (in the original sense of the word), an *ethnos*" (p. 3).

While Israel has a largely Jewish population and a dominant Jewish culture, those facts in themselves do not determine whether such a state can or cannot be democratic. The democratic nature of a state, according to Dowty, depends on whether the majority of the population practices democracy among themselves, and whether they are willing to extend it to citizens of other ethnic backgrounds. The political focus of a state, then, depends on the nature and characteristics of its population, and it is to the identity of the citizens of the Jewish State to which we now turn to understand the relations between religious and nonreligious Jews.

Eighty percent of Israel's citizens are Jewish. About 15% are Muslims. The rest include Christians, Druze, and other small groups.[7] Ultra-Orthodox, or Haredim, comprise about 5% of the Jewish population. These persons are characterized by rigid adherence to religious law. The Haredi community includes small groups that do not recognize the state and do not even vote in parliamentary elections. The idea of secular Jews trying to usurp the role of the Messiah in the Jewish return to Zion is anathema to them. Moderate Orthodox Jews who are more receptive to modernity and who seek to balance their religious life with participation in general society comprise another 15% of the Jewish population. Many of these persons live a compartmentalized life, restricting their religious practices to particular times and places, as they take part in "secular," modern society. Based upon various Israeli surveys, Dowty concludes that about 29% of the Jewish population describe themselves as religiously traditional, and the remaining 51% say they are nonreligious (p. 174). The religiously traditional observe a mix of religious practices, but then so do those who say they are nonreligious. We have to understand these groups better in order to comprehend the nature of religion as a social problem in Israel.

Very few good national studies of Jewish identity and practices have been conducted in Israel. Limited resources often lead researchers to focus on small groups that are not representative of the overall Jewish population.[8] (Israel's Central Bureau of Statistics does not include questions relating to religious practices and levels of religious identity in the census or in its ongoing surveys because of its desire to refrain from becoming involved in sensitive political issues.) This situation led Avi Chai, a philanthropic foundation, to commission two studies of Israeli Jews, in 1991 and in 1993. The foundation hoped that the information gathered would be useful in helping it to determine how to achieve its two goals: to encourage mutual understanding and sensitivity among Jews; and to encourage Jews toward greater commitment in Jewish observance and lifestyle. The Louis Guttman Israel Institute of Applied Social Science, for so many years the leading, and basically the sole institution specializing in quality quantitative national data collection, was commissioned to conduct the studies.

The studies are summarized by Shlomit Levy, Hanna Levinsohn, and Elihu Katz, the principal researchers in the Guttman Institute, in Charles S. Liebman and Elihu Katz, *The Jewishness of Israelis: Responses to the Guttman Report*.[9] The main finding emphasized by the researchers, and by Avi Chai in press releases, is that many Jewish Israelis observe quite a bit of ritual and Jewish practice. For example, 80% light Shabbat candles at least occasionally and even 78% of the respondents classified as nonobservant always or frequently participate in a Passover seder of some kind.

Almost all of the Jewish Israelis circumcise their male children (*brit milah*),[10] and 60% visit a synagogue on the high holidays or on special occasions. The authors conclude that only 7% of the respondents are *objectively* nonobservant in terms of ten major precepts compared to 20% who *describe* themselves as totally non-observant (p. 15). The overall conclusion suggested is that

> the rhetoric of secular and religious polarization generally used to characterize Israeli society is misleading from a behavioral point of view. It would be more accurate to say that Israeli society has a strong traditional bent and, as far as religious practice is concerned, that there is a continuum from the strictly observant to the nonobservant rather than a great divide between a religious minority and a secular majority. (p. 31)

Furthermore, the study concluded that almost all Jewish Israelis are committed to the Jewish character of Israeli society, although many are critical of the religious status quo.

The results of this study were reported quite extensively in the Israeli media, and many commentators expressed their surprise regarding the finding of a lack of polarization. Liebman, professor of political science at Bar Ilan University, analyzed the media reactions to this report, as well as those of academics. (Avi Chai held an academic conference for discussing the findings, and ten of the papers presented at that conference are included in the appendix to *The Jewishness of Israelis*.) Aside from questions challenging the methodology of the report and selective reporting (to fit a reporter's preconceptions, such as what was done in the Haredi press to demonstrate that Israeli Jews are "really" religious), the most interesting discussions relate to the interpretation of the data. Does "observance" indicate being part of, or even just accepting the religious camp? One example of the reaction to the study will suffice: Eliezer Schweid, professor of Jewish thought at the Hebrew University, Jerusalem, claims that the difference in attitudes between religious and nonreligious groups is not defined only by the quantity of commandments observed. What is more important is the significance, authority, importance, and scope that individuals assign to such commandments as a way of shaping their outlook and way of life (in Liebman and Katz). Israelis mean all sorts of things when they say they attend a Passover seder. To be sure, many read the traditional *Haggadah,* but others tell stories and jokes, or complain about the fact that they have to eat matzah. Still, it is on the night of Passover eve that they get together and celebrate their collective life. Consider, too, that some nonkosher restaurants in Tel Aviv no longer serve bread, but matzah only, on Passover, in deference to the preference of their customers. Does this indicate a continuum of *religious* observance? Perhaps, but quite possibly, it is not because of their desire to adhere to God's commandment regarding unleavened bread that these people avoid bread as they eat their *treif* meals.[11] Liebman and Katz, who was the scientific director at the Guttman Institute and who is Emeritus Professor of Sociology and Communication at the Hebrew University of Jerusalem, and who is also a recipient of the Israel Prize for his work in communication, respond to the critics in their book. They specifically deal with such issues and how the data should be understood.

The Jewishness of Israelis is a very important work, both for the factual information it imparts about the study (although the reader is better referred to the full report), and because it is a study in the sociology of knowledge. The Avi Chai study results do need to be analyzed and interpreted independently. They should be distinguished from what Liebman calls the "Guttman conception of the report," or the "interpretation of the significance of the study" as opposed to the "raw data." Considering how significant this study has become in describing Jewish Israelis—it has been cited by almost every student of Israeli religious life since its publication—it would be most welcome to understand the factors that actually dictated how the study was done. Avi Chai determined the topics to be included in the survey, and apparently the questions as well. Perhaps that is why respondents were not asked to characterize themselves as religious, traditional, or nonreligious—a very common method of self-classification in Israel. Such categorical identities (as problematic as they admittedly are) would have made it more difficult to argue that Israeli Jews are *not* divided from one another.

Accommodation

We have already indicated that Israelis believe the relations between religious and nonreligious Jews constitute a social problem. The Avi Chai data suggest that the clear-cut distinction between religious and nonreligious Jews is one that is difficult to make. Let us continue from this point to understand what is the nature of religion as a social problem, and how the character of the Jewish collective mitigates this problem.

Interaction among members of two groups can be characterized either by interpersonal relations or by intergroup relations. Interpersonal relations take place when the contact between individuals is based on their personal characteristics and identities. Intergroup relations take over when the group identity of at least one of the actors (even in an interaction situation of just two persons) is called into play. Arab-Jewish relations in Israel are almost invariably characterized by an intergroup perspective—the collective identity of the other is quite salient and central to the social exchanges that take place. On the other hand, much of the daily contact between religious and nonreligious Jews is characterized by interpersonal relations. It takes a particular event or occasion to transform such contact into an intergroup relationship, when one of the sides will draw on the degree of religiosity as a factor in the identity of the other and relate to "you, the religious" or "you, the nonreligious." Interaction between religious and nonreligious Jews does not incorporate the physical fear that characterizes the relations between major antagonistic groups in the world: nonreligious Jews and Haredi or religious Jews do not feel they have to cross the street when they see one another late at night because of the fear of a hate attack. So what is the problem?

The main controversy regarding Israeli religion, according to Dowty, as well as to Bernard Susser and Liebman, in *Choosing Survival: Strategies for a Jewish Future,* is the application of Jewish religious law to the public domain. This is what is labeled as *religious coercion.* Bus transportation is curtailed in most cities on Shabbat; El Al, Israel's national airline, is not permitted to fly and most stores and institutions are required to close on that day. Public institutions must observe the laws of *kashrut.* Bread cannot be publicly displayed for sale on Passover. Various ordinances proscribe the sale of pork—the list goes on and on. Most problematic is the fact that laws of personal status are under the domain of religious law—that is, marriage and divorce. Only Orthodox marriages are sanctioned in Israel, which means that persons who are not allowed to marry under Orthodox law (e.g., a Cohen—a descendant of the tribe of priests—who wishes to marry a divorcée) cannot undertake a marriage ceremony in Israel that is recognized by state agencies. Reform and Conservative marriage ceremonies and conversion procedures performed in Israel are similarly not recognized by the state.[12]

If we analyze the relations between religious and nonreligious Jews with regard to the specific complaints each side has, it seems that different theories of intergroup relations explain the orientation of each side toward the other. The orientation of religious Jews toward nonreligious Jews is based on identity theory.[13] Their feeling is that Orthodox Judaism represents the proper way of Jewish life, and that it is their religious definition of Judaism, and identification as religious Jews, which will ensure Jewish continuity, indeed, preserve Israel as a Jewish State. Not infrequently one hears very condescending attitudes expressed by some Orthodox persons against the nonreligious. For example, a rabbi in a Tel Aviv synagogue stated in a sermon in honor of a newly marrying couple, that "they [the nonreligious] get divorced all the time, but our children know how to conduct proper family life and establish stable homes that are based on the Torah. Our sons and daughters know how to raise children who are loyal to Israel, *baruch hashem* [thank God]." I have often heard Orthodox youth indicate that "we have values, but *they,* they have no values." This motif was one of the themes used by the National Religious Party in the 1999 election campaign to attract votes from the nonreligious population—"ensure the preservation of values, in dress and in public behavior, by voting for the party that instills values in its children."

The orientation of the nonreligious toward the religious is based on realistic conflict theory. The nonreligious population complains about specific interests that relate to the inequitable allocation of limited resources. The two main topics of controversy in the 1999 election campaign were money, demanded by religious parties to support their institutions, and military service (see plate[14]). Israel is unique in having created a system whereby all Haredi Jews attend yeshivas, so that they will not have to go to the army. Never before was there such a community of scholars, where every Orthodox boy was sent to yeshiva to study full time for such an extended period of time.[15] This has created a system of dependence that requires substantial funding. There is a tremendous feeling of inequity specifically felt toward the Haredi population, as opposed to the national religious population. National religious males—the *kipot srugot* (wearers of crocheted skullcaps)—serve in the military, and work for a living. It is the Haredim who are labeled as "parasites" by their detractors, inasmuch as they are depicted as only

One People—One Conversion [Orthodox]

Those "killed" in the tent of Torah—Live very well with 90% reductions in kindergarten payments

Secular Mezuzah (Obverse: Israel Defense Forces—Protectors of the Doors of Israel)

One People—One Military Induction (Protest against non-induction of haredim)

taking from society, and not providing any useful contribution to society in return.

The significance of this situation is that the religious/nonreligious problem is increasingly becoming identified as a Haredi/nonreligious problem. If the Haredim would cease making "unjustified" claims, the nonreligious population would have less cause to complain. The "strange" dress of the Haredim does not really bother the nonreligious, nor do their stringent religious practices.[16] Their attitude toward them is generally "if it works for you, it's OK with me," as long as they do not try to impose their lifestyle on them.[17] In this regard, the fact that the Haredim, and increasingly the national religious population also, wish to live in separate neighborhoods and communities is acceptable to the nonreligious. Dowty cites statistics from a 1973 doctoral dissertation (p. 160) indicating considerable social distance between religious and nonreligious youth. The respondents indicated, in general, that they do not want friends or even neighbors who differ from their own levels of religiosity. It appears to me that this social segregation, in contemporary Israel, is considered legitimate and, for many nonreligious as well as religious persons, even desirable. Housing advertisements "for religious persons only" are generally not considered to be discriminating. "Discrimination" is a label applied to unequal treatment when it is seen to be unjust and unfair. Since the nonreligious population anyway prefers not to live with the religious, they do not view the housing practices as discrimination. Conflict arises when religious Jews, and especially Haredi Jews, are seen as trying to take over a neighborhood. The presence of a small number of religious Jews in a predominantly nonreligious neighborhood generally does not lead to friction. Nonreligious Jews fear that the character of the neighborhood will change once Haredi Jews constitute a critical mass. They dread that religiously based demands, such as motor vehicle restrictions on Shabbat, will impinge on their lifestyles, so many nonreligious Jews are happy that religious persons create and reside in their own neighborhoods and settlements.[18] Whether a segregated residential pattern contributes to the ability of religious and nonreligious Jews to get along with one another on a macrosocial level, or leads to more polarized attitudes because of decreased exposure to the other group, is an unresolved question.

In *The Jewish State,* Dowty analyzes the history of the Yishuv and the factors that led up to the present situation with regard to religious/nonreligious relations. The excellent and lucid presentation deserves its own reading. His book is on a par with, if not better than, the late S. Zalman Abramov's penetrating analysis of religion in Israeli society published in 1976,[19] especially since he deals with the broader issue of democracy and how religion impacts on this topic. Dowty looks at Israel from within and from without, having spent time in Israel and now, in the United States (like Liebman, Katz, and Susser, for that matter). Dowty notes that Zionism was viewed by traditional religious leaders as yet another threat to Jewish unity, and as a continuation of the secularizing Haskala movement (pp. 162 ff.). The Zionist movement made efforts to reach religious Jews by enlisting them as Zionists, or in the case of the ultra-Orthodox non-Zionists, just by drawing them into practical cooperation. As Dowty notes, the difference between religious Zionism and Haredim is basic to Israeli politics, but it is also a part of the broader religious-secular accommodation on religious issues.

Drawing on the work of Eliezer Don-Yehiya,[20] Dowty notes three elements that contribute to the accommodation of religious and nonreligious Jews. These are proportionality on the political level, with an equitable division of all the goods that the political system has at its disposal; the autonomy of religious institutions and culture, which protects the religious subculture from the threat of assimilation; and mutual veto, or the recognition that there is a limit to how much each side can push the other past a certain point without threatening Jewish unity.

Each of these points, it will be noted, requires a fundamental acceptance of a wish for Jewish unity. None of the individual patterns would work if the sides did not initially accept one another. The large-scale immigration of non-Jews, and Jews with little Jewish identity threatens to upset the balance. The Russian ethnic parties in the 1999 elections ran on a platform that basically negated the role of religion in public life. (Natan Sharansky's party, *Yisrael ba-Aliyah,* has since been accused of reneging on its election promises, but it now emerges that Sharansky himself was against some of the party's more blatant demands against religious involvement in the state. Apparently Sharansky supports the Orthodox stance on conversion—not a popular view among the party's supporters.)

It is interesting that autonomy contributes to accommodation. One wonders, however, whether there might be long-term effects that contraindicate the beneficial effects. For instance, the Haredim have managed to survive, despite the encroaching impact of modernity on religious life, by vigilantly separating themselves from the rest of society. In addition to rigid socialization patterns, there is a tremendous amount of social control. Internalized belief, coupled with fear of being perceived to be deviant, is a very powerful method of ensuring compliance. The socialization pattern also makes it quite difficult to leave even if one wants to exit. The creation of a community of Talmudic scholars among the men is also related to a community that is functionally illiterate as far as general education goes. These persons have little, if any, knowledge about how to function in the modern, secular world. The economic well-being of this society is dependent on the inflow of monetary resources that are not self-generating. The money put into the Haredi community is not an investment that will bring economic returns, but a contribution that once used, is gone. This is recognized in Israel today. A high percentage of Haredim are below the poverty level, and efforts are underway to enable Haredi men to seek legal employment without losing their full exemption from military service.

Modernity and the Collective

Fundamentalism threatens to move the religious away from the center. Modernity threatens to move the nonreligious away from the collective. This is the issue raised by Susser and Liebman in *Choosing Survival*. Like Liebman, Susser is a professor of political science at Bar Ilan University, and he also moved to Israel from the United States. Having been brought up Orthodox, Susser tells us that he no longer practices ritual—he describes himself as "post-Orthodox." He is, he says, "too skeptical to believe, yet too committed to leave" (p. 7). Liebman tells us that he is not Orthodox, but philo-Orthodox, part of the Orthodox community if for no other reason than because it would be difficult for him to separate himself from the community to which some of his immediate family belong. He would join a Conservative synagogue if there were one in his neighborhood. These authors, in short, are people steeped in tradition, and yet removed from it. These are academicians who are knowledgeable about the two societies they write about in this book, the United States and Israel, and have the ability to look at both societies as insiders and also as outsiders. What analysis awaits us from scholars who can be so candid about their religious identities?

A damning one. While admiring “the denseness and richness of Jewishness as it plays itself out in the Orthodox world,” they write,

> Our reluctance (at times it rises to bona fide repugnance) is with the increasingly militant and aggressive ultra-Orthodox as well as with the politically uncompromising and messianic National-Zionist Israeli strain of Orthodoxy. The ultra-Orthodox intolerance of alternate expressions of Jewishness is matched only by their attempts (in Israel at least) to coerce the non-Orthodox to submit to their religious will. Ultra-Orthodoxy increasingly embraces outlandish superstition and, in its current triumphalist mood, does it with an “in your face” belligerence. Worse still, its practitioners tend to revel in those undeniably present dark sides of the tradition that celebrate Jewish self-aggrandizement and xenophobia. (p. 169)

Susser and Liebman begin their analysis by discussing the impact that the Enlightenment had on Judaism and on Jewish life. Jews felt that universalism and equality required them to change their dress, language, and diet, in short, their whole way of life. For Jews as a persecuted group, the invitation to join a universal fellowship mitigated the suffering of centuries; the Jewish odyssey was ending in reconciliation and harmony. The irony of the Enlightenment, as the authors note, is that when faced with pogroms and crusades, the Jews held out to the end, but when given the opportunity for assimilation, many embraced it with hardly a second thought.

The idea of belonging to a humanity that transcends national boundaries was a radical change for the Jews, for throughout history they had been “a people dwelling apart,” which incorporated persecution and suffering as part of their religious ideology. For Susser and Liebman, this is the crux of the dilemma for contemporary Judaism. The inevitability of Gentile oppression has become reified, transformed into a mental construct independent of its empirical referent. An “ideology of affliction” had been woven into the fabric of Jewish life and formalized in Jewish theology, and it has consequently insinuated itself into the very psychology of Jewish existence. Susser and Liebman explain that it is not persecution per se that has preserved Judaism, but the fact that the Jews internalized and interpreted it in a specific way. This pattern was established by the rabbinic elite whose victory over all its rivals determined the basic form of Judaism following the destruction of the Second Temple in 70 C.E. One of the patterns that developed was the establishment of Judaism's character as an ethno-religion. By fusing religious with ethno-national identity, the rabbis created a community of faith that resists easy distinction between religious beliefs and peoplehood. This unity—communal existence as a religious category—helped the Jews overcome discrimination, degradation, pogroms and massacres. Jewish religiosity furnished a vindication of Jewish suffering, and Judaism rendered Jewish misfortunes endurable. When the Gentiles persecute the Jews, they are doing so as agents of God, as He punishes Israel for its sins. Of course in the end, righteous Jews will enjoy their rewards in the world to come. Messianic deliverance will arrive at the "end of days." At that time, the Jews will be returned to the Land of Israel, whereupon the entire world will recognize the mission of the people of Israel and worship the God of Israel.

Susser and Liebman tell us all this, but as it happens, Orthodox Jews "know" this is true, because they have learned this from their parents. But there are two corollaries that the authors put forth that Orthodox Jews do not hear much about. Were Jews to abandon their religious convictions, their oppression would be rendered meaningless. Indeed, Jewish history would be a mortifying tale of impotence and humiliation. In addition, were Gentile oppression to cease, the ethno-religious civilization of the Jews would have to be reformulated in order to retain credibility. In fact, the adversity-centered segment of the Jewish heritage resists attenuation. The ideology of affliction becomes the surrogate for almost all Jewish content, and this prevents the creation of a culturally self-affirming and psychologically autonomous understanding of Jewish existence.

While I have attempted to combine snippets of Susser and Liebman's book in order to present their basic ideas, anyone interested in these topics just has to read this volume in its entirety. One has to sense the pain felt by the authors and their fear for Jewish survival to appreciate their penetrating, if acerbic, analysis. The authors do state at the outset that this is not a "regular" academic analysis, but a reflective work. They use the ideas presented thus far (and others) to analyze American Judaism and Israeli society. In doing so, they have gone beyond Liebman's work on the ambivalent American Jew, his work with Don-Yehiya on Israel civil religion, and his work with Steven Cohen, comparing the Israeli and American Jewish experience.

American Judaism (aside from Orthodoxy and the peripherally Jewish), write Susser and Liebman, has become privatized. It is characterized by universalism, moralism, personalism, and voluntarism (pp. 72 ff.). It is removed from traditional religious law. Rituals are not mandated, nonobservance is not sinful, and what is more important is that one feel Jewish, as opposed to actually being Jewish. The authors' evaluation of this situation is that it does not bode well for the survival of Judaism in America. This is because the logic of these factors undermines Jewish particularism and accelerates the tendency to assimilation. Privatism "cannot be a vehicle for Jewish survival in America because it already represents the unconditional victory of the American" (p. 89). Similarly, synagogues may try to fill their pews by camouflaging or even subverting Jewish content, but in the end "since synagogues can never be more American than America, the appeal of the original will always be more potent than that of the clone" (p. 89).

Why is the situation different in Israel? Because Israelis are still preoccupied with the precariousness of their existence, and they live in propinquity with other Jews. In fact, Israel can be described as the largest Jewish neighborhood in the world (pp. 92–93). Israeli realities recall traditional forms of Jewish existence, and even secular Jews are affected by this and recognize the importance and value of the connection between Jewish tradition and Israel's cultural identity. The entire Jewish experience in Israel leads to a situation in which parting from the Jewish context requires mutiny aforethought, whereas in the United States, just being neutral means leaving the Jewish fold (p. 97). Israeli Jews view their society as a perpetuation of the past. Indeed, Zionism is now associated with the religious right in Israel (p. 101). This is an interesting phenomenon, considering the fact that Zionism originally entailed a rejection of Orthodox tradition. Even more significant, and this is probably the most important point to be made with regard to Israeli Jews, religious and nonreligious, is that they feel they are a beleaguered people. They view their conflict with the Arabs as an ethno-religious struggle with themselves being the victims of oppressors. In fact, the authors continue, "the conception of a normalized Jewish existence is an intolerable affront to a people whose entire history bespeaks unparalleled uniqueness—whether in tragedy or in cultural distinction" (p. 110). The situation of a country being surrounded by hostile forces leads Israelis to feel that social solidarity is essential for society. An element of Israel's civil religion, which became a hit song, states, "The whole world is against us; it's an old tale but true."[21]

Susser and Liebman are very pessimistic about American Jewish life. They feel that it is a sinking ship. They suggest a series of remedies including increased Jewish learning, and the development of communal boundaries between Jews and the host American culture. The non-Orthodox, they say, should be taught that the championing of Jewishness is a historical responsibility to be shouldered, rather than just a choice to be made. Additionally, leaders should ask for sacrifice and passion, since asking for little means getting even less. "When a rabbi speaks to a Bat or Bar Mitzvah asking 'only' that s/he attend services occasionally and affiliate with a Jewish organization, an act of profound self-deflation, almost self-ridicule, has taken place" (p. 151).

I imagine that American Judaism would be greatly strengthened were these recommendations to materialize but I wonder who the authors had in mind regarding their implementation. The suggestions seem to contradict American individualism. Susser and Liebman propose that rabbis seek more commitment. In their chapter on Israeli religion they note that there is no pressure on Orthodox rabbis to be responsive to the needs of the Israeli public. The situation is quite different in the United States where rabbis are employed by the congregations. Susser and Liebman do not tell us what "commitment" is, but I wonder how long a rabbi who seeks more of it will last.

Are Israelis better off? Susser and Liebman certainly think so. The community experience in Israel leads to bonding. The civil and religious practices adopted by Jewish Israelis constitute a "system of community-sustaining folkways . . . that amplify the sense of belonging and identity (p. 161).[22] But observers of the Israeli scene (including Susser and Liebman) also note a change in Israeli society that threatens to undermine unity and social cohesion among the Jews. There is a small, but quite vocal group of Israelis who are ideologically secular. These persons include post-Zionists whose universalistic message and negation of the collective ideology of Zionism puts them on a Jewish par with the individualism of unaffiliated American Jews. Liebman suggests that persons with such an orientation are overrepresented in the media and in the arts, and for that reason, their number appears to be greater than in reality. Yet there is a sense that the number is increasing. There is a perception of a strong correlation between the political right and Orthodox Jews. While not all of the politically right supporters are Orthodox, it is relatively rare to find an Orthodox Jew who (openly) supports the political left.

I sense that there are several factors that account for the increased intolerance of religious coercion among native Israeli Jews. As Liebman and Susser, Dowty, and other scholars like Eliezer Schweid, and Baruch Kimmerling note, Israeli society is increasingly individualistic.[23] The role of the collective is declining, and personal autonomy increasing. Susser and Liebman note that "the era in which the Jewish national movement developed took for granted that nations, as well as the states bodying them forth, were associations that linked individuals sharing roots and a common past" (p. 132). They explain that the question for the founders of Israel was not whether it should be a Jewish State or a Jewishly neutral state, but rather, the degree to which the Jewish heritage was to be incorporated in the state. Individual, liberal, democratic conceptions have now delegitimized the ethno-national state. The Shinui party's televised election commercials in 1999 fit in with this claim very well. Party leader Tommy Lapid castigated religiously based laws as inappropriate for a modern society. He presented a series of practices that contrast Israel with "normal" states. "In a *normal* state, no one tells you whom to marry; in a *normal* state, no one tells you what you can eat and what you cannot eat; in a *normal* state. . . ." The advertisement closed with the question of who will rule: the majority *(rov)*, or the rabbis *(rav)*. Today, write Susser and Liebman, "'normal' states avoid doing just what was [once] considered the central duty of nation-states; pursuing collective goals" (p. 133).

There were always some Israelis who rebelled against the collective goals. Various leagues against religious coercion have been established since the early years of the state. But it is quite possible that some of those who might have been bothered by the situation were inhibited from actually acting, because they felt that they could not effect social change. It is also possible that some of the persons who were most bothered by religious laws left the country. The number of Israelis who live outside of Israel today is estimated to be between 700,000 and 1,000,000.[24] A common assumption is that economic factors served as a primary factor in their decision to leave, but we really do not know why they left or what impact any combination of factors might have had on their motivation. In any case, political parties, such as Shinui, may well give nonreligious Israelis a sense of empowerment that they lacked in the past.

We can also speculate that a new "breed" of Israeli Jew, further removed from the values of the founding fathers, has developed. One can differentiate between first-generation and second-generation nonreligious Jews. The phrase, "first-generation nonreligious Jews," refers to those persons who grew up in a religiously traditional home, but who identify themselves as nonreligious. These persons tend to have a more positive affective orientation toward Israel as a Jewish State and more tolerance for religiously based laws. Second-generation nonreligious Jews grew up in homes that were also nonreligious. These persons are not only cognitively removed from Jewish tradition, but are also characterized by a more negative affective attitude toward Jewish life, especially in the public domain.[25] Though we lack appropriate statistical data, it is plausible to surmise that the number of such persons is on the rise.

Another factor impacting on Israeli religion is the addition of some 800,000 emigrants from the former Soviet Union who arrived in the period between 1989 and 1999. At least 200,000 of them are not Jewish. In fact, the nature of the Jewish identity of even Jewish Russians is unclear, after so many years in a Communist regime. Pragmatically, this is essentially a culturally and religiously non-Jewish population that is characterized by an individualistic orientation. Apparently, a significant number of these persons view their Russian cultural background with pride, and, while this is not necessarily related, they also view religious coercion negatively.[26] Many of the issues of religion in Israel public life, especially those dealing with family status (marriage and divorce, and, of course, the definition of who is a Jew), and Shabbat and *kashrut* observance, affect them particularly. How tolerant will these persons be of religious coercion? Ethnic Russian parties won ten seats in the 1999 election. Meretz-Democratic Israel, a civil rights oriented party won ten seats. Shinui, a strong antireligious party won six seats. These parties call for a renegotiation of the relationship between religion and state, not necessarily completely abolishing the bond, but altering it to considerably circumscribe religious law and to limit its impact on the general public.

Conclusion

The "nation that dwelleth alone" in the title of this essay is under threat of becoming a state that dwelleth alone. While the collective orientation of the state still has a strong hold on the majority of its citizens, the relations between Israel and Jews abroad are becoming strained. Reform and Conservative Judaism, the dominant religious movements outside of Israel, are disenfranchised in Israel, and Israeli political decisions have an impact on the orientation toward those denominations as religious movements. Increasingly, non-Orthodox Jews outside of Israel question their relationship with Israel as a Jewish State. The factors that contribute to internal cohesion, a traditional, religious orientation, thus divide Jews around the world.

As bad as the situation might appear to the outsider, it really could get much worse. The prediction is that it indeed will. There are too many macro-level changes in Israel combined with a rapid influx of immigrants who are not part of the Jewish dream that undermine solidarity in the ethno-national state. A movement to alter the Law of Return, the law that grants migration and citizenship rights to Jews and to their descendants down to a third generation, was the subject of Immigration and Absorption Parliamentary Committee meetings in 2000. Shas is opposed to the immigration of non-Jews, and the fact that many of the immigrants from the former Soviet Union are not Sephardim does not help their cause with this party. Former Prime Minister Ehud Barak stated that he would not allow the law to be amended. He was ostensibly fearful of the impact that any change might have on the question, once again, of "who is a Jew?" and the implications that any change might have on the recognition of non-Orthodox conversions. Indeed, representatives of the Reform and Conservative movements regularly participate in the parliamentary subcommittee meetings (leading some ultra-Orthodox political leaders to boycott the meetings). An extreme antireligious sentiment on this issue, on the other hand, was expressed by Arie Caspi, a noted columnist in *ha-Aretz,* who has declared his support for the continued migration of non-Jews inasmuch as these persons will assist in limiting the impact of Haredi Jews on Israeli society.[27]

The question, for some, is no longer how to combine state and religion, but whether the ruling force should be the state or religion. Shas, the Sephardi ultra-Orthodox political party, is mentioned by all analysts as a rising force, but it is doubtful whether anyone really envisaged that it would succeed as forcefully as it did in the 1999 elections, winning seventeen seats (up from ten).[28] I suspect that the emotion in the citation from Susser and Liebman quoted above is somewhat affected by the rise of Shas (which went from six to ten seats in the 1996 elections). Shas used amulets and promises of rabbinic blessings for their voters to attract supporters (including a call for support from a Sage *[Mekubal]* who had passed away fifteen years earlier). The strong educational institutions established by Shas attract large numbers of heretofore nonreligious youth and turn them into Orthodox, Shas supporters. The fear of this situation is altering the basis of the attitude of the nonreligious population from one based on realistic conflict over interests and material resources, to one that is based on identity theory, and on the very nature of the Jewish State. Dowty looks at this situation and the implications it has for the survival of democracy, while Susser and Liebman look at the impact the changes in Israel have for the survival of Judaism. They have all performed a valuable service by providing us with insightful volumes that shed light on the processes under way, and the factors that will have an even greater impact in the future.

Notes

1. "Religious" and "Orthodox" are often treated as overlapping in Hebrew. Non-Orthodox Israeli Jews commonly describe themselves as nonreligious. Reform and Conservative Jews and their denominational movements face a dilemma in this regard, because by definition, they are treated (at least by some persons) as nonreligious inasmuch as they are non-Orthodox. See Ephraim Tabory, "The Identity Dilemma of Non-Orthodox Religious Movements: Reform and Conservative Judaism in Israel," in *Jewishness and Judaism in Contemporary Israel*, eds. Zvi Sobel and Benjamin Beit-Hallahmi (Albany: State University of New York Press, 1991), 135–52.

2. See Eliezer Ben-Rafael and Stephen Sharot, *Ethnicity, Religion and Class in Israeli Society* (New York: Cambridge University Press, 1991).

3. In this essay I refer only to Jews in Israeli society. The impact of Jewish Israel on Arab citizens has not yet been sufficiently studied.

4. For an engrossing study of what constituted Jewishness in antiquity, see Shaye D. Cohen, *The Beginnings of Jewishness: Boundaries, Varieties, Uncertainties* (Berkeley: University of California Press, 1999).

5. Dr. Yossi Beilin, while serving as Israel's minister of justice, suggested that it be sufficient for a non-Jewish candidate for immigration to

Israel to bring witnesses who testify that the candidate is interested in being part of the Jewish community. See: Beilin, *The Death of the American Uncle* (Tel Aviv: Miskal-Yedioth Ahronoth Books and Chemed Books, 1999) (in Hebrew).

6. This is one of the more popular topics for Israeli symposia and colloquia. See, for example, *The State of Israel as a Jewish and Democratic State: a Symposium and Related Documents*. The Twelfth World Congress for Jewish Studies (Jerusalem: World Congress for Jewish Studies with the Cooperation of the Avi Chai Foundation, 1999) (in Hebrew).

7. Statistical Abstract of Israel 1998 No. 49 (Jerusalem: Central Bureau of Statistics).

8. See, for example, Carol Gordon, "Mutual Perceptions of Religious and Secular Jews in Israel," *Journal of Conflict Resolution* 33:4 (1989): 632–51; Ephraim Tabory, "Avoidance and Conflict: Perceptions Regarding Contact between Religious and Nonreligious Jewish Youth in Israel," *Journal for the Scientific Study of Religion* 32:2 (1993): 148–62. Several unpublished national studies have been conducted, for example, by Gesher, in 1985, and by the Ministry for Religious Affairs in the early 1990s. Probably the most often cited study of a representative sample of the Jewish population prior to the Guttman report was Yehuda Ben-Meir and Peri Kedem, "Index of Religiosity of the Jewish Population of Israel," *Megamot* 24:3 (1979): 353–62 (in Hebrew). This study also found no clear-cut dichotomy between religious and nonreligious Jews, but rather a continuum of religiosity running through from the extremely religious through the completely nonreligious.

9. For the full report see Shlomit Levy, Hanna Levinsohn, and Elihu Katz, *Beliefs, Observances and Social Interaction among Israeli Jews* (Jerusalem: Louis Guttman Israel Institute of Applied Social Research, 1993).

10. An Association Against Circumcision has been established to encourage Jewish Israelis to refrain from this practice, but it has failed to attract many members. In fact, even some of those who belong to the association nevertheless circumcise their male children. See Sharon Erez, *"Circumscribed Circumcision": The World of Parents Who Do Not Circumcise Their Sons* (master's thesis, Bar-Ilan University, 2000) (in Hebrew).

11. There are other examples of behavior and attitudes in the report that can be derived from alternate motivations. Seventy-four percent of the "totally nonobservant" say that "to help others in need" is important or very important to them as a guiding principle in their lives, and 50% say that giving money to charity is important. Eighty-five percent of this group says that living in Israel is important and 81% say that feeling part of the

Jewish people is important. All of these data appear in a table titled "ranking Jewish values by the totally non-observant" (p. 28).

12. This subject constitutes the main issue of contention between foreign Jewry and Israeli authorities.

13. For a basic exposition of the theories discussed here see Donald M. Taylor and Fathali M. Moghaddam, *Theories of Intergroup Relations: International Social Psychological Perspectives,* 2d ed. (Westport, CT: Praeger, 1994). See also Kenneth D. Wald and Samuel Shye, "Interreligious Conflict in Israel: The Group Basis of Conflicting Visions," *Political Behavior* 16 (1994): 157–78.

14. The secular *mezuzah* pictured in the plate is a replica of a military dog tag. The distributor of these secular *mezuzot* is identified as "the Voice of the Silent Minority." The advertisement for these states, "With your hand on the *mezuzah,* who really deserves a kiss [for protecting the people?]." The Hebrew text on the obverse of the dog tag translates as "keepers of the gates of Israel." The original Hebrew is *Shomer Dlatot Yisrael*. Together, the first letter of each of the words (*shin* [ש], *dalet* [ד], and *yod* [י]) spells God's sacred name.

15. Menachem Friedman, "The Religious and Haredi Communities in Israel following the 12th Parliamentary Elections: Trends and Processes," *Skira Hodshit* 36:5 (1989): 22–34 (in Hebrew).

16. In some respects, the Haredim are treated like a quaint sect by tourist groups who, to the resentment of the Haredim, visit their enclaves much as tourists visit the Amish in the United States.

17. Some of the most vocal opposition to the Haredi community has been expressed by families of children who have become "penitents" and "returned" to Haredi Judaism, when the children refuse to visit their parents because the grandchildren will be exposed to a nonreligious lifestyle. See Sophia Mahler and Dan Mahler, *The Souls' Hunters* (Tel-Aviv: Zemira-Bitan, 1998 (in Hebrew: *Tzayadei ha-Nefashot*). The clever Hebrew subtitle, "*Tshuva le-Tshuva,*" translates as "A Response to Penitence."

18. I suspect that many religious persons would consider housing "for the non-religious only" to constitute a discriminatory practice and as another indicator of how the non-religious population just cares about itself. Housing "for the nonreligious only" would probably be interpreted as a denigration of religion and Judaism, and lead to charges of anti-Semitism and Jewish self-hatred.

19. S. Zalman Abramov, *Perpetual Dilemma: Jewish Religion in the Jewish State* (Jerusalem: World Union for Progressive Judaism, and Rutherford, NJ: Fairleigh Dickinson University Press, 1976).

20. Eliezer Don-Yehiya, "The Resolution of Religious Conflicts in Israel," in Stuart Cohen and Eliezer Don-Yehiya, eds., *Conflict and Consensus in Jewish Public Life* (Ramat Gan: Bar Ilan University Press, 1986), 203–18.

21. Song performed by Lahakat Pikud Dizengoff, Hed Artzi Records (in Hebrew), 1970.

22. Liebman compares secular Judaism and secular Jewishness in "Secular Judaism and its Prospects," in Dan Urian and Efraim Karsh, *Jewish Aspects in Israeli Culture* (London: Frank Cass, 1999), 29–48.

23. Eliezer Schweid, "Judaism in Israeli Culture," in Urian and Karsh, *Jewish Aspects in Israeli Culture,* 9–28; Baruch Kimmerling, "Between Hegemony and Dormant *Kulturkampf* in Israel," in *Jewish Aspects in Israeli Culture,* 49–72.

24. Estimate presented by Rabbi Michael Melchior, minister responsible for Diaspora and Social Affairs in the Office of the Prime Minister, at a meeting with the Israel directors of the World Jewish Congress, 22 December 1999.

25. Shai Rosenberg, *A Comparison of First and Second Generation Non-Religious Jewish Israelis* (master's thesis, Bar Ilan University, 2000) (in Hebrew).

26. Russian immigrants were not included in the Avi Chai-Guttman study, and thus the study really no longer presents a true picture of Jewish society, or to put it more accurately, a picture of the Jewish nature of non-Arab society.

27. "The Legion of Goyim," *ha-Aretz*, 26 November 1999 (Weekend supplement), p. 12 (in Hebrew).

28. The National Religious Party and United Torah Judaism, a Haredi party, each won five seats in the 1999 election. Shas, it should be noted, did not envisage the degree of success. Some of the elected candidates on its slate would not have been placed so high on the party list, had it been realized that the party would win so many seats.

Part 3

Israeli Society: The Arab Community

5. Palestinians in Israel: Social and Educational Conditions in the 1990s

Ilham Nasser,
Trinity College, Washington, D.C.

This essay considers several new books that shed light on the social and educational conditions of the Arab citizens of Israel, a topic about which there has been only scarce research until now. The author uses an analysis and comparison of these recent publications to make the argument that discussion of the status of the minority always involves a political agenda. Research that reflects an Israeli government perspective emphasizes improvements in social and educational conditions since 1948; studies reflecting Palestinian perspectives emphasize discriminatory policies against the minority and gaps between the minority and the majority communities in terms of educational and employment opportunities, and the allocation of economic resources.

Al-Haj, Majid, *Education, Empowerment, and Control: The Case of the Arabs in Israel,* Albany: State University of New York Press, 1995.

Haidar, Aziz, *On the Margins: The Arab Population in the Israeli Economy,* New York: St. Martin's, 1995.

Haidar, Aziz, *The Palestinians in Israel and the Oslo Agreement*, Beirut: Institute for Palestine Studies, 1997 (in Arabic: *Al-Falastiniyun fi-Isra'il fi thell Ittifaqiyat Oslo*).

Stendel, Ori, *The Arabs in Israel,* Brighton, England: Sussex Academic Press, 1996.

This review essay has been inspired by the scarcity of academic and empirical research on the social and educational conditions of the Palestinian citizens of Israel, and especially on the institution of the family and the changes it has gone through since the establishment of the State of Israel.[1] In the last decade, there has been an increased effort to explore these topics while examining the economic and sociopolitical conditions of this minority.[2] However, many of the recent studies are on Israel as a democracy and its relation to the Palestinian minority.[3] Such articles mainly analyze the political status of the Arab minority and its relations with the state. The topic of social and familial conditions is still a neglected one among scholars.

The present essay evaluates the contributions of four recent books to the understanding and discussion of the Arab minority's social and educational conditions. It examines the books' methods of inquiry and the validity of their conclusions. In addition to offering in-depth analysis of the major issues introduced, this review aims to examine the underlying assumptions of the three authors, and to uncover their theoretical and academic claims and frameworks.

Two of the books in this review were written for a variety of audiences, while the other two mainly targeted educators and specialists. Ori Stendel's book is a basic general review on the Arab community. Aziz Haidar's Arabic book is a general review of the sociopolitical impact of the 1993 Oslo Accords on the Arabs in Israel. In the remaining two books, social and educational issues are more central. Majid Al-Haj focuses on the Arab education system in Israel, while Haidar's *On the Margins* deals with the status of the Arabs in Israel's national economy. Unlike Stendel's introductory text, both Haidar and Al-Haj target an audience that is more specialized about the issues under investigation.

Socioeducational conditions are an essential factor in measuring and understanding the status and development of an ethnic minority. A close examination of educational systems, the allocation of economic resources, and other conditions help us determine the attitudes and views of the majority (especially the establishment) toward its minority.[4] In addition, educational and social processes are interrelated and both play a significant role in shaping the features of a community and its ability to deal with the majority. Learning more about social structures and values, including familial factors, can shed light on the impact of the education system on minority members (Al-Haj, pp. 6–7). Al-Haj highlights the relationship between the need for social change and the education system. Stendel focuses more on sociocultural factors rather than on educational ones, while Haidar's two books offer a socioeconomic viewpoint.

As in any research on minority affairs, discussion of the social and educational conditions and status of Palestinians in Israel always involves an undisclosed political agenda by both Jewish and Palestinian scholars as well. The three reviewed authors make several different, often undeclared, assumptions. Stendel, a former Israeli government official who served as a deputy advisor on Arab affairs in the 1970s, intends to draw a positive view and to emphasize the efforts of the government toward improving the conditions of the "minorities." He neglects to review the urgent problems and needs facing the Arabs as a minority. On the other hand, Al-Haj and Haidar consistently and systematically compare the Arab and Jewish sectors to illustrate existing gaps.

Arabs in Israel: An Official Perspective

Stendel's book, *The Arabs in Israel,* attempts to examine the status of the Palestinian minority in Israel from different angles and aspects including education, political activity, the status of women, employment, and language and literature. It is informative to readers who are interested in understanding the conditions of the Arab minority and their modern history from a mainstream governmental perspective. Throughout the book Stendel shares his insights and his personal accounts of interactions with members of the Arab community. He reviews the development of the Arab minority since the establishment of the Israeli state and also evaluates major political events and political parties among the Arabs. In addition, Stendel describes Arab society in Israel and analyzes the social and family/clan structure among the Arabs and the Beduin. He focuses, too, on the legal status of the Arabs as a minority within the Jewish State, and the relations between the Arabs in Israel and the rest of the Arab world. All along, Stendel emphasizes the importance of controversial laws, such as the Law of Return, underpinning the Israeli state as a homeland for Jews. He explains the necessity and importance of these laws for the state and justifies their existence. For example, while recognizing that the Law of Return "unquestionably gives clear and distinct preference to Jews whoever they may be to immigrate to Israel," Stendel argues that "[t]his is not discrimination against the Arab citizens of Israel, but rather a clear statement of the desire to realize the idea of turning Israel into the national homeland of the Jews from the Diaspora" (p. 193). He, therefore, does not view Israel as discriminating against its minority either in law or in practice.

Stendel concludes his book with an analysis of the role of the Arab minority in the peace process with an emphasis on the complexity of their loyalties and the duality of their relations with the rest of the Palestinians. He assures his readers that the Arabs of Israel will never declare total hostility toward Israel, affirming that they "will not automatically answer any call of the PLO, Hamas, or the Islamic Jihad. Their own existential considerations will serve as a necessary 'filter' of the various expectations entertained of them" (p. 236).

Stendel provides information about the Arabs before the establishment of the state and describes the changes that occurred with regard to schools and health and social services after 1948. He emphasizes, for example, what he calls the "demographic revolution" among Arabs resulting from education, and especially the education of women about family planning (p. 41). He states, "While the rate of live births has remained steady, there has been a dramatic decrease in mortality among Muslim Arabs since the establishment of Israel, declining from 8 per thousand during 1955–59 to 4.3 per thousand in the most recent census" (p. 39). Stendel points also to the steady rise of the number of youngsters attending schools in rural and urban centers, including girls and Beduin, and to the increase in government expenditure on Arab education, which has in turn brought about a higher standard of living in the Arab sector. Thus, Stendel accurately describes the improvements achieved by Israeli laws and services, but he neglects the impact of the 1948 "Exodus" on Palestinian society. He ignores the fact that this society was torn apart, left with no infrastructure or any economic basis. When reviewing the changes in communal structure, he overlooks the massive confiscation of lands that the government conducted, despite the fact that an explanation of this issue is indispensable for understanding changes in agricultural resources and their impact on Palestinian society.[5]

With the aim of highlighting the improvements that Israel brought to the Palestinians since 1948, Stendel chooses to break down the Palestinian community into several ethno-religious groups and denominations such as Beduin, Muslims, and Christians (p. 45). This official governmental classification is perceived as offensive by the Arab minority because it ignores their rights as a national minority and as part of the Palestinian people. It also serves as a way for the government to discriminate against one religion over another, as both Haidar and Al-Haj argue in their books. Stendel's approach corresponds consistently with governmental attitudes of "divide and rule," distinguishing between different sects and religions among the Arabs.

Stendel continues highlighting the positive changes in the Arab society since the establishment of the state, disregarding some of the central factors playing a role in these changes. For example, he emphasizes the new building trends and major developments in the *suqs* (markets) as an indicator of modernity brought by the state since 1948, but he totally overlooks the proximity and density in buildings and the changes of employment patterns among Arabs—issues that are specifically addressed by Al-Haj and Haidar. His views on these issues are descriptive and lack an in-depth and complex examination of events and underlying reasons for such changes. For example, Stendel ignores the fact that 50 percent of the Arab population lives under the poverty level and that 13 out of the 14 cities with the highest unemployment in Israel are Arab villages and towns.[6]

Stendel's description of the status of women is the most selective and biased in his analysis. He chooses to focus his discussion on the "sensitive" and yet unresolved issue of "family honor" that always attracts readers from Western cultures and is typical of an orientalist research approach that neglects the complex internal dynamics of indigenous cultural practices, regardless of their sociopolitical functions. In addition, it is important to indicate that his source of information on this topic comes from a book written by Joseph Ginat in 1982.[7] Although 14 years had passed between the publication of Ginat's book and Stendel's writing, Stendel makes a minimal effort to examine a variety of recent social developments and changes in Arab society. He only briefly mentions the "Al-Fanar" organization that aims to protest honor killings among the Palestinians (p. 65). Furthermore, he neither relates to the complexity of these issues nor considers the success stories of women in the Arab community. He goes on with his lengthy description of the inferior status of Arab women, especially Muslim women, and explains the recent improvements in their status as being merely influenced by, or an outcome of, Western civilization brought to Arabs through Jewish-Israeli influence. It is not my intention here to underestimate the issues under discussion nor the contribution of the Israeli government's social policies to the status of women, but to highlight the fact that Stendel relies on outdated texts and doesn't initiate any in-depth analysis of such issues from different angles.

Stendel adds two sections on Arab society. The first is on the Beduin, whom he insists on treating separately from the rest of the Arabs in Israel. The second is about the Arab intelligentsia (he uses this term to refer to the educated or college graduates among Palestinians). Stendel briefly refers to some statistics about higher education among the members of this community, and then describes the characteristics of Arab students in Israeli universities. He discusses their continuous attempts to become spokespersons for the Arabs in Israel, pointing to the fact that students have the freedom to express themselves on a national level in Israeli universities. This is a freedom they exercise by demonstrating whenever controversy erupts (over issues such as Land Day, guard-duty on campus, and the Lebanon War). Again, Stendel ignores issues of discrimination, unemployment, housing, and many others factors that the Arab students and graduates face. Instead, he concludes this section with an explanation of intermarriage between Arab intellectuals and Jewish women by saying, "it sometimes seems that the minority intellectual, who sets out to fight for his people, needs the personal backing from one of the 'daughters of the majority' in his confrontation with the majority" (p. 79). Such statements that are apparent throughout Stendel's book are based on his own speculations about the Arabs and their behaviors rather than on solid arguments and fieldwork.

The Arabs in Israel is clearly motivated by Stendel's personal political views, attitudes, and experiences as a former government official. He provides detailed information about his dealings with some of the Arab mayors, offering his impressions of their character, personalities, and families. On many occasions he uses his own political judgment in admiring whom he likes and disregarding others. He is also uninhibited in criticizing some of the Arab student leaders based on his own political judgment. For example, in one of his many anecdotes, he describes the disrespectful behavior of Arab students at Haifa University toward S. Khamis, a leader of the Communist Party: "They [the Arab students] sat and laughed in [Khamis's] face, and he seemed to close his eyes to their ridicule. They showed no respect for his white hair" (p. 11).

Despite the wealth of personal experiences that Stendel shares with his readers, his book lacks the complex perspective of the Arab reality in all its aspects. *The Arabs in Israel* does not identify the social and educational needs of the Arabs and makes no attempt to provide conclusions or recommendations for development. On the contrary, it paints a positive picture of the status of the Arab minority in Israel, as most Israeli government agencies do when presenting the affairs of this minority.

Arabs in Israel: A Critical Perspective

Al-Haj's book, *Education, Empowerment, and Control: The Case of the Arabs in Israel,* provides an analysis of the education system, including a discussion of curriculum issues, physical facilities, and key formal policies starting with the Ottomans, the British Mandate, and finally the State of Israel. Al-Haj presents the readers with a theoretical framework that assumes interrelation between education and social change. He provides general background information on the Arabs in Israel, including details on the demographic, social, economic, and political aspects of this community during the three periods just mentioned. Al-Haj emphasizes the changes in government educational policy toward the Arabs, including the creation of separate Druze and Beduin education systems. He describes the process in which the government created what is called the "Druze education unit." "The particularism characterizing Druze education," he writes, "was not restricted to the administrative level; it included the content of education, despite the absence of autonomy in this area" (p. 74). Throughout the book there are comparisons and examinations of the Jewish and Arab sectors in the areas of institutions and pupils, physical and educational facilities, policy, goals, curricula, teachers, and social control.

Unlike Stendel, Al-Haj highlights the neglected issue of Arab graduates' employment and the Israeli government's inability to absorb the educated and professional Arab graduates in the job market, which is evident in the high unemployment rate among this sector of the population. He describes what happens to Arab students after graduation including their employment and social status. He provides demographic information that is based mainly on the Central Bureau of Statistics. In addition, he provides valuable information about Arab students and their religious and socioeconomic makeup based on survey data that he gathered in 1989 "to investigate the employment situation of all Arabs who graduated from the university of Haifa between 1982 and 1987" (p. 2). According to Al-Haj, the survey revealed that "employment distress among Arab university graduates has increased during the 1980s. . . . 42 percent are either unemployed or underemployed; another 30 percent work in fields far removed from their education and training" (p. 209). Furthermore, his survey suggests that those who are better educated have less of an opportunity for employment in the Jewish sector (p. 210).

Al-Haj's information on the demographic, social, economic, and political aspects of the Arab population provides an in-depth analysis of social-educational changes that have occurred after the establishment of the state. He comes to his conclusions through close examination of government reports (including government archives, educational goals, and curriculum for the Arab sector) and interviews with people involved in the education system. He identifies the developments and accomplishments due to the exposure of the Arab minority to the Jewish majority, but he also notes the complexity and mistreatment of the minority by the different governmental agencies and their influence on education. Al-Haj relates to these developments in education and economic resources in a factual way while emphasizing the pressing need for change, and the discriminatory practices used by the government.

In his book he constantly makes a connection between education and its usage as a tool of control by the government. His main argument is that education is utilized as a political control mechanism by the dominant group, in this case, the Jewish-Israelis. More specifically, Palestinians see education as a tool of empowerment while the government employs it as a mechanism of social control.

He suggests that over the century, the Palestinians have been denationalized by their Ottoman, British, and Israeli rulers. Al-Haj claims that, today, education has lost its function as an agent of social change and has become an institution for literacy (p. 215). Social change, according to him, has been restricted by three main factors: "social localization, economic delocalization, and political marginalization" (p. 25), all of which were products of government policies.

Al-Haj dedicates a significant part of his analysis to the changes that the typical Arab extended family went through since 1948. He emphasizes the transition from agricultural work to hired labor outside the village, which caused the weakening of the extended family. Al-Haj relies on previous studies on the family structure to convey the changes that the nuclear family went through. He writes, "The individual needs of family members have come to play an important part in determining these patterns, and women and children whose influence in this area was limited, even marginal, in the past, now have an important role in the decision-making procedures of the family" (p. 23).

Al-Haj points out the formal policy of control that is adopted by the Israeli government to restrict the development of Palestinian Arabs in Israel (p. 23). Examples of this policy include the government's failure to develop new and local avenues of employment following the massive loss of agricultural lands and the transformation of the Arab agricultural labor force to an industrial one. Government policy also involved confiscation of land and neglect of infrastructure, both of which have resulted in economic marginalization.

Overall, Al-Haj's analysis captures many of the structural causes of the existing economic and social gaps between Arabs and Jews in Israel. However, he does not take a stand on essential issues and fails to address controversial problems such as the Jewishness of the state as a root cause of the discrimination embedded in Israel's laws and pronouncements. Such factors have been the main focus of many Arab scholars in their analysis of Arab-Jewish relations in Israel.[8] Al-Haj's study would also have benefited from a comprehensive analysis of the Palestinian national movement and its impact on changes within the Arab minority in Israel.

In *The Palestinians in Israel and the Oslo Agreement*, Haidar provides an analysis of the recent conditions of the Arab-Palestinian minority in Israel. He focuses on the economic and political relations between the Arab-Palestinian minority and the State of Israel but he also reviews the political, economic, cultural, and social systems within the community as well. Haidar's unique contribution lies in his addressing the efforts of the Palestinians toward improving their living conditions, including the establishment of action committees, such as a higher education committee and a committee for the protection of Arab-owned land, to deal with different problem areas. He also deals specifically with political attitudes toward the Palestinian uprising of 1987–1993, and the Oslo Accords and their impact on the voting trends among Palestinians. Haidar concludes his book with a vision for the future of the Palestinians in Israel by closely examining the peace process and its impact on the economic, social, and political conditions of the Palestinians. His main claim is that the Arabs will remain marginalized in the future as a result of the Oslo Accords. But he concludes with a positive note by saying,

> We believe there is a possibility to diverge from marginalization by continuing to strengthen the human, individual and economic energy we have and by forming social, political, and cultural patterns that are unique and different. We have to strengthen the belief that our political destiny is different from the rest of the Palestinians and that we need to look for new formulas for our existence as individuals and groups. (p. 247)

Unlike Stendel and Al-Haj, Haidar analyzes the relations of this minority living in Israel with the rest of the Palestinian people, and its attitudes toward the Palestinian Authority. The Arab minority in Israel, he claims, has come to realize that their belonging to the Palestinian people doesn't necessarily mean that they are committed to the same actions as all Palestinians. Their destiny must be affected by their special status as citizens of the Israeli state (p. 221). According to Haidar, socially and politically the Palestinians in Israel (whether on an individual or the collective level) view and admire the Jewish majority—and not the rest of the Palestinians—as their role model.

Haidar also discusses the reasons behind the Palestinians' lack of assimilation into Israeli society, especially the absence of interest in such a process among the Jews and Palestinians themselves. "Jewish Israeli society," he writes, "is sealed from the beginning against any non-Jewish individuals and groups" (p. 22). In his description of social and educational conditions, he highlights the discriminatory practices of the different Israeli ministries in the allocation of resources, budgets, and employment patterns. He emphasizes the gaps that exist in all areas of living, such as education conditions at all levels, students' achievement, social services, health services, and housing. Haidar documents the discrimination against the Arab sector in Israel, using government data to support his arguments.

Contrary to Stendel, Haidar's main goal is to reveal the facts about government policies toward the Palestinian community and the influence of various political events on their educational, economic, and social conditions. Haidar states that "it is not simple to distinguish between the political and social in the government's policy towards the Palestinian minority; they are interrelated in most cases because policy in the social realm is influenced by and devoted to serving political agendas" (p. 16). According to Haidar, the policy of treating the Arabs as members of different religious groups is a classic example of that difficulty. When the Israeli government decides to continue recruiting Druze youth into the Israel Defense Forces (IDF), such a decision has major implications for the social networks and conditions of the Arab Druze in Israel. This decision also feeds into the government's policy to grant special status to Druze towns.

Haidar argues that the Israeli cultural system aims at applying two different ideologies: one for the settlers (by which he refers to all immigrants to Israel, such as the new Russian and Ethiopian immigrants), and another for the Arab population. For the first ideology, there are two justifications: The need for immigrants and the establishment of a unique political system, and the need to justify discriminatory policies toward the minority. The policy toward the minority focuses on aiming to convince them that they don't constitute one group of people and that their individual interests will be met only by collaborating with the government. According to Haidar, this ideology "attempts to persuade the minority that their inferiority is a result of their own culture and that they live in a better reality and standards than their fathers" (p. 20).

In the book, there is a tendency to present a general overview of the social, political, economic, and educational conditions among the Palestinians. Although Haidar analyzes the recent changes among the Arabs in Israel such as economic and social changes, his book lacks an in-depth examination of factors that led to the conditions of Palestinians after Oslo. His constant attempt to provide an overview overshadows the importance of providing more comprehensive description and analysis of the subject matter.

In his second book, *On the Margins: The Arab Population in the Israeli Economy,* Haidar reviews the status of the Arab minority in Israel's economy. He discusses in depth the government's policy toward the Arabs and the methods it has used to manipulate their economic status and employment patterns. Haidar examines the political system and the foundations of Israel as a Jewish national state, and he criticizes the lack of basic individual rights and the emergency regulations used by the government toward the Arab minority.

Throughout the book, Haidar analyzes the relationship between economy and politics. He emphasizes (a) the government's control over resources such as land and water; (b) the stagnation of the Arab economy as a result of discrimination; (c) control over financial institutions; and (d) changes in the Arab labor force, especially with regard to agriculture. He provides demographic information about employment patterns and land confiscations, and compares the allocation of resources in both the Arab and Jewish sectors. Haidar provides a striking example of government control in a case where 180,000 dunams owned by Arabs were annexed to the regional council of the settlement of Misgav, thereby preventing the Arab owners from tending to their land (p. 31).[9] He shows how the Arab population reacted to these policies by getting organized as a community, and by putting pressure on the Ministry of the Interior to allocate more budgets and resources to Arab local councils—a significant aspect that is not mentioned in the books by Stendel or Al-Haj. He reviews the development of Palestinian activism, from actions by individuals to organized national-collective action, and describes the establishment of several public committees to address the needs and desires of the Palestinian minority.

On the Margins systematically follows the economic development among the Arabs and its impact and relation to the government's economic policy. Haidar reveals the Israeli government's consistent efforts (since the establishment of the state) to change the Arabs from farmers to blue-collar workers. He reviews a sample of four Arab towns and examines them closely, thereby familiarizing the reader with the economic conditions of the community, and he provides an empirical basis for his assumptions and analysis. The strength of Haidar's book stems first from his use of these four case studies and second, from his analytic abilities and the supportive data he provides from different sources. The book's weakness lies in its inability to address internal economic problems, for example, by providing more detailed analyses of women's employment patterns and the existence of underage employment.

Same Population, Different Views

Among the four books under review, the Palestinian authors present the critical "minority" point of view, while Stendel presents official government policy regarding the Arabs.[10] This is evident first in the ideological framework and analytic approach used by each of the authors. Even though Stendel does not specify a theoretical framework for his book, it is clear that he adopts the "modernization" theory that is popular with many other Israeli-Jewish scholars (cf. Haidar, *On the Margins*, p. v). This is a theory that emphasizes the changes and transitions that Arab society has undergone in its social, economic, and educational conditions. It examines these changes in a linear fashion, with an inherent assumption that modernization and industrialization are positive while tradition is negative and backward.

In contrast, both Haidar and Al-Haj adopt the "control" theory—that is, the theory that Israeli governments intentionally implement policies that restrict and limit the Arab minority; they achieve this by controlling resources (as Haidar points out) and by controlling the education system (as Al-Haj demonstrates). In addition, Al-Haj chooses to present a "positivist approach" to explain the relationship between education and social change; this approach views school as an agency of socialization. Al-Haj stresses the fact that "through the school system, individuals are trained to be motivated and technically capable of performing adult roles. The school also functions as an allocation system, contributing to the allocation of specific roles in society to individuals" (p. 5). Within this framework, Al-Haj concludes that formal education is vital for development and social change.

The books under review address social and educational conditions of the Palestinians in Israel and their relations with the Israeli governments' policies in different ways. Stendel's text includes some very general demographic information on birthrate, education, and ethno-religious subcategories. Haidar focuses mainly on the interrelation between Israeli governments and the Palestinian minority, and official attitudes to the Arab community's sociopolitical and economic conditions. He emphasizes social and educational segregation in the State of Israel, and the discriminatory policies adopted by Israeli governments toward their Palestinian citizens. Al-Haj focuses on the educational system and social change within this community, providing demographic data and survey results to support his claims of injustice and discrimination.

All three authors fail to emphasize the interrelation between political context and family structure. Scholars concerned with the Arab minority in Israel rarely work on or identify the connection between family life (including the socio-educational aspects) and political context. More specifically, there is an issue that for too long has gone unaddressed: How does the status of the Palestinians as a minority influence the social and family values among Arabs in Israel? The impression created by many scholars is that the Palestinian minority is only a collective response-mechanism to actions undertaken by the State of Israel. All of the books under review here convey the impression that this population lacks initiative, dynamics, and diversity. The problem is most acute in Stendel's and Al-Haj's writing (Al-Haj briefly discusses this issue on p. 31) and less in Haidar's, which provides an analysis of the responses of the Arab minority to government policy.

These books differ in the depth of their coverage. Al-Haj examines the education system across many years, from the Ottoman period to the Israeli state of today. Stendel's book is an introductory review that attempts to cover as many issues as possible that are of concern to the Arab minority. Haidar's two books are targeted more toward the division of labor and the place of Arabs in Israel and Israel's economy, and the conditions of Arabs in general after the Oslo Accords. While Stendel's book and Haidar's *Palestinians in Israel and the Oslo Agreement* are geared to a wider audience, Al-Haj's book and Haidar's *On the Margins* target educators and policymakers. They offer concrete examples of inequalities in the government's policies—in allocation of resources for Arab schools, in distribution of land, in employment opportunities, and so forth—affecting the social and educational conditions of the Arab minority.

The complexity and politicization of the subject under discussion are revealed in the different terminology used in these books. Stendel chooses to define and identify this minority as the "Arab minority," "Arab minorities," or "Arab Israelis." Furthermore, he insists on relating to the Beduin as an entity separate from the Arabs or from the "rest of the minorities" (p. 58). Such an approach is conveyed, too, by other Israeli-Jewish scholars who have reflected on government policy toward Arabs by relating to them as religious groups (Muslims, Christians, and Druze) or as regional and cultural entities.[11] Also, by using "Yehuda" and "Shomron" (Judea and Samaria), Stendel consistently sticks to official government terminology when referring to the West Bank (pp. 11, 21, 73).

Al-Haj follows a different strategy in defining the Arab community by consistently addressing them as the "Arabs in Israel" or as "the Arab minority in Israel." He also refers to public figures as "Arabs" unless it is significant to convey the religion of the person. Furthermore, Al-Haj makes a distinction among the different Arab sectors only when he addresses the issue of separate curricula for Druze and Beduin and the allocation of time for religious studies. This terminology, when used by a Palestinian, suggests either that the author wishes to be cautious in downplaying differences among religions, or else that his target audience is the Israeli public. This approach is certainly not evident in Haidar's writings.

Both Haidar and Al-Haj emphasize the discriminatory policy of the Israeli government toward the Palestinian minority when they lay out the official policy and its actual implementation in the allocation of sufficient budgets, physical plants, and economic resources, to name a few areas. Al-Haj's thorough examination of the education system reveals the impact of the underlying Ministry of Education official policy on Arab schools. He compares the Jewish and Arab curricula in terms of their goals and purposes, and repeatedly emphasizes the government's efforts to weaken Arab-Palestinian identity by neutralizing the curriculum and emptying it of any national symbols. Al-Haj compares the Ministry of Education's general goals and curricula for the Arab and Jewish sectors, and also closely examines the specific goals for teaching history, Hebrew, and Arabic in both sectors. For example, the goals of strengthening Jewish national identity (one of which is "to implant a Jewish national consciousness, and strengthen the feeling of a common Jewish destiny") have no parallel among the goals for Arab schools (Al-Haj, p. 129). Both Al-Haj and Haidar reiterate that education is of prime importance in shaping the identity of Arab youth. Furthermore, they both identify an explicit and implicit Israeli policy to create a "disoriented and oppressed youth" (Haidar, *Palestinians in Israel and the Oslo Agreement*, p. 79; Al-Haj, p. 140).

Conclusion

In the early nineties the political, economic, and social conditions of the Arab-Palestinian citizens of Israel went through major changes—chief among which was the peace accord between the Palestinian Liberation Organization and the government of Israel. Some of these changes were driven in part by the Labor-Meretz government (1992–1996) which aimed to improve the conditions of the Arab minority in Israel. Nevertheless, these improvements did not significantly minimize the economic, educational, and social gaps that continue to exist until the present day between the Arab and Jewish sectors in Israel.[12] The lack of equal distribution of social and educational resources between these two groups has become more distressing after the Oslo Accords and the start of the "peace process," largely because the high hopes for change have clashed with the reality that the peace accord brought nothing essential to improve the living conditions of the community. Palestinians in Israel were excluded from any participation in the post-Oslo discussions by both the Palestinians and Israeli negotiators, leaving them to defend their interests by themselves. The clashes between Israeli police and Arab protesters in October 2000, in which thirteen Arabs were killed, are but one indication of that.

Even though education is highly valued among Palestinians, the community is still not sufficiently involved in the education system. Parents and the public in general are not involved or aware enough of the policies and practices that underlie their children's education.[13] Research on this topic has repeatedly suggested that the education system is used as a "control system" over the Palestinian community.[14] Still, it doesn't seem that the general public appreciates its own potential impact and role in the process of initiating and taking responsibility for their children's education. Nevertheless, there is more recent public awareness of the gaps in social and educational resources between the Arab and Jewish sectors. This is reflected in the increasing number of newspaper reports and conferences on the subject, but the impact has yet to be felt. The formation of committees to monitor the educational system of the Palestinian community in Israel is one of the collective methods that the community is using to improve their conditions.[15]

There is no single book or study devoted entirely to an examination of both the social and educational conditions of the Arab community in Israel. The books reviewed here relate only in part to these matters. Furthermore, none of the authors suggests a specific solution to solve the long-standing issues within the Palestinian minority. In general, lack of empirical data on social and familial conditions of the Arab minority is one of the major shortcomings of the field. Some of the reasons for this are related to internal and social factors in the Arab community. Within the Palestinian-Arab community there is an implicit resistance on the part of school officials, teachers and principals, parents, and the public in general when asked to respond to research agendas and questionnaires. Minorities, in general, are often suspicious of researchers because of concerns about their motives and their relations with the establishment.

Scholarly work on the subject of social and educational conditions of the Arab minority in Israel will always be influenced by the political ideologies and dynamics in the country. Changes of regime and major political upheavals (from the British Mandate to the Israeli state, the occupation of the West Bank and Gaza, the Lebanon War, the Oslo "peace process," the immigration of Soviet Jews, the Gulf War, etc.) have influenced the socio-educational situation among the Arabs in terms of goals, resources, physical plants, and the curriculum itself.

The question remains whether the impact of this set of political factors alone is blocking or determining the possibilities of social change. According to Al-Haj and Haidar, the government's control over the Palestinian minority is the sole factor responsible for delaying social and educational progress in this community. For both of them, Arab minority actions are always in response to discriminatory government policies. Only recently have there been some pioneering attempts to organize various interest groups of Arabs on a national-ethnic level regardless of Israeli government policies.[16]

The risk of constantly drawing the connection between the government's practices and the general conditions of the Arab minority is that Palestinian scholars lose the ability to examine themselves and, as a result, neglect the importance of addressing internal factors contributing to gaps and underdevelopment of their social and educational conditions. Some areas for further research are (1) the family structure and how it is being influenced by social, educational, and economic factors; (2) the role of local leadership in determining the social and educational conditions of the Arabs in Israel; and (3) the responsibilities of teachers, school principals, parents, and local authorities for the educational situation.

Notes

1. In this review I will use the terms "Palestinians in Israel" or "Palestinian Israelis" to denote the Palestinian-Arab minority in Israel.

2. An example of the new focus in these studies is the examination of self-help groups among the two populations. See Ari Ben and Adital Tirosh, "Understanding of and Attitudes towards Self-help: Views from Palestinian and Israeli Members of Self-help Groups," *Journal of Social Service Research* 24:1–20 (1998): 131–48. See also Ben, Tirosh, and Azaiza Faisal, "Commitment among Arab Adolescents in Israel," *Journal of Social Psychology* 138:5 (1998): 655–60.

3. See Asaad Ghanem and Nadim Rouhana, "The Crisis of Minorities in Ethnic States: The Case of Palestinian Citizens in Israel," *International Journal of Middle East Studies* 30 (1998): 321–46.

4. Majid Al-Haj, *Education and Social Change among the Arabs in Israel* (Tel Aviv: International Center for Peace in the Middle East, 1991) (in Hebrew).

5. Ian Lustick, Majid Al-Haj, Noah Lewin-Epstein, and Moshe Semyonov are among the scholars who have written on this issue.

6. *Fasl al-Makal* (an Arabic weekly newspaper), 24–30 December 1999, quoting a report of the National Insurance Company.

7. See Joseph Ginat, *Women in Muslim Rural Society* (New Brunswick, NJ: Transaction Books, 1982).

8. See Nadim Rouhana, *Palestinian Citizens in an Ethnic Jewish State: Identities in Conflict* (New Haven: Yale University Press, 1997).

9. Overall, the Arab population lost 960,940 dunams while retaining 4,809,206 dunams. Haidar, *On the Margins,* 44.

10. A review of earlier books on the subject of Arabs in Israel revealed some more challenging work written by Jewish Israeli writers and others. See Ian Lustick, *Arabs in the Jewish State: Israel's Control of a National Minority* (Austin: University of Texas Press, 1980); Noah Lewin-Epstein and Moshe Semyonov, *The Arab Minority in Israel's Economy*, Social Inequality Series (Boulder, CO: Westview Press, 1993).

11. See Shmuel Toledano, "Report of the Committee for the Investigation of Delinquency in The Arab Sector" (Jerusalem, 1984, mimeographed) (in Hebrew), 197.

12. Based on a 1996 study conducted by Beit Berl, the Institute for the Study of Arab Society in Israel, Haidar argues that during the rule of the

Labor-Meretz coalition economic conditions of the Arabs actually deteriorated, with more Arab families joining the ranks of the poor (192).

13. In my study of Palestinians in Nazareth, 99 percent of mothers and fathers in the sample chose “school skills” as the most important group of skills for their children. See I. Nasser, *Parents' Ideas about Child Development among Palestinians in Israel* (University of Maryland, Dissertation Abstracts, 1997).

14. I. Lustick, S. Mari, and M. Al-Haj came to the same conclusions many years ago.

15. *Fasl al-Makal* published several reports on the subject in November and December 1999.

16. See Rouhana, *Palestinian Citizens in an Ethnic Jewish State,* for further information on such organizations.

6. Research on Welfare and Well-being in Israel: A Palestinian Perspective

Khawla Abu Baker,
Emek Yezreel College

This review essay focuses on the issues of social welfare and well-being for the Arab minority in Israel, a topic that has attracted minimal research during the first fifty years of Israeli statehood, despite its pressing importance. The books under review here are unique for their attention to the structural deficiencies and inequities that work to the detriment of Israel's Arab citizens, and for their authorship by Arab scholars. Based on their findings of institutional discrimination against Arabs in Israel and the wide gap between Arab and Jewish Israelis in the areas of education, social welfare, and psychological services, this essay argues that no positive change can be expected without national affirmative-action laws favoring the industrialization of Arab towns and a vigorous enforcement of antidiscrimination laws already on the books.

Al-Haj, Majid, *Education among the Arabs in Israel: Control and Social Change*, Jerusalem: Magnes Press/Floersheimer Institute for Policy Studies, 1996 (In Hebrew: *Hinukh be-Kerev ha-Aravim be-Yisra'el: Shlita ve-Shinuy Hevrati*).

Amara, Muhammad, and Sufian Kabaha, *Divided Identity: A Study of Political Division and Social Reflections in a Split Village*, Givat Haviva: Jewish-Arab Center for Peace, 1996. (In Hebrew: *Zehut Hatsuya: Haluka Politit ve-Hishtakfuyot Hevratiot Be-Kfar Hatsuy*).

Atrash, A'as, *Days Go By: Unemployment among Arabs in Israel*, Beit Berl: Institute for Israeli Arab Studies: 1995 (In Hebrew: *Yom ve-Od Yom: Avtala Aravit be-Yisra'el*).

Dwairy, Marwan, *Cross-Cultural Counseling: The Arab-Palestinian Case,* New York: Haworth Press, 1998.

With the establishment of the State of Israel in 1948, one of many new considerations for Palestinian Arabs was the social welfare and general well-being of those who remained in Israel and became citizens. The four books reviewed here, which focus on social and educational services in the Arab sector, were all written by Palestinian residents of Israel. They raise a number of important questions:

1. When the State of Israel was established, what plans did the government have for shaping the political, national, religious, cultural, and economic lives of its Arab citizens?
2. Bearing in mind that Israel was established as a welfare state, what were the negative implications of living under military administration (1948–1965) for the social, psychological, and educational welfare of Israel's Arab citizens?
3. If Israel is indeed a welfare state for all of its citizens, who determines welfare policies for the Arab population, and on what basis?
4. Finally, and most critically, how has welfare become a means of social and psychological control and oppression over the Arabs in Israel?

Very few books have been devoted to studying welfare issues concerning the Palestinians living in Israel. Indeed, during the first fifty years of Israel's existence, there were no more than fifteen, and only a few written by Palestinians. Early research studies written by Palestinian citizens of Israel centered mainly on politics and the social sciences.[1] The first research study on education among the Arabs living in Israel, published in the mid-1970s, exposed for the first time numerous facts about the poor educational situation of Israel's Arab population. In addition, its results pointed out the state's salient educational bias toward treating the Arabs as a cultural rather than as a national minority, thus cutting them off from their Palestinian and Arab history, nationality, and heritage.[2]

Books published in the 1990s adopt a similar line, wherein the main efforts of the investigators are focused on presenting data. Though most of the conditions tabulated stem from the political situation of the Arab population in Israel and result directly from political decisions, the investigators have not declared their political positions. Even though the state is directly and exclusively responsible for the lack of social welfare services in the Arab sector, not one educational or social welfare study specifically makes this claim. In other words, these researchers are writing books with political messages, but without taking a clear-cut political stand.

Reflecting a shared Palestinian perspective, the four books reviewed here demonstrate many commonalities, but the one most prominent characteristic is that, while their arguments are shaped by political factors, the authors' political convictions are only implied, not openly stated. All of these books indicate that Israel has undertaken a consistent and deliberate policy that perpetuates the lack of social welfare for the Arabs in Israel, a condition that originates from the establishment of the state. Despite Israel's self-declaration as a social-welfare state, over the years its Arab population has not benefited as has the Jewish population. Recently, as the result of political agitation and legal action by its Palestinian citizens, the Israeli Supreme Court has forced some government ministries and programs to adopt more egalitarian policies. Nevertheless, the books under discussion reveal a variety of policies that preserve discrimination and perpetuate the inferior status of the Arabs in Israel.

For the purposes of this analysis, the concept of "welfare" refers to the social services, mental health treatments, and educational opportunities available to Israel's Arab citizens. Each of the books constitutes a small piece of the very large puzzle that affects the well-being of the Palestinians living in Israel. A'as Atrash discusses unemployment; Majid Al-Haj focuses on education; Muhammad Amara and Sufian Kabaha deal with both of these issues as well as leisure time, family structure, and identity; and Marwan Dwairy considers mental health and psychological services. Despite the importance of the welfare issue, studies have yet to touch on other important aspects such as housing, addiction, crime, prostitution, and mental health in Arab families, particularly Arab refugee families, and violence in Arab villages. One of the problems facing researchers in this field is that Israeli government ministries either do not keep accurate records of current statistics regarding the Arab population in Israel, or consider such data classified and do not make it available to researchers.[3]

These books can be read as case studies that together present a broad insider's picture of the overall social welfare and educational situation in Israel's Arab sector. Atrash discusses the city of Shfaram, the second largest Arab city in Israel, inhabited by three religious groups (Muslims, Christians, and Druze) in order to illustrate the significance of Arab unemployment. Amara and Kabaha focus on the village of Barta'a as an instructive example of sociopolitical and educational changes resulting from macropolitical decisions. Al-Haj, in dealing with education, illustrates the well-known link between education and the advancement of the social conditions of minorities—in this case, the Palestinian minority in Israel. Dwairy focuses on the mental health of Israel's Palestinian population to point out the significance of cultural sensitivity during psychological treatment. Following a summary of the main points of each book that will emphasize the political context of welfare with respect to the Arab sector in Israel, this essay will consider the correlations among the central themes of all of these books.

Unemployment and Poverty among Arabs in Israel

In *Days Go By: Unemployment among Arabs in Israel,* Atrash describes his method of "comparative research," in which he compares the Jewish and Arab populations in Israel in order to identify the causes of unemployment within the latter. This section begins with a general discussion of unemployment among the Arabs and presents the major trends specific to that population (p. 8). Atrash examines the effectiveness of government policies for granting unemployment compensation to Arabs versus increased wage-earning opportunities available through projects launched to expand employment in the Arab sector. He concludes that, whereas most

Jewish employees earn more than the minimum wage and are motivated to find new work when they become unemployed, Arabs, who are more likely to earn only the minimum wage, have no incentive to seek new jobs when they can receive the same wage through unemployment payments. These findings indicate that the differences in social, familial, economic, and political structures between the Arab and Jewish sectors require that the Ministry of Labor and Social Affairs differentiate between the two sectors in its employment and unemployment policies.

Atrash does not analyze his data in terms of the historical, sociological, and political status of the Arabs living in Israel; his starting point is rather to analyze unemployment in light of various economic theories, such as classical economics versus Keynesian economics (p. 84). But the book is riddled with facts that beg thorny political questions that the author neither explicitly verbalizes nor answers. For example, what are the consequences of the striking unemployment figures on the welfare of the entire Arab sector? Atrash reveals a significant average wage gap between Jews and Arabs, but does not address questions such as, Why is the average salary of Arab males so close to the amount the state pays for unemployment compensation? (p. 27) Or, why has the percentage of Arab males in the work force in Israel always been lower than that of Jewish males? Why is the percentage of Arab women in the workforce lower by dozens of percentage-points than that of all other Arab and Jewish population groups? (p. 12, table A-1) Why hasn't the unemployment rate in the Arab sector declined even though the level of education has increased? (p. 37, table A-6). If the highest rate of Arab unemployment is among the illiterate and uneducated (p. 42, table A-8), why haven't employment bureaus offered adult-education courses to Arabs in addition to professional training?

Atrash's study demonstrates how the severity of unemployment in the Arab sector in Israel leads to a deterioration of individual well-being. Without a job and a permanent and secure income, the effort to meet existential needs becomes an economic and emotional burden for the individual. When unemployment strikes an entire community, it causes an acute social problem. Chronic unemployment is often accompanied by a host of social ills, among them family violence, low self-esteem, apathy, hopelessness, drug and alcohol abuse, and widespread anger and despair. Since unemployment is usually a long-term problem, its deleterious effects on the economic and emotional welfare of the unemployed and their families usually require systemic treatment. In the introduction, Atrash hints that "since unemployment has particularly harmed one of the two ethnic groups in our society, it is clear that emphasis should be placed on treating this problem within that sector. In this context, it would not be redundant to point out the negative political significance of unemployment differences among different sectors" (p. 7). In other words, the state must stop treating unemployment in the Arab sector as equivalent to unemployment in the Jewish sector, and must relate to it as a political, and not purely as an economic, issue.

Even though the Arab and Jewish populations live in the same country, fluctuations in the economy affect these two groups differently. Atrash proposes several reasons for this, among them the fact that close to 59% of the Arab population is over the age of fifteen, as compared to 71% of the Jewish population. That is, the potential Jewish workforce is larger than the Arab workforce. Also, Arab families have more children than Jewish families, which constitutes a larger drain on their resources. Additionally, Arab towns and villages cannot meet employment needs. Because of a shortage of industrial development, almost 50% of employment opportunities for Arabs are outside their residential area.

To demonstrate the severity of the problem, Atrash carried out a more comprehensive survey of the residents of the city of Shfaram, in which he examined the employment structure and its effect on unemployment and the degree of mobility of the city's workforce. The results of the Shfaram survey confirmed his conclusions regarding unemployment in the Arab sector at large. Most Arabs are "blue-collar workers" (professional laborers and construction workers) with 4–11 years of schooling; unemployment hits first and foremost older males (over the age of 45); and since most Arab families have a single breadwinner only, an unemployed father means disaster for the entire family. Shfaram, however, is something of an exception to these rules. A city with many educational institutions, employment opportunities for educated Arabs did increase in response to a modicum of private Arab investment within the community. But only Shfaram, Nazareth, and Um el-Fahm have local investors with enough capital to build institutions and industries capable of absorbing an educated Arab workforce. Had the state similarly invested in Arab towns, the unemployment rate would be much less severe than at present.

Atrash proposes the following solutions to the unemployment problems:

1. increased investment in employment opportunities in Arab towns and villages to not only reduce the rate of unemployment among males, but to also encourage Arab women to enter the workforce;
2. investment in educational and professional training in the Arab sector;
3. reorganization of unemployment services in the Arab sector;
4. encouragement of traditional occupations that are currently dying out, such as agriculture, by ceasing discriminatory policies.

Atrash believes that the adoption of these solutions can narrow the employment and welfare gap between Israel's Jewish and Arab population groups.

Change and Control: The Two-edged Sword of Education

Al-Haj's *Education Among the Arabs in Israel: Control and Social Change*[4] relies on two main theoretical approaches: a positivist approach, which is based on the functionalist school of thought, and a conflict approach, which sees education as an agent for maintaining the power of the ruling group and for legitimizing the authority of those who dominate society. The first treats education as a sociohistorical agent which, on the one hand, shapes values and behavior, leads to social change, and trains elite groups and political leaders, and, on the other hand, preserves intellectual systems (pp. 4–5). For the second approach, school is an institution used by the government to control society and to maintain the existing power ratio, and change is possible only if the official system chooses change or if it comes under an unusual amount of pressure applied by minority groups demanding change (p. 10).

Al-Haj notes that both of these approaches disregard ethnicity and its interaction with nationality and education in countries that have adopted philosophies of multi-ethnicity and multiculturalism. He highlights the impact of British colonial requirements on setting educational goals, which even today influence the structure and contents of the Arab educational system in Israel. Throughout the book, the author attempts to answer this question, Does education serve to catalyze social change within the Arab community, or does it serve as a mechanism for social control by the Jewish majority over the Arab minority?

The book integrates qualitative and quantitative research methods. The author relies on three field studies that investigated the physical conditions in Arab schools, educational trends within the Arab population, and the employment status of Arab graduates of Haifa University. The qualitative method consisted of analyzing the contents of documents from the Israel State Archives; the archives of Arab local councils; Ministry of Education reports; the minutes of the Follow-Up Committee on Arab Education in Israel; and relevant articles in the Israeli press (in Hebrew, Arabic, and English). In addition, Al-Haj interviewed people active on all levels in the field of education. The author's objective is to investigate the "function and nature of formal education among the Arab-Palestinian minority in Israel" (p. 11).

Al-Haj briefly summarizes the macrosociological conditions in which the Arab population developed from the late Ottoman period through 1948, emphasizing the changes in social, familial, and economic structure wrought by the creation of the State of Israel. Overall, the status of Palestinian Arabs within Israel immediately became marginal. He then discusses how this macrosociological background constitutes the basis for explaining the development of the educational system during the Ottoman period and the British Mandate. Under the Ottomans, education attracted little interest within the Arab population, especially for girls, despite the fact that schooling was free. The Arab elite's interest in education focused on a struggle to change the system from a Turkish one to an Arab system, with Arabic as its official language. During the Mandate, the British considered education a way to maintain the existing status quo and prevent an Arab national awakening. Thus, educational programs stressed universal values and avoided political content and national ties. The adoption of different educational curricula for urban and rural populations widened the existing social, class, and economic gaps within the Arab community. British officials believed that this trend was necessary in order to "maintain a balanced employment structure" (p. 40).

Like Atrash, Al-Haj also compares the Jewish and Arab populations. This is clearly an effective method for researchers to utilize in order to underline the historical, institutional, and resource gaps between the two. For instance, whereas the Israeli objective of education for Palestinian society was to prevent the development of nationalist sentiment, in the Jewish sector the goal was to instill Zionist ideals as part of building the nation, in spite of the variety of trends in Hebrew education during this period (pp. 42–46). In Israel, both the Arab and Jewish educational systems fell under the auspices of the same Compulsory Education Law (1949). Among its many other stipulations, the law dictates that local government units must erect, maintain, and furnish school buildings. The lack of Arab local government units led to an initial gap between Jewish and Arab education in Israel. That is, although Israeli law required that the Arabs must send their children to school, the law also prescribed that the Arabs set up and maintain their own educational institutions, even though the Israeli government knew full well that at the time most Arabs lived in rural and unincorporated areas. Many other laws have similarly discriminated against Arab education.

Al-Haj demonstrates that Jewish control of education serves as a means of social control over the Arab population. When the Arab educational system was set up, a Jew was appointed as its head; Jews also made up the entire professional staff, with the exception of one inspector. Jews dominated the committees that formulated educational programs and goals for Arabs. Al-Haj writes that at one time the Ministry of Education even tried to convince Arab citizens that setting up high schools was not worthwhile (p. 65).[5] The ministry consistently avoided developing professional and technological education in the Arab sector, thereby maintaining the Arabs as an unskilled labor force. The Ministry ruled over its Arab teachers with an iron hand, threatening to dismiss anyone who was involved in political activity or who refused to officially identify with the declared policies of the State of Israel. Not surprisingly, it banned educational materials with Palestinian or Arab nationalist content (p. 101).[6] Al-Haj argues that Israel purposely instituted educational programs designed to create submissive Arabs who would lose their Palestinian identity and accept the superiority of the Jews. He quotes Jonathan Peres et al., who concluded that

> policy makers [in the Ministry of Education] sought a compromise for contradictory trends: . . . Equality vs. Jewish superiority, development of general values vs. development of national values, granting autonomy to Arab education vs. aspiring for full integration into the Jewish educational system. . . . Instead, Arab national identity was blurred, and

> Arabs were educated to inferiority and mediocrity within the Jewish majority. (p. 103)

While Al-Haj makes no recommendations or suggestions for changing the gloomy situation in Arab education, his study can be considered an "operative research study." Policymakers, educators, and politicians in the field can make excellent use of the comprehensive statistics from the Ottoman and Mandate periods, while the comparison with the Jewish sector can spur the Arab sector to demand improvements in the educational situation in every town and village.

Splitting Up Arab Families: National and Psycho-Social Consequences

The village of Kfar Barta'a, the focus of the study by Amara and Kabaha, *Divided Identity: A Study of Political Division and Social Reflections in a Split Village,* provides an instructive and rare example of how arbitrary political decisions made on the macrolevel can affect every aspect of the everyday lives of individuals, families, and clans. Even though its arbitrary division puts the village in a rather unique situation shared by only a few others in the "Triangle" region (the concentration of Arab villages in the center of Israel), Barta'a's situation presents a particularly salient illustration of how the lack of governmental investment in basic services directly affects welfare in the entire Arab sector.

The 1949 Rhodes Armistice Agreement between Jordan and Israel allowed the international frontier to run right through Kfar Barta'a, dividing the village between the two countries until 1967. Western Barta'a remained under Israeli jurisdiction, and Eastern Barta'a was transferred to Jordanian jurisdiction, although the two villages continued to draw water from the same well. Oddly enough, no border fence was ever erected; instead, the wadi that ran through the center of the village became the international border, and Jordanian and Israeli military patrols prevented residents from crossing from one side of the village to the other. Clearly, the wishes of the Kabaha clan, which comprised the village's inhabitants, east and west, were not a factor for the decision makers.[7]

The political agreement dividing the clan changed its members' lives enormously. The authors' objective in studying the Barta'a case is "to examine the social repercussions of the political changes" caused by the division (p. 11). Prior to 1948, the Kabaha clan eked out a meager living from three sources: agriculture, animal husbandry, and forestry. After 1948, the economic situation of those who remained in Israel seriously deteriorated as a result of Israeli policies toward the Arab minority, particularly martial law that limited mobility and work, along with the confiscation of thousands of dunams of Barta'a's land and the lack of even a paved road connecting Western Barta'a to the neighboring Jewish settlements.

For Amara and Kabaha, the case of Western Barta'a constitutes an example of the interactive relationship between the policies of the ruling Israeli government and the welfare of the Arab population. The most salient connections between national policy and Arab social, economic, educational, and psychological welfare can be summarized under the following headings, which can be but briefly treated here.

Discrimination

During the period of Israeli military administration, the state regarded the Arab minority as a hostile fifth column and placed restrictions on Arab mobility within Israel. For Barta'a this meant that its inhabitants' freedom of movement was limited beyond the village's boundaries. Thus, levels of employment, income, education, and basic infrastructure development in the village were extremely low. When the state decided to integrate Arabs from the region with a special professional training program for construction, the residents of the village slowly began integrating into the life of the nation (p. 43). The 1956 war brought resignation to the fact of Israel's existence; at the same time, the state eased its requirements for work permits and the village became more proletarian and less agricultural. After the 1965 abolition of martial law and the 1967 war, most of the residents of the region became construction workers, largely abandoning agriculture.

The State's Failure to Provide Basic Services

Even today Western Barta'a has no official local government. It was not until 1970 that the government paved the village's main road; in 1985, the internal roads were paved, but at the residents' expense. The village was connected to the Israeli telephone system only in 1979, and to the national electricity grid in 1981. The villagers themselves set up a private water system unconnected to the national water system. Private associations developed preschool education; the village school is maintained by a local committee called the "Education Authority," which hires and pays the salaries of school employees other than teachers, who are employed by the Ministry of Education.

The authors compared the socialization of schoolchildren from Eastern Barta'a (the Jordanian educational system) with that of those from Western Barta'a (the Israeli educational system), arguing that the behavior of the children reflects the civic socialization of each population group. For instance, pupils in Eastern Barta'a participated in the 1987 Intifada, losing numerous teaching days but demonstrating a high maintenance of pan-Arab values and a Palestinian identity. Their peers in Western Barta'a, however, were kept out of the streets by their parents, who insisted on their maintaining regular school and extracurricular activities, despite the unrest raging across the wadi. One can conclude that the Jordanian educational system thus constituted an agent for Palestinian social preservation, while the Israeli educational system worked to mute the community's indigenous identity and served instead as an agent to instill and preserve the civic values of the state (p. 81).

Secure Family Relations within a Clan as a Factor in Psycho-social Welfare

The case study of Barta'a also shows how the dynamics of clan relations are affected by macropolitical decisions. In 1949 the reigning powers' decision to split the village severed clan relations between east and west; in 1967 Israel's occupation of the West Bank led to clan reunification. Despite the elimination of the physical border, a psychopolitical border had developed between the citizens of the two halves of what had once been one village and one clan. The renewed contact only served to underline the differences and the degree to which each group had become integrated into the culture and institutions of the ruling country (p. 57).

In their discussion of the 1987–1993 Intifada the authors provide an outstanding example of the clear difference between the existential needs of Barta'a's residents of the occupied territories and those of Barta'a's citizens of the State of Israel. At the beginning of the Intifada, with the army keeping a close watch on activists in Eastern Barta'a and warnings from the police, the residents of

Western Barta'a chose to stay within the boundaries of Israel, and daily contact between the clan members declined. Interestingly, Eastern Barta'a's Intifada leaders accommodated their Western Barta'a' relatives' desire to avoid run-ins with Israeli law, and asked for their moral, economic, and media support only. Even while distinguishing between them, the Intifada also brought Barta'a's western and eastern clan members closer together. Clan leadership passed from the elders to the young leaders of the Intifada; as this new generation gained power, strength, and authority within their families, relatives from Western Barta'a hastened to renew their ties with family members whose sons were leading the uprising in the eastern side of the village. In addition, the authors were amazed at how the citizens themselves had revived the significance of the international border running through the wadi, which, more than anything else, came to symbolize the presence of the state within the collective consciousness of the residents of Western Barta'a.[8]

The Intifada both strengthened family relationships within the divided village and emphasized the civic differences between the residents of the two halves. Amara and Kabaha examine the dynamics of developing a collective social identity, as opposed to a national civic identity, based on the relationship with the state over time. They conclude that, for the residents of Western Barta'a, "the Islamic identity remained extremely significant, followed, in descending order, by Arab and Palestinian identity, identity with the Kabaha clan, and, in last place, identification with Israel and with the village" (p. 143). Most of those claim that they did not consider themselves Israelis, but rather citizens living in the State of Israel, and they differentiated between their civic identity, as holders of Israeli identity cards, and their national identity, as Arabs, not Israelis. The villagers perceived Israel as the country of the Jews, and believed that they were being treated as inferior to the Jewish population. In their discussions with researchers, villagers expressed deep psychological grudges against Israel, claiming that they were not interested in defining themselves as "Israelis" because they regarded the state as a military power that had conquered Arab lands in the 1948 and 1967 wars.[9] The book mentions this only in passing. In general, very few such assertions appear in the research literature because of the thin line between respondents' freedom of expression and what the authorities might define as denial of the right of the country to exist or attempted provocation and rebellion *(hasata ve-hamrada).*

The Relationship between the Level of Public Services and Identity

An examination of the development of identity in the two halves of the village of Barta'a underlines the depth of the relationship between institutional intervention and identity. As government institutions became more prevalent in the village, traditional alternatives diminished. For example, because the lives of villagers in Western Barta'a are bound by the laws of Israel, they did not preserve or develop their tribal laws. In comparison, Jordan allowed tribes and large clans to chose between the laws of the state and those of the tribe. Thus, Eastern Barta'a residents preserved and developed their clan identity.

Because of a serious shortage of public institutions and welfare services in Western Barta'a, the extended family became the critical source for childcare, financial assistance, psychological support, care for the elderly and disabled, and so on. Not surprisingly, the authors report that "most of those surveyed see the extended family as a shared base and as the source of moral and material support" (p. 36) It is clear that as Israel shirks its obligation to provide welfare services to its Arab citizens, the role of the extended Arab family intensifies, and its influence on the life of the individual continues to be central. As a result, the identification of the individual with his extended family is of utmost importance.

In Search of National and Cultural Sensitivity

Marwan Dwairy, of Haifa University's School of Education, is an educational, developmental, and clinical psychologist and an integral figure overseeing the Ministry of Education's program for gifted Arab pupils. In *Cross-Cultural Counseling: The Arab-Palestinian Case,* Dwairy argues that cultural insensitivity constitutes another means of state control over the Arab population. His methodology is inductive, using his clinical experience to reexamine Western psychological theories and axioms. He supports his ideas with the results of several studies conducted within Palestinian Arab society in Israel. Like the authors of the other three books, Dwairy uses the conjoint approach of relating to Palestinian mental health as a case study for cross-cultural counseling, and to his clinical cases as more specific case-study examples.

Dwairy begins by presenting the history of the Palestinians and their relationship with Arab nationality and Islam as important aspects for understanding their cultural and psychosocial well-being. He then deals with the influence of Arab family structure on developing the "self" and "personality" among Arabs. Dwairy's argument relies upon results of research conducted on large numbers of Palestinian-Arab families living in the Nazareth region.

Dwairy exposes the disadvantages suffered by Arab clients when they are diagnosed and treated according to the norms of Western psychology. He claims that modern psychology has developed with an emphasis on understanding the qualities of the individual, who emerges as an independent entity in individualistic societies. Individuation, according to Western psychology, is the main process that takes place during the course of a human being's development. After adolescence, a person is expected to have accomplished the process of individuation and to begin conducting his or her life through an independent personality construct. Behavioral as well as psychological disorders are explained, according to Western psychology, by intrapsychic constructs or processes driven by elements such as ego, self, conflicts, and defense mechanisms. Psychological problems are defined as intrapsychic disorders. Psychotherapy intervenes to restore the "normal" intrapsychic order. The ultimate objective of all Western psychotherapy is to allow the patient to be aware of his or her unconscious and to achieve self-fulfillment.

Dwairy argues that this form of psychology is able to offer only a partial explanation for the behavior of Arabs and for other peoples living in close-knit traditional communities, and may cause more harm than good in treatment. People who live in an authoritarian and collective social structure are directed by an external authority that defines for the individual "shoulds" and taboos. Therefore, Dwairy argues, cultural norms and other external oppressions will explain behavior in Arab society better than intrapsychic constructs and processes. In his view, personality development and structure in authoritarian and collective societies differ substantially from the assumptions embodied in Western personality theories. He describes Arab personality development, structure, and dynamics, which are collective rather than individuated and have two main layers of personality: social and private. He summarizes a large body of cross-cultural research into the substantial differences in the prevalence of, and diagnosis of, psychological disorders across ethnicities.[10] He argues that many normal behaviors among Arabs may be pathologized and misdiagnosed by therapists relying exclusively on Western psychotherapy.

Psychotherapy that targets an intrapsychic order, according to Dwairy, actually misses the main source of conflict and anxiety which, in Arab societies, is interpersonal rather than intrapsychic. Dwairy claims that focusing on the intrapsychic with a traditional Arab client may bring forbidden drives and emotions to consciousness. Fulfilling these drives in a conservative society is likely to lead to individual-family conflicts that are unsolvable, and may cause an acceleration of oppression for the client. Therefore, culturally insensitive psychotherapy may transform a minor intrapsychic conflict into a major familial one, which may proceed to extended family conflicts and violence. Dwairy presents several cases that demonstrate this process and the open wounds left after supposedly "successful" psychoanalysis. Such therapies were not culturally sensitive to the structure of the Arab family and norms.

In his book, Dwairy proposes a new model of psychotherapy that is systemic, short-term, problem-focused, and based on outreach. Because mind and body, as well as individual and family, are inseparable in Arab society, he suggests a biopsychosocial approach to therapy that utilizes cultural values and metaphoric language. Central to his approach is the genuine readiness of the therapist to respect and empathize with the client's cultural background and to fit his or her tools to the client.

In the last two decades, many Western societies have become aware of cultural differences in mental health and have started to revise their approaches. Cross-cultural psychology is now the fourth dimension in psychology, after the psychoanalytic, behavioral, and humanistic dimensions. While cross-cultural counseling courses are obligatory in every recognized program for mental heath training in academic institutions in the United States, Israel's insistence on the Zionist vision of a cultural "melting pot" means that Israeli academic programs lack even elective cross-cultural counseling courses. Dwairy concludes that the psychological services available to Arabs in Israel, as provided by Israeli-trained therapists (Jewish or Arab), do not serve the best interests of the Arab individual or community. One can extend the same argument to Israeli Jews who also live in tightly knit conservative and authoritarian communal circumstances, such as the ultra-Orthodox or the traditional Ethiopian or Yemenite communities. It is indeed a great misfortune for people in pain to have their problems compounded by inappropriate treatment.

Welfare, Well-being, and the Mechanisms of Political Inferiority

While all four books reviewed here deal with matters in the fields of social, educational, and mental welfare, political elements are quite apparent, to differing degrees, in all of them. A careful reading of each book, including an emphasis on the data presented in the tables, leads to one unequivocal conclusion: a strong political bias dominates the educational and social services in the Arab sector in Israel. While none of the books argues against Israel's right to exist, they all challenge, implicitly or explicitly, the veracity of Israel's professed status as a democratic and egalitarian country.

All of the volumes reviewed also reveal the phenomenal complexity of the "identity" of Arabs living in Israel. The authors rightly perceive this identity as interactive and contextual. In certain situations, Arab citizens ask to be recognized as a national minority, while in other contexts they seek to be considered as a cultural or religious minority. One identity does not negate any other; rather they all complement one another.

At the time of Israel's establishment, the state regarded the Arab minority as a hostile national community and related to it accordingly. The provision of normal welfare services to that minority required special political decisions at the highest echelons of the Israeli government. Those decisions, made in the antagonistic atmosphere of that time, have continued to have a negative impact on the welfare and well-being of Arabs in Israel to the present day. The books under discussion here give innumerable examples of official government neglect, inaction, or malevolence which, over the years, have allowed (or even encouraged) severe social problems to fester within the Arab sector. For example, despite the fact that unemployment among the Arab population has constituted an acute social problem for decades, there has never been an official government recovery program for this sector. The official welfare services have never confronted the mental and familial problems that have developed as a result of chronic unemployment and have disregarded the psychological aspects of these economic problems, at the cost of great suffering to Arab individuals, their families, and the community.

Unemployment compensation payments have helped Jewish unemployed workers return to the workforce because these payments have been accompanied by the creation of proper conditions, such as the development of industrial areas close to residential districts, the provision of advanced technological education and professional training and the availability of Hebrew-language education, and a high basic wage. One of the most striking findings of Atrash's study is that in the Arab sector, in contrast, unemployment compensation payments perpetuate unemployment because none of the aforementioned additional conditions exist. This is an outstanding example of the ecological, symbiotic, and comprehensive relationship linking welfare issues and politics, education, and economics. In order to find a genuine solution to the Arab unemployment problem, the state must put together a comprehensive program that targets all of these fields.

Another example of the government's irresponsibility to its Arab citizens lies in the field of education. Looking at Al-Haj's research, we must ask why all documents and decisions regarding education for Arabs made at the time the country was established have been treated as "confidential" material all these years, and why it required legal action on the part of researchers to open the State Archives in order to examine these documents. Al-Haj stresses the fact that the educational system in Israel is first and foremost a *Jewish* system, and that the *Arab* educational system is a tool in the hands of the state that is in no way organically derived from Arab society. The title of Al-Haj's book summarizes the goal of this system, namely, "control and social change" in order to serve the needs of a country that controls a national minority constituting nearly 20 percent of its citizens. It is impossible to speak simply in terms of social welfare when the central axiom of the education system is based on dominance over an entire population group and total disregard for its national and cultural uniqueness. By itself the law for free compulsory education is a good thing; unfortunately, the educational system for Arabs has become an effective mechanism for long-term control to shape the identity and mental constitution of the Arab citizens of Israel.

Amara and Kabaha's book is illustrative of the rift within Palestinian society caused by the imposition of artificial political borders by the State of Israel on several levels: self, spiritual, familial, clan, and national. The research difficulties faced by the authors—the suspicions expressed by those interviewed and their lack of cooperation, particularly during the time of the first Intifada—indicate the Palestinian Arab citizens' fear and perception of the state as a hostile institution.

Lack of equal state services for Arabs in Israel preserves the collective, authoritarian social structure of Arab society because it retains the family as the main source for providing for the basic needs of individuals. Therefore, psychological problems caused by the oppressive social and political structure are highly prevalent among Arabs. On the other hand, lack of suitable mental health services prevents professionals from providing the most effective help for people who suffer from psychological disorders.

Palestinians in Israel have experienced a traumatic ordeal caused by political, military, and social upheaval, especially during the events of 1947-1949. Amara and Kabaha's case study of the divided village of Barta'a highlights the social, economic, psychological, and political dislocations that Palestinian citizens suffered after the establishment of Israel. While the new state made a social welfare policy for its Jewish citizens a major national goal, it had a different sociopolitical agenda for its Arab citizens. Land confiscation, martial law, internal migration, and poverty caused by the loss of property during the war required a state project for the psychological, social, economic, and educational rehabilitation for Arab citizens. Instead, as Al-Haj's research shows, the state used the education system and martial law to establish subservience among its Arab citizens. Jewish political leaders determined policy toward the Arab educational sector and controlled it by appointing Jewish policymakers who dictated its contents by controlling the curriculum. They also exerted control over the employees through the security forces, creating an education system that was a de facto arm of the security services in Israel. As a direct result, education for Arabs in Israel has long been a mechanism for control instead of a mechanism of social change.

The disadvantages of the Arab educational system in comparison to the Jewish sector have continued since their original establishment. Even though the Arab system is controlled by the same state legislation as the Jewish one, in the Arab sector many of these laws are routinely flouted, such as those pertaining to compulsory education, special education, and welfare services. In this system, up to 55 percent of Palestinian Arab students do not finish high school. Despite this, no major state project has ever been prepared to treat these unhealthy phenomena. According to Israeli law, psychological and educational counseling and social services are obligatory components of the educational system. Nevertheless, programs were never prepared to meet the needs of the Arab population in this regard, and no Arab mental-health workers were trained to work within the national and cultural needs of the Arab minority. Atrash's research points out the results of the Arab educational system: a high percentage of unemployment, a high percentage of untrained workers, and all the concomitant social problems.

In reviewing the prevailing conditions of the Arab community in Israel, one may conclude that educational programs and unemployment policy are designed so that Arabs in Israel will continue to re-create the culture of poverty, thus maintaining their status as a deprived, inferior national minority. Culturally insensitive psychological therapies and counseling programs compound the situation. The result is that most young Arab families in Israel are occupied with solving their everyday social, economic, and psychological problems, instead of becoming involved as active and equal partners in running the state. The documentation of this phenomenon by the authors reviewed here is an important early step in bringing the multifaceted problems of the Arabs citizens to light. The condition of the Arabs in Israel will never be truly resolved, however, as long as the state puts the political priorities of the Jewish population above the welfare and well-being requirements of its Arab population.

Notes

1. See especially Sabri Jiryis, *The Arabs in Israel* (New York: Monthly Review Press, 1976).

2. Sami Mari, *Arab Education in Israel* (Syracuse: Syracuse University Press, 1978).

3. For details on this issue, see Aziz Haidar, *Social Welfare for Israel's Arab Population* (Boulder, CO: Westview Press, 1990).

4. This book appeared earlier in English as *Education, Empowerment and Control: The Case of the Arabs in Israel* (Albany: State University of New York Press, 1995). (See the review essay by Ilham Nasser, in this volume, in chapter 5.)

5. Through the mid-1970s, many villages lacked secondary schools. This led to dropouts among poor students, whose families were not able to pay for travel expenses, and girls, who were forbidden to leave their villages without an escort. In villages with high schools the percentage of highly educated people, both men and women, is much greater.

6. The Israeli Security Services had to confirm the nomination of all new Arab teachers, and the Ministry of Education fired teachers who participated in political activities. For a more detailed picture, see Majid Al-Haj, 134–40.

7. This review focuses only on social change and on the social and educational welfare of the citizens of Western Barta'a, since the goal of this essay is limited to studying welfare conditions for Palestinians in Israel.

8. For more details on this important aspect of the research, see Amara and Kabaha, 107–13.

9. See ibid., chapters 7–9, dealing with the "identity question."

10. *Diagnostic and Statistical Manual of Mental Disorders,* 4th ed. (Washington DC: American Psychiatric Association, 1994).

Part 4

Whither Post-Zionism?

7. Does Post-Zionism Have a Future?

Deborah L. Wheeler,
University of Washington

This essay explores post-Zionism as a cultural, political, and ideological movement. The texts reviewed are examples of recent contributions to the growing literature on this phenomenon. Paying special attention to historiography, politics, the visual arts, and cinema, the author asks whether Zionism will continue to shape the collective memory of future generations of Israelis, or whether classical Zionism has been superseded by forms of post-Zionism.

Fuhrer, Ronald, *Israeli Painting: From Post-Impressionism to Post-Zionism,* New York: Overlook Press, 1998.

Hitchhikers (in Hebrew: *Trampistim,* with English subtitles). Produced by Vered Sapir. Directed by Asher Talman. Distributed by Ergo Video, 1998.

Morris, Benny, *Righteous Victims: A History of the Zionist-Arab Conflict, 1881–1999,* New York: Alfred A. Knopf, 1999.

Shlaim, Avi, *The Iron Wall: Israel and the Arab World since 1948,* New York: W.W. Norton & Co., 2000.

Silberstein, Laurence J., *The Postzionism Debates: Knowledge and Power in Israeli Culture,* New York: Routledge, 1999.

Sternhell, Zeev, *The Founding Myths of Israel: Nationalism, Socialism, and the Making of the Jewish State,* trans. from the French by David Maisel, Princeton: Princeton University Press, 1998.

Post-Zionism is a term coined by Israeli journalists to describe the deconstructive efforts of the "New Historians" that gained currency in the late 1980's.[1] Post-Zionism began as an attempt to revise (undermining, according to committed Zionists) the foundations of Israeli collective memory. It has grown into an all-encompassing cultural, political, and ideological movement. Post-Zionism has changed the face of Israeli society in significant ways—from the revision of public school curricula, to the transformation of Palestinian-Israeli relations. This essay reviews some textual examples of the entrenchment of the post-Zionist mentality. In order to clarify some of post-Zionism's complexities, the movement is considered in light of politics, scholarship, and art/culture.

I argue that the texts reviewed in this essay represent a few of the many challenges presented Zionism by the post-Zionist currents running through the Israeli intellectual and political scene in the 1990s. As Laurence J. Silberstein observes in *The Postzionism Debates: Knowledge and Power in Israeli Culture,* "[f]or a significant social and cultural transformation to occur, a change must first occur in the discourse through which events are framed and assigned meaning" (p. 208). Together these texts reveal aspects of the post-Zionist effort to clear space for new discourses, and thus new power relations in Israel. In light of this analysis we might pose the question, What role will Zionism past play in the shaping of future collective memory? This question took on more importance than ever with the outbreak of the September 2000 "al-Aqsa Intifada" that put on trial the spirit of compromise and dialogue that permeates the post-Zionist agenda.

Defining Post-Zionism

Post-Zionism has many meanings, not only because it is an "ism," but also because it is a politically loaded term. Post-Zionism encompasses "all those who have revised or criticized the work of the mainstream Zionist academic community in Israel," including "artists, novelists and others using a new cultural discourse."[2] In terms of life beyond academia, post-Zionism is symbolized by a new openness to global culture, including pop culture icons Madonna and the Big Mac, and the removal of old grudges and refusing to live in fear.[3] In general, post-Zionism is "an attempt to de-idealize Zionist history."[4] It also constitutes an attempt to "make Israeli society an open, liberal and secular society" (Sternhell, p. xii).

Part of the reason why post-Zionism is difficult to define in a uniform fashion is the diversity of participants in the movement. Post-Zionist narratives include those crafted by Jewish Israelis, Jewish Americans, and Palestinian citizens of Israel, among others. The post-Zionist movement includes a dominant contingent of Jewish Israeli academics, disillusioned with Zionist discourses. These include Baruch Kimmerling, professor of sociology at the Hebrew University of Jerusalem; Ilan Pappé, professor of history at Haifa University; Benny Morris, professor of history at Ben Gurion University, Beersheva; and Zeev Sternhell, professor of political science at the Hebrew University. Politically, Kimmerling and Pappé are associated with the far left, while Morris and Sternhell are more moderately left of center and maintain many of the traditional perspectives of Labor Zionism. Post-Zionist discourses are also enhanced by Jewish citizens of the Diaspora including Israeli expatriate Avi Shlaim, professor of history at Oxford, and Jewish American Laurence Silberstein, professor of Jewish studies at Lehigh University in Pennsylvania. Though he does not see himself as a post-Zionist, Prof. Joel Migdal of the University of Washington has also been labeled and denounced as such by some on the Israeli right because of his writings on the Palestinians.

While some argue that a prerequisite for being a post-Zionist is being Jewish, others disagree. Silberstein devotes an entire chapter to the Palestinian post-Zionist critique, focusing on the work of Anton Shammas and the late Emile Habiby. Habiby was a novelist (author of the popular modern fable, *The Secret Life of Saeed: The Pessoptimist*[5]); editor of *al-Ittihad* newspaper published in Haifa; former Member of the Knesset, and winner of the 1992 Israel Prize for Literature. Shammas is a Palestinian citizen of Israel, a novelist best known for his Hebrew-language novel, *Arabesques: A Novel,*[6] a journalist, a former employee of Israeli television, and currently professor of comparative literature at the University of Michigan. Silberstein argues, in agreement with Migdal and Kimmerling, that "no critique of [Z]ionism would be adequate . . . without allowing Palestinians to tell their own story" (p. 129). In this respect, Silberstein considers both Shammas and Habiby "extremely effective in revealing the colonialist effects of [Z]ionist practices and discourse" on their community; their voices "render a major contribution to the formation of postzionist discourse" (p. 129).

Those who use post-Zionism as a kind of slur are reacting to what they see as "attacks on Zionist objectives" (Sternhell, p. xii). In the face of such criticisms, those who have been labeled *post-Zionists,* like Sternhell, defend their intellectual projects stating that "[t]here can be no greater error than to associate scholars' questioning of accepted ideals about Jewish nationalism, Jewish socialism, or the place of universal values in the Jewish national movement with post-Zionism" (p. xii). And yet such questionings in their very articulation are considered by the right and the traditional Zionist elite as a de facto attempt at sanctifying "Jewish disempowerment."[7]

Some have observed that, in many intellectual circles, post-Zionism in the 1990s rapidly became a new form of Israeli political correctness.[8] Others have argued that post-Zionism remains a minority intellectual position that does not reflect Israeli public opinion as a whole (Silberstein, p. 166). In any case, post-Zionism generated a cultural and political climate in which, as Ronald Fuhrer observes, collective memories of the past were rapidly fading (p. 192). This collective forgetfulness was especially present among the younger generations who were instead, "armed with the critical tools and the new philosophy (French deconstructionism and ideas of the Frankfurt School) imported from its workshops in France and Germany" (p. 192). With these weapons, they "conducted" ethical inspections of Zionist language, imagery and media" (p. 192), thus unraveling a "uniformity in Israeli art" and a shared commitment to the Zionist project in culture, politics, and everyday life (p. 193).

Political Post-Zionism

Just as post-Zionism has many meanings, its political expression is also varied. The category can include former Education Minister Shulamit Aloni's decision to de-emphasize the place of Jewish religion in the public school curriculum, and, at the same time, any peace plan designed to take Israel back to its pre-1967 borders. Some post-Zionists are politically committed to the repeal of the Law of Return, or any other law that distinguishes between ethnic communities and categories of citizenship (Pappé). Others argue that Israel is a settler colonialist state and is in need of decolonization, similar to the dismantling of Apartheid in contemporary South Africa (Kimmerling and Gershon Shafir). Post-Zionists are not recognizable as a single political constituency, but instead form a fluid and dynamic community of individuals who are separately struggling to make Israel a more secular, democratic nation where the rule of law is applied to all citizens equally.

According to critics like Anita Shapira, professor of Zionism at Tel Aviv University and a staunch Israeli nationalist, post-Zionism is by nature politically, rather than historiographically motivated. She supports her position by observing that among post-Zionists, "the past is not discussed in and of itself to be explained on the basis of the data and evaluations of the contemporaries of that period, but rather in accordance with the considerations and political agenda of the present."[9] Another critic, Yoram Hazony, observes that "instead of creating a new balance in Israeli historiography, the new academics have waged what amounts to a scorched earth campaign against the past, joining author and artist in a wholesale effort to wreck the basic faith of the Israeli public in its own history."[10]

Zionism, Post-Zionism, and Scholarship

From its inception, the Zionist movement understood and capitalized upon the close relationship between discourse and a will to power. With such knowledge, Zionist narratives created a foundation for collective mobilization and provided a new mapping of Jewish identity as a form of contemporary nationalism. In the process Zionist organizers relied heavily on all kinds of discourse: songs and slogans, stamps and posters, newspaper articles and diplomacy, declarations and official endorsements, press releases, text books, art and scholarship.[11] If scholarship was an important element in the Zionist movement's consolidation of power, then we might expect counternarrative to play an important role in post-Zionist revision.

In terms of Zionism and scholarship, Shapira notes that many of the first historians who studied the foundation and early history of the state were employed in the history section of the Israel Defense Forces (IDF). This status gave them full access to a wide range of classified documents, but at the same time required them to practice self-censorship to protect the emerging collective memory of the state.[12] As Yael Zerubavel has observed, sometimes "deliberate suppression of memory" was required to sustain this collective memory, which was the cement for Israeli society and national identity.[13] Thus historiography becomes a decisive tool in the creation and suppression of Zionist memory in the service of the national cause. The pioneering ethos and the hero epic were often more important than what "really" happened. The rewriting of history, which is an important element in the post-Zionist movement, is an attempt in part to stir up these suppressed memories and to reformulate collective identity through counternarratives. It is to this scholarship that we now turn.

Silberstein's text provides a broad "mapping" of the intellectual history behind post-Zionism, and depicts the discourses that have struggled from the mid-1960s to deconstruct and reconstruct a sense of Israeli-ness, both within and beyond Zionism. Some of the intellectuals he discusses, like Amos Oz, Martin Buber, and Meron Benvenisti, provide critiques "from within" Zionist narratives, seldom challenging the moral right of Israel to exist as a Jewish State. These writers "insist on [Z]ionism's viability" and reject "the calls of critics outside [Z]ionism for the dismantling of the [Z]ionist apparatus" (p. 47). Instead this group of critics, which Silberstein describes as the precursors of post-Zionism, remains "within [Z]ionist discourse" while seeking to rid it of what they consider to be "its perversion," especially focusing upon the Palestinian problem that Zionism helped to create (p. 66). These pre-post-Zionist writers "insist that Zionism has the capacity to bring about the changes and reforms needed to end the conflict," whereas post-Zionist scholars "reject the [Z]ionist label and position themselves outside the spaces of [Z]ionist discourse" (p. 66). In Silberstein's view, post-Zionist writers like Tom Segev, Pappé, Shafir, Uri Ram, Shammas, Habiby, and contributors to the Hebrew-language journal *Teoria u-Vikoret (Theory and Criticism)* have produced "the most recent, and to date, most effective effort within Israel to problematize [Z]ionist discourse and the historical narratives it has produced" (p. 89). Three representative cases of historiographical "problematization" are examined in more detail in the next section: Sternhell's *Founding Myths of Israel: Nationalism, Socialism, and the Making of the Jewish State;* Morris's *Righteous Victims: A History of the Zionist-Arab Conflict, 1851–1999;* and Avi Shlaim's *Iron Wall: Israel and the Arab World Since 1948.* Each of these texts attempts to revise a different part of Zionist history. Two of the texts however, show some discursive signs of remaining "within" rather than "beyond" Zionist discourse. These texts were selected because they are the most recent contributions to the debates at this writing.

Sternhell's *Founding Myths of Israel,* unlike Silberstein's general intellectual history of the post-Zionist movement, is a carefully focused case study. It examines the relationship between Jewish nationalism and orthodox socialism in Israel, arguing that the movement was more nationalist than it was socialist. Instead, Sternhell suggests that "the lack of a social vision rooted in a comprehensive outlook and universal values" as one would expect from orthodox socialism "became fully apparent" as soon as the nation became a formal state, facing new demands of governance (p. 46).

> The pioneering ideology, with its central principles—the conquest of land, the reformation of the individual, and self-realization—was not an ideology of social change; it was not an ideology that could establish a secular, liberal state and put an end to the war with the Arabs. With the end of the War of Independence and the completion of the great waves of immigration, it became apparent that the labor movement was not equipped with a conceptual framework that permitted it to move beyond the national revolution it had led and presided over with such conspicuous success (p. 46).

According to Sternhell, had the Zionist movement been true to its socialist leanings, rather than to its Jewish nationalist agenda, then the state might have had a general social vision with which to run a just, secular, and democratic state. Instead, Zionism bred war with the Arabs, dangerous religious nationalism, and particularistic politics, all of which are dimming the light unto the nations.

As with most post-Zionist literature, Sternhell's suggested solution to the problem he describes is to create a secular, liberal state, to put an end to war with the Arabs, and to solve problems created during the pre-state period. Sternhell argues that the Israeli Declaration of Independence, for example, has no jurisprudential authority, and was mainly an article for export (p. 320). Thus if Israel wants to create a vision for the future, a real discursive foundation for viable statehood, then it must have a constitution that has the power to enforce its ideals of equality and human rights for all citizens.

In spite of his biting critique of Zionism and his strong revisionist vocabulary, Sternhell remains what I call a "soft-core post-Zionist," given his interpretations of the Holocaust. Sternhell remains within the fold when he states that "in 1933, Hitler began to vindicate Zionism" (p. 338).

For soft-core post-Zionists, when the security of Jews in the Diaspora was in jeopardy, that is, before 1948, Zionism was morally justified in creating a home for the Jews, even if it meant the creation of a Palestinian refugee problem as a result. The most common argument for this hierarchy of values is that Palestinians could easily live among their other Arab brethren, whereas a life in exile for the Jews meant the possibility of extinction. Hard-core post-Zionists, although they don't deny the perilous situation of Jews before 1948, view Zionism as settler colonialism that disenfranchised another community, and they refuse to view it as a moral solution to the Jewish problem. In their view, the Holocaust is used by Zionists as a political weapon "to legitimate unjust acts against the Palestinians" (Silberstein, p. 118). From the hard-core post-Zionist perspective, the Holocaust, although a tragedy, becomes in the Palestinian-Israeli context a tool for "silencing critical debate" about whether or not Israel was born in sin (p. 118). The Holocaust thus becomes an important dividing line among categories of Zionist and post-Zionist scholarship. If readers locate a history, like Sternhell's, which uses the Holocaust as an explanation for Zionism's morality in 1948, then they can use this perspective to graph the scholar's degree of commitment (or lack thereof) to post-Zionism.

When we look at how these scholars interpret the history of Israel after 1967, the line that divides hard- and soft-core post-Zionists blurs. Both sides of the divide, and even some dovish Zionists, claim that arguments regarding the need for more territory, the West Bank and Gaza, the Golan Heights, and/or Lebanon, to save the Jews from extinction were morally unjustified. What makes a post-Zionist, according to Sternhell, is not an abolition of a commitment to Israel's moral right to exist for the Jewish people, but rather, the concomitant position that the Palestinians have an equal right "to freedom and independence" (p. 339). But defining what freedom and independence mean further divides post-Zionists. Some more conservative members of the movement, like Sternhell and Morris, argue that the 1949 boundaries of Israel offer a model for future compromise with the Arabs. Thus Palestinians, regardless of their origins, will need to pursue their freedom and independence within the West Bank and Gaza. For hard-core post-Zionists this position is intellectually lacking because it is not going beyond Zionism. Instead, what is needed is decolonization, as in South Africa. Jews must renounce all moral claims supporting their rule over Arabs, and the end result will be some form of binational and/or nontribal, democratic relationship.

Both Silberstein's and Sternhell's works participate in the post-Zionism debates (although to varying degrees) by interrogating the relationships between knowledge and power, and by encouraging "the distinctive and specific effects" of "emergent new configurations of power-knowledge relations" (Silberstein, p. 6, quoting Hall). The works of Morris and Shlaim enhance and entrench this trend toward new configurations of power-knowledge relations. The authors do so, and to varying degrees, not in terms of recasting Zionist ideology and methodology, as in the case of Sternhell and Silberstein, but rather in terms of rethinking the implications of Zionism for Israel's multiple relationships with the Palestinians.

Morris's text begins with a tone-setting epitaph—a portion of a poem by W. H. Auden, "Those to whom evil is done / Do evil in return" (p. viii). But who are the righteous victims, we are left to wonder? From a Zionist perspective, like that of Shlomo Aronson,

> the Shoah destroys this claim [that Israel was born in sin] insofar as it establishes who were the real victims, how far the tragedy extended, who were the secondary victims, and to what extent they were sealed off from the suffering of others and their right to a piece of land to which their culture was linked for two thousand years. (quoted in Silberstein, p. 118)

The righteous victims were the persecuted, homeless Jews who needed to settle in the Land of Israel, to reach safe haven in a land that gave birth to their culture and formed the foundation of their communal imagination for twenty centuries. Victimized in Europe, Jews are righteous in their displacement of others who are secondary victims. From a post-Zionist perspective, it's the Palestinian Arabs who are the righteous victims because they lost their territorial identity in 1948 and often their possessions, when the Jews "came home." From Morris's perspective, both Jew and Arab are righteous victims, whose struggles for viability embed one another in dialectics of violence.

Attempting a balance reflected in the title of his book, Morris thus maintains a middle ground between the two victims, or at least attempts to do so. He claims that "Zionism was a colonizing and expansionist ideology and movement" (p. 652). "Besides the emergence of the State of Israel," Morris writes, "the other major result of the 1948 war was the destruction of Palestinian society and the birth of the refugee problem" (p. 252). Morris's strong revisionist vocabulary, his use of words like *settler-colonialism* and *expansionism,* along with his pointed descriptions of the Palestinian plight and his recognition of the Arabs' claim to part of the land (at least within the West Bank and Gaza), all indicate his affiliation with post-Zionist space-clearing enterprises.

On the other hand, much of Morris's text reads like a classical Zionist narrative. He stresses the protocols of Umar (eighth-century, Damascus) to describe Muslim mistreatment of Jews throughout Islamic civilization. This is a common discursive strategy among Zionist scholars attempting to justify Israel's treatment of its Arab minority.[14] He talks about Arab "pogroms" waged against the Jews in 1929 and 1936 (p. 147), in a way that sounds much like classical Zionist exaggeration. Morris also claims that Palestinians were not, in his words, "a distinct people" until 1920 (pp. 653–54). This somehow makes their claim to the land (pre-1967) seem less legitimate than that of the Jews, who were simply trying to get back to the land that God promised them, that they ruled as early as the first millennium, and that would save some from the gas chambers of Hitler's Europe.

Since Morris does not consider the rich (although dispersed) archive of Palestinian and Islamic narrative ties to the land (his explanation is that Arab perspectives are not as well documented and as organized as Jewish ones), it is difficult to view this account as one that attempts to go beyond Zionist narratives. Moreover, pogroms and the Holocaust still dominate Morris's narrative and obliterate any consideration of Palestinian reasons for loving the land. As Morris notes, "[a]s the pogroms in Russia in the 1880s had launched modern Zionism, so the largest pogrom of all, the Holocaust, was to propel the movement, almost instantly, into statehood" (p.161). Reading history backward in this way makes it difficult to argue against Zionism, even for a post-Zionist. Thus Morris, although he attempts to present both Palestinian and Israeli views of righteous victimization, still maintains a framework which, in light of the Holocaust, makes Jews more righteous than Arabs.

Avi Shlaim's *The Iron Wall,* which appeared in Hebrew in late 1999 simultaneously with Morris's *Righteous Victims*, goes the furthest of the three works considered here in revising Zionist narratives. The book questions the intentions and attitudes of Israel's leaders toward the Arabs. It is a diplomatic, political history and, if it has any weakness, it is his narrow focus upon the elite core of Israeli statesmen. Rarely if ever does Shlaim include popular narratives, or the ideas of the common Israeli/Jew in his revision. Neither does he speak for the Arab side. Since the text attempts to document Israel's relations with the Palestinians, some expectations for data beyond the views of Jewish-Israeli leaders are raised without being met.

To his credit, however, Shlaim, in contrast to Morris, relies mostly on primary source material. He provides a balanced treatment of the events leading up to statehood and thereafter in light of the narratives of Zionist leaders and their personal subtexts from diaries, letters, communiqués, speeches, and interviews. Shlaim points out, for example, that Theodor Herzl felt that Zionism would economically benefit the Arab natives; thus he expected, wrongly so, that local Arabs would welcome the Jewish national movement (p. 4). Herzl viewed the Arabs as "primitive and backward," a perspective that Shlaim tempers with his revision (p. 4). Similarly, Shlaim challenges Chaim Weizmann's view that "Palestinian Arabs were not a separate political community with national aspirations of its own" (p. 6), although Shlaim does not mince words in charging the Arab national movement with disorganization that was in part responsible for their poor performance in 1948 and beyond. For example, Shlaim observes that "[t]he inability of the Arabs to coordinate their diplomatic and military plans was in no small measure responsible for the disaster that overwhelmed them" (p. 36). This critique and familiarity with the Arab side helps to reinforce the balance of his narrative. In Shlaim's view, the Zionists took advantage of Arab weakness and disorganization, and collaborated with Arabs who would sell the Palestinians short for their own advantage, like King Abdullah I of Jordan. Shlaim argues that the Palestine question was not a genuine concern for Arab regimes who remained self-interested, aiming to consolidate their hold on their own national populations through the rallying cry of anti-Zionism/anticolonialism.

Demonstrating his firm commitment to post-Zionism, Shlaim, unlike Morris and Sternhell, does not begin with a view of Israel as a moral imperative based upon the Holocaust. We see this in his criticism of Israeli leaders who equate the Nazi threat with the Arab threat. For example, Shlaim observes that Golda Meir's attitude to the Arabs was based upon "emotion and intuition rather than on reason and reflection" (p. 284). Similarly, Shlaim explains Menahem Begin's commitment to a Greater Israel and lack of interest in compromising with the Arabs in light of emotion and fear linked to the loss of his parents and brother in the Holocaust (p. 353).

Yitzhak Shamir shared with Meir and Begin a Holocaust legacy that colored his attitude toward the Arabs (p. 463). Part of the post-Zionist project seeks to sever the linkage between Arab national anger and Israeli fears of a future Holocaust in order to create a foundation for dialogue. Shlaim's presentation, especially his critique of Meir, Begin, and Shamir, suggests that the creation of the State of Israel was not free from sin, and that the Holocaust was not linked with the morality of the Palestinians' dispossession. Shlaim argues that when Israelis are obsessed with security, Arab sensitivities are not figured in to the equation, and this is dangerous for Israel's future (p. 398).

Shlaim, unlike Morris or Sternhell, is careful to use a post-Zionist discourse when describing political events. For example, he explains that while 1948 was Israel's year of Independence, for the Palestinians it was known as *al-Nakba*—"the disaster" (p. 28). Similarly, what Zionist discourse labeled *riots* and *disturbances* (a.k.a. the Intifada) in 1988, Shlaim calls "the Palestinian War of Independence" (p. 450). Whereas Zionist discourse calls the IDF's efforts to "restore order" to the territories justified in light of the uprising, Shlaim calls such measures "draconian" (p. 453). This vocabulary acts like a flag, identifying the scholar's perspective in the study of this conflict. In many ways post-Zionism is a movement designed to change narratives, and thus mentalities. Words configured in a way that goes against convention or shatters national myths are taken as a serious threat to the state, or as an enabler of democratic society, depending on one's perspective. In this case, Shlaim's choice of words distinguishes his scholarship as the most "post-Zionist" of the three revisionist histories reviewed here.

Zionists gain rich imagery from the Holocaust for justifying their intransigence vis-à-vis the Arabs. We see this linkage in the following passage:

> Arafat, were he stronger, would do to us things that Hitler never even dreamed of . . . Hitler killed us with a measure of restraint. . . . If Arafat were to reach power, he would not

> amuse himself with such "small things." He will cut off our children's heads with a cry and in broad daylight and will rape our women before tearing them to pieces and will throw us down from all the rooftops and will skin us as do hungry leopards in the jungle . . . without the famous "order" of the Germans. . . . Hitler is a pussycat compared to what Arafat will bring upon us. (Herzl Rosenblum, editor of *Yediot Aharonot,* quoted in Morris, pp. 514–15)

These same strategies of linkage between Arab intentions and the Holocaust were used to justify Israel's bombing of the Iraqi nuclear reactor in 1981. In explaining his reasons for acting, Begin wrote in a letter to President Reagan that

> [a] million and a half children were poisoned by the Ziklon gas during the Holocaust. Now Israel's children were about to be poisoned by radioactivity. For two years we have lived in the shadow of the danger awaiting Israel from the nuclear reactor in Iraq. This would have been a new Holocaust. It was prevented by the heroism of our pilots to whom we owe so much. (quoted in Shlaim, p. 387)

The extreme language of both of these passages reminds us all how much public discourse shifted during the 1980s and 1990s. No longer was Arafat portrayed as a vicious animal, but acknowledged as a head of state by many, if not a majority of, Israelis. No longer was the Holocaust invoked as a de facto explanation for why Israel cannot make peace with its neighbors. Although fear of the future and its unknowns continued to plague both Jew and Arab alike, bold steps were being made by both sides toward some realm of compromise before the al-Aqsa Intifada. Some of this common ground had, no doubt, been prepared and enriched by the deconstructive efforts of post-Zionist scholarship, even if in some cases, revisions of Zionist narratives remained incomplete. To some degree, art helped to foster this culture of compromise and it is to these influences that we now turn.

Art, Culture and Post-Zionist Expression

Historically, there has been a close relationship among art, Zionism, and post-Zionism. As Ronald Fuhrer observes in *Israeli Painting: From Post-Impressionism to Post-Zionism,* "as the need emerged for a visual tradition with which to document the Zionist project of reconstruction, the task was shouldered by artists . . . whose work helped to shape a national epic that hailed the exertions of the Zionists, along with idyllic kibbutz life" (p. 9). As is the case with scholarship in a post-Zionist context, in the realm of artistic expression a sense of service to the Israeli national cause has dissipated. Art has, like the broader postmodern movement of which post-Zionism is a part, taken a turn toward individual self-expression. Art exists for the sake of art, for the sake of the individual and his or her introspection, for social critique rather than national celebration. Fuhrer laments the passing of the Zionist period in Israeli art, arguing that, in the present period, "[t]he scene was now characterized by a pluralism of trends, styles, techniques and media. . . . This pluralism also extended to political and social pre-occupations. . . . Gone were the days of innocent representations of the ways of Israeli society. . . . Sensitivity to "the other" (Palestinian) . . . opened up Israeli art to post-Zionist self-scrutiny" (p. 192).

Fuhrer describes the art scene in Tel Aviv as representative of this new cosmopolitanism that both gave birth to and nurtured post-Zionism. In Tel Aviv—"New York in the Middle East"—coffee shops are "thronged with youngsters shaven-headed, multi-hued of hair and pierced with ornamentation like the models of either sex that adorn billboard advertisements":

> It's a new, cosmopolitan generation of computers and video games, hip to the Internet and wired to MTV. A generation that reads less but knows much more, even if its memory has greatly declined. . . . They are a "now" generation of instant satisfaction, yuppies engrossed exclusively in their own affairs. As for ideology and ideals, Israeli army officers will tell you, in strict confidence, that motivation in the national cause has greatly decreased in the secular population, while increasing among those religious youngsters sporting the yarmulke. (p. 190)

Fuhrer's tone of dismay with post-Zionist art, and the decline in national commitment among young artists, is in part explained by the overall purpose of his book. This text, in the author's own words, "is to be seen as an invitation to visit Israel and its abundance of museums, galleries and art workshops" (p. 7). It is difficult to encourage committed Zionists to visit an art scene that is increasingly critical of the Jewish national movement and the state that created it. Moreover, Fuhrer's dismay springs from his shock over the failure of the army to instill Zionist ideals and national commitment. Historically, the IDF "was regarded as a school of national conduct" (Sternhell, p. 327). This school of national conduct trains most of the nation's youth, including artists and intellectuals, as well as military leaders and future politicians. Part of the post-Zionist trend in art, therefore, reflects the army's failure to inspire national commitment and Zionist memory among its conscripts.

Fuhrer documents in an informative way the kinds of ideological crisis described in the rest of this essay. When the Zionist movement needed imagery with which to consolidate collective memory, artists were in line to serve the cause. Painters such as Menachem Shemi celebrated the ingenuity and commitment of the pioneers, "who were confronted with immediate pioneering tasks connected with the redemption of the land, such as draining swamps, constructing roads, building homes and planting trees" (p. 7). We see the spirit of pioneering commitment in the gaze of a young man in Shemi's *A Pioneer*, ca. 1924 (p. 46) and in Joseph Zaritsky's portrait of a new immigrant in his painting *On the Ship's Deck,* 1923 (p. 59). Also giving Zionist imagination textual expression are artistic celebrations of the redemption of the land of Israel. In the art of the Yishuv there is a preoccupation with landscape, with images of fertility, with Mediterranean breezes, and with the countryside (although most immigrants lived in cities).

In the post-1948 period, one Israeli painter become well known as a consolidator of Israeli collective memory—Marcello Janco. This artist made a great contribution to Israeli art not only through his paintings, but also through his efforts to establish an artist colony at Ein Hod in the remains of an Arab village in 1950. Images contained in Janco's paintings reinforce a collective memory based upon the security challenges of running a state surrounded by a sea of Arab territorial and political opposition. His *Wounded Soldier* (1948) and *Air-Raid Alarm* (1948) remind Israelis of the sacrifices made in establishing the state (pp. 94–95). Images of insecurity reinforce a collective consciousness of the need to guard future generations from the anger of Arab reprisals. Images of Arabs as a natural part of the landscape are collectively "forgotten." Instead, replacing the Arab are images of violence, of bleeding, of bombs, all conveying a psychology of being under siege. In light of Arab might, the Israeli pioneer becomes even more heroic in his or her successful quest for independence.

After the 1967 war, Israeli art became increasingly characterized by levels of abstractness and complexity, which in turn reflected the increasing divisiveness of Israeli society and politics. Symbolic of this new Israeli art scene—and new politics—is the painting of David Reeb, an Israeli artist committed to "increasing social and artistic dialogue with Palestinian artists" (p. 191). In Reeb's painting *Tel Aviv Landscape with Green Line* (1986) we see this mingling of artistic and political dialogue with "the other" (p. 224). An impulsive green outline of the State of Israel is superimposed on frames of a tranquil Tel Aviv street scene, evoking images of how the conflict over the boundaries of the state interrupt day-to-day life. Reeb overtly embeds the conflict in his art and thus forces the discussion of politics in order to grasp the meanings of his art. In addition to the display of dialogue in his paintings, Reeb satisfied the need to grapple with the conflict in his daily life through his close relations with his Arab student Abu-Shakra. Abu-Shakra, inspired by Reeb, pursued his own form of dialogue with "the other" through representations of the *tzabar*. *Tzabar (sabra)* is the Hebrew word for cactus fruit, and also the word for native-born Israelis. In the latter case, the word is meant to evoke an imagery that guides day-to-day behavior—prickly on the outside, sweet on the inside. For Abu-Shakra, this inside is bittersweet. For the cactus symbol, which early Zionists adopted as their image of future generations, had a long history in the land. Like Walid Khalidi's photo-documentary *Before Their Diaspora: A Photographic History of the Palestinians, 1876–1948,*[15] Abu Shakra's paintings remind observers that the cactus is subject to multiple meanings. It's one community's hope for future empowerment; it's another's reminder of past rootedness. Post-Zionism in art is about clearing space for dialogue and diversity of voice similar to what we observed in the post-Zionist political and scholarly realms. As a whole, these cultural and political movements are spokes in the same wheel. Together they promise an interesting ride toward the future. But the road is still rocky, and filled with uncertainty.

The Future of Post-Zionism, The Future of Israel

Zionism, writes Yoram Hazony, is the "ingredient that was the cement in the wall of [Israeli] national identity."[16] How, then, might

Israel maintain bonds of community in the post-Zionist context? Some have suggested that in a post-Zionist context an ideology of globalization replaces traditional nationalist Zionism. Like any other nation, Silberstein observes, Israel lost its control over public narratives with the advent of cable and satellite television in the 1990s, which in turn led to a public demand for "expanded cultural options" (p. 95). As a result, Israel, like nations around the world, experienced a rapid process of Americanization. Silberstein remarks,

> This is evident in the rapid growth of shopping malls and the increasing presence of such American franchises as McDonald's throughout the country. Caught up in the pursuit of the good life, a growing number of Israelis, particularly among the younger generation, increasingly find the collectivist values of labor [Z]ionism to be unrelated to the realities of their daily lives.
>
> Not surprising, the rapidly changing cultural, economic, and social landscapes and political conditions have led a growing number of Israelis to regard [Z]ionism as irrelevant to the new Israel. . . . On every front, the Israel of which previous generations had dreamed and for which they had fought seemed to be crumbling before their very eyes. (p. 95)

In the film *Hitchhikers,* we see another example of what a post-Zionist Israel might look like. *Hitchhikers* is a wonderful film constructed as a "day-in-a-life" type narrative, but with a twist. The film begins with a man driving from Haifa to Tel Aviv to visit the gravesite of his deceased brother. Along the way, he decides to pick up a hitchhiking soldier, and soon gets more than he bargains for. An Arab, standing nearby, also asks for a ride, but both the driver and the soldier say they don't have any more room in the car. This is clearly a lie, since the car is a Volvo station wagon and easily fits five people or more. However, while getting into the car, the soldier inadvertently drops his gun's bullet case in the gutter. The Arab, watching this, hesitates for a moment, then flags down the car and rushes to return the ammunition to the soldier. This act establishes his identity as "the good Arab" and he is thus given a ride in the car. When they stop to let the Arab in, a young female hippie also asks for a ride, and so the plot is set with a cast of characters representing the Labor Zionist past (the driver), the non-Jewish minority in Israel (the Arab), religious conservatism and the ideals of national service (the soldier wearing a *kippa*), and the new post-Zionist Israeli, peace loving, antiracist, disdainful of Jewish identity and nationalism that breeds militarism and anti-Arab racism (the hippie).

Discourse within the car symbolizes the broader context of Israeli self-critique occurring in the larger society. Music playing on the radio and conversations between passengers all help to develop this theme. One song celebrates that "In Israel we're all Jews and we're all friends." The present company is testimony to the problematic nature of this view: the Arab is not Jewish; the hippie does not love the soldier, at least not his opinions; and the driver does not understand the disaffection of younger generation. Another song by an Israeli punk band carries the message, "We're a screwed-up generation." The first set of lyrics is laughed at in embarrassment, while the second is received with grim contemplation. In an ensuing conversation between the hippie and the soldier, the former observes,: "prejudice and stereotypes are what is killing Israeli society." This statement is given time to make its mark, before the radio drowns out all other conversations with guarded optimism thanks to the soothing lyrics of Stevie Wonder's "I Just Called to Say I Love You." This creates a lighter mood within the cramped physical and ideological space of the car interior, and a common ground emerges. Within the microcosm of an old Volvo, Arab, Labor Zionist, young religious-nationalist soldier, and post-Zionist hippie can reflect together, lulled by a global culture. While their dialogue remains strained at best—the soldier making fun of the hippie's multiple facial piercings and she mocking his *kippa,* the Arab making fun of himself, verbalizing "what might have been said had he not been present"—there is dialogue and some stereotypes are broken. While the soldier takes offense at the hippie's comparison between his adornment and hers, the audience is left thinking about the meaninglessness of symbols in the value-free space within the automobile.

In addition, the automobile contains a society in which appearances are not what they seem. The religious soldier has a secular girlfriend he keeps in the closet, so to speak. The driver, who represents the old Zionist pioneering spirit, is on a journey to a memorial service for his brother who died, not (as we were led to believe) in the service of his country, but instead by committing suicide over the unrequited love of a woman. To everyone's surprise, the Arab turns out to be a homosexual, signifying not one but two levels of marginalization. Old discursive space is penetrated by new narratives and, at the end of the journey, we see that the truths of the past give no hint of what the future may hold. The film illustrates an observation made by Pappé, that Israeli society today is stuck in "a phase in which most of the Zionist truths have collapsed but there is no sign of what would replace them."[17]

An ambiguous conclusion to the film provides an eerie foreshadowing of political events that characterize the present Palestinian-Israeli conflict and the uncertain future of post-Zionism. While Shlomo Artzi's somber lyrics "what a price we pay to live here," resound, the lines between fact and fiction break down. We learn in the last few minutes of the film that *Hitchhikers* is a metanarrative, a film about making a film. The Arab character ends up threatening to commit an act of violence, by stealing and wielding a gun from a police officer at a security checkpoint. The hippie is shot dead in the standoff between the Arab and the rest of the characters when she tries to stop the soldier from firing on the Arab, perhaps suggesting a grim future for post-Zionism. Incidentally, it is the soldier's bullet, not the Arab's, that kills the hippie. When the tension builds to a breaking point, the director yells, "cut" and he asks for the shooting scene to be a retake. So fact is revealed as fiction, and the audience feels the relief that "this is just a movie." The hippie is not dead from the gun wound; in fact, she and the Arab character are friendly on the set; he helps her up from her dusty place on the ground. The hippie and the conservative soldier are a couple off screen. During the break from filming they call their son on the phone and tell him they'll be home soon.

To build tension again, however, real security forces that are clearing the road where they are filming interrupt the break the film crew and actors are taking. The security forces explain that there has been a hijacking of a bus and it's heading right for this area. The actors disperse; the soldiers prepare their weapons and take positions. Artzi's lyrics, "They both give me chills, terror and love . . . what a price we pay to live here," are the last words of this film. The ambiguous conclusion of the film *Hitchhikers* is symbolic of the same ambiguity that characterizes post-Zionism's future in the wake of the September 2000 "al-Aqsa Intifada."

Conclusion

In September 2000, violent clashes between Palestinian demonstrators and Israeli security forces in Jerusalem triggered a chain of events with no end in sight at the time of this writing. The escalation of the violence that engulfs both sides in daily losses of life has scholars and activists increasingly pessimistic regarding the chances for compromise and dialogue. This pessimism has dealt a serious blow to the post-Zionist platform. Some committed Zionists use the al-Aqsa Intifada to justify their opposition to post-Zionism, stating that "Though many Israelis had flirted with post-Zionism, evidently a strong majority of Jews in Israel awakened [following the September 2000 outbreaks] to realize that a secular triumph at home and a dreamy belief in the good will of implacable enemies on their borders would lead to the doom of a Jewish state."[18] Post-Zionists are divided in their responses. Some say that the al-Aqsa Intifada is the product of a Zionist approach to "compromise" that gave the Palestinians so little as a peace dividend that they became desperate and chose violence instead. Others were surprised by Palestinian violence, and are confused by Arafat's apparent lack of commitment to ending or preventing attacks such as suicide bombings. Even Tom Segev, one of post-Zionism's founders notes, "The recent uprising forced us back into a Zionist consciousness."[19] During the battle between Zionism and post-Zionism, Israel was "in the midst of a cultural civil war."[20] In the post-al-Aqsa Intifada context, the stakes are higher. Observers remain, like the film *Hitchhikers,* conflicted about the future, both in terms of the meaning and possibility of peace and compromise, and the ability or inability to trust appearances.

Notes

1. For examples of works by so-called new historians see Benny Morris, *The Birth of the Palestinian Refugee Problem, 1947–49* (Cambridge: Cambridge University Press, 1988); Ilan Pappé, *Britain and the Arab-Israeli Conflict, 1948–1951* (New York: Macmillan, 1988); Avi Shlaim, *Collusion across the Jordan: King Abdullah, The Zionist Movement and the Partition of Palestine* (Oxford: Clarendon, 1988); Simha Flapan, *The Birth of Israel* (New York: Pantheon, 1984). The Spring/Summer 1995 issue (7:1) of the journal *History and Memory,* subtitled "Israeli Historiography Revisited" and edited by Gulie Ne'eman Arad, focused on the intellectual challenges of the new historians.

2. Pappé, "Post-Zionist Critique on Israel and the Palestinians—Part 1: The Academic Debate," *Journal of Palestine Studies* 36:2 (Winter 1997): 30.

3. Yoram Hazony, "The End of Zionism?" *Azure* (Summer 1996): 2. See also his book that developed from this article: *The Jewish State: The Struggle for Israel's Soul* (New York: Basic Books, 2000).

4. Pappé, "Critique and Agenda: The Post-Zionist Scholars in Israel," *History and Memory* 7:1 (Spring/Summer 1995): 85.

5. Emile Habiby, *The Secret Life of Saeed: The Pessoptimist,* translated from the Arabic (first published in 1974) by S. K. Jayyusi and T. LeGassick (London: Zed Books, 1985).

6. Anton Shammas, *Arabesques: A Novel*, translated from the Hebrew (first published in 1986) by V. Eden (New York: Harper, 1988).

7. Hazony, "The End of Zionism?" 2.

8. Hazony, "The End of Zionism?" 3.

9. Anita Shapira, "Politics and Collective Memory: The Debate over the New Historians in Israel," *History and Memory* 7:1 (Spring/Summer 1995), 17. See also her chapter on the politics of interpretation at work in the new historians' interpretations of the War of Independence in *New Jews, Old Jews* (Tel Aviv: Am Oved, 1998), 46–85.

10. Hazony, "The End of Zionism?" 4.

11. For more on this subject see Michael Berkowitz, *Zionist Culture and Western European Jewry* (Durham: University of North Carolina Press, 1996).

12. Shapira, "Politics and Collective Memory," 12. Cf. the debates over this still-delicate issue between Benny Morris and Motti Golani in Chapter 1 of the present volume.

13. Yael Zerubavel, *Recovered Roots: Collective Memory and the Making of Israeli National Tradition* (Chicago: University of Chicago Press, 1995), xv.

14. For an example of this general trend, see *Jews among Muslims: Communities in the Precolonial Middle East,* eds. Shlomo Deshen and Walter P. Zenner (New York: New York University Press, 1996), especially 55–58.

15. See Walid Khalidi, *Before Their Diaspora: A Photographic History of the Palestinians 1876–1948* (Washington, DC: Institute for Palestine Studies, 1991).

16. Hazony, "The End of Zionism?" 3.

17. Pappé, "Post-Zionist Critique," 30.

18. Wiliam Safire, "The New Sharon," *Denver Post*, 9 February 2001, p. B-7.

19. "An Interview with Tom Segev," *Tikkun,* January/February 2001, p.1.

20. Meyrav Wurmser, "Can Israel Survive Post-Zionism?" *www. allenpress.com / mieq / issues / vol06 / ftr-0601.html,* p. 1.

8. The Open Society and Its Enemies: Changing Public Discourse in Israel

Leah Rosen, *Emeq Yezreel College*
and Ruth Amir, *Emeq Yezreel College*

Contemporary scholarship about Israel is fully cognizant of the deep fragmentation within the Israeli body politic. Increasingly, political discourse and the public agenda recognize, and are shaped by, ethnic, national, and economic divisions within the state. This essay explores Israel's current identity crises, outlining the positions of those who adhere to a long-standing statist ideology and hold a melting pot model as an ideal versus those who advocate multiculturalism and display a new interest in identity politics.

Ben-Ami, Shlomo, *A Place for All,* Tel Aviv: ha-Kibbutz ha-Meuhad, 1998 (in Hebrew: *Makom Le-Kulam*).

Bishara, Azmi, ed., *Between "I" and "We": The Construction of Identities and Israeli Identity,* Tel Aviv: Van Leer Jerusalem Institute and ha-Kibbutz ha-Meuhad, 1999 (in Hebrew: *Bein ha-Ani le-Anakhnu: Havnayat Zehuyot ve-Zehut Yisra'elit*).

Ezrahi, Yaron, *Rubber Bullets: Power and Conscience in Modern Israel,* New York: Farrar, Straus and Giroux, 1997.

Gavison, Ruth, and Issam Abu-Ria, *The Jewish-Arab Cleavage in Israel: Characteristics and Challenges,* Jerusalem: Israel Democracy Institute, 1999 (in Hebrew: *Ha-Shesa ha-Yehudi-Aravi be-Yisra'el: Me'afyenim ve-Etgarim*).

Mautner, Menachem, Avi Sagi, and Ronen Shamir, eds., *Multiculturalism in a Democratic and Jewish State*, Tel Aviv: Ramot, 1998 (in Hebrew: *Rav-tarbutiyut be-M'dina Demokratit ve-Yehudit*).

Peres, Yochanan, and Ephraim Yuchtman-Yaar, *Between Consent and Dissent: Democracy and Peace in the Israeli Mind,* Jerusalem: Israel Democracy Institute, 1998 (in Hebrew: *Bein Haskamah le-Makhloket: Demokratiya ve-Shalom ba-Toda'a ha-Yisra'elit*).

Rabinowitz, Dan, *Anthropology and the Palestinians,* Ra'anana: Institute for Israeli Arab Studies, 1998 (in Hebrew: *Antropologiya ve-ha-Falastinim*).

During the 1996 elections Israel adopted a unique system of a direct election of the prime minister within an otherwise parliamentary regime. Voters cast two ballots, one for the prime minister and one for the party of their choice. The result was an increased fragmentation and a decline in the vote-share of the two large parties that had traditionally dominated the elected parliament. Furthermore, three groupings—the right-wing Zionist-religious, Shas (Sephardi, Orthodox), and Arabs—increased their representation significantly, while Russian immigrants made substantial gains with a newly formed party. (See table 1.)

After these elections, commentators conveniently attributed the "excessive" representation of Sephardi (Oriental) Jews and new immigrants from the former Soviet Union to the electoral reform. While some may claim that this fragmentation is an undesirable side effect of electoral reform, we maintain that it is in fact a reflection of a deeper social transformation. The further accentuation of this trend in the May 1999 elections (see table 1) is slowly beginning to disturb the hegemonic structure of political discourse; the public agenda is finally recognizing that Israel exhibits troubling ethnic, national, political, and economic divisions. In particular, the elections focused public attention on the crisis of identity within Jewish society, highlighting the tenacious nature of ethnic and religious identities in defiance of the Zionist project.

There is a growing understanding in Israel that the melting-pot ideal is in crisis. However, there is a clear distinction between, on the one hand, those who suggest that this crisis is structural and that the project should be abandoned and, on the other hand, those

Table 1

Representation in the 120-Seat Israeli Knesset, 1984–99 (seats)[1]

	Left-wing Liberal	*Labour*	*Likud*	*Ultra Right-wing*	*Zionist-Religious*	*European-Orthodox*	*Shas / Oriental Jews*[2]	*Arabs*[3]	*Russian Jews*	*Others*[4]	*Number of Parties*
1984	6	44	41	6	4	4	5	6	—	4	15
1988	7	42	40	7	5	7	6	6	—	—	15
1992	12	44	32	11	6	4	6	5	—	—	10
1996	9	34	32	2	9	4	10	9	7	4	11
1999	10	26	19	4	5	5	17	10	10	14	15

Source: Israeli Knesset Internet Site.

1. Parties are divided into categories according to national, ethnic, and political identity.
2. This category consists mostly of the Shas party, except for 1984 when an additional MK was elected from another ethnic party (Tami).
3. This category consists of the mainly Arab Communist Party and various nationalist, Arab parties.
4. Others consist of small splinter parties. In 1984 Others include Ometz (1MK) and Yahad (3 MKs); in 1996 The Third Way (4MKs); in 1999 the Centre Party (6MKs), Shinui (6 MKs), and AM (2 MKs).

who wish to intensify the efforts to make it successful.[1] Others, both citizens and professional commentators in academia, journalism, and political life, express concern and frustration at the growing fragmentation of Israeli politics. For them the problem is mainly a political one, reflecting a faulty electoral system that translates itself into a fragmented parliament that results in a problem in governance.

The books we review offer a fair summary of the range of arguments summoned by all these groups. Since the assassination of Prime Minister Yitzak Rabin in 1995 there has been a marked proliferation of academic and semiacademic publications on Israeli society. Characteristically, and in contrast to past trends, these are written in Hebrew and often by academics daring to come out of the security of the ivory tower and to participate in political debate. A distinct pattern emerges in these works. Yochanan Peres and Ephraim Yuchtman-Yaar, Ruth Gavison and Issam Abu-Ria, and to a lesser extent Yaron Ezrahi are less impressed by these social and cultural changes, adhering to Israel's official melting-pot and statist ideology. But Shlomo Ben-Ami, Dan Rabinowitz, and the edited volumes by Azmi Bishara, and Menachem Mautner, Avi Sagi and Ronen Shamir make up a diverse group, representing a great variety of disciplines—law, sociology, anthropology, history, and philosophy—and displaying a new interest in multiculturalism and identity politics. These more responsive writers, adopting new concepts and theoretical frameworks, seek to influence the public agenda. Perhaps the most striking indication that public discourse in Israel is undergoing a radical transformation is the entry of two of these prominent intellectuals onto the political stage: one a Palestinian and one a Jew. In the 1999 elections, Bishara, a philosopher, ran for prime minister; Ben-Ami, an historian, became a leading Labor Party Knesset member and Cabinet minister.

The volumes by Ezrahi, Peres and Yuchtman-Yaar, and Gavison and Abu-Ria reflect the ambivalence of mainstream academia toward the social and political transformations in Israel. While acknowledging that Israel is in crisis, each in its way reaffirms the values and interests of the melting-pot ideology. Gavison and Abu-Ria map the main issues dividing Jews and Arabs in Israel. The authors point out two interrelated problems. The first concerns the definition of Israel as a Jewish State, the implications of that definition for Israel's collective identity, and the conception of the general good. The second focuses on the considerable inequalities between Arabs and Jews both in social and economic terms and in political power.

Like many academic works produced in Israel, *The Jewish-Arab Cleavage in Israel: Characteristics and Challenges* is written in a cautious mode. In its own words, it does not commit itself to any one position on the "many important dilemmas that are on the agenda today" (p. 10). On the one hand, its review of recent scholarship offers a critical outlook on the inferior status of Arab citizens in Israel. Following liberal opinion, it attributes this state of affairs to two main causes, the Israeli-Arab conflict and the fact that Israel is a Jewish State. The same liberal approach, on the other hand, precludes the writers from acknowledging particular collective identities within the Jewish community, reaffirming Israel's melting pot and statist ideology. Consequently, they fail to link the position of Arab citizens in Israel to that of Oriental Jews, for example. For, contrary to official opinion, Arab citizens in Israel are not faced with a monolithic Jewish collective; where Gavison and Abu-Ria write of the superiority of Jewish ethnicity they are in effect referring to the superiority of *European* Jewish ethnicity (p. 13). This oversight is especially striking in view of the fact that the authors refer to Sammy Smooha and Yoav Peled, each of whom, in his own way, criticizes the predominance of European Jews in Israel.[2]

Peres and Yuchtman-Yaar's study, *Between Consent and Dissent: Democracy and Peace in the Israeli Mind,* is an extensive and thorough survey of attitudes and preferences in Israel on such subjects as democracy, peace, and the Israeli-Arab conflict. It attempts to explain these attitudes by correlating them with various demographic variables such as education, income, religion, and ethnicity. The authors also aim to examine the links between different attitudes in order to construct a hierarchical value system. Like Gavison and Abu-Ria's work, this study is grounded in a statist ideology. This is reflected especially in the authors' conception of democracy. In their introduction, they note that in Western democracies "the stable consensus . . . was threatened by new issues and new political contenders" (p. 21). In particular, they argue that the recent rise of various "extremist" social, national, and religious movements in Western Europe, America and Israel might create an "anti-democratic political atmosphere" (p. 21). For Peres and Yuchtman-Yaar, a threat to the consensus equals a threat to democracy. Together with other conservative liberals, they confine democracy to a narrow political, and largely procedural, definition. In the Israeli context, this means that, when examining commitment to democracy, they emphasize the will of Jews to extend civil and political rights to Arab citizens *on an individual basis*. While important, this issue can no longer be said to be the only one dividing democratic and antidemocratic forces in Israeli society today. New voices are raised against the hegemonic consensus about democracy, demanding that democracy incorporate new groups with their own needs and concerns. Thus, their surveys find that European Jews are more "democratic" than Oriental Jews, while different surveys, with different conceptions of democracy, would find that this commitment of European Jews to "democracy" presumes an Israeli form of democracy that reflects exclusively their own cultural preferences. In other words, their view of democracy, one that the authors share with other well-educated affluent European Jews, conditions the full inclusion of other groups in Israeli democracy on their will and ability to adopt the hegemonic consensus with its Eurocentric bias. Moreover, despite their liberal attitudes toward the Arab minority in Israel, these writers, like most other Israeli social scientists, do not include them in their samples.

Yaron Ezrahi's *Rubber Bullets: Power and Conscience in Modern Israel* is a stirring semi-autobiographical account of the struggle between collectivism and individualism in Israel today. The book echoes the bewilderment of the prosperous, liberal, and Ashkenazi Israel in the face of the resurgence of religious and right-wing forces in Israeli politics and culture. The book, beautifully written and well versed in both Jewish culture and Western intellectual traditions, is one of the more remarkable works to have been produced by an Israeli academic in recent years. Ezrahi's stance is halfway between the two groups of authors we review. For, unlike Gavison and Abu-Ria or Peres and Yuchtman-Yaar, he is acutely aware that the Zionist dream may be shattering. Challenged by the Palestinian Intifada in the occupied territories, Ezrahi engages in some private soul-searching, which evolves into an exercise of the collective conscience and a reevaluation of Israel's collective memory. Ezrahi identifies three areas in which the Israeli self-image is inflicted by self-righteousness: the relationship with the Palestinians, attitudes toward new immigrants, and the commitment to liberal democracy. These concerns, however, betray Ezrahi's own "blind spot." In his "battle of stories" one story is conspicuously missing; Oriental Jews remain voiceless. In this respect, *Rubber Bullets* echoes the official Zionist narrative, a story told by and of European Jews. It is their various internal conflicts that concern Ezrahi. The "pendulum," in his words, might swing between "left and right governments, between liberal-democratic openness to the world and ethnocentric, nationalistic entrenchment." A balance might be struck between "men and women, public and private lives, the community and the individual, the national home and the private home, state and society" (p. 265). But Oriental Jews remain outside his reflections on the past and future Israel.

The remaining four volumes by Rabinowitz; Bishara; Ben-Ami; and Mautner, Sagi, and Shamir reflect a growing disenchantment with the melting-pot and statist ideologies. Vital to these works is the abandonment of the official Zionist narrative and with it the pretense of an objective perspective. Rather than regarding Jews as forming a monolithic collectivity against "the Arabs," they examine the multiplicity of rival and overlapping particular identities. Moreover, they acknowledge the legitimacy of the demands made by these ethnic and national collectivities to shape Israeli democracy according to their needs and values.

Rabinowitz, one of Israel's more influential anthropologists and a prolific contributor to a leading newspaper, offers a critical review of the state of anthropological scholarship about the Palestinians in *Anthropology and the Palestinians*. This work aims to wean Hebrew readers of their anachronistic stereotypes about the nature of anthropological study. It introduces them to an anthropology which, in the wake of Edward W. Said's *Orientalism*,[3] has lost its naïveté and has come to reflect on its own methods. Following Said, Rabinowitz turns this reflexive mode onto the study of Palestinians as "the other," beginning in the second half of the nineteenth century. *Anthropology and the Palestinians* is a critique of a great variety of anthropological genres and topics, such as the journal, the scientific essay, modernist ethnography, Palestinian agriculture, the Palestinian village, and the theory of modernization. The last three chapters discuss the work produced by Israeli and Palestinian anthropologists. Of particular interest is Rabinowitz's exploration into the ways in which Orientalist anthropological practices were employed in the services of two related purposes: the construction of Israeli national identity and the marginalization of Arab citizens in Israel. Rabinowitz's critique of anthropology has wider implications. It bears directly on the Israeli public agenda and undermines the self-congratulatory conceptions of Israeli liberals in their battle with the nationalist right-wingers. *Anthropology and the Palestini-*

ans exposes the Eurocentric premises underlying the views of liberals who habitually see Palestinians and Oriental Jews in terms of an inferior culture that is said to obstruct their integration into a progressive Israel.

Multiculturalism in a Democratic and Jewish State, edited by Mautner, Sagi, and Shamir, is an excellent example of the newly emerging interest in multiculturalism and the politics of identity. Many of the chapters warn against the view of Israel as consisting of rigidly divided communities. The authors emphasize, instead, the instability of private and collective identity and interaction among cultures. The book consists of twenty-nine articles by scholars from a wide variety of disciplines and is dedicated to the memory of Ariel Rosen-Zvi, the former dean of the Law Faculty at Tel Aviv University. In contrast to Peres and Yuchtman-Yaar's argument,[4] the collection is inspired by Rosen-Zvi's aim of reconciling Judaism and democracy. Thus Gavison, for example, writing in Mautner, Sagi, and Shamir, examines the practical ways in which the Zionist determination to establish a Jewish State can be maintained while upholding the democratic objective. In order to reconcile the "Jewishness" of Israel with its commitment to democracy, she suggests that we recognize the many different possible meanings of democracy as well as of "a Jewish State." Some of these meanings are obviously exclusive of one another. However, she argues, by relinquishing the "all-or-nothing" approach Israel can be democratic to an extent and Jewish to an extent, while not being purely democratic or Jewish. For example, Israel cannot be democratic and fully Jewish in the sense of being a theocracy in which Jewish law (*halakha*) dictates all aspects of public and private life. But, in her view, democracy can be reconciled with other important meanings of "Jewishness," such as a Jewish majority, immigration patterns, language, symbols, and culture. Similarly, Israel cannot be Jewish and wholly democratic in the liberal sense of maintaining neutrality and not favoring any one conception of good and any one of the identities of its citizens. Thus, Gavison notes, Israel cannot be both Jewish and democratic if democracy is taken to mean "a state of all its citizens" and the abandonment of a "statist affiliation" between Israel and a Jewish distinction.

In "Amalek's Punishment: How Jewish Traditions Cope with the Moral Problem and the Status of Morality in Jewish Tradition" (also in Mautner, Sagi, and Shamir), Avi Sagi, like other contributors, proposes to set Jewish traditions in a new light, arguing that

Judaism can be seen to reaffirm democracy and multiculturalism. Pnina Lahav, writing about the High Court decisions in the Shalit case ("Personal Identity and Collective Identity, Modernity and Jewishness in the Shalit Case,") addresses the impact of Jewish law on the collective identity of Israeli Jews. Although highly theoretical and without specific reference to Israeli reality, Mautner's "Law as Culture: Towards a New Research Paradigm" bears directly on the increasingly controversial role of the High Court in Israel under Chief Justice Aharon Barak. We see in Mautner's comprehensive and inspiring analysis a welcome retort to those who, in defense of the High Court, emphasize the status of its members as neutral and objective experts. For if, following Mautner, we recognize that the Israeli High Court is part of the cultural system, then we cannot ignore the values and preferences that shape its rulings and the ways in which it seeks to construct the consciousness and practices of its citizens. Mautner's article is particularly pertinent where it outlines the impact of the Enlightenment on the legal system. The fact that the legal system is shaped by the "Enlightenment model of reason" and the Cartesian assumption that reason alone can produce universal and objective truth has had substantial effects in Israel. The High Court has become the voice of reason, and, as such, is called upon to denounce the practices of various cultural groups as the manifestation of unreason or, at best, as relics from less enlightened times.

Shlomo Ben-Ami, a renowned historian and leading politician, offers his analysis of the most acute problems in Israeli society today and unveils his proposals for the future. This book, *A Place for All,* introduces a refreshing political outlook, which incorporates the lessons of multiculturalism into a forceful reformulation of social democracy. Written in the form of a lengthy dialogue with a fellow historian, it confronts questions neglected by both the academic and the political agendas in Israel. These include such topics as social justice and the global economy, immigrant workers, the infusion of "communitarian values" into social democracy, and the reform of market forces.

Azmi Bishara, a philosopher and member of the Knesset, has edited a volume, *Between "I" and "We": The Construction of Identities and Israel Identity,* which reflects the recent interest in Israeli academia in how national and ethnic identities are formed and transformed. Of particular interest here are the essays by Henriette Dahan-Kalev, Avner Ben-Amos, Ilana Bet-El, and Bishara that highlight the historic nature of national and ethnic identity and the role played by power relations in shaping the collective identities of both Jews and Arabs. We will address these issues in some detail in the following sections.

This review essay focuses on the processes that transformed collective identity in Israel, beginning with the development of the melting-pot ideology, and outlines the reactions of various scholars to the newly emerging realities. The first part offers an account of the melting-pot project and statist ideology. The second part examines the crises that undermined the melting-pot perception. In the third part we explore the conservative backlash to newly constructed particularist collective identities. The final section addresses the prospect of whether Israeli political culture is conducive toward the creation of a multicultural society.

The Melting-Pot Project and Statist Ideology

Zionism had always been ambivalent toward the multiplicity of identities gathered in Israel. Like all national movements, Zionism represented itself as a movement for the regeneration of an ancient, preexisting nation rather than for the invention of a new one. According to both Ben-Amos and Bet-El, in "Commemoration and National Identity: Commemoration Ceremonies in Israeli Schools" and Dahan-Kalev, in "Identity, Memory and Ethnicity" (both in Bishara), reality was quite different. Both argue that the Israeli nation had to be forged, deliberately and imaginatively, constructing one uniform, universal collective identity for all Jews out of the multiple, particular identities of the immigrants that made up Israeli society.[5]

The early Zionist settlers soon developed a hegemonic system that controlled the form and content of public discourse. The construction of the Israeli nation in one melting pot was called *kibbutz galuyot* (the ingathering of exiles). An essential part of the melting-pot ideology was the delegitimization of the particular identities of the various groups of immigrant Jews. A national collective memory was carefully assembled, predicated on the self-image of the pioneer Zionist settlers (the *halutzim*). The Israeli collective identity was similarly fashioned after the particular identity of the Jewish community who settled in the pre-1948 Palestine. For the hundreds of thousands who immigrated to Israel after 1948, full membership in the community meant exchanging their own identity with this new national identity. Far from being allowed to participate in the construction of their collective identity, the new immigrants were forced to abandon their own particular identities as irrelevant to the newly forming modern nation.

As the work of Dahan-Kalev, Rabinowitz and Ella Shohat[6] suggests, Israeli nationalism had a built-in bias toward Western, European culture. At the same time, however, it also propagated a belief in unbroken ties to an ancient Israel and an immemorial past. In the Orientalist fashion, Oriental Jews were cast in the role of enacting that ancient past in the present. Consequently, Oriental Jews were forever associated with the "primordial,"[7] not to say, the primitive; their history and cultural practices a hindrance to integration into a modern and enlightened Israel. This Western bias is particularly jarring when one considers the fact that in Israel even European Jews were largely immigrants from Eastern, rather than from Western, Europe. However, for the bulk of European Jews who immigrated to Israel after 1948, the melting-pot experience was different than that of most Oriental Jews for another reason altogether. Most Oriental Jews immigrated to Israel in large extended families, embedded in rich cultural traditions. Jewish immigrants from Europe, after 1948 were, in contrast, Holocaust survivors. Their identities, their heritage, were already erased—together with their families—by the Nazis. Pulverized by the Second World War, they were more pliant than Oriental Jews, more disposed, even eager, to adopt a whole new collective identity.

In the political sphere, unlike the cultural one, a more tolerant approach was adopted. Thus, the new regime established a semi-competitive party system, with the historical Labor (Mapai) Party as the dominant party, controlling a fragmented parliament by means of a patronage system. Under its auspices political discourse, rather than deliberating the formation of national identity, was reduced to the discussion of the division of the spoils, mainly in terms of partisan control over budgets and civil service positions. In addition, military and economic adversity combined with the absorption of large immigration served to suppress the problematic issues of identity, keeping them well away from public discourse.

The formal term for this ideology was *mamlakhtiyut* (statism). Its expressed purpose was to instill in all state institutions a disposition to uphold universal rules toward all citizens, banishing all special and particular interests and all attempts at segregation. In practice, translated into a government directive after 1948, this ideology covered a myriad of contradictory policies. Thus, the state extended recognition to the political division between the historical Labor movement and the Revisionist Right, to religious groups—both Zionist and non-Zionist ultra-Orthodox—and to Arabs. A similar recognition, however, was denied to ethnic divisions among Jews, both politically and culturally. Attempts by different Jewish ethnic groups to organize politically were considered a challenge to the state and to the principles of statism, and were quickly contained by co-optation.[8] In contrast, Orthodox Jews, religious-Zionist Jews, and Revisionist Jews formed their own parties without incurring ideological censure. On the cultural plane, Israel established a state education system *(mamlakhti)* which permitted special streams for two groups only, the ultra-Orthodox non-Zionists and the Orthodox Zionists. The ultra-Orthodox non-Zionists established their independent system, while the Orthodox Zionists were allocated a stream within the state education system. Likewise, in its early years Israel saw a proliferation of newspapers, both privately owned and party affiliated. While there were numerous publications in various European languages, this was not an "ethnic press" that cultivated distinct collective identities for the diverse immigrant communities. Rather, mostly published by the dominant Labor Party, these papers disseminated statist ideology. While European languages were well represented, Oriental Jews did not have similar newspapers.[9]

Arab citizens were exempt from statist ideology. The melting pot was a Zionist project and hence entry into it was confined to Jews only. Unlike Oriental Jews, Arabs were denied even the hope of full membership in society. They were excluded from the collective identity. In effect, as Rabinowitz notes, the Israeli collective identity was constructed in opposition to the Arabs as the "other." Oriental Jews fared slightly better. Although part of the Israeli collective identity was constructed in opposition to the Oriental as the "other"—conceived as nonmodern, decadent, and irrational—Oriental Jews were offered, at least formally, the opportunity to abandon their "redundant" identity for a modern and enlightened Israeli one.

In short, statist ideology censured particular ethnic identities, frowning on both political and cultural expression of the different immigrant communities in Israel. It curbed public discourse, restraining political disagreement, and in particular delegitimized controversy surrounding the emerging national collective identity. Public discourse in Israel—whether in academia, in politics, or in the media—tended over the years to draw attention away from overlapping cleavages, ethnicity, and social justice. Instead we find that its agenda is taken over mostly by narrow political discussions, concentrating on personal rivalries and the division of spoils among partisan politicians. Those controlling public discourse today—although quite unlike the Founding Fathers—are on the whole still faithful disciples of the melting-pot and statist ideologies, and thus quick to denounce and explain away displays of particular collective identity and organization.

Cracks in the Melting Pot

Cracks in the melting pot and its corresponding statist ideology can be traced back to the first "National Unity" government of 1967, which legitimized the Herut Party as a government party, heralding the end of Mapai dominance.[10] Herut ran on the anti-establishment ticket, using the discrimination against Oriental Jews for electoral gain. It was, however, in complete agreement with the Labor party on the need to uphold the uniform Jewish identity and statist ideology and thus on the delegitimization of a separate collective identity for Oriental Jews.

Only after 1988, with the emergence of Shas in the general elections, were Oriental Jews openly recognized as a distinct and legitimate group in society and thus in the electorate.[11] Yet, we must emphasize that Shas, throughout its long years in government, did little or nothing toward the structural amelioration of the social and economic disadvantages of Oriental Jews in Israel. Shas is in many respects an establishment party; like Mapai in the past, it preserves Oriental Jews in the position of clients, replacing Mapai's patronage system with its own.[12] Shas' constituency has grown by leaps and bounds from one parliament to another because the party was determined to approach Oriental Jews in a rather novel way—to address their collective identity as Oriental Jews. In the rather tedious Israeli political life Shas is undoubtedly an intriguing phenomenon, bewildering most commentators by collapsing their well-rehearsed models. Shas has transformed public discourse irrevocably. After the extensive efforts expended at its suppression, the media, academia, and the political elite are now forced to grapple with ethnic heterogeneity and its consequences.

An additional impetus to the downfall of statist ideology and to the transformation of public discourse came with the mass immigration of Jews from the former Soviet Union in the late 1980s.[13] Israel encouraged the immigration of Russian Jews with the hope of both strengthening the Jewish majority and the secular, European element within it. Thus, in general, the European middle classes welcomed the Russian immigrants as a means of Westernizing Israel. They were expected to counterbalance the awakening of ethnic identity among Oriental Jews, the heightening demand for equal citizenship among Arabs, and the strengthened political leverage of Orthodox Jews. But the Russian immigration failed to fulfill these expectations. Ironically, rather than dampening the awakening of Oriental Jews, the quick organization of Russian immigrants as a distinct group worked to intensify the struggle of Oriental Jews. Secondly, the aim of increasing the Jewish majority was also frustrated. Russian immigrants, rather than bolstering the Jewish, European collective identity, challenged it with a strong conception of their own superiority over what they perceived as a primitive, Levantine culture.

Hence, for the first time in Israel, three markedly different groups—Russian immigrants, Oriental Jews, and Arabs—confront the hegemonic structure. Despite an underlying animosity among them, they share a common agenda: an insistence that their own collective identity and cultural heritage is at least as worthy as, or even "superior" to, what is propagated by the melting-pot and statist ideologies. More significantly, they all share in the demand to participate in the shaping of the collective identity of Israel. As both Bishara and Gavison and Abu-Ria show, Arab citizens, while defining themselves as Palestinians, are nevertheless more forceful than ever in their demand for full and equal citizenship in Israel. In other words, like Oriental and Russian Jews, they demand to preserve their own collective identity without relinquishing their right to be full members of society *as Arabs*. All three groups share in the belief that citizenship should not be conditioned upon the abandonment of their own particular identity, collective memory, and cultural heritage. This was evidenced in the 1999 elections when, in addition to the rise of Shas and the Russian parties, the Arabs, in a surprising but calculated move, decided to put forward their own candidate for prime minister.

Changing Public Discourse

Israeli society is reluctant to relinquish its belief in the Zionist project, the melting pot, and statist ideology. Many find consolation by explaining away the success of Shas. Firstly, some argue, Shas is but an additional ultra-Orthodox party, a new mantle for an old phenomenon, that is, non-Zionists who can be appeased by allocation of public moneys. Secondly, they insist that Shas' growing constituency does not represent any significant social processes, but is merely the unpleasant result of unsightly but insignificant factors, such as the spoils system and electoral corruption. This analysis, widespread among lay citizens as well as among professional commentators, resonates with the forlorn hope that ethnic divisions in Israel will eventually evaporate. It is often expressed in the passionate but naive call to restore "the ethnic demon" to its bottle.

This conception of reality is embedded in longing for a time when the Zionist project of constructing a uniform, homogeneous national identity for all Jews was able to contain the attempts of different immigrant groups to cultivate their own distinct collective identity. It is the frustrated cry of those who have long been favored by the hegemonic value system and are now perturbed by the prospect of Israel becoming something they can no longer regard as their private dominion. For now, all kinds of different groups demand to be heard in and by the political and cultural institutions that determine the shape and image of Israel.

Peres and Yuchtman-Yaar are correct in identifying this demand as a threat to the stable consensus. But, contrary to their belief, it is not necessarily a threat to democracy. Russian immigrants, Oriental Jews, and Arabs all challenge the state to uphold its commitment to democracy and equal civil rights. Their demands defy some of the most sacred elements of the hegemonic value system. Oriental Jews and the ultra-Orthodox criticize decisions of the Israeli High Court; Russian Jews campaign to control the Ministry of the Interior; and Arabs press to change the constitutional definition of Israel as the state of the Jewish people. Liberal democracy is ill-equipped to deal with the multiplicity of particular collective identities. The emergence of individualism in Israel, welcomed by Ezrahi, does not offer the remedy required by those groups that have long been excluded by the hegemonic culture. As both Gavison and Shamir argue in separate chapters (in Mautner, Sagi, and Shamir), the resort to the language of rights and the frequent reliance on the legal system alienate large segments of society and tend to devalue their particular cultural practices. A democratic Israel must be responsive to the needs and concerns of all its citizens and not only to those of the affluent, educated, and secular European Jews.

But the center is not yielding without a fight. In the 1999 election a vociferous journalist and TV personality succeeded in mobilizing the margins of the beleaguered center against the rising periphery, gaining six seats in Parliament.[14] In addition, Meretz, a usually moderate-liberal party with a largely middle- and upper-class constituency, launched a campaign against the inclusion of Shas in the coalition government.[15] Likud politicians persisted with their by now familiar campaign to draw attention away from their failure to alleviate the economic disadvantages of Oriental Jews, first, by focusing on the Israeli-Arab conflict, and, secondly, by emphasizing Labor's alleged contempt for Oriental Jews and reminding us of the "injustices of the past" perpetrated by Labor's precursor, Mapai. Labor, on the other hand, sensed that its campaign should address "social issues." Hoping to draw Oriental Jews away from the Likud, it promised a redistribution of resources in favor of the lower classes. However, the inclusion of Shlomo Ben-Ami in the government notwithstanding, it is doubtful whether Labor's commitment to social justice is any greater than that of the Likud. The gap between rich and poor in Israel has grown in the last twenty years, regardless of who was the ruling party.[16]

Epilogue—A Multicultural Society?

Israel at the close of the twentieth century appeared to be a fragmented society, a society that had lost its common ground. In "Reflections on Multiculturalism in Israel," Mautner, Sagi, and Shamir note that every Israeli—and not only Russians, Oriental Jews, and Arabs—seemed to belong to a different cultural, ethnic, or national group (in Mautner, Sagi, and Shamir, pp. 67–68). But, as always, appearances can be misleading; boundaries between different groups are not as rigid as they might seem. In effect, the life of the manifold groups in Israel is dominated by similar or even identical cultural contents. We might say, in short, that although groups might be well defined, their values, and the practices they observe tend to overlap. This should reassure those worrying that the awakening of particular collective identities signals a loss of national collective identity and even a breakdown of society.

But the ascent of particular collective identities, though indicating turbulence in the melting pot, does not necessarily herald the dawning of multiculturalism in Israel. Following Mautner, Sagi, and Shamir (pp. 75–76), we note that whereas multiculturalism implies a dialogue among groups that respect one another, in Israel the characteristic pattern is of mutual negation and devaluation. In recent years different groups have tended to conceive of their own identity as not only distinct but as opposed to that of the other groups. Indeed, in Israel today the devaluation of the beliefs and practices of other groups plays a key role in the construction of identity—a process which, according to Bishara, is now common in the Arab community as well. The devalued group is not selected at random; it is usually the one group that is perceived as dangerously and competitively close. Thus, rather than developing in dialogue with other relevant groups, groups tend to adopt patterns of separation and isolation. In the political arena, they often engage in a struggle for exclusive control over state, cultural, and economic institutions.

Israel is at a crossroad. The fact the various religious, ethnic and national groups share common values, myths, and practices gives us reason to believe that, under certain conditions, the creation of a multicultural consciousness and modus vivendi is possible. However, there is in Israel, as yet, neither the understanding nor the will necessary for such conditions to be satisfied. Indeed, history and political culture contrive to impel different groups on the road to "life-or-death" battles, or at least struggles for control over the central institutions of the state. A good example is the belligerent rhetoric surrounding the government coalition formation following the 1999 elections, where parties competed in launching the most virulent invalidations of other groups and parties. Parties sought not only to seize control over state resources but also, and even more vehemently, threatened to exclude other parties and thus other cultural and ethnic groups from access to regulatory and redistributive powers.

Israel's political culture does not in fact provide an alternative to this strategy. Emulating the statist doctrine of the Founding Fathers, each group is attempting to shape Israel's collective identity in its own image, rather than accepting the multiplicity of particular collective identities. Often proffered as a miracle cure, a "National Unity Government" is not really a multicultural alternative but part and parcel of statist practices. In effect, "National Unity" governments have always worked to reinforce the practice of invalidation and devaluation. The prospects of multiculturalism in Israel depend on the development of political and cultural mechanisms that enable groups to engage in struggle while renouncing the hope of dominating one another. Multiculturalism does not signal the end of disagreement about the future character of Israel's public space but should be seen, instead, as the ushering in of a different kind of public discourse, one in which more groups can participate than under the melting-pot and statist ideologies.

The intense display of emotion during the 1999 elections could be seen as the rearguard action by the followers of the Old Order. These could best be characterized by their adherence to statist ideology in fear of either the unknown or the prospect of losing their hegemonic structure. Their loud protest notwithstanding, the political system is now multipolar, consisting of groups of roughly the same size, reinforcing the significance of particular identities. Different people are beginning to play different tunes. Oriental Jews might become disillusioned with Shas but they are unlikely to relinquish their new confidence in their particular collective identity.[17] The struggle of Arabs in Israel for equal and full citizenship will suffer many more setbacks; but public discourse today no longer ignores their demand that Israel should be redefined as "the state of all its citizens." Combined with their growing electoral power, this has already borne some significant results. For the first time the Knesset Foreign Affairs and Security Committee has had several Arab members, one of them an outspoken member of a nationalist Arab party.[18] From the Zionist perspective, Israel at the turn of the millennium was certainly a strange and distant entity. But for many of its inhabitants, it was slowly becoming a less estranged one.

Postscript

Following the outbreak of the September 2000 "al-Aqsa Intifada," Israeli public space underwent yet another transformation. To the bewildered spectator it looked as if Israel had been taken over by mischievous ghosts from the past. The sounds of gunfire scared off the new social forces who had ventured into the public arena; questions of identity were banished beyond the pale. Public discourse regressed to its earlier narrow boundaries.[19] The former wrestling among various ethnic, national, and cultural groups was replaced by a vigilant consensus. Political discourse endorsed only those participants who associated themselves with the one legitimate collective identity, that is embattled Israel confronted yet again by the Arabs and—in the shadow of the summer 2001 United Nations conference on racism in Durban, South Africa—by the whole world.

The discussion over the various constituents of Israeli identity came to an abrupt end. However, this transformation affected the two national collectivities differently. The al-Aqsa Intifida exposed the fragility of multicultural discourse and in particular the half-hearted commitment of Jewish citizens to its principles. It silenced the demands of Oriental Jews, religious Jews, new immigrants from the former Soviet Union, and Palestinians to participate in the construction of Israeli collective identity. These Jewish collectivities seem to have adapted to the newly exhumed nationalistic agenda, retreating into the background and leaving the stage to the representatives of the "old" Israel and of their belligerent rhetoric. This option was not open to Palestinians citizens of Israel, cast in the role of the enemy by the new-old discourse. This newly exhumed agenda includes, among other things, the return to the myths and phraseology of the War of Independence. Thus, Palestinian citizens of Israel—for whom the 1948 war represents their *Nakba* (disaster)—find themselves at best as outcasts in their own country and at worst threatened with exile. The past has become the present and will probably persist into the near future.

Notes

1. For the more liberal-conservative contributions by academics to public discourse see, for example, Baruch Kimmerling, "Elections as a Battle over Collective Identity," in *The Elections in Israel—1996,* eds. Asher Arian and Michal Shamir (Jerusalem: Israel Democracy Institute, 1999), 57-83 (in Hebrew); Arian, *The Second Republic: Politics in Israel* (Chatham, NJ: Chatham House, 1998). For a different view, see, for instance, Ilan Pappé, "Zionism in Light of the Theories of Nationalism and Historical Methodology," in *Zionism: A Contemporary Controversy,* eds. Pinhas Ginossar and Avi Bareli (Sde Boker: Ben Gurion University of the Negev Press, 1996), 223-63 (in Hebrew); Uri Ram, "Elections '96: Images and Amulets," *Teoria u-Vikoret* 9 (1996): 199-207 (in Hebrew); Yoram Peled, "Strangers in Utopia: The Civic Status of Palestinians in Israel," *Teoria u-Vikoret* 3 (1993): 21–29 (in Hebrew).

2. See Sammy Smooha, "Minority Status in an Ethnic Democracy: The Status of the Arab Minority in Israel," *Ethnic and Racial Studies* 13:3 (1990): 389–413; Smooha, *Arabs and Jews in Israel,* 2 vols. (Boulder, CO:

Westview Press, 1992); Smooha, "Class, Ethnic and National Cleavages and Democracy in Israel," in *Israeli Society: Challenges and Perspectives,* ed. Uri Ram (Tel Aviv: Breirot Publishers, 1993), 172–202 (in Hebrew; an English version of this article was published in *Israeli Democracy under Stress,* eds. Larry Diamond and Ehud Sprinzak [Boulder CO: Lynne Rienner, 1993]); Yoav Peled, "Strangers in Utopia," in *Israeli Democracy under Stress,* 21–38.

3. Edward W. Said, *Orientalism* (New York: Pantheon, 1978); Said, *Culture and Imperialism* (New York: Vintage Books, 1993).

4. Yochanan Peres and Ephraim Yuchtman-Yaar contend that, in their own words, between Jewish identity and democratic regime there exists a tension bordering on contradiction (29).

5. See Ernest Gellner, *Nations and Nationalism* (Oxford: Basil Blackwell, 1983); Benedict Anderson, *Imagined Communities: Reflections on the Origin and Spread of Nationalism* (London: Verso, 1991); Maoz Azaryahu, *State Cults: Celebrating Independence and Commemorating the Fallen in Israel 1948-1956* (Sde Boker: Ben Gurion University of the Negev Press, 1995) (in Hebrew).

6. Ella Shohat, *Israeli Cinema: East/West and the Politics of Representation* (Austin: University of Texas Press, 1989).

7. See, for example, the reference to the primordial in Kimmerling, "Elections as a Battle over Collective Identity" 57–83.

8. For example, by the creation of satellite parties such as the Yemenite Party and the Sephardi Party in the First and Second Knessets.

9. Until the early 1970s, the state and, in effect, the historical Labor Party (Mapai), controlled the electronic media.

10. Asher Arian and Yonathan Shapiro, "The End of a Dominant Party System," in *The Elections in Israel 1977,* ed. Arian (Jerusalem: Jerusalem Academic Press, 1980), 23–38.

11. Signs of this transformation could be observed even earlier, with the success of Tami in 1981 and 1984, and of Shas in the municipal elections in Jerusalem in 1983.

12. In the periphery Shas has stepped in to fill the gaps left by a retreating and an inadequate welfare state. A poignant example is its success in establishing an alternative to the state school system and to the public day-care system, *Ma'yan Ha-Hinukh Ha-Torani.*

13. Unlike the recent immigrants from the former Soviet Union, the 1970s immigrants encountered a more forceful statist ideology, which dis-

couraged them from preserving a distinct collective identity. Indeed, some of leaders of the two newly formed Russian parties immigrated in the 1970s.

14. Yosef "Tommy" Lapid took over the moderate Shinui party before the elections under the slogan of "government without the ultra-Orthodox," in which category he included the European ultra-Orthodox non-Zionists and Shas.

15. Enlightened left-wing Israelis do not admit that they have prejudices against Oriental Jews. They justify their animosity toward Oriental Jews on political grounds, that is, they "blame" them for their allegedly crude nationalism, ethnocentrism, and hatred of Arabs. See Smooha, "Class, Ethnic and National Cleavages and Democracy in Israel," 172–202.

16. Zvi Zusman, "Poverty and Economic Gaps," *Economic Challenges for the Next Four Years* (Jerusalem: Israel Democracy Institute, 1996) (in Hebrew).

17. The school system established by Shas might lose its popularity among Oriental Jews and give way to an Oriental stream within the State schools, such as has been initiated by the Kedma schools in Tel Aviv and Jerusalem. See Tamar Barkay and G. Levy, "Kedma School," in *Fifty to Forty-Eight: Critical Moments in the History of the State of Israel* (Tel Aviv: Van Leer Jerusalem Institute and ha-Kibbutz ha-Meuhad, 1999), 433–40 (in Hebrew).

18. In the past, membership in this committee was restricted to Jews from Zionist parties only. This was achieved by adjusting the key for allocating seats in this committee in such a manner as always to exclude Arab parties. Up till now, Arab parties have not participated in any coalition and no Arab citizen has served as Cabinet minister.

19. Even the system of elections has moved toward the status quo ante. Direct election of the prime minister was repealed by the Knesset in 2001. The next election will be conducted under the more conventional parliamentary system.

9. Literature as a Response to Paradox: On Reading A. B. Yehoshua's *A Journey to the End of the Millennium*

Stephen Schecter,
Université du Québec à Montréal

This essay offers personal reflections on A. B. Yehoshua's A Journey to the End of the Millennium, *along with an assessment of the critical and interpretive attention that novel has attracted. The author discusses Yehoshua's fictional account of Ashkenazi-Sephardi encounters, ostensibly from a period over a thousand years ago, in terms of themes that illuminate contemporary Israeli dilemmas. The author also considers the historical and moral lessons to be learned from imaginative literature laden with paradox.*

Shamir, Ziva, and Aviva Doron, eds., *"A Journey to the End of the Millennium": Studies in A. B. Yehoshua's Novel,* Tel Aviv: ha-Kibbutz ha-Meuhad, 1999 (in Hebrew: *"Masot 'al Tom ha-Elef": Iyyunim be-Roman shel Alef Bet Yehoshua*).

Yehoshua, A. B., *Mas'a el Tom ha-Elef,* Tel Aviv: ha-Kibbutz ha-Meuhad, 1997 (translated from the Hebrew by Nicholas de Lange as *A Journey to the End of the Millennium,* New York: Doubleday, 1998).

In A. B. Yehoshua's novel, *A Journey to the End of the Millennium,* the principal protagonist's Ishmaelite partner is described at the end of the book as clinging "to his view that the whole of this great journey, on sea and by land, was totally unnecessary, for Jews by their very nature are incapable of achieving a final and decisive judgment" (p. 263). The judgment to which he refers is the one the hero of the novel, Ben Attar, sought in his contest with his nephew's wife. The contest hinges on the question of polygamy. Ben Attar, a North African Jew living in the tenth century, has a thriving commerce going, one end of which penetrates into the Atlas Mountains via his Ishmaelite partner; the other reaches the towns of Western Europe via the diligent efforts of his nephew, who left his native Tangier after his wife committed suicide. But when the nephew marries a woman from the lands of Ashkenaz, the partnership is placed under a ban by the nephew's new wife, who cannot stomach the fact that Ben Attar has two wives. Ben Attar hires a ship and sets out for Paris with his two wives and his Ishmaelite partner to prove to the woman that dual matrimony can and does work. On the way they pick up a rabbi from Seville, who was to argue Ben Attar's case before the Bet Din that was to judge the matter.

In a winery outside of Paris a court is set up and the verdict goes in Ben Attar's favor. When the nephew's wife then threatens to divorce him, they all agree to journey to Worms and submit to a second trial, there in the wife's hometown. This time the verdict goes against Ben Attar. On the journey back to Paris his second wife dies, enabling the partnership to be resumed. But even though Ben Attar seems to come to some kind of emotional insight with respect to his singular matrimonial status, he returns with a bitter sense of defeat and irreparable loss. As he tells this to the rabbi from Seville on the ship that is now on its journey home, the latter merely takes up his quill and starts to pen the first line to another poem. The line reads as follows: "*Is there a sea between us, that I should not turn aside to visit thee. . . .*" (p. 309). And on that note the book ends.

Such are the barest of the story's bones, but enough to give the reader of this essay some idea of its fantastical nature. When one has finished it, one is amazed and perplexed. I find myself nodding at the Ishmaelite's words, as would anyone who knows anything of the workings of a Jewish organization. What Jew ever listens to another Jew? What Jew is ever persuaded by another Jew of anything? What Jewish organization ever sticks to a decision when someone always has a better idea after the decision was taken? And yet, Jewish organizations thrive, a Jewish country exists, and was built from scratch out of the dream in a Viennese journalist's head who said that if you shall want it, it is not a dream, even though in another Yehoshua novel, *Mr. Mani*,[1] Herzl is described as a man who lives, especially with respect to the Land of Israel, in dreams, not in reality. So too a storyteller, and so too a reader, who sits in the *galut,* the Jewish "exile," and reads fantastical stories like *A Journey to the End of the Millennium* and then dares to offer some perspective on Israeli society gleaned through the prism of the story. Is it fair? Of course. "For the Jews," Yehoshua writes early on in this story, "even those who had never traveled far from their town, always knew something about Jews from other towns, just as they always knew something that the gentiles did not yet know themselves" (p. 53).

So what do I know? I know that this story, ostensibly about polygamy, is not about polygamy, nor even about love, except insofar as love is a story that always calls for interpretation. When I first read the story in Hebrew I rebelled against the verdict, and my reaction did not change after I reread it twice in English. And why should it, since the author himself places our allegiance on the side of Ben Attar and his entourage, and subverts whatever moral tale on love lies embedded in this story with his acute psychological observation? But if it is not a moral tale about love, perhaps it is a moral tale about cultural difference and how to live it. No one who has read the novel can fail to observe that the contest between Ben Attar and his niece by marriage is also a contest between South and North, between Sepharad and Ashkenaz, between those two branches of Jewry that have rivaled each other in different ways for two millennia and now take up the contest again within the frontiers of the reborn nation-state. If Yehoshua goes back a thousand years to take up this question, perhaps it is to show us that the current ethnic divide in Israel is not simply a matter of access to resources, but a question of learning to live with cultural difference and appreciate it. And this question is one that haunts not only Israel, but every country that buys into modernity, for the logic of modernity is global and inclusive. As modern society unfolds, more and more people are drawn into its activities, new dimensions of selfhood open up, and multiple identities clamor for expression and recognition.

It is interesting to see how this cultural divide is portrayed, for it reverses the dominance we associate with the hegemony that Ashkenazim have exercised over the Zionist project for most of this century. In *A Journey to the End of the Millennium* Sepharad is described as a land of gay and vibrant colors where the scent of double marriage clings to your clothes "like cinnamon" (p. 145) and where the desire of a second wife can be sprinkled upon a husband "like fragrant powdered garlic" (p. 21), while Ashkenaz is that land where dead Jewish scholars watched "over living scholars, who in their turn were preparing the world for future generations of scholars still unborn" (p. 75). And it is a representative of Sepharad, the rabbi from Seville, who puts forward the argument in favor not of uniformity, but of pluralism. In his concluding plea on Ben Attar's behalf at the Beth-Din set up outside Paris, he musters these words that echo in a thousand years' retrospect:

> *We have not crossed the mighty ocean to enrage your spirit, nor have we any thought of urging you to double or multiply your wives. If we have judged aright by appearances, the land in which you dwell is bleak, with such small houses and such meager produce, and the Christians who surround you inflict fear upon you beyond your control, so it is small wonder that you lack the power that flowers in a thousand roses in the southern lands basking in the light of the wise sun. But just as we refrain from judging you from our strength, so you too have no right to judge us from your weakness. Therefore, let each remain true to himself and faithful to his own nature; restore the old partnership and do not damage it further.* (p. 136–37)

Is Pluralism Enough?

Is pluralism enough to solve our contemporary ills, in Israel or elsewhere? Probably not, but then it is not literature's task to resolve social problems. At best, it will only register them, sometimes obliquely, sometimes directly, and if successful, thereby thematize what seems to be on people's minds. To judge by the essays in the collection edited by Ziva Shamir and Aviva Doron, *A Journey to the End of the Millennium: Studies in A. B. Yehushva's Novel,* the issue of pluralism is very much on Israelis' minds, but how that is to be achieved, and how it will sit with the desire for unity, is not all that clear. Not for the critics, not for Israelis, not for humanity itself, this dilemma being a fairly new one, foisted on us by the latest twist in the evolution of modern society. But perhaps it is also an age-old dilemma, for it seems to haunt the characters in Yehoshua's story, who did not have any greater success at squaring this circle than we do. Still, as many of the critics in the compendium of essays pointed out, looking at the problem from the vantage point of literary characters set in a period a thousand years ago might give us some inkling of how to approach this problem in our times. At least, exploring it in a literary context gives us the breathing space to examine its many facets and so to think about it free of the compulsion to act. But as with any journey, what we find at the end of our exploration might very well surprise us.

Let me therefore take up my dialogue with this book once again, this time from the vantage point of its critics. Inevitably I shall go over some of the themes I have already raised, but in a book whose major theme is duplication, such an exercise is only to be welcomed with the irony that is its due.

The first task, as I already mentioned, is deciding what this book is about and what, if anything, it has to teach us, in the widest sense of that word, about the issues it raises. And deciding what this book is about requires understanding something about its characters. But how to decide? Adi Tzemach, for one ("Yehoshua between North and South"), argues that Ben Attar is far from the philosopher of love the Andalusian rabbi portrays him as. Nor, Tzemach argues, is he much of a lover. Yehoshua, he suggests, deliberately sets out to deflate the myth of the warmhearted passionate southerner, and this because, appearances to the contrary, the basic thesis of this book is an argument in favor of monogamy. But another critic, Avraham Balaban ("Between One Lack and Another"), argues just the opposite. There is no irony in the author's voice, the writer is one with his hero, and everything in the novel, from the ship's sails to the two synagogues in Worms, evokes the joy and serenity of double marriage. Esther-Minna, the woman from the north, is seen from Ben Attar's perspective, doubly suspect as one who would disturb the harmony of his Jewish home, possibly because she herself, blond-haired and blue-eyed, is, it is hinted, of Viking lineage.

The debate is equally fierce about the character of Esther-Minna. As the only woman with a name and a voice, she is taken by many to be the emblem of individuality, although others (Eli Yassif, "*A Journey to the End of the Millennium*—In Those Days, In Our Times"; and Yossef Tuvi, "The Problem of Time in the Guise of a Historical Novel") have stressed her rigidity, her sexual abstinence, her jealousy and shame, and her fear of the unknown, all symbolized in the repudiation of the partnership that she decreed to her husband.

These critics, and others, have then gone on to point out that in some ways it doesn't matter, the point of the whole novel being to shatter the stereotypes about Ashkenazim and Sephardim (Avidav Lipseker, "The Artist in his Studio"; Nissim Calderon, "Two Tongues"; and Yedidia Yitzhaki, "Unity Within Multiplicity"). If the Sephardim's emotional makeup overflows with bounty, the Ashkenazim burn with intensity (Calderon); and yet the southerners' generosity does not extend to the nephew Abulafia's deformed daughter, while the northerners' intensity turns to scrupulous obedience to the law, even if it should result in the sundering of family ties and, ultimately, the death of one of its members (Dalia Ophir, "The Sea Between You and Me—Between East and West in *A Journey to the End of the Millennium,*" and Shulamit Almog, "The Failure of the Judgment as the Downfall of the Journey"). What, then, is the point of shattering these stereotypes?

This is a question Gilead Morahg raises ("It Is Not an Israeli Story—*A Journey to the End of the Millennium*") and answers by claiming that the historical anachronisms so many others have alluded to only go to show that there is little in this book of relevance for the analysis of Sephardi-Ashkenazi relations in contemporary Israel.[2] Rather, he argues, this book is an allegory about the dilemma of national unity as it confronts the entire Jewish people in the world today. Others, on the other hand, have argued the opposite: that in breaking down the stereotypes, the author encourages the reader to think anew about the other in his or her midst, Sephardim for Ashkenazim, Arabs for Israelis, and vice versa. Some, like Ziva Shamir ("From Repudiation to Compromise: A Different Reading of *A Journey to the End of the Millenium*"), even argue there is a political lesson to be learned here, namely, that those who brick themselves up behind their own cultural heritage rather than open themselves up to the encounter with others, however opposed and threatening the others' way of life, are doomed to historical disaster. One must, in short, risk, for the sake of peace and for the sake of life.

It is certainly testimony to the author's literary talent and to the novel's rich texture that this book can yield so many different, sometimes even opposed, readings, and on nearly every level. Each reading bears scrutiny, for each reveals something even as its argument breaks down, given the novel's own parameters or what we know from history. Let us consider, for a moment, the argument that one of the novel's main themes is the problem of the unity of the Jewish people, not in the year 1000 but in the year 2000. Let us also consider that this problem extends beyond the border of Israel itself, to include not only relationships between Ashkenazim and Sephardim, or religious and secular Jews, within Israel, but also those between Israel and the Diaspora, subsumed by the contemporary debate: who is a Jew?

In his essay Morahg suggests that Ben Attar's real motivation for embarking on his voyage, as incomprehensible to his communal contemporaries as it is to us, has to be seen in his irresistible attraction to Esther-Minna, an attraction that is metaphoric for the longing of Sephardic Jewry to reunite with its sundered, Ashkenazi half. One is tempted to add that this longing is the age-old longing of the Jewish people for reunification and return, expressed in the Zionist project and concretized in the establishment of the State of Israel. Yet hardly is this millennial dream realized than the unity starts to explode all over again. Debate ravages Israeli society about how to deal with its Arab enemies, and this debate is conflated with how to deal with its own two major communities. To which is added the divide in contemporary Israel between religious and secular conceptions of the Jewish State, a divide that extends not only to the thorny issue of territorial concessions to the Palestinians, but also to religious and civic pluralism within Israel, and between Israel and the Diaspora. This issue is further complicated by the hard to ignore fact that after two thousand years of longing to return, many Israelis now decide to emigrate, adding to the mix of the Jewish Diaspora.

When they emigrate, moreover, they do so to countries where the separation between church and state is a de facto, if not always de jure, reality, and where modern pluralism exerts its pull, leading more and more Jews to define themselves in nonreligious terms. How, then, shall a dialogue between all these separate elements of international Jewry go on? How shall unity be achieved? Is it possible? That these questions are not merely academic can be seen in the concrete decisions taken by various actors that constitute answers to these questions. Settlements in the occupied territories are clung to with tenacity. Conversions performed by Reform and Conservative rabbis are not recognized. In Jerusalem, the buses do not run on Shabbat. In the Diaspora intermarriage between Jews and Gentiles is on the rise. Is there a future to the Jewish people, let alone a unity? And is it not ironic that this question gets posed once the return to Zion becomes a fait accompli?

In his reading of Yehoshua's novel, Morahg suggests that there are three possible bases for uniting the Jewish people. One is the Hebrew language, for in the encounter between North and South in this novel, were it not for the Hebrew language communication would have been well-nigh impossible. As matters stood, few were the protagonists who mastered the tongue, but enough to enable translation and so permit the courts of law to be convened. Another is religion, for although the Ashkenazi and Sephardi rites differed, the joint celebration of festivals—the novel occurs around the Jewish New Year—gave the Jews a common framework of prayer within which the different traditions found a way to blend. The third such basis is the link between family and nation, which drove Ben Attar to such lengths to restore his partnership with his nephew. Yet, when the Andalusian rabbi Elbaz made this the basis of his plea, it fell on deaf ears. Indeed, Morahg points out that none of these three possible bases seemed to suffice then. And the reader is quick to conclude that they are no more likely to suffice now. In his search for what is missing, Morahg would fall back on a partnership between men and women within the family, but the ambiguous ending of the novel, not to mention the parlous state of relations between the sexes today, let alone the rising divorce rates in Israel as elsewhere, do not give too much room for hope.

It is hard to decide if Morahg concludes his essay with pessimism or qualified optimism. The oscillation between these two tonal poles is typical of all the essays in this book. In that respect, how one is tempted to deduce it reflects rather well the mood of contemporary Israeli society. But surely it also reflects the mood of anyone faced with the dilemmas of societal and personal unity in today's world. Not for nothing do many commentators (Calderon, and Yitzhaki quite explicitly) remark on the grotesque dimension in Yehoshua's novel, as though by making it clear to us that things could not possibly have been historically as they were presented, the author enforces upon the reader the stance of the critical observer who comes to recognize that his or her own world may very well be equally grotesque. Or perhaps, for those more inclined to be hopeful, to understand that for contemporary life to be more intelligently met than it was by the novel's protagonists, we shall have to learn to see differently all the time (Yassif, Tuvi, Ophir, Shamir, but also Amiya Lieblich, "On the Deed of Double Love: A Reading in the Psychology of Men and Women"; and Aviva Doron, "To the Earthen Flowerpots").

Literature and the Law

But is seeing differently enough? And may it not be the case that it is only in literature that we have the luxury of seeing thus? Let me approach this matter through one of the essays in this collection that takes on this issue directly. Shulamit Almog argues that although both sides sought a solution to their conflict in a court of law, a legal verdict was totally inappropriate to resolving their dilemmas. She makes this argument in part from a feminist perspective, but the implications of her argument go beyond that. The legal domain, she claims, is a masculine one. It is not open to arguments grounded in emotional realities. Esther-Minna, portrayed as the representative of the female voice in the novel, errs in grounding her challenge to bigamy in a rabbinic edict. Upheld, the edict leads to the death of the second wife, the one who dared to demand the right to dual matrimony for women as well. Not only did the judgment kill two people, the second wife and the judge himself, Almog argues, it also did nothing to foster dialogue. The southerners leave with anger in their hearts, while the northerners learned nothing about their southern cousins. The judge who pronounced the ban did so, Almog points out, out of panic at his own desire that the second wife's claim elicited. The words the author puts into the judge's mind to justify his prohibition are: "*Duplication inevitably leads to multiplication, and multiplication has no limits*" (p. 211).

Others have disputed this take, arguing that, if nothing else, northerners and southerners each learned something about themselves (Dorit Hof, "From a Divisive Brightness to a Secret that Combines—A Reading of *A Journey to the End of the Millennium*"). In a way, both are right. Opening yourself to the other is indeed a painful process, in love and in politics. To do so one has to leave home, abandon one's cultural and psychological moorings with no guarantee that the enterprise will bring success or happiness.

Indeed, chances are it will bring disappointment, as it did to every character in this novel. What one has given up may well turn out to be not worth the voyage, and what one has gained may be bitter indeed, with no one that much the wiser. Except, perhaps, some critics suggest (Yassif, Doron, and Ephraim Rosen, "Sephardic Poetry and Culture in the Work of A. B. Yehoshua in the wake of *A Journey to the End of the Millennium*"), for the artist, and for those who accept a literary verdict instead of a legal one.

Almog herself points out that Elbaz's initial victory in the winery at Villa Le Juif was more a tribute to his poetic skills than to his rabbinic lore. Shamir considers the whole episode a parody of populist politics in Israel, but Doron remarks that the Andalusian rabbi was the most open character in the novel, the one who could listen to people's feelings beyond their declaration of principles, and thereby managed to speak to what the whole community wanted, even if they couldn't articulate it: a resumption of the partnership as symbolic of the unity of the Jewish people. Perhaps, then, we ought to pause a minute and consider that an aesthetic verdict, won by charm and humor, has something to recommend itself with respect to the dilemmas we have touched on.

The Unity of Paradox

In the late modern world, the pluralism that results from social differentiation has as its corollary the increasing insulation of each social sphere, characterized by the medium that circulates within it and the codes that govern that circulation. Rights circulate within the judicial system according to the code of legal/illegal, while art circulates within the realm of literature according to the code of pleasing/displeasing. Each can influence the other, but to do so the claims that emerge from one sphere have to translate themselves into the media and codes appropriate to the other one. How relevant, then, is literature to the world of action exemplified by the law? And how can its relevance make itself felt?

The answer, I would suggest, lies in the boundaries that separate the spheres. In the world of pragmatic action, judgments are made, decisions are taken that are irreversible and whose consequences are felt, bringing with them, often as not, undesired, and unanticipated, results. In the world of literature, no judgments are made, no actions are taken, and the decisions are reversible. If we don't like the story, we can rewrite it. One of the critics in the volume of essays (Israel Jacob Yuval, "The Silence of the Historian and the Imagination of the Writer: Rabbi Amnon from Mayence and Esther-Minna from Worms") did just that. But all the other interpretations to which this novel gave rise, including this essay, are also another form of rewriting the text. As we do so, we play with history. We dispute the meaning of characters, motives, situations, and reverse our own positions as we dialogue with other readers. Our allegiance goes now to the south, now to the north; to bigamy and to monogamy; to the rule of law and to the charms of song. We yearn for unity, but we embrace diversity. We consider openness a virtue, but we fear what we know only too well has already come about. We are moved by the southern melodies that entwine themselves into the northern prayers, but we cringe, when we don't smile, at the crabbed and dun tones of the north. We accept historical anachronisms even as we register them. In the novel we can hold all that together as paradox because in the novel we don't have to decide, don't have to take sides, can even shift them as we see events in a new light. And there perhaps lies not only its advantage, but also its benefit for the world of social action where decisions have to be taken and choices made.

Since we now know that life is full of the unintended consequences of our actions, perhaps it is worthwhile to linger somewhat in the world of literature where we have the luxury to think things through, to think about the complexity of what confronts us before rushing headlong into action. The author wondered in the prologue to his book whether it is possible to write history, to enter into the world of people who lived so long ago and so differently from us. But, as a few critics (Yassif and Yitzhaki) mentioned, it is precisely because those people's issues are ours, because their emotional life taps into our fears and desires, that the reading of their story is helpful to our own. Not that it tells us what to do about the issues that confront us. Rather, this story, this voyage to the end of that millennium, shows us that things are indeed complex and that we, no less than that story's protagonists, have an entire skein of motivations propelling us to act to which we are blind. In a world that allows more and more of us to act out these unconscious motivations, perhaps it behooves us to think again and again before we act.

If both Ben Attar and Esther-Minna sought a judgment from the wellsprings of their unconscious, and if the judgment they sought brought unintended sorrow to them and their entourage, why should we think that we are any different with respect to the judgments we seek in order to settle the disputes that divide us? And how shall we enter the murky world of our unconscious unless we step outside ourselves? And how shall we step outside ourselves and enter into the world of the other, unless we brave our inner world? Of course, one could say that we need not worry. The postmodern world is so busy that events will come knocking at our door and we will be forced to start up. But that is precisely the dilemma. On the terrain of late modernity, the knock at our door always comes too early and quickly, clamoring for a decision. This cautionary tale would have us wait a minute, have us take a slightly longer view, one informed by reflection—historical, psychoanalytical, and literary—one that remembers that passions are dangerous and that decisions always carry with them unanticipated, and potentially lethal, consequences. We might, so I am suggesting, allow ourselves the luxury of living our lives as a story, especially now that postmodern life has not only made that possible, but even necessary.

This is all the more necessary in a world where the choices no longer present themselves in an either-or framework. If none of the bases for the possible unity of the Jewish people that Morahg drew from his reading of this novel seems possible, that is because the postmodern world has changed the way in which we have to confront this issue. In the novel, the different religious rites of the south and the north were not insurmountable barriers because members of both communities shared a common religious belief. In our times, however, religion is no longer the shared basis for Jewish identity, not in Israel and not in the Diaspora. It is part of our cultural heritage, but without pertinent moral orientation for much of world Jewry. Rabbi Elbaz could invoke rabbinic authority to transform the land into sea in order to permit Ben Attar to voyage on Succoth and to bring his second wife's corpse to Paris as quickly as possible. But many today would not seek rabbinic dispensation for a comparable action. The continuous modernization of religion works only as long as tradition governs social behavior. Once modernity gets to work, the unity of the world, or at least the perceived unity of the world, is torn asunder. Today we live with the consequences. And yet most Jews still feel Jewish in some way or another.

It used to be thought that Zionism would replace religion. Certainly this was the ideology that infused those of the Jewish Enlightenment who sought to reconstruct a viable Jewish identity within the framework of a modern, Jewish nation-state. But today the Zionist project is called into question by the very society Zionism brought into being. The success of modernity in Israel has brought to the fore all the issues that confront the citizens of modernity everywhere else. What does it mean to be Jewish if more than half of world Jewry refuses to make aliyah? Is Jewish identity, like all identity, something that is constructed, pragmatically, out of the remnants of history, something that is there after all the illusions are shattered, and captured only in literature, symbolized in this novel by the line of verse with which it ends: *"Is there a sea between us, that I should not turn aside to visit thee? . . ."* (p. 309). Perhaps one of the paradoxes of Zionism itself is that as the society it brought into being causes its ideological unity to unravel, the unity that is nonetheless felt, whose metaphoric equivalent in this novel finds expression in the resumption of the fragile partnership (Yitzhaki), can best, and only, be grasped in literature. And how ironic, but also how wonderful, that the renaissance of Hebrew literature to which Zionism also gave rise should turn out to be its most enduring achievement!

No reader can ignore in Yehoshua's book the smoldering menace of Christian Europe with its Crusades to come. The supreme irony of this novel is that although Ashkenazi Jewry won, both in this story and in history, and won by allying itself with its Christian neighbors who were destined to produce modernity itself, that alliance in the end proved fatal. In the novel there is the figure of an apostate physician, who had converted from Judaism to Christianity in order to save his children from the messianic fervor he knew would come. Prophetically, he tells the rabbi from Seville that the North African entourage shall be saved, but not the Jews from Metz. And we know, of course, that a thousand years later even apostasy would not save Jewish children from the death camps.

Drawing Lessons from Literature

Yet because literature allows us that breathing space to confront it, we can select from history that which we think most relevant to our times. Shamir, who in the collection of essays argues on behalf of European modernity, rides roughshod over its darker side; but perhaps she has to do so because she is interested in deducing from Yehoshua's novel some prescriptions for action. The irony of her stance is that she chooses to emphasize not the lethal consequences of the choice that Ashkenazi Jewry made, but the life-enhancing ones. She too, in fact, effects a historical reversal, but one that is evoked by the novel itself, and so uses the paradox of literature to reflect on the choice that confronts her society in the here and now. The Rhineland from which Esther-Minna came and to which she returned for the second trial does not conjure up for Shamir the pogroms of the eleventh century, but the flowering of Jewish learning associated with Rabbi Gershom and Rashi. Nor on a world historical scale does she choose to emphasize the clash between French and German culture, but rather the meeting of Western Europe on the lands of Alsace-Lorraine. Indeed, Worms reminds Shamir of the "eternal peace" decreed by the emperor Maximilian I, even though she is quite aware of the irony of the epithet "eternal." For what she chooses to underline is that the peace decreed did last for a limited time, enough to allow a certain number of generations to flourish. And therein, she suggests, lies the lesson of history embedded in this novel for us.

In a world where we know our decisions produce irreversible and unforeseen consequences, perhaps the best we can do is try and make the most intelligent decisions for the short run we can hope to foresee. In the context of contemporary Israel, the lesson concerns the question of peace. Not an eternal peace, nor one that will immediately eradicate the accumulated hurts and wrongs of generations, but a peace that will enable Israel and her neighbors to get on with the business of life and so escape from their current nightmare of history. But to do so, one has to overcome the natural tendency to repudiation that surfaces in our encounter with the other. Such is the way to read the novel, Shamir suggests. It is a historically selective reading, even a metahistorical one, but it certainly is credible, within the context of the novel and within the context of contemporary Israel.

In this welter of paradox, the novel then lends itself to multiple and opposing interpretations, such that those who argue it is an allegory about our times are no more right or wrong than those who claim it is a novel about the past because it is a novel about the future (Calderon), the future being the possibility that lies like an embryo in the present. Hence the symbolic importance of the children, and especially the rabbi's son, in this novel (Nitza Ben-Dov, "For This Boy Have I Prayed"). The child embodies the possibility of a future for the Jewish people, but the child is like contemporary Israel, unmoored from tradition though not totally; a link to the others, Jews and Ishmaelites, with whom his parents must live, yet whose survival is an open question. For the sins of the fathers, going all the way back to Abraham, who, like Ben Attar, set out on a voyage (Yitzhaki) with a form of noble fanaticism in his heart, weigh heavily on our people, as they do on all people.

Sadness inhabits all the characters at the novel's end and extends even to the reader, leaving no one unscathed by the voyage that has been undertaken. Everyone has come to understand that life exacts its price, and the price is death. Unity is needed, but can only be approximated. One must dream to be alive, but one must also bury one's dreams or our unleashed passions go on a rampage. We see what Sigmund Freud already told us: everything leaves traces and we keep on pursuing the lack that drives us to more (Balaban). And so we are left with the question that forms the title of Yair Mazor's article: "With What Shall His Heart's Love Be Extinguished? And How Shall His Shattered Hope Be Lamented?".

To which, it would seem, we can only offer the solace of literature. And not any kind of literature now, but a postmodern literature, adequate to the task of rendering the human condition on the social terrain where it now presents itself. A book such as *A Journey to the End of the Millennium,* which, for all its fantastical playing with history and characters, for all its grotesque reversals and the others it permits, for all its grim and bitter truths, is, as many critics have observed, a highly lyrical and comical novel. This is so, I would suggest, because there is no other way to deal with the postmodern condition. Tragedy does not seem to be the appropriate mode for people who have seen through everything. Comedy, on the other hand, does, for it reconciles us to paradox, to impossible truths, to a world in which a change in perspective teaches us only another way of seeing things, bereft of the illusion of overcoming.

The novel ends with the line of verse taken from a poem by Shmuel Hanagid: "*Is there a sea between us, that I should not turn aside to visit thee. . . ?*" (p. 309). The poem was composed, in reality, forty-one years after the events that occurred in the book. For Rosen, this little fact is an eloquent reminder of the redeeming power of literature, if not of its role as a cultural source of unity. For Ophir, the line itself is pregnant with a double entendre: on the one hand, it represents a definite break between Sephardi and Ashkenazi Jewry; on the other hand it holds out the promise of a resumption of the partnership. But preferably, she suggests, both. Again a paradox. To which I would add another, since every good book always calls forth another, especially in a book whose theme is duplication. Consider this: the words with which *A Journey to the End of the Millennium* ends are the very words Ben Attar could have uttered before setting sail himself. Like another fantastical, late modern novel, *Finnegan's Wake,*[3] the end is also the beginning. But only in literature or art can the end also be the beginning and still make sense of sorts.

Notes

1. A. B. Yehoshua, *Mr. Mani* (New York: Doubleday, 1992).

2. For an English version of this essay see Gilead Morahg, "Testing Tolerance: Cultural Diversity and National Unity in A. B. Yehoshua's *A Journey to the End of the Millennium,*" *Prooftexts* 19:3 (1999): 235–56.

3. James Joyce, *Finnegan's Wake* (New York: Viking, 1958).

Part 5

Peace Process

10. Anthologizing the Peace Process

Mira Sucharov,
Carleton University, Ottawa

This essay considers the state of scholarship about the Arab-Israeli and specifically Palestinian-Israeli conflicts as revealed in three recent anthologies whose many contributors examine both conflicts from many angles. The author concludes that many social science treatments of the Israel-Arab-Palestinian triad lack methodological rigor and theoretical coherence. She also argues that although most analyses look to external elements to explain why conditions in the 1990s favored a continuation of the peace process, domestic determinants within Israeli society are equally important. Finally, she attributes Israel's 1993 decision to reach a peace settlement with the Palestinians to a cultural identity shift within Israeli society, including the wide dissemination of revisionist views of Israeli history, the changing role of the Israeli soldier, and reconsidered narratives about the role of the state in the region. The author suggests an integrative approach, combining external and internal factors, in understanding the development of a state's political culture and its capacity to make peace. The breakdown of the Oslo process and the escalation of Palestinian-Israeli violence after September 2000 make the question and the requirements of the protagonists' readiness to make peace all the more important.

Freedman, Robert O., ed., *The Middle East and the Peace Process: The Impact of the Oslo Accords,* Gainesville: University Press of Florida, 1998.

Peleg, Ilan, ed., *The Middle East Peace Process: Interdisciplinary Perspectives,* Albany: State University of New York Press, 1998.

Sela, Avraham, and Moshe Ma'oz, eds., *The PLO and Israel: From Armed Conflict to Political Solution, 1964–1994,* New York: St. Martin's, 1997.

The Arab-Israeli peace process has spawned a virtual industry of peace-watching, the fruits of which range from polemic to journalistic to academic. And while the recent crisis in the region has cast the future of the process into doubt, the policy shift undertaken by Israel and its neighbors in the early-to-mid-1990s remains a significant phenomenon worthy of study. Despite the cycle of violence that was unleashed in September 2000, Israel and the Palestine Liberation Organization (PLO) have indeed shifted their basic policy from total belligerence and mutual nonrecognition to attempts—however flawed or imperfect—at reconciliation. The outbreaks known as the "Al-Aqsa Intifada" have served as an example of a peace process that has become derailed; yet, understanding its origins can help us better appreciate the conditions that will have to be met in order for the parties to resume their aborted efforts at resolving their long-standing conflict.

This essay examines three anthologies on the peace process, with a special focus on the Israeli-Palestinian domain. The chapters focus on the causes of the process and the regional and domestic effects of whatever agreements have been—or have yet-to-be—reached. The essay is organized around three questions. First, what is the state of theoretically informed research on the Arab-Israeli and Palestinian-Israeli conflict? Second, in the long-standing debate between "domestic" and "external" determinants of foreign policy, to which side does the evidence in the Israeli-Palestinian case point? Finally, what are the dominant trends, if any, within Israeli society that in the 1990s enabled a shift toward peace with its closest neighbor, the Palestinians?

On the question of theory and data, I argue that the state of social science treatments within Middle East studies could be better served by more attention being paid to theory. With notable exceptions,[1] many of the authors in this field neglect the rich theoretical tradition in their respective disciplines that can help to situate the case within a broader empirical context. Some of the chapters I will address do, in fact, succeed in this task. However, many others do not; and even the ones that do so could be more explicit and sophisticated in their theoretical pursuits.

On the second and third questions, I note that, while most of the chapters point to external factors as representing background conditions favoring the peace process, the primary determinants lay within Israeli society itself. I build on this explanation in two ways. First, I suggest that our thinking about unit-level determinants be expanded to include a more regionally contextual view of international relations. Thus, rather than cast domestic determinants as the conceptual opposite of "international" factors, I suggest that we understand a state's political culture as being developed within the context of interstate interaction, rather than being insulated from it. Second, I expand on the domestic-level explanation to elaborate on the cultural shift identified by some of authors within these volumes. A number of the chapters posit that an Israeli identity shift—evidenced by evolving views of history, the changing role of the Israeli soldier, and reconsidered narratives about the role of the state in the region—is what facilitated Oslo. I elaborate upon this claim through a streamlining of the idea of national narratives. To conclude, I suggest potential avenues for further research in the Arab-Israeli domain, and summarize the potential theoretical directions that our robust body of empirical research might take.

The Peace Process and Social Science

While so much of social science is wracked by methodological disputes, a common theme underlying the social scientific enterprise is to attempt to understand social phenomena through the tools of theoretical analysis (positivist or otherwise). As the Arab-Israeli peace process represents one such social phenomenon, this section attempts to highlight instances where theory has been used productively in the books under review, as well as to identify areas where more generalizable analysis is possible.[2]

The first book under discussion is Ilan Peleg's *Middle East Peace Process: Interdisciplinary Perspectives.* Laura Zittrain Eisenberg and Neil Caplan's piece provides an explanatory framework through which they forecast the likelihood of whether the Oslo process will ultimately succeed, but the framework does not appear to rest on any larger theoretical principles. Neither is it particularly parsimonious, resting as it does on no less than eight factors.[3] However, this type of scholarly pursuit is consistent with the aims of much of history as a discipline, historians' explanations often being derived inductively from intensive case research. Indeed, the authors make explicit that their project rests on comparing "the current Israeli-Palestinian peace process with the traditional patterns of unsuccessful Arab-Israeli diplomacy" (p. 7). Nevertheless, it would be useful to know whether their framework (derived from a 1978 article by Caplan) is inductively derived from regional particularities, or deductively from conflict resolution in general.

Mordechai Bar-On's chapter (in Peleg) engages the question of whether the "new historians" in Israel (those who seek to reinterpret the conventional wisdom in Israeli history) have succeeded in their task of "reeducating" the Israeli public. This question has wider political relevance, for, as Bar-On shows, the debate over historiography in Israel transcends scholarly circles, even making "media headlines" (p. 22). While presenting a useful overview of the new historiography in Israel, Bar-On does not ultimately answer the question that he poses; How successful have the historians been?

Bar-On's chapter would also benefit from a discussion of the broader issue of historiography and identity that he alludes to. Here, it would be fruitful to probe the disciplinary objectives of the new historiography. Does the discipline of history exist solely to uncover the "truth," or does it function to understand how citizens of a particular polity understand their past?[4] Engaging this question would help to situate history within the broader context of the humanities versus social sciences, and therefore would augment the "interdisciplinary" aims of the volume. While most social scientists are probably more concerned with how history is conceptualized at a particular point in time, or else over time[5] (in order to understand its effects on subsequent social phenomena), historians themselves may have other aims. Indeed, Bar-On cites one of the preeminent Israeli "revisionist" historians, Benny Morris, as claiming that the historian's task is simply "to try to reach the historical 'truth'" (in this case, rather than serving any political function) (p. 23). Here, it would be useful to glean Bar-On's take on this question, with the accompanying research to substantiate it. Moreover, it would be useful to further explore the relationship between politics (as

Morris seems to use the term) and "identity." Specifically, although Morris claims that he does not undertake his historical projects in order to bolster any particular ideological group in the country, how would he (and other revisionist historians) view the relationship between his work and the identity of the state in question?

A related issue is the question of what new historical research brings to those who seek to measure identity: an oft-pursued, yet elusive, task of an increasingly large pool of social scientists, as well as of Israel Studies scholars. Specifically, should national identity be determined from the "actual" historical record of the people under study, or via the collective memory of that people? Again, it seems that the latter view would be more amenable to social scientific research, as it is difficult to measure identity if the subjects in question are not aware of a particular historical event, or else understand its meaning differently from that put forward by a new historical interpretation. Here, what has become consistently important to identity-oriented scholars is the idea that material reality is "socially constructed,"[6] that material "facts" or "events" are only important insofar as they are collectively understood by the actors. It would be useful to determine whether Bar-On subscribes to this "constructivist" view of social phenomenon, and if so, what the relevance of new historiography is to the polity under study.

Myron Aronoff and Pierre Atlas's essay (in Peleg) fruitfully employs a social-psychological framework to analyze the question of what will emerge as the dominant Zionist discourse. Their case study, however, could benefit from an attempt at generalization, especially given the problem in Israel Studies between considering Israel to be a case worthy of comparison, or one that is sui generis. For instance, the fault line that the authors identify within Israeli collective consciousness (that of "Jewishness" versus "Israeliness") could be situated more broadly, perhaps using concepts such as "ethnicity" versus "civic identity." Even here, however, the idea of ethnicity is problematic, as Israel comprises Jews of multiple ethnicities (namely, Sephardim and Ashkenazim). Given the fact that Israel was founded as a Jewish State, it may be that attempts to examine the collective consciousness of this particular state is limited by the uneasy relationship between the two (or more) forms of identity. On closer consideration, however, it seems that many other states experience similar dilemmas between "civic" and "ethnic" identity, and thus it could help our ability to analyze identity by attempting a more widely situated explanation.

Stuart Cohen's article on societal-military relations (in Peleg) traces a detailed narrative between the relationship between the peace process and the role of the Israel Defense Forces (IDF) in society. Cohen points to an interesting (if potentially circular) cause-effect phenomenon relating to the effect that a changing view of the IDF has wrought on the peace process, and the ability of the latter to further entrench that change. In so doing, he highlights a crucial link between national security decisions and state identity, but it is circular in that he notes that changes in societal-military relations were "apparent long before" the Oslo process began, yet a successful peace process will likely "accelerate the trends." While it is certainly the author's prerogative to note this multilayered dynamic, it might be useful to attempt to focus on how much of the peace process of the 1990s was caused by this changing relationship. Moreover, given that Cohen's thesis is that the peace process engendered tensions between the government and the IDF, it is curious to note Mark Rosenblum's partially competing claim that governmental relations with the army significantly worsened under Prime Minister Benjamin Netanyahu (in Robert O. Freedman, *Middle East and the Peace Process: The Impact of the Oslo Accords*). This calls into question the causal relationship between the advancement of the peace process and governmental-military relations.

Peleg's epilogue to his edited volume also deals with issues of political culture in Israel and specifically for the prospects for a *kulturkampf* to ensue between advocates of "universalism" and "particularism" in the country. While explicitly grounded in theories of political culture, Peleg's essay suffers from a lack of focus in its guiding claims. Peleg takes pains to state his central "hypothesis" no less than three times within the first part of his essay, but in each iteration he presents a slightly different version. Ultimately, he presents a radical claim: that violence is likely between two political cultures uneasily coexisting within Israel, a divide encapsulated by Yitzhak Rabin's 1995 assassination by a disgruntled religious nationalist (p. 238).

While provocative and fruitful in its attempt to forecast wide-reaching changes to be wrought in the event of a successful peace process, some of Peleg's predictions seem misguided given what we know about both theory and data in the Israeli case. Specifically, Peleg suggests that the conclusion of peace could lead to the creation of a verse in *Hatikvah* (The Hope, Israel's national anthem) "celebrating Jerusalem's sanctity as [a] symbol of universal peace" (p.

260). Yet given the highly charged atmosphere surrounding the negotiation of symbols in the Middle East,[7] it is unlikely that Israel would agree to recast Jerusalem into such a universal light. Moreover, the claim raises problematic though important questions surrounding the issue of (political) culture and its malleability. If culture is considered to be the repository of national or ethnic symbols, then it follows that a given culture will be hesitant to redefine these same symbolic places or events. Finally, there remains the problem of whether the "peace process" is so ideationally revolutionary as to advance a radical shift in a polity's culture. The snail's pace of the implementation phase of Oslo followed by violent unrest and the apparent unraveling of the process since 2000 suggest otherwise.

Another identity-related question is that of the role of force in shaping national identity. Tracing the use and achievements of the "armed struggle" by the PLO over the last three decades, Yezid Sayigh (in Avraham Sela and Moshe Ma'oz, *PLO and Israel: From Armed Conflict to Political Solution, 1964–1994*) argues that the use of force was instrumental to Palestinian nation-building, and, subsequently, to state-building under the Palestinian Authority. Sayigh alludes to the importance of other anticolonialist and revolutionary struggles in shaping national consciousness—such as in Algeria and Cuba (p. 26), and as such provides a broader context in which to generalize his claims. However, he could go further in grounding his thesis in the wider literature on identity construction.

Mark Rosenblum's essay on the prospects for peace under Netanyahu (in Freedman) brings to light the fleeting nature of incumbent governments. The rapid changing of the guard between Labor- and Likud-led governments since Oslo—shifts that have mirrored the radically fluctuating pace of the peace process—bears this out.

Finally, Leonard Binder's article (in Sela and Ma'oz) on strategic reciprocity in Israeli-Palestinian negotiations is the most theoretically self-conscious of all the essays under discussion here, employing multiple game theoretical models to analyze the dynamics of the Israeli-Palestinian negotiations and prescribing an optimal course of action for the actors. Whether or not one subscribes to the tenets of game theory as encapsulating all the facets of decisionmaking (e.g., cognitive biases and emotional factors are necessarily left out), it is clear that Binder succeeds in generalizing the Israeli-Palestinian negotiating context beyond the regional specificity of the Middle East.

What these chapters suggest is that the state of our empirical knowledge of Israeli politics and culture is growing at an amazing pace. However, this abundant data-rich research needs to be joined with theory; otherwise, the twin poles of theory and data in the context of Israel Studies will forever be ships passing in the night. From a scholarly perspective, the embedding of empirical questions within a theoretical framework allows us to generate new questions, as well as to have the best tools at our disposal to address them. From a professional perspective, it is in the interests of Israel-oriented social scientists to be explicit in their theoretical agendas, so as to secure Israel Studies a place on the hiring, publishing and tenure "maps," as well as to cultivate and maintain academic conversations among scholars concerned with similar issues being played out in different regions.

Domestic Factors and the Peace Process

As with much of the writing on regional problems from scholars steeped in one particular case or region, most of the essays under discussion here admit a place for domestic variables in understanding the peace process, as, at minimum, crucial supplementary factors to the underlying systemic conditions. True, many of the essays do not specifically engage the question of what led to the peace process, but rather focus on its domestic effects. This latter approach nevertheless draws attention to the importance of domestic variables in understanding foreign policy events. Three of the essays explicitly address the question of what led Israel to pursue an altered foreign-policy course with the Palestinians, leading to the 1993 Oslo agreement: Myron Aronoff and Yael Aronoff's "Domestic Determinants of Israeli Foreign Policy" (in Freedman), Susan Hattis Rolef's "Israel's Policy Toward the PLO" (in Sela and Ma'oz) and Baruch Kimmerling's "Power-Oriented Settlement" (in Sela and Ma'oz). Naomi Chazan (in Sela and Ma'oz) discusses the role of women in working toward peaceful change. From the Arab perspective, Muhmmad Muslih ("Palestinian and Other Arab Perspectives," in Freedman), maps the Arab reaction to the Israeli-Palestinian peace process, while Raymond A. Hinnebusch ("Syria and the Transition to Peace," in Freedman) traces Syrian policy toward Israel.

In "Domestic Determinants of Israeli Foreign Policy" Aronoff and Aronoff point to governmental composition coupled with an evolving political culture as the central factors in explaining Israel's shift toward peace with the PLO. Echoing Aronoff and Atlas in the Peleg volume, they stress the fact that challenges to the dominant Zionist discourse (particularly by Arab Israelis and the young guard of the Labor Party) elicited a change in Zionist ideology, thereby facilitating the shift toward peace. The authors note the difference between Rabin's view of Israel as a "light unto the nations" versus his Likud predecessors' vision of the country as a "nation that dwells alone" (pp. 22–23). What is left unexplored, however, is the question of what elicited these ideological challenges. The simplest, but least parsimonious, explanation would rely on the idiosyncratic differences between any two individuals in power (i.e., Rabin versus his Likud predecessor, Yitzhak Shamir). However, nowhere do the authors rely on personality-based explanations as such.

Another explanation would posit that different political parties nurture different ideologies among their members, such that each group of elites possesses a separate worldview. While this is likely what the authors were implying with their domestic politics explanation, it is not explicitly presented. And if this is the case, it would be useful to investigate the relationship between "worldview" and "culture." Does the former imply a certain morality, or at least a view that is created and held at the personal level, or is it something that arises from collective consciousness? Certainly, in the case of Israel, religion plays a large part in framing policy options for the actors, and as such suggests collective thinking. However, for those Israelis who are explicitly secular, from where does the scope of what they see as legitimate policy choices arise? A more sophisticated reading might look to patterns in the behavior of the state over time, and attempt to determine what kind of domestic reaction might be elicited from this. In the next section, I will propose an explanation in line with this argument.

Kimmerling presents a more critical explanation for Israel's turn toward the Oslo process (in Sela and Ma'oz). Indeed, Kimmerling—whom Bar-On (in Peleg, p. 22) labels a "radical"—argues that Israel's decision to pursue Oslo was based on a power-politics calculation by which Israel concluded that "indirect control of the Palestinians is a better and cheaper strategy than direct control. . . ." (p. 237). Curiously, Kimmerling alludes to the "high costs" of occupation within Israeli thinking, without much explication as to the nature of these costs—that is, whether they are measured by blood or treasure, or by domestic or international moral standing, or something else. Kimmerling does discuss the problems facing the IDF in continuing the occupation, including a changing "mentality" from "blitzkrieg"-type warfare to "policing," as well as the economic and strategic costs resulting from the maintenance of the settlements (p. 237). However, a large stone is left unturned in Kimmerling's analysis: that of the relationship between a changing military mentality and a strict geopolitical and economic calculation. That is, if the military's mission was indeed called into question, then perhaps part of the explanation for the Oslo process lies in issues of Israeli national identity. Kimmerling does allude to the importance of political culture in understanding the Oslo process; he identifies the Zionist as, first and foremost, a self-perceived "warrior" (p. 229). However, he does not follow this analysis through to its logical conclusion: the effect of a particular political culture on foreign-policy shifts.

Second, Kimmerling's argument could be well served by incorporating the issue of the effect of scholarship on changing elite perceptions. If Israeli scholarship emanates from the ranks of "radical" critics such as Kimmerling himself, then perhaps Kimmerling (and others like him) are part of the explanation. As Bar-On's astute analysis shows, any attempt to call into question the Zionist project has the possibility (however slim) of altering actual state policy through a reconsideration of the relationship between foreign policy and collective self-image.

Hattis Rolef (in Sela and Ma'oz) is more eclectic in her investigation of the question of what led to Israel's changing attitude toward the PLO in the 1990s; indeed her essay is more of a chronological account than an analytic exploration. She posits that the factors influencing the shift in attitude were pragmatism, changing threat-perception based on evolving statements by the PLO itself, the elimination of the Jordanian option (based on King Hussein's disengagement from the West Bank in 1988), domestic challenges to the Israeli law forbidding contacts with the PLO, and Yitzhak Rabin's electoral promise to bring about a peace settlement with the Palestinians within six to nine months of coming to power in 1992. Her long list of domestic factors still begs the question of what led to these domestic challenges. She does point out that many of the challenges to the law forbidding contact with the PLO stemmed from pro-democracy forces (p. 266). But we are left unsure as to why Rabin felt he had to promise a peace settlement with the Palestinians to garner favor with the electorate, and why a general mood of pragmatism took hold within the Israeli government. Furthermore, we know that Rabin himself experienced what might be termed a sea-change in his policy stance toward the Palestinians (from his infamous "break their bones" directive as defense minister during the first half of the Intifada to his ultimate support for negotiating directly with the PLO).[8]

Finally, a much neglected topic—although one that has garnered increased attention since the first Intifada years—is the role of women in the peace process. Naomi Chazan, herself a Member of Knesset from the dovish Meretz bloc, briefly sketches a chronology of efforts by Israeli and Palestinian women to press for peaceful change, sometimes through interparty dialogue, and sometimes separately (in Sela and Ma'oz). Missing from her account—particularly since the article is entitled, "The Role of Women and Female Leadership in the Intifada and the Peace Process"—is a discussion of the role of women's groups that work to oppose the peace process, such as "Women in Green," that arguably arose as a response to the anti-occupation group known as "Women in Black." Furthermore, while she does mention that not all the women's groups are motivated by feminist concerns (p. 215), it would be useful to explore the relationship between the needs of women in society and the aims of the peace movement, including potential peace dividends. It has long been assumed that given Israel's pressing "national security" concerns, domestic issues have been cast to the side. Under this reasoning, peacemaking could end up freeing resources that could be used to address a plethora of social issues, the status of women being one example.

The escalation of violence associated with the second Intifada certainly cast the Israeli-Palestinian peace process into doubt, and with it, the prospects for a settlement between Israel and Syria. With hindsight regarding the aftermath of Oslo but without the ability to reflect on the crisis begun in 2000, Muhammad Muslih (in Freedman) discusses the attitudes of Arabs—both elites and masses; both Palestinian and non-Palestinian—to the peace process. What emerges is a dual picture of pessimism about the fate of the Palestinians among the public at large, including prominent intellectuals, coupled with a pragmatic view toward propelling the peace process espoused by political elites. The latter attitude was notably enshrined in the 1996 Arab Summit held in Cairo. While Muslih does not explicitly engage the question of the relative weight of domestic versus international determinants of foreign policy, his observations suggest that, despite the fundamental dissatisfaction of the masses, Arab leaders will have reasons for continuing to pursue a path of peace with Israel.

Raymond Hinnebusch draws a similar picture of Arab policy toward Israel proceeding without hindrance from the masses—an assessment that goes against the conventional scholarly wisdom regarding Arab politics[9]—in his examination of Hafez al-Asad's policy making in the Israeli-Syrian peace process. His analysis is detailed and informative, although the argument would benefit from a discussion of the merits of rational-actor analysis versus domestic politics explanations. Is the Syrian case merely an outlier, or was Asad's relative decision-making latitude a phenomenon representative of Arab foreign policy making in the post-Cold-War era? Moreover, an updated analysis (his was written before Hafez al-Asad's death) would want to compare Bashar al-Asad's policy making process with his father's, in order to determine the relative weight of the individual versus the Syrian (or broader Arab) political system in shaping policy outcomes.

As is apparent from many of these essays, domestic variables in the Israeli context—and somewhat in the Arab context—largely play a complementary role to regional or systemic factors, such as the Intifada, the Gulf War, and the end of the Cold War. In the ongoing battle within International Relations between domestic and external factors, there is a dearth of literature meaningfully integrating the two. The simplest way of admitting a role for both types of factors is to argue that systemic conditions serve as underlying factors while domestic variables serve as more proximate factors. However, I would suggest that we can conceive of a framework in which domestic and external factors are more than just discrete parts of an interlocking puzzle; where domestic factors are conceptually embedded within international realities. I will illustrate this framework using Israel's original decision to engage the Palestinians in the Oslo process.

Israel and Oslo: Integrating Domestic and International Variables

While much of domestic politics theorizing focuses on the needs of the leadership for reelection,[10] attempting to integrate domestic with international factors often means that it is difficult to propose a new framework wherein each side of the coin is mutually contextualized. This section will attempt to illustrate how the Israeli-Palestinian peace process can be understood as a product of factors at both levels.[11]

Following the identity-politics tradition in international relations, I would argue that national self-image is crucial to the way in which states craft policy choices and subsequently change them. Two related processes shape a state's self-image in the international system. The first is the early interstate experiences of the state in its regional environment, such as acceptance or rejection by other states. These experiences bestow upon the state a *role* that is, in turn, fundamental in shaping the state's behavior, and that leads to complementary behavior by other states. Israel's formative years were characterized by acute rejection by its regional neighbors (the Arab states) coupled with friendly relations with most of the Western powers.

The second process relates to the *narratives* that a polity develops about itself that serve to define both the members' relationship to the collective, and the state's image of itself in the international environment across time. Seen functionally, narratives are forces intended to bind nationals together socially and culturally; they are the glue of sociocultural "imagination." Operating at a deeper level are unconscious "counternarratives" that the conscious narratives have arisen to either mirror, or conceal. The counternarrative is not palatable to the collective for its challenging of the polity's vision of itself. In the Israeli case, the conscious narrative approximates the notion of "defensive warrior" touting "purity of arms." This narrative is embodied by the identity of the IDF, and is encapsulated by significant historical events that occurred on the territory of what is now Israel—including the fall of Masada (73 C.E.), the Bar Kokhba revolt (132–135 C.E.), and the Battle of Tel Hai (1920), all of which cast the Jewish/Israeli (defensive) fighter as outnumbered by foreign aggressors.[12]

Where a shift toward conflict resolution may occur is through a "cognitive-emotional realization" resulting from the enacting of policy choices that contradict the self-image of the state—such as adopting a more aggressive stance than the state's self-perceived military doctrine would dictate. In the case of Israel, this series of policies stretched from the aftermath of the 1967 war, when Israel first became an "occupying power," through the 1982 Lebanon war and the first Intifada, both of which led Israel to be in the position of a self-perceived "aggressor" rather than an "embattled state" pursuing only defensive goals—from the "lamb" to the "wolf" as one Israeli commentator has observed.[13] Similarly, Eyad El Sarraj ("Mental Health Challenges for the Palestinian Authority," in Sela and Ma'oz) discusses this reversal of the hitherto Israeli-Palestinian relationship of victim-aggressor, as perceived by the Israelis (p. 167). Once this lack of "fit" emerges, the state attempts to realign its policy behavior with its self-image in order to reduce the cognitive dissonance that arises from unconscious counternarratives coming to the fore.[14] However, given that the second Intifada has involved the widespread use of Palestinian suicide bombing against civilian targets within Israel's pre-1967 borders, Israelis have arguably reverted to experiencing themselves as the beleaguered ones, a self-perception that partly explains Israel's harsh reprisal raids. Thus, in the case of Oslo, while other external and internal factors—such as the evolving pacifying stance of the PLO, the influx of Soviet Jewish immigration, and Israel's need to expand its commerce to broader markets—were relevant to Israel's decision to pursue peace with the Palestinians, this discussion has attempted to highlight a hitherto neglected variable: the relationship between Israel's role-identity and its policy actions.

In that this account posits that foreign policy is a product of "roles" and "collective memory" based on outside experiences, we can see that international factors are a crucial part of the composition of domestic identity. In addition, this framework successfully integrates the various domestic variables introduced in many of the essays under discussion: the identity of the IDF alluded to by Cohen, Israeli political culture discussed by Peleg, and the use of "power" by Israel over the Palestinians posited by Kimmerling. Thus, when Cohen notes the introduction of conscientious objection during the Lebanon War and continuing with the first Intifada (in Peleg, p. 117), we are left to wonder what, exactly, is the relationship between this phenomenon and Israel's pursuit of peace? Similarly, Kimmerling raises difficult questions regarding the use of power by the Jewish State; and while others have drawn links between that and foreign policy,[15] Kimmerling's analysis does not go as far as it could in connecting these larger issues.

My analysis also provides a generalizable analytic framework for the question posed by Susan Hattis Rolef, Why did Israel shift its policy stance vis-à-vis the PLO? And specifically, why was a more dovish government elected, and why did the Labor party experience new thinking among its younger-generation leadership? Similarly, the new historiography investigated by Bar-On can be understood as a cause of the coming to light of the "counternarratives" posited here. Such domestic forces as new historians, along with peace movements and the media, serve as a "mirror" enabling elites to see the disconnection between their foreign policy patterns and the collective "self-image" of the state.

Conclusions

The publication of scholarly appraisals of contemporary events can be easily overtaken by changes in the real-world arena. Such has been the case—tragically for the actors in the Middle East—since the outbreak of the al-Aqsa Intifada in September 2000. As noted at the outset of this essay, this crisis, however frustrating for peace proponents within and without the region, does not mitigate the importance of understanding the decisions taken by Israel and its neighbors since the beginning of the Madrid peace process in the early 1990s. Nor are such analyses irrelevant for predicting the prospects for future peace. Specifically, the various societal shifts outlined in the essays point to important factors in determining the potential for Israelis and Palestinians to extricate themselves from standoffs and setbacks, even devastating ones, that will inevitably occur. Take, for instance, the *kulturkampf* that Peleg predicts and the importance Bar-On attributes to revisionist historians. Both would appear to have been cast into question since the violent outbreaks of autumn 2000. Yet these factors are still immanent and may again become relevant, with a potential impact in navigating Israelis back to the peace table. On the Palestinian side, Sayigh's claim that the use of force has facilitated the state-building process within the Palestinian Authority (PA) raises the question of whether the "Al-Aqsa Intifada" has bolstered or atrophied the credibility of the Palestinian leadership. If the PA has indeed been strengthened by its population's use of arms, then perhaps we can expect Arafat to enjoy more domestic legitimacy if and when he returns to the negotiating table—domestic support being crucial for any agreement to succeed. However, to the extent that the IDF's incursions into the Palestinian areas destroy the administrative organs of the Palestinian Authority, Arafat could see his popularity, and his ability to execute any subsequent agreement, lessened.

In terms of scholarship, the three volumes are excellent cases of data-rich discussions on the peace process, yet their essays could benefit from a greater attention to theoretical concerns. By drawing on insights already available to scholars of other areas, the marrying of generalizable theory and case-specific analyses in Middle East Studies can help us better understand the particularities of the region. In the foregoing pages I have offered an alternative way of conceptualizing domestic and international variables in Israel's decision to pursue peace with the PLO. It seems clear that certain societal variables—namely, the changing role of the IDF, the use of power in the Israeli psyche, and the evolving identity of the Israeli state—have not only been highlighted within the recent Israel Studies literature, but have played an important role in Israel's decision to shift its policy stance from one of conflict to compromise with the PLO. Further research is needed to shed light on the relationship between these factors in order to better explain Israeli and Arab attempts at peacemaking, as well as to lay out the prospects for overcoming the current—and daunting—hurdles in the region. These sorts of analyses can help us understand the possibilities not only for renewed peace efforts between Israel and the Palestinians and for meaningful peace processes to begin between Israel and Syria and Lebanon, but between actors in other conflict-ridden regions as well.

Notes

1. See, for instance, Michael Barnett, "Culture, Strategy and Foreign Policy Change: Israel's Road to Oslo," *European Journal of International Relations* 5:1 (1999): 5–36; Stephen Walt, *The Origins of Alliances* (Ithaca: Cornell University Press, 1987); Ian S. Lustick, *Unsettled States, Disputed Lands: Britain and Ireland, France and Algeria, Israel and the West Bank-Gaza* (Ithaca: Cornell University Press, 1993); Michael Brecher and Jonathan Wilkenfeld, *A Study of Crisis* (Ann Arbor: University of Michigan Press, 1997); as well as Barnett, ed., *Israel in Comparative Perspective: Challenging the Conventional Wisdom* (Albany: State University of New York Press, 1996), which argues that Israel should be viewed as one case within the comparative tradition of political science, rather than as an "exceptionalist" data point.

2. Of course, many historians advocate a less generalizable, more interpretive view of past events. For discussions of how history and theory

may be bridged, see John Lewis Gaddis, "History, Theory and Common Ground," *International Security* 22:1 (Summer 1997): 75–85; Michael Brecher, "International Studies in the Twentieth Century and Beyond: Flawed Dichotomies, Synthesis, Cumulation," *International Studies Quarterly* 43 (1999): 219–21.

3. These factors are "a wealth of experience, dubious purposes and ulterior motives, problems of timing, negative impact of third-party involvement, a wide gulf between proposed terms of agreement, problematic status of negotiating partners, dynamics of deadlock, and psychological obstacles." Laura Zittrain Eisenberg and Neil Caplan in Peleg, *Middle East Peace Process,* p. 4.

4. The recent revelation by Israeli archaeologists that much of what Jews have taken to be their ancient history is unsubstantiated empirically raises similar issues of historical "fact" versus contemporary "identity." See Ze'ev Herzog, "Deconstructing the Walls of Jericho," *Ha'aretz Magazine*, 2 November 1999 (internet edition). See also David Biale, *Power and Powerlessness in Jewish History* (New York: Schocken Books, 1986).

5. An example of this from the Israeli case is the recent governmental directive to rewrite high school history textbooks to include Israeli atrocities against local Arabs, such as the Kafr Kassem massacre of 1956. See Lee Hockstader, "Israel Explores Dark Pages of Its Past," *Washington Post,* 31 October 1999, p. A1.

6. See Alexander Wendt, *Social Theory of International Politics* (New York: Cambridge University Press, 1999); in the Israeli-Palestinian case, see Baruch Kimmerling in Avraham Sela and Moshe Ma'oz, *PLO and Israel* 243.

7. See Danny Rubinstein, "Exploring the Terminology Gap," *Ha'aretz* (English edition) 15 November 1999, p. 5.

8. [See also the analysis by Hemda Ben-Yehuda, "Policy Transformation in the Middle East," in *Review Essays in Israel Studies: Books on Israel, vol. 5*, eds. L. Z. Eisenberg and N. Caplan (Albany: State University of New York Press, 2000), 178–87.—eds.]

9. See Michael C. Hudson, *Arab Politics: The Search for Legitimacy* (New Haven: Yale University Press, 1977).

10. See Anthony Downs, *An Economic Theory of Democracy* (New York: Harper, 1957).

11. This section draws on ideas contained in Mira Sucharov, "The International Self: Israel and the Palestinians, 1948-1993," Ph.D. diss., Georgetown University, 2001.

12. See Yael Zerubavel, *Recovered Roots: Collective Memory and the Making of Israeli National Tradition* (Chicago: University of Chicago Press, 1995); David C. Jacobson, "Mythmaking and Commemoration in Israeli Culture," in Eisenberg and Caplan, *Review Essays in Israel Studies,* 99–117.

13. Yaron Ezrahi, *Rubber Bullets: Power and Conscience in Modern Israel* (New York: Farrar, Straus and Giroux, 1997). While the 1956 Sinai Campaign was arguably an aggressive war, a view no doubt bolstered by the participation of Britain and France, what is important is that Israelis, on the whole, did not see it as such; thus, there would have been no reason for cognitive dissonance to arise in the wake of the campaign. In his speech to the Knesset in the aftermath of the Six-Day War, Israeli Prime Minister Levi Eshkol proclaimed that "three wars [the reference undoubtedly to 1948, 1956 and 1967] have been forced upon us in twenty years." See Col. Mordechai Bar-On, ed., *Israel Defence Forces: The Six Day War* (Tel Aviv: Israel Ministry of Defense, 1968), 233.

14. This dissonance between self-image and military behavior is discussed in the context of the 1987–1992 Intifada in Tamar Liebes and Shoshana Blum-Kulka, "Managing a Moral Dilemma: Israeli Soldiers in the Intifada," *Armed Forces and Society* 21:1 (Fall 1994): 45–68.

15. See Ezrahi, *Rubber Bullets.*

11. Power-Relations, Recognition, and Dialogue: The Dynamics of Israeli-Palestinian Peace

Amal Jamal,
Tel Aviv University

This essay, which was written in 1999 (more than a year before the outbreak of the "al-Aqsa Intifada"), addresses the inability of the Israeli-Palestinian peace process as begun in Oslo to genuinely diminish mutual hatreds, fears, and distrust between the protagonists. The author argues that the Oslo peace process ignored the deeply rooted antagonism between Israeli and Palestinian national identities, and instead restricted its focus to regulative issues based on the existing balance of power. An authentic reversal of Israeli-Palestinian enmity, he argues, requires a deeper mutual recognition between the two sides than the kind provided by a legalistic focus only. The insider accounts of the Oslo peace process offer readers insight into not only the political-strategic aspect of the negotiations, but also into the emotional-communicative dimension of the talks. Finally, in reviewing a study of Arab-Jewish dialogue and encounter groups in Israel, the author concludes that it is within an improved form of this type of conflict-resolution that one may find the basis for true peace that is missing from the official Israeli-Palestinian negotiation process.

Abbas, Mahmoud, *Through Secret Channels: The Road to Oslo,* Reading, England: Garnet, 1995.

Abdel-Malek, Kamal, and David C. Jacobson, eds., *Israeli and Palestinian Identities in History and Literature,* New York: St. Martin's, 1999.

Abu-Nimer, Mohammed, *Dialogue, Conflict Resolution, and Change: Arab-Jewish Encounters in Israel,* Albany: State University of New York Press, 1999.

Savir, Uri, *The Process: 1,100 Days That Changed the Middle East,* New York: Random, 1998.

Peace talks and reconciliation efforts by Israelis and Palestinians have attempted to transform the conflictual relationship between them. Real efforts have been made to abandon the consequences of the colonial condition that had "chained the [two parties] into an implacable dependence, molded their respective characters and dictated their conduct" for a long period of time.[1] This essay demonstrates the way in which the peace process between Israelis and Palestinians has mirrored the "puzzling circulation of desire around the traumatic scene of oppression."[2] It follows the dynamics of the implacable enmity between the two parties seeking to examine the way they have chosen out of their deeply rooted antagonism.

This review essay argues that the relationship between Israelis and Palestinians, developed in the last century by systematic policies of the powerful party, will not be resolved by artificial solutions that avoid the dialectics of hatred and desire, on the one hand, and the basic need for sincere mutual recognition, on the other hand. The historical rapprochement reflected in the Oslo peace process mirrors a complex situation of power-relations, with "power" being understood not only as a matter of coercion but also as a subjectivized imaginative space that turns individuals from "its points of application" to its vehicles.[3] Israel has not only colonized Palestinian land and "body"; it has also invaded the Palestinian mind and presented itself as a cultural model capturing the imaginative space of many Palestinians. Israel has created, as occupier, a complex relationship of hate and admiration among its subject Palestinians.

This relationship, as seen in particular from one of the books reviewed, is not limited to conflictual situations but is also engraved in the peace efforts made by both sides. Why, we may ask, has the historic act of "talking peace" failed to transform the conflictual relationship into a mutually constructive and cooperative effort to overcome the damage of the past? Israel's security-consciousness determines the framework of the negotiations and undermines the Palestinians' need for recognition. As a result, the peace efforts face obstacles on both sides that prevent a real historical reconciliation. The books reviewed here make it clear that the Oslo peace process has not addressed the sources of the Israeli-Palestinian conflict but, rather, has sought regulative mechanisms aimed at maintaining and legitimizing existing power-relations.

Israeli and Palestinian Identities in History and Literature, a collection of essays edited by Brown University professors Kamal Abdel-Malek and David C. Jacobson, illustrates the extent to which Israeli and Palestinian identities are constructed and reconstructed in mutually exclusionary terms. The authors clearly show that the conflict between Israelis and Palestinians is not only over territory, but is also embedded deeply in each people's psyche. The situation created after 1948, and especially after the Israeli occupation of the West Bank and Gaza Strip in 1967, has led to dynamics that have influenced both sides' self-perceptions and has imposed an essentially colonial condition laden with stark violence and counterviolence.

Mahmoud Abbas's *Through Secret Channels: The Road to Oslo* and Uri Savir's *The Process: 1,000 Days that Changed the Middle East* provide us with firsthand information by participants in the Oslo and post-Oslo negotiations. The direct involvement of these two figures enables us to examine the political-strategic as well as the emotional-communicative dimensions of the negotiations. What were the considerations of each side in the process, and how were these considerations reformulated during the negotiations? The two accounts enable us to gauge the motivations, views, and conceptions of the people involved in the process, while exposing the dialectics of enmity-desire relations and their impact on the prospects of a peaceful settlement in the future.

Greater skepticism regarding Israeli-Palestinian reconciliation emerges from *Dialogue, Conflict Resolution, and Change: Arab-Jewish Encounters in Israel,* written by Mohammed Abu-Nimer, a Palestinian citizen of Israel. The book deals with Jewish-Arab relations and encounters in Israel and describes the way in which educational methods become part of a broader control system used by the dominant Jewish majority to maintain the status quo and reinforce taboos. The book illustrates the hegemonic ways in which Israel deals with the Palestinians as separate communities. According to Abu-Nimer, the intervention models used for Arab-Jewish encounters are not directed toward dealing with the basic sources of the conflict, and fall short of introducing change on either the structural or policy levels. Abu-Nimer's examination includes a rich variety of theories of conflict-resolution models which, in my view, help us to better frame and draw conclusions about the two eyewitness books on the Oslo peace negotiations.

Identity Construction, Nationalism and Conflict

Since the end of the last century nationalist Jews and Palestinians have viewed each other in antagonistic terms. Both sides have built up their national identities by disavowal of the other's political rights. The Zionist movement followed Western nationalist thought where national identity was "constructed in terms of differentiation from devalued others . . . reinforcing social and cultural hierarchies and providing the legitimation for expansionary projects, military preparedness, and even war."[4] Despite the multiplicity of political and ideological streams within the Zionist movement, all of them have instrumentalized the "spiritual bond" of the Jewish people with the Land of Israel. The Zionist aspiration for a Jewish homeland depicted the State of Israel in religious terms, as a "Jewish State," and thereby excluded those Palestinians that remained in Israel from being an integral part of Israeli society.

The Palestinians, on the other hand, constructed their identity in opposition to Western colonialism. The imposition of the British Mandate on Palestine and its promises to guarantee a homeland for Jews conditioned the process of Palestinian national identity-formation.[5] Despite the different political narratives that constituted Palestinian identity and the internal rivalries within the national movement, Palestinians based their national aspirations on what they saw as their fundamental right to the land of Palestine.[6] Their efforts to maintain their historical relationship with their land determined not only the way in which they viewed themselves, but also the way in which they conceived the immigrant Jews—namely as a direct existential threat, whose economic and cultural impact was to be feared and resisted.[7]

Despite their opposing trajectories, Zionism and Palestinian nationalism have influenced each other mutually, something that is usually ignored in the literature of both sides. The collection of essays edited by Abdel-Malek and Jacobson illustrates the dialectical relationship between Israeli and Palestinian identities after 1948. They draw on disciplines ranging from history, sociology, political science, film studies to literature in order to pinpoint "the dynamic process of the definition and redefinition of identity that both Palestinians and Israelis have undergone" (p. xv). The book is divided into three main parts. The first part, on identity formation, includes five chapters, only one of which deals with Palestinian identity. The remaining six chapters focus on the inter-relationship between Palestinians and Israelis as seen through literature. Together, they demonstrate the overlapping, shifting, and counter-dynamics of Palestinian and Israeli identities.

Salim Tamari ("The Local and the National in Palestinian Identity") demonstrates that the development of Palestinian identity has been fragmented as a result of the various historical experiences of the different Palestinian communities after 1948. Tamari illustrates the way in which external circumstances such as the Egyptian occupation of Palestine in the nineteenth century, the British Mandate, and Zionism transcended Palestinian identity beyond local boundaries and transformed it into a national one. However, as a result of the confrontation with the Zionist movement and later with the State of Israel, the politics of exile became the decisive marker of Palestinian identity for a long period of time. This marginalized those Palestinians who remained on Palestinian soil, either in the West Bank and Gaza Strip or within the borders of Israel. Tamari does not pay enough attention to the way in which establishing the Palestinian Authority have changed the dynamics of identity-formation among Palestinians. In my view, the integrative policies of the Palestinian Authority have led to new forms of stratification within Palestinian society, leaving Diaspora Palestinians and Israeli Palestinians outside the new processes of identity-construction.

Tamari's contribution is followed by a detailed account of the transformations taking place among Palestinians living in Israel. Sammy Smooha's analysis ("The Advances and Limits of the Israelization of Israel's Palestinian Citizens") deals with the coexisting, sometimes contradictory, processes taking place among Palestinian citizens of Israel. This population is "subject to the cross-pressures of Israelization and Palestinization" (p. 28). While they have adjusted to their minority status, accepted Israel's right to exist, and adopted the dominant Israeli culture through their use of the Hebrew language, they are, according to Smooha, increasingly drawn to Palestinian nationalism and to feeling greater affinity and loyalty to the Palestinian people. Smooha's account of these processes is based on his yearning for better coexistence between Palestinians and Jews within Israel. He demonstrates how the Jewish-Zionist character of the State of Israel has "turned Arab citizens into unequal outsiders" (p. 29). In order to overcome this situation, Smooha suggests the reexamination of classical Zionism, which is depicted as an "outdated nationalist ideology" (p. 30). Smooha leaves no doubt about his aspiration to maintain Israel's Jewish character, but he espouses a more liberal conception of Jewishness that is more open to Arab-Jewish coexistence.

The exclusionary nature of Zionist ideology and its impact on Israeli politics is demonstrated in the essays by Nurith Gertz, Neil Caplan, and Gershon Shafir and Yoav Peled. Gertz ("The Others in Israeli Cinema of the 1940s and 1950s: Holocaust Survivors, Women, and Arabs") demonstrates how the cinema of the 1940s and 1950s helped in shaping Israeli-Jewish identity by rejecting its "others." The discourse used by the cinema of the time, asserts Gertz, "attempts to nullify the dynamism of [the differences among Jews of different origins], to organize them in such a way as to liken the 'others' to each other, and to create a hierarchy meant to support the homogeneous appearance of the new Hebrew identity" (p. 35). The Israeli films of the time are a translation of the Zionist ideology into the language of cinema, trying to persuade Israelis as well as others of the justness of the Zionist project. The films analyzed by Gertz mirror a modernizing conception of Jewish history where a coherent history of progress is presented. The films reflect the attempts of Zionism to transcend two thousand years of history by connecting the Jewish biblical past with the flourishing Zionist future. Building on Homi Bhabha's understanding of national discourse, Gertz shows how the Zionist project is undermined when the "others"—Holocaust survivors, women, and Arabs—shatter the coherence of the dominant Zionist narrative. Therefore, they must be marginalized and rendered outsiders.[8]

Caplan ("Victimhood and Identity: Psychological Obstacles to Israeli Reconciliation with the Palestinians") deals with one side only of the psychological obstacles that obstruct a real reconciliation between Israelis and Palestinians: namely, a "mutual sense of victimhood [that] has become one of the most serious psychological complications bedeviling Arab-Zionist and Palestinian-Israeli relations" (p. 65). Caplan outlines Israeli perceptions and self-image as victims, leaving to specialists on Palestinian nationalism and identity to construct the Palestinian equivalent of this phenomenon. He demonstrates clearly the way in which the experience of the Holocaust became a prominent factor in Israeli public discourse. The "sense of siege" is turned into an explanatory factor for Israeli politicians and the public. Despite the fact that Caplan does not intend to justify Israeli treatment of Palestinians, his account unfortunately contributes ammunition to those who manipulate the Israeli self-image as victim into a vindication of its treatment of Palestinians. Despite its important academic contribution, this chapter presents historical circumstances as an overwhelming force that impose themselves on human groups. By downplaying the role of leadership in utilizing such "master-stories" as the Jewish Purim story (Haman the villain) or the modern Holocaust (Hitler as villain), Caplan contradicts some of the recent theoretical literature on nationalism.[9]

Israeli citizenship has recently drawn a lot of attention and has become a central issue in sociopolitical debates and judicial cases in Israel. The establishment of the State of Israel as a Jewish State created inherent differences between Jews and Arabs in Israeli citizenry. The "Law of Return," which was enacted for Jews only, as well as the "Citizenship Law," have established the juridical foundations of the Jewish State. Both laws articulate the priority that Jews have over non-Jews in access to state resources. Sociologist Gershon Shafir and political scientist Yoav Peled ("Citizenship and Stratification in an Ethnic Democracy") seek to break the Jewish-Palestinian divide in their analysis of Israeli citizenship. They demonstrate how new theories of citizenship enable new analyses of ethnic relations in Israel and can apply to the incorporation of both Arabs and Jews into the Israeli polity. They argue that three discourses of citizenship—the liberal, the republican, and the ethnonationalist—were combined in Israeli political culture as a result of a "number of social processes that intersected at critical historical turning points" (p. 91). The intersection of the three citizenship discourses is analyzed as "a pattern of interaction between the exclusionary dimensions of Israel's colonizing and nation-building practices and the inclusionary aspects of its democratic state institutions" (p. 91). Based on the need to nationalize an ancient religious community and to legitimize its settlement project, the Zionist movement emphasized ethnic Jewish identity. It utilized the virtuous republican character of the settler community for the moral purpose of state-formation. This interconnected purpose has established the hegemony of an ethno-nationalist citizenship discourse. Shafir and Peled demonstrate the way in which the dominant ruling elites have advanced this discourse and utilized it to maintain their political hegemony. In the authors' view, "the declining influence of the republican citizenship discourse has caused fierce competition for hegemony between the adherents of the other two [citizenship] discourses" (p. 102). This process reflects the rising power of new social forces in Israeli society that seek to establish their hegemony in Israeli politics. Based on such an analysis, one could claim that Israeli politics is characterized by a deep contest between two opposing poles: those who emphasize the religiously articulated ethno-nationalist discourse, and the adherents of a liberal citizenship discourse. This polarized political culture can explain the tense political situation in Israeli politics with regard to the peace process. The future of the occupied Palestinian territories is one of the main axes around which liberals and ethno-nationalists contend. Shafir and Peled are optimistic about the future in which they foresee the triumph of the liberals as a result of the rising influence of global forces on the shaping of Israeli society.

Despite the deep and thorough analytic aspects of Shafir and Peled's argument, their essay has some theoretical and empirical shortcomings. Their analysis is functional, making the state and its role in shaping society seem marginal. But the Israeli state has proved itself most able to play a central role in determining the nature of Israeli politics and the dynamics of its society and economy. Despite the liberalization processes taking place in Israeli society, the dominant elite is not willing to give up the ethno-national character of the state. Shafir and Peled do not pay enough attention to the dominant "national-security" discourse and its impact on Israeli politics. These two facts condition the dynamics of the peace process and block any real possibility of historical reconciliation between Zionism and Palestinian nationalism.

The essays in the second part of this collective work expose the interconnectedness between literature and politics. They attest to the thesis that it is no accident that literatures bear the names of nations.[10] Palestinian as well as Hebrew literature have played a central part not only in reflecting the experience, agonies, and raptures of Palestinians and Israelis but also in constructing their memories and identity. As one critic has pointed out, nations themselves are narrations.[11] In the words of Edward Said, "the power to narrate, or to block other narratives from forming and emerging" is a political act, central to the relations between different nations.[12] While the later essays in the book deal with Palestinian and Jewish writers separately, one notices similarities between them. Both Palestinian and Jewish writers have portrayed the aspirations of their peoples as much as they sought to express their confusion regarding the existing reality. The essays of David C. Jacobson ("Patriotic Rhetoric and Personal Conscience in Israeli Fiction of the 1948 and 1956 Wars"), Arnold J. Band ("Adumbration of the Israeli 'Identity Crisis' in Hebrew Literature of the 1960s"), and Ami Elad-Bouskila ("Arabic and/or Hebrew: The Languages of Arab Writers in Israel") demonstrate the ways in which the establishment of the State of Israel have brought Israeli writers, Jews and Arabs, to reflect on the historical and moral implications of the new circumstances, while establishing a new cultural discourse that seeks to accommodate the tensions of the new political reality.

Essays by Issa J. Boullata ("Mahmud Darwish: Identity and Change"), Salma Khadra Jayyusi ("Palestinian Identity in Literature") and Kamal Abdel-Malek ("Living on Borderlines: War and Exile in Selected Works by Ghassan Kanafani, Fawaz Turki, and Mahmud Darwish") deal with the portrayal of Palestinian identity in literature. Through these analyses of Palestinian writers and poets, we can see how Palestinian identity has been shaped and reshaped by changing circumstances in Palestine and the Middle East. Heroic figures emerged in the Palestinian political discourse of the 1960s and 1970s. According to Jayyusi, memory played a big role "in the staying power of the Palestinians' struggle to preserve their identity" (p.168). Memory was preserved in fiction, personal accounts, and poetry, which helped in defining Palestinian cultural and literary identity. The Palestinian cause occupied a central place in Palestinian literature, as demonstrated clearly in the writers and poets selected for analysis in the three essays. According to Abdel-Malek, Palestinian literature "include[s] characters, techniques, and literary tropes that can be characterized as liminal entities that, in turn, represent the central Palestinian experience of living a marginal existence on literal and figurative borders" (p. 180).

Not surprisingly, war and exile have conditioned the consciousness of Palestinian writers, something that is reflected in their writings. Jayyusi drives this point home:

> The semantics of such concepts as resistance, courage, honor, duty, patriotism, and responsibility have been a driving force in the Palestinians' spiritual survival. It must be emphasized here that in *good* Palestinian literature the verbal utterance of these abstracts has faithfully been avoided; the contemporary sophisticated aesthetics and the modernizing agents that have become a religion to contemporary writers would not tolerate such a verbal utterance of abstract concepts. Instead, they are conveyed in the tone, the subject matter, and the descriptive account of what has happened and still happens to Palestinians. (pp. 171–72; emphasis in original)

Power-relations, Negotiations and Recognition

A review of Mahmoud Abbas's and Uri Savir's personal accounts of the initial stages of the peace process between Israel and the Palestine Liberation Organization (PLO) plunges us immediately into the psychological, cultural, and political motivations that steered Palestinians and Israelis into negotiating their now-ill-fated Oslo accord. Seen in the light of the subsequent uprisings that began in September 2000, Abbas's *Through Secret Channels* and Savir's *The Process* are especially effective illustrations of the contrast between the inflammable situation on the ground and the warm meetings between Israeli and Palestinian negotiators who worked to achieve mutual recognition between sworn enemies.

Savir's and Abbas's accounts express the agonies of the past and the longing for a better future for both Israelis and Palestinians. Besides being a political review of the breakthrough in Israeli-Palestinian relations, their books expose the political reasoning behind the diplomatic maneuvers in Oslo and afterward. The authors detail the rapprochement between two enemies and present a reliable account of the process, with all its progress and regressions. Despite the similarities, one should indicate that the vantage point of the authors is different. Whereas Savir was directly involved in the negotiations, Abbas (a.k.a. Abu Mazen) was detached from them, monitoring developments from Tunis based on the notes made by those Palestinians who were actually at the negotiation tables. Furthermore, Abbas' book covers the Oslo process only, while Savir's goes into the implementation of the Declaration of Principles (DOP)[13] and the difficulties that the two sides faced in attempting to reach a common interpretation of the ambiguous formulations agreed upon in Oslo.

The Oslo track was not taken seriously at first; it was presumed to be an attempt to bypass the difficulties that characterized the public negotiations in Washington D.C. and to test the seriousness of the two sides. Both authors situate the negotiations in their respective context. Abbas sees the accord signed on the White House lawn on 13 September 1993 as resulting from

> a cumulative build-up to which the media and the political and military activities of the Palestinian revolution had contributed . . . the immense contribution of the six years of uprising, . . . [t]he end of the Cold War and its consequences, . . . [and t]he extensive networks of the contacts which the PLO had set up with local Israeli and international Jewish factions. (p. 18)

Savir, on the other hand, says

> [t]he Middle East had changed in the previous five years. The Soviet Union . . . had disintegrated. Moreover, the Arab world itself had fragmented after the Iran-Iraq war. Religious fundamentalism . . . was now a serious threat to most of the regimes in the region. . . . The United States was being courted by almost every country in the area. . . . Many Arabs had begun to view Israel as a potential partner in their endeavors. The Palestinians understood that years of terrorism and the intifada . . . had brought them neither political nor economic gains. The PLO, in fact, seemed on the verge of bankruptcy. (pp. 4–5)

Despite these contrasting accounts of the circumstances that led to the initiation of talks between Israelis and Palestinians, they reveal the parallel logic that motivated each side. Despite the fact that each party thought that the changes played in his favor, the results were a historic breakthrough. Both wanted to exploit the opportunity to squeeze the maximum out of the occasion; realpolitik was the dominating logic in the negotiations.

Both accounts illustrate that the negotiations were much easier than the implementation of the agreements agreed upon. The personal and intimate friendships that developed between negotiators and their willingness to overcome psychological barriers did not become the legacy of all. Reality was much stronger than the power of a few visionaries to transform longtime enmities into successful cooperation. Savir states that

> [e]ach side hailed the agreement as a historic step. Each spoke of the great hopes it inspired for its people. But neither expressed a true change of feeling toward its erstwhile enemy. This fusion of long habit with the anticipation of revolutionary change led to an often ambivalent process, one that alternated between retreat into the familiar and bursts of constructive creativity. (p. 93)

Savir and Abbas both accept the balance of power between Israel and the Palestinians as their point of departure. They speak of the negotiations as a real historical reconciliation between the two parties, yet their books contain much evidence of the ways in which the existing power relations dictated the results of the negotiations. Abbas, who represents the Palestinians, the weaker side at the negotiating table, reflects the imbalance of power, elegantly stating that

> [w]e [the Palestinians] were of course negotiating with a seasoned and able [Israeli] delegation, long-practiced in negotiations with other parties, especially the Egyptians. It could also fall back on many teams that could provide it with data, analysis, ideas and alternatives. By contrast our delegation had neither the experience nor the resources of the Israelis. (p. 162)

He adopts the position of the underdog without taking any responsibility for the poor composition and performance of the Palestinian delegation in Oslo.

Savir's account of the subsequent meetings of the Israeli and Palestinian delegations assigned to the implementation of the

Israeli redeployment in Gaza and Jericho exposes, even further, the imbalance of power between the two sides. He states plainly that the powerful Israeli position dictated the implementation of the agreements. He pinpoints the Israeli emphasis on security needs and the way in which these needs set the direction of the negotiations. Describing the first meeting between Yasir Arafat and Prime Minister Yitzhak Rabin in Cairo, Savir explains, "For the rest of the session Rabin lectured Arafat about security as the key test for the Palestinians. . . ." In his view, the positions of the two sides

> remained essentially fixed, even as the gap between them incrementally narrowed, mostly to the benefit of the stronger side. That Israel's approach was dictated by the army invariably made immediate security considerations the dominant ones, so that the fundamentally political process had been subordinated to short-term military needs. (p. 99)

Both books also illustrate the fact that the Oslo Accords avoided specifying concrete solutions to most of the controversial issues, with the result that negotiations over implementing the DOP became very tense. Gaps between the positions of the two sides abruptly ended the cheerful opening of the October 1993 Taba talks. In Savir's words, "the honeymoon in Taba was short-lived. For upon setting forth their opening positions, both sides grasped that there was a huge gap between their interpretations of the DOP" (p. 98). The differences between the Palestinian and Israeli positions were also seen in the economic talks held in Paris, with Israel intending to create an economic partnership at minimal cost to its economy. Furthermore, as Savir bluntly notes, "[a]bove all, . . . Israel wanted it understood that the free movement of Palestinian goods and citizens be subject to security considerations. In short, the Palestinians would be wholly dependent on Israel's economy and security—or, to be more precise, on Israel's *sense* of security" (p.100).

In such an atmosphere, the agreements between Israel and the PLO were sent off the track of historical reconciliation under the impact of existing power-relations. The widening gaps between Israeli and Palestinian positions and Israel's ability to impose *its* understanding of the ambiguous clauses in the agreements contradict Abbas's statement that "[t]he presumption of Israeli superiority is unfounded" (p. 219). His basic optimism regarding the future seems to be undermined, step by step, in the implementation phase, something that he never confronts in his book. With today's hindsight, it is easy to dismiss the accuracy of his perception of the DOP as a first step toward attaining full independence.

Mutual recognition is a fundamental issue in conflict-resolution.[14] As in every colonial situation, the policies of the powerful party are crucial to a peaceful solution of the conflictual relationship. In this light, the form, content, and degree to which the dominant party, Israel, recognizes the Palestinians as equal partners in the process of settling the conflict in the region is central. Both authors view the mutual recognition between Israel and the PLO as the peak of the whole process of negotiations; but the substance of that recognition does not reach the degree of mutuality that is required for transforming the dominant colonial condition.[15] Despite the fact that both authors stress the importance of recognition, their perspectives as the dominant and the subordinate party suggest different meaning of the concept. Savir clarifies that

> [t]he Palestinians had no problem recognizing Israel in the context of the peace process. But here we [Israelis] were speaking of recognizing it unconditionally, or at least without reference to its borders. We were prepared to recognize the PLO as the representative of the Palestinian people but not the PLO's version as leaders of a Palestinian state. Thus we insisted, on orders from Jerusalem, that Arafat would sign his letter to Rabin as the chairman of the PLO and not, as he had been accustomed to signing his correspondence since 1988, as the president of Palestine. (pp. 74–75)

Abbas, on the other hand, does not deal with the crucial gap between the PLO's and the Israeli government's positions regarding mutual recognition: namely, that whereas the PLO recognized an already-existing state and its right to live in security, Israel's recognition was limited to the PLO as representative of the Palestinian people. The Palestinians' national right to self-determination as equal partners was not fully accepted. Israeli policies of creating facts on the ground in the West Bank and Gaza Strip continued as if nothing had happened. Abbas's treatment of the issue of mutual recognition does not reflect any sensitivity toward the moral power of the Palestinian experience. He thinks and acts as a player whose aim is to reach a deal that maximizes what he has at stake at the moment. His book is a good illustration of the yearning for Israeli and American recognition of the PLO. In his reminiscences of the trip to Washington D.C., Abbas says that "[t]he PLO and its leadership had moved very swiftly from being a terrorist organization (according to the American administration) to one worthy of the White House's interest" (p. 3). In Abbas's account, the PLO elite felt great relief after being accepted as the representative of the Palestinian people.

Savir describes the haggling over terminology as being met with typical Palestinian leniency, a pattern that repeated itself several times during the negotiations. Whereas the Israeli delegation was fully prepared and had worked out every word, the Palestinian negotiators had to return to their bosses in Tunis each time that the Israelis changed a formulation.[16] Abbas reflects on this issue, noting,

> I remember that while we were discussing the matter of the displaced Palestinians and after the Israelis had agreed in principle to make reference to them, we disagreed on the use of one word. The Israelis' wording was: "The future status of the displaced Palestinians . . . will not be prejudiced *because* they are unable to participate in the election process, . . ." while we [the Palestinians] wanted it to read: "The future status of the displaced Palestinians . . . will not be prejudiced *if* they are unable to participate in the election process. . . ." A lengthy debate ensued about the use of the word "because," but in the end we could not have our way. (p. 162; emphasis in original)

Savir views this quibbling differently, when he comments, "On the part of the Palestinians, this was done by playing for time and avoiding an examination of details. On the Israeli side it was done by exploiting time and becoming obsessed with minutiae. The contrast reflected not just different approaches to reality but differences in the two political cultures" (p. 82). Such clashing descriptions of similar events illustrate the different ways in which Israelis and Palestinians understood the process they were involved in.

Abbas formulates every possible argument to justify the historical process that led to the Oslo agreement, uncovering the economic, political, and diplomatic labyrinth in which the PLO found itself. The eruption of the Intifada in December 1987 was a major factor that pushed the Palestinians toward accepting UN resolutions 242[17] and 338. Abbas considers the PLO's concern for not losing the momentum created by the Intifada as a vital part of the leadership's new strategy. Merely boasting about the achievements of the Intifada would not have served Palestinian interests. The PLO had to think of new possibilities that would offer the "children of the stones" a real solution. In this regard, Palestinian leaders agreed to reconsider UN resolutions that were once entirely rejected by the PLO. According to Abbas, the principal aim of this change was to "stifle the pretexts that Europe, America and Israel had been employing to justify their position vis-à-vis the PLO and the Palestinian issue" (p. 23). Abbas was obviously pleased with the opening of the dialogue between the PLO and the U.S. government after fourteen years of American holding aloof from contacting any PLO official. The PLO had now become "an official and integral part of any dialogue on the Middle East conflict" (pp. 33–34).

Abbas views the secret contacts between PLO delegates and representatives from the West Bank and elsewhere with top-ranking officials and members of both left-wing and right-wing parties in Israel as legitimizing the change in the PLO's historical positions toward recognizing Israel. Those secret contacts, for Abbas, amounted to mutual recognition and marked a change in Israeli political thought. Yet, notwithstanding his claims of deep changes in Israeli society, it seems that Abbas is really describing a process that was taking place within himself. The changes he attributes to Israeli society do seem to reflect the real position of Israeli officials as much as they mirror his own wishful thinking.

Developments on the ground were disturbing enough to change the whole enthusiastic atmosphere that developed after the signing of the agreements. Abbas points to the limitations of the diplomatic achievement, saying "I did not think that signing would end everything, but saw it rather as a beginning for many things particularly since the accord did not settle many issues and did not clarify many points that still required continuous hard work" (p. 5). The difficulties that both sides had to face were illustrated by, among other things, the tragic February 1994 massacre in Hebron, when a fanatic Jewish nationalist entered the al-Ibrahimi Mosque and shot dead thirty-one worshipers. This, as we now know, was but one tragic event in a series that was still to come.

Savir does a better job than Abbas in describing the ways in which the realization of the DOP caused difficulties for both sides.

He shows how the radical nationalist parties in Israel led a massive campaign against the implementation of the agreement. In many demonstrations organized by the right-wing parties, opposition politicians such as Benjamin Netanyahu and Rafael Eitan remained silent when the mob called Rabin a murderer or a traitor. Savir formulates his fears about the rising tension in Israel as follows: "I feared for the fate of the entire process. You can conduct negotiations under any circumstances, I mused, but at the end of the day, what counts is the determination to make peace by not allowing fanatics to undermine it" (p.128). This description of the rising opposition to the peace process within Israeli society serves to cool down Abbas's cheerful enthusiasm.

Arafat, on the other hand, had to face rising demands in the West Bank and Gaza Strip and throughout the Arab world. At first, in Savir's eyes,

> Arafat had shown himself to be a true partner in the quest for peace and—once more—the one man in the PLO capable of making difficult decisions. These qualities strengthened his ties with the only men on the Israeli side who were capable of doing the same, so it became possible once more to implement the declaration despite the serious problems that lay ahead. (p. 133)

After the Palestinian leader's emotional return to Gaza in July 1994, and the accompanying redeployment of the Israeli army, Savir assesses the newly established Palestinian Authority (PA) with a mixture of satisfaction, on the one hand, and concern, on the other:

> Arafat began his journey as the chairman of the Palestinian Authority by relying on the methods that had served him so well in Tunis: trying to centralize his power through divide and rule tactics. His first objective was to create an instrument for policing Gaza and Jericho, manned mostly by veterans, loyalists and members of the Palestine Liberation Army who were brought in from abroad and integrated with local supporters into a cluster of roughly a dozen sometimes redundant, or at least overlapping, security organs. (p. 145)

Savir does not connect Arafat's options and policies to the tough security conditions imposed on him by the Israeli side, betraying an orientalist view of Palestinian politics and governance.[18] His view is exemplified in the Israeli expectation that Arafat should crush the organizational infrastructure of Hamas. He states plainly that "our security people usually pressed Arafat, on every possible occasion, to send his policemen from house to house confiscating illegal arms. . . ." (p. 147). These expectations reflect the paternalistic way in which Israelis viewed their Palestinian peace partners.

Apart from his treatment of the negotiations, Savir includes a chapter on the developments that led to the assassination of Yitzhak Rabin. The progress in the peace process and the evacuation of the Israeli army from Palestinian cities was accompanied by rising violence. The terrorist attacks conducted by Islamic fundamentalists in Israeli cities were met with severe Israeli measures of closure and collective punishment. Right-wing radicals in Israel heated up the atmosphere and incited against the government and its prime minister. The rising tension led a Jewish nationalist fanatic to end the life of one of the prime symbols of the peace process. Savir's dramatic account of the assassination demonstrates the centrality of this incident in Israeli society, but his closing chapter concerning negotiations with the Palestinians and the Syrians illustrates his belief that personal acts of terrorists cannot stop the course of history.

Dialogue and Change

The fourth book under review is based on a thorough research of six intervention models applied in Arab-Jewish encounter programs in Israel. The study examines the underlying presumption of these programs, which is that it is possible to improve the relationship between the two parties by helping to create "more tolerant, democratic, and culturally sensitive generations" (p. xviii). Mohammed Abu-Nimer points out that "initiatives of encountering adversarial parties are usually considered to be an integral part of the forces that act for change in the relations between the conflicting parties or the different ethnic groups in divided societies" (p. xvii). His study examines whether the intervention programs are actually directed to promote political change, or whether they support the existing status quo control-system.

Abu-Nimer thoroughly reviews the intergroup-relations approach, pointing out drawbacks regarding its effectiveness at the structural level. This approach, based on individual and interpersonal encounters, falls short of addressing interethnic conflict and asymmetrical power relations. He favors, instead, conflict-resolution theory and its basic assumptions. Despite the shortage of adequate conceptualization in this field, Abu-Nimer stresses the usefulness of certain intervention models that are based on the conflict-resolution approach. He discusses the benefits and shortcomings of negotiation processes, mediation processes, problem-solving models, and conciliation processes, and demonstrates that intervention models have the ability to introduce systematic and structural change by reeducating the parties involved in a conflict.

After an analytic introduction focusing on conflict-resolution theory and the main models applied by its proponents, Abu-Nimer examines the intervention models applied to Arab-Jewish relations in Israel. In presenting the historical, social, and political background, he points out the central role the state plays in shaping the relationship between Arabs and Jews. Arab-Jewish coexistence programs have been responses to rising tensions in Israeli society. For example, the rise of radical and extreme racist attitudes among Jewish youth in the early 1980s marked the peak of the need for intervention models to reeducate the new generations in Israel and to reduce the impact of radical views espoused by Meir Kahane and others. This background helps explain the dominant role of Jewish organizations and individuals in the coexistence programs. It also explains the fact that the flow of resources to finance these programs comes from Jewish and state sources. Abu-Nimer shows how the organizational map of Arab-Jewish encounter programs mirrors Jewish domination over them. This factor reflects the structural bias embedded in these programs, and limits their possible impact on structural and social change.

These deficiencies are complemented by the biases in the research methods and approaches used to study coexistence programs (see, e.g., pp. 53–54). Besides remaining vague in terms of the effectiveness of encounters in changing the attitudes of the participants, their evaluation of positive and negative change derives from the definition of the State of Israel as a Jewish State with an Arab minority. Researchers always assume the existing ideological framework remains stable and is not an issue that should be also discussed in the encounters. Furthermore, previous research has relied on social-psychological approaches that concentrated on perception and attitudinal change, rather than on structural and political change. Therefore, no real attention was paid to the impact of structural constraints on the quality of relations between Arabs and Jews.

Following his critical review of existing research, Abu-Nimer presents his own comparative-qualitative research that describes, explores, and explains six existing intervention models that operate in the field of Arab-Jewish relations. He examines the selection of the participants; the underlying assumptions and goals of those involved; the structure (advance preparation, number of encounters, format of meetings, and follow-up activity); the issues discussed in the meetings; the process that takes place in the meetings, and the type of third-party intervention (activator, instructive, or facilitative). The central conclusion of this part of the study is that, despite the rising awareness that the conflictual relationship should remain central within coexistence programs, there is a lack of organizational support in all intervention programs that provide legitimacy and recognition for the existence of the conflict (pp. 93–94).

Abu-Nimer describes the contextual and interorganizational conditions that prevent the incorporation of the conflictual approach into Arab-Jewish intervention programs. The need for support from the Ministry of Education to enter schools, and the sources of funding that are mainly from Jewish individuals and organizations (whose main aim is to promote the positive image of the Jewish State), are among the main structural factors that influence the character of the intervention programs. Furthermore, the professional orientation of the Jewish, as opposed to Arab, interveners plays a crucial role. For most Jewish mediators or facilitators, this type of work is either used to help pave their way to managerial-level jobs or is viewed as a transitory period in their career. For many Arab interveners, these jobs are a last resort in cases where they could not find professional jobs or were not enrolled as educators in the regular school system. These conditions determine the typical design and process of interaction in Arab-Jewish encounters.

One of the important findings of this study is that the intervention programs do not always reflect the perceptions of the interveners and the participants. This is illustrated by the fact that many interveners expressed, on the one hand, their desire to introduce political change and promote the solution of the Arab-Jewish conflict and, on the other hand, thought that the changes produced by Arab-Jewish encounters were insufficient for resolving the conflict. Indeed, Abu-Nimer's study demonstrates the limited impact of intervention programs. While they may increase an awareness of Arab-Jewish relations, they fall short by not going beyond the immediate circle of the individual, in the case of students, or the immediate circle of the school and professional domain, in the case of teachers. Intervention programs were not influencing the larger political context, and were not facilitating social or political change.

Abu-Nimer sums up his study by stating that the intervention models in their current structure, framework, process, and content "are operating in a manner that . . . contributes to preserving the status quo of the control system which the Israeli government imposes on Arabs in Israel" (p. 158). He demonstrates the ways in which encounter programs strengthen the separation between the political, on the one hand, and the personal or psychological-cultural, on the other hand, thereby educating students to avoid political issues. In his view, "schools and educators are charged with maintaining the status quo, rather than with producing changes that might upset the existing economic, social and political equations" (p. 158).

Dialogue, Conflict Resolution, and Change is the first comprehensive and critical study of the "conflict industry" which, despite its contribution to the creation of a positive atmosphere among some Arabs and Jews, serves as a sophisticated source of income to a limited number of people who usually belong to the same political elite that dominates the Israeli political system. Abu-Nimer's contribution provides us with new critical analytic tools that enable a better understanding of the other books reviewed here. It helps readers develop a deeper appreciation of Abbas's and Savir's accounts of the peace process, and demonstrates why the current peace process is not following a promising track toward conflict resolution.

Conclusion

An observer of the conflict with long experience in organizing informal meetings between Israelis and Palestinians has very accurately pointed out the shortcomings of the peace process begun at Madrid and Oslo:

> Over the decades, the parties [Israelis and Palestinians] have engaged in systematic denial of each other's national

> identity, with the aim of delegitimizing the other's national movement and political aspirations. . . . [I]f the parties are to conclude a principled agreement, conducive to sustainable peace and reconciliation, they will have not only to reverse this pattern, but also to take active steps to acknowledge the other's nationhood and humanity in word and deed.
>
> The mutual recognition of the Oslo agreement represented an initial step in that direction. It did not go beyond a pragmatic acceptance of the fact that the other exists and must be accommodated in order to achieve a mutually satisfactory solution of the conflict.[19]

The mutual recognition described by Savir and Abbas as the crown of the Oslo peace talks was not an acceptance, in principle, of the mutual needs of the two parties. While the Oslo Accords were a clear sign of a change in the attitude on both sides, this change was far from the end of the struggle, as we have learned from the mounting frustrations and disappointments in the implementation of the 1993 accords.

The realities inside Israel, and in the West Bank and Gaza, indicate that there are deeper unresolved problems that cannot be discarded in the twinkling of an eye. Irreconcilable differences may be creatively bypassed, in the short term, by mutual ambivalent postures and vague formulations of the various agreements that have been signed.[20] But, ultimately, these differences will remain to hamper true reconciliation until they are effectively dealt with by wiser and more successful strategies than the ones recommended thus far by many of authors covered in this review.

The Palestinian-Israeli peace talks begun at Oslo were based not on the willingness of the two parties to transform their antagonistic conceptions of national identity; rather, they served to institutionalize the existing asymmetrical power-relations between them. They failed because they were based on the desire by both sides to achieve the recognition of the other party without directly confronting the uncomfortable historical sources of the conflict. With the existing status quo as the point of departure, hopes for peace were built on the principle of graduality and on the postponement of the most controversial issues (settlements, Jerusalem, and refugees) to the "final-status" negotiations. But developments on the ground and the efforts made by the powerful side to preempt the results of the final-status negotiations by creating facts during the interim period have contributed to the failure of the Oslo process.

The four books under review expose the reader to the full complexity of the relationship between Israelis and Palestinians. The critical reader will be rewarded with sobering evidence of the impossibility of overcoming a long-standing colonial condition by mere technicalities and organizational manipulations imposed by the powerful party on the weaker one. The tendency of the powerful party to establish its historic gains at minimal costs without accommodating the demands of the weaker party has turned the peace process into a mechanism to institutionalize the occupation. Such a tendency may prolong the "process" but is very short on "peace."

Notes

1. Albert Memmi, *Dominated: Notes Towards a Portrait* (London: Orion Press, 1968), 45.

2. Leela Gandhi, *Postcolonial Theory: A Critical Introduction* (New York: Columbia University Press, 1998), 11.

3. Michel Foucault, *Power/Knowledge: Selected Interviews and Other Writings 1972-1977* (Hertfordshire, England: Harvester Press, 1980), 98.

4. J. Ann Tickner, "Identity in International Relations Theory: Feminist Perspective," in *The Return of Culture and Identity in International Relations Theory,* eds. Yosef Lapid and Friedrich Kratochwil (Boulder, CO: Lynne Rienner, 1997), 147.

5. Rashid Khalidi, *Palestinian Identity: The Construction of Modern National Consciousness* (New York: Columbia University Press, 1997).

6. Edward Said, *The Question of Palestine* (New York: Times Books, 1979).

7. Khalidi, *Palestinian Identity*.

8. Homi K. Bhabha, *The Location of Culture* (London: Routledge, 1994).

9. See, for instance, Benedict Anderson, *Imagined Communities: Reflections on the Origins and Spread of Nationalism* (London: Verso, 1991); Eric J. Hobsbawm and Terence Ranger, *The Invention of Tradition* (Cambridge: Cambridge University Press/Canto, 1983).

10. Paul Gilbert, "The Idea of National Literature," in *Literature and the Political Imagination,* eds. John Horton and Andrea T. Baumeister (London: Routledge, 1996).

11. Homi K. Bhabha, ed., *Nation and Narration* (London: Routledge, 1990).

12. Edward Said, *Culture and Imperialism* (London: Chatto & Windus, 1993), xiii.

13. For the text of the "Declaration of Principles on Interim Self-Government Arrangements," dated 13 September 1993, see Laura Zittrain Eisenberg and Neil Caplan, *Negotiating Arab-Israeli Peace: Patterns, Problems, Possibilities* (Bloomington: Indiana University Press, 1998), 212–16 (doc. 13).

14. Charles Taylor, "The Politics of Recognition," in *Multiculturalism: Examining the Politics of Recognition,* edited and introduced by Amy Gutmann (Princeton: Princeton University Press, 1994), 52–73.

15. Ashis Nandy, *The Intimate Enemy: Loss and Recovery of Self Under Colonialism* (Delhi: Oxford University Press, 1983).

16. See, for instance, the Israeli request to replace the word "accordingly" with "consequently" in the letters of mutual recognition, described in Uri Savir, *The Process,* 75–76.

17. For the text of the UN Security Council Resolution 242 adopted on 22 November 1967, see Eisenberg and Caplan, *Negotiating Arab-Israeli Peace,* 157 (doc. 1).

18. For the meaning and evolution of orientalist views, see Said, *Orientalism* (New York: Pantheon, 1978).

19. Herbert Kelman, "Building a Sustainable Peace: The Limits of Pragmatism in the Israeli-Palestinian Negotiations," *Journal of Palestine Studies* 28:1 (Autumn 1998): 47.

20. Aharon Klieman, *Constructive Ambiguity in Middle East Peace-Making* (Tel Aviv University: Tami Steinmetz Center for Peace Research, 1999).

12. Economics as a Security Tool in an Era of "Peace" in the Middle East

Maen F. Nsour,
The School of Public Policy,
George Mason University

This essay explores the economic implications of the Arab-Israeli political peace process and the implications for each state's complex security considerations. A review of recent literature in Arabic indicates that reactions to proposals for Arab-Israeli economic cooperation are mixed, displaying more suspicion and contempt than enthusiasm. The author proposes that the quality and extent of regional cooperation between Israel and the Arab states will be dependent upon the development of a common perception that cooperation is in everyone's interest. Under current political conditions, Arab analysts argue that allowing Israel to export to Arab markets will actually enhance Israel's capabilities for maintaining its greater military spending. Only a comprehensive political settlement with real "peace dividends" can bring about long-term stability and a reduction in tension. Until then, a purposeful policy of Arab-Israeli economic interdependency is unlikely. Instead, scholars suggest that the Arab states will either continue to seek security through the modernization of their armed forces, or attempt an integrative arrangement among themselves as an option for counteracting Israel's current perceived economic and security dominance.

Kayali, Majid, *The "Middle-Eastern" Scheme: Its Dimensions, Basis, and Contradictions*, Abu-Dhabi, U.A.E.: Emirates Center for Strategic Studies, 1998 (in Arabic: *Al-Mashrou' al-Sharq al-Awsati: Ab'aduh, Murtakazatuh wa-Tanakudhatuh*).

Kaylani, Haitham, *The Peaceful Settlement for the Arab-Israeli Conflict and its Impact on the Arab Security,* Abu-Dhabi, U.A.E.: Emirates Center for Strategic Studies, 1996 (in Arabic: *Al-Tasweyah al-Silmiyah l-il-Seraa' al-Arabi al-Isra'ili wa-Atharuha 'ala al-Amn al-Arabi*).

Sahli, Nabil, *The Development of the Israeli Economy: 1948–1996,* Abu-Dhabi, U.A.E.: Emirates Center for Strategic Studies, 1998 (in Arabic: *Tatawor al-Iqtisad al-Isra'ili: 1948–1996*).

Yamout, Abdul-Hadi, *The Arab Economy and 'Middle Easternism',* Tunis, Tunisia: Arab Development Institute, 1997 (in Arabic: *Al-Iktisad al-Arabi wa al-Sharq Awsatiyah*).

In international politics states are primarily concerned with preserving their national security. For a state to safeguard its security, or to continue to survive, possessing a strong economy, which is manifested by a relatively high gross national product (GNP), advanced high-technology industries, and an abundance of human and natural resources is inevitable. A state's ability to establish and sustain an agile military force depends, to a great extent, on its continuous ability to divert adequate resources to such an endeavor. Military strength—in certain circumstances—is also a means by which the state can preserve its national wealth and prosperity. Security, for any state or a group of states, can be based either on the weakness of rivals or on higher relative capabilities. The most effective way to preserve national security will be through creating a state of military capabilities so that potential adversaries, by reason of their relative weakness, will not contemplate the idea of aggression. As the power of the state is measured by its relative standing in comparison to other states, a nation might enhance its power not only by expanding its own capabilities, but also by conspiring to weaken its potential enemies. Either course would improve its relative strategic standing among nations. Once in a dominant position, states usually embrace economic coercion as an integral element of their foreign policy and grand strategy, thus jeopardizing security and stability of the system simply because conflict escalation may well take place as a result of coercion through economic means.[1] Klaus Knorr maintains that "[l]ike all power, material economic power can be used for coercion, for influencing the behavior of the weaker actor, or for directly achieving a desired effect, harmful in an adversary relationship, supportive between friendly or allied countries."[2] Surely, under crisis conditions, vulnerable states always become targets of economic coercion and their policies fall hostage to the dominant actor in the system.

The Security Dilemma

Nation-states want many of the same things—survival, sovereign freedom, status, and wealth. To ensure their own self-preservation, most states are motivated to acquire as much military might as their resources allow. The predicament that such behavior creates is the security dilemma: Arms acquired are perceived by others as threatening, which then provokes similar behavior by those threatened.[3] According to Glenn Snyder, the security dilemma results because

> [e]ven when no state has any desire to attack others, none can be sure that others' intentions are peaceful, or will remain so; hence each must maintain power for defense. Since no state can know that the power accumulation of others is defensively motivated only, each must assume that it might be intended for attack. Consequently, each party's power increments are matched by the others, and all wind up with no more security than when the vicious cycle began, along with the costs incurred in having acquired and having to maintain their power.[4]

Underlying the security dilemma are two important assumptions: (1) security is a function of power and (2) power is a function of economic and military capabilities. The security dilemma explains why states that might be sharing a common interest engage in individual actions that prevent them from obtaining it. According to the four authors under review here, the security dilemma in the Middle East explains why the Arab states should refrain from indulging in economic relations with Israel. Majid Kayali, Haitham Kaylani, Nabil Sahli and Abdul-Hadi Yamout all subscribe to Robert Baldwin and

David Kay's argument that "[i]ncreased trade enables . . . countries [to achieve a dominant competitive position] to strengthen their security position not only by accelerating their rate of income growth but also by creating dependency relationships on the part of the other countries through trade and investment ties."[5] The central thesis in the reviewed works is the vital importance of the economic element to national security. National security can be furthered by weakening the economies of rivals or potential rivals as well as by strengthening and organizing its own and those of its allies. Nations—even the best of allies—engage in different forms of "economic warfare"[6] and in different intensities, the purpose of which is to increase their economic strength or to weaken or disrupt the ability of enemies or potential enemies to provide economic support for their national policies. These actions include economic, political, and psychological measures. All strategies require economic resources in some form or other for their preparation and execution. Thus Kaylani, a former Syrian ambassador to the United Nations and the editor of the Arab League's Arabic periodical *Arab Affairs,* speaks for all our authors when he states in *The Peaceful Settlement for the Arab-Israeli Conflict and Its Impact on the Arab Security* that

> [a]ny discussion of a common market or free trade in the Middle East, or any cooperation in the areas of environment, transportation, tourism, science and technology, and other fields should not be looked into unless the elements of security are enhanced and trust is established between the states that intend to cooperate. Surely, these elements can not materialize if the Israeli nuclear umbrella continues to dominate the horizons of the area and as long as Arab security continues to be the hostage for the Israeli nuclear weapon. . . . The persistence of this dangerous imbalance of power between the participants in the peace process retards the Arab drive to achieve a settlement with Israel. . . . There is no meaning for peace in the shadow of nuclear capabilities possessed by a single party that can use it to impose its will on the other parties. (pp. 61–62)

Economics and Security

The relationship between economics and security is pervasive, profound, and extremely complex. Economic factors play a clear role in determining the basic structure of geostrategic systems. It is the relative economic strength of a state in a system that ultimately defines the status of the state. Economic strength is the single most important index of national power. It is the ability of national economies to sustain high levels of growth, to generate and capitalize on advanced technological products and processes, and to engage competitively and energetically in the international marketplace that will determine rankings in international power lists. Our authors recognize the determinate role of economic factors in shaping the structure of security in the Middle East. This recognition is surely behind the apparent unanimity of our authors in basically all their positions vis-à-vis the utilization of economics as a security tool. Sahli, a researcher at the Central Bureau for Palestinian Statistics in Damascus, argues in *The Development of the Israeli Economy: 1948–1996* that "[b]ecause of the grave implications of the "Middle Easternism" scheme . . . the devising of an appropriate new economic Arab strategy to respond to the new perils is an absolute necessity that is dictated by the daunting regional developments" (p. 86). Similarly, Dr. Abdul-Hadi Yamout, in *The Arab Economy and 'Middle Easternism'* points to the persistent emphasis among Arab states to reduce vulnerabilities by maintaining or increasing their relative power position in the international system and by maintaining as much autonomy as possible. The Arab states, according to Yamout, continue to measure their vulnerabilities by comparing military capabilities mainly with Israel, by assessing their dependence on strategic resources located on the territory of other states, and by assessing their economic and diplomatic entanglements on their power to control outcomes in such a way as to maintain their capabilities and reduce dependencies (pp. 328–29).

For Yamout, control of markets by Israel becomes a new threat to replace the threat of territorial control. He maintains that just because threats to a nation's territory and resources do not arise in the form of military aggression, the threats themselves have not disappeared. Nations in intense competition with one another will seek to manipulate markets to control the resources of others (pp. 303–8).

Haitham Kaylani, on the other hand, reminds his readers that

> Israeli strategic thinking literature points clearly to the fact that the peace process should not affect the vigorous military technology and industrialization. On the contrary, it emphasizes that this industry should develop for both eco-

> nomic and security reasons. Israeli scholars stress that the post-peace era requires the continuous sustenance of military superiority over the Arabs, and to them, that ensures stability and guarantees state security. (p. 60)

Technological leadership is the basis of economic power, and economic power is the foundation of military might.[7] Kaylani maintains that "The advanced Israeli military technology will continue to be the source of anxiety for [Arab] participants in the settlement process and the focus of their main concern when devising strategies to preserve their national interests" (p. 59). Those states where commercial innovation flourishes and that provide the source of production for another's industrial base are those that are economically competitive and thus increasingly powerful. And their power is a growing source of political influence and can, under the right conditions, be adapted to bolster national military capabilities.

National Security and Economic Cooperation in the Arab-Israeli Context

Growing economic ties between adversaries may affect threat perceptions and shift national security interest calculations. In some circumstances, interdependence is as likely to cause resentment and tension as to promote mutual trust and confidence.[8] Much depends on the maintenance of equitable economic growth and the absence of security threats. If significant differences in economic growth exist, then interdependence is unlikely to be a constraint on disputes, but leads to mutual recriminations and to a tense strategic environment. There are many important economic issues that have significant security dimensions in the Middle East. Among these security-related economic issues are the relationship between economic growth and defense expenditures; the implication of economic interdependence for regional security; and issues such as trade diversion, tariffs and other forms of protection, and violations of international trade agreements that could lead to disputation and conflict. Sahli argues that

> [t]he rise of a "Middle Eastern system" will inevitably lead to the weakening of the Arab position and to the collapse of the Arab national idea and will serve the integration of

> Israel in a regional system made of multi-nationalities. . . . This scheme will allow Israel to become a partner in regional resources. Integration into the [Arab] region will lead Israel to benefit in the areas of water, oil, financial resources, human power, markets and investments. . . . This scheme, if it materializes, will help in the development of the Israeli economy, after it was about to suffocate because of limited markets, labor shortage, limited investment and financing opportunities and, most importantly, colossal military spending. (p. 63)

Regional reactions to Arab-Israeli economic cooperation are mixed, although there is more suspicion and derision than enthusiasm.[9] Regional cooperation between Israel and the Arab states is dependent upon the development of a common perception that cooperation is in everyone's interest. Kayali, press director at the International Union for Arab Labor Syndicates based in Damascus, maintains in *The "Middle-Eastern" Scheme: Its Dimensions, Basis, and Contradictions* that the realities of economic dynamism and increasing interdependence, and the opportunities and challenges they present, do not autonomously generate cooperative mechanisms. People are not persuaded that multilateralism is the most appropriate approach to managing this economic dynamism and increasing interdependence. In the era of both the post-1993 peace process and ongoing conflict in the region, people are obviously far from perceiving economic relations between Israel and the Arab states as beneficial. In fact, there is widespread persuasion that allowing Israel to access Arab markets will enhance its capabilities to maintain a garrison state. Sahli claims that

> [t]he main objective of integrating the state of Israel [into a Middle Eastern market]—apart from the political purposes—is to launch the mechanisms of growth of an Israeli economy that is facing difficulties. . . . [T]his economic relationship with Israel—within the context of the suggested market—will boost the Israeli economy and will, consequently, lead it to become the pivotal economy in the region. (p. 83)

The Arab authors under review echo the findings of Simon Kuznets, who suggests that uneven growth in an international system leads states toward conflict. Kuznets argues that rates of economic growth and wide differences in rates of growth "cumulate rapidly into marked shifts in relative economic and political power among nations—a situation usually provocative of international strain and conflict."[10] He points out that such uneven growth increases political influence and economic advantage, thus creating parallel disadvantage and a decrease in other nations' power, inclining them toward conflict. Kuznets maintains that rapid growth in some nations, consequent to industrialization, paired with stagnation in others, could vitiate the security regime binding the global community together.[11]

Categories of Economic-Security Interaction

There are three categories of economic-security interaction: the national strength of a country, which depends upon both its economy and its military; national preferences (e.g., the choice of military allies or trade partners), formed from both economic and security interests; and economic or military actions that can be used as policy tools to affect one another.[12] Within these three categories (strength, preferences, and tools), influence can run either from economics to security or vise versa.

National Strengths

A relatively large economic surplus allows for diversion of resources toward achieving security goals. Economic surplus can be spent directly on increasing the prowess of a nation's military, either quantitatively or qualitatively. A nation's technology level enhances and is enhanced by its military might. To quote Kenneth Waltz, "great power status cannot be maintained without a certain economic capacity" or "without a considerable economic capacity no state can hope to sustain a world role."[13]

These reviewed works consider this line of reasoning and respond to the question, does the opening of Arab markets to Israel's exports enhance the latter's economic capabilities which, in turn, account for growth in military spending in Israel? The answer to this question is unanimously yes. However, the literature on this subject does not address whether higher levels of military spending account for higher levels of economic growth. The implications of the latter issue are substantial and have deep policy implications for economic cooperation between Israel and the Arab world. If relatively high military expenditure in Israel cannot be used to generate economic growth in the country, policymakers in Israel must, therefore, be making military spending decisions for security purposes only. Obviously, the Arab states are primary objects of Israeli security. Had Israeli policymakers been concerned only about economic growth a better policy would be reallocating government resources from the military sector toward civilian purposes. Military expenditure could prove to be exclusively subject to the strategic environment facing Israel. Consequently, the Arab states could find that economic cooperation with Israel would jeopardize their national security and restrain the development of any meaningful economic interaction. This issue will be addressed later on in this essay.

National Preferences

The central premise here is that foreign policy preferences within a nation depend to a certain extent on its economic structure. There are several ways in which this relationship might play out. High levels of foreign trade and investment might increase costs of war to a country and thus motivate it to maintain peaceful foreign relations. Or the structure of a nation's trading relationships could lead to a set of preferences regarding its allies and enemies. According to Robert Keohane and Joseph Nye, "Transnational relations affect interstate politics by altering the choices open to statesmen and the costs that must be born for adopting various courses of action."[14]

Thus, according to this line of thought, economic interdependence can create a set of domestic interests that are translated into policy through the domestic political process. Such increased economic interaction might affect the security preferences of nations through the creation of a sense of "regionhood" that eases feelings of insecurity. This interaction can certainly work the other way as well. For a nation with certain security preferences regarding a particular neighbor, it is expected that its economic policies and relationships would be structured accordingly. The economic impact of security concerns is evident in domestic economic development strategies and can be seen in the structure of international economic relations. Examples of the latter are Arab attempts to prohibit trade with Israel through the use of the Central Boycott Office (CBO).[15]

Policy Tools

Another view of the economics-security connection acknowledges that both can be used as tools by one nation in order to change the behavior of another nation.[16] An increase in defense expenditure is dependent on the rate of increase in gross domestic product (GDP) and an increase in perceived external threats. Threat perception and sense of vulnerability have some bearing on defense spending. According to the reviewed works there is one major power looming on the horizon in the Middle East: Israel. Our Arab authors believe Israel could bolster its hegemonic position and create regional instability. This evolving and uncertain strategic scenario will produce new security threats for the Arab states. In the face of such an uncertain security situation, the authors advocate, Arab countries should turn more toward security self-reliance, best pursued through modernization of armed forces and the adoption of deterrence strategy. These authors argue that economics will continue to be an indispensable tool in the Arabs' strategy for national security. In fact, the quantity and quality of arms presently being acquired by the Arab states require favorable economic performance.[17]

Economic development and defense expenditure are positively linked. The ability of Israel and the Arab states to increase their acquisition of military hardware can stem from a vibrant economic growth. Economic growth means not only that a country can spend more on the military, but also that an increase in military spending is not perceived to be a social burden. The policy implication that our authors attempt to field is obvious: security policy cannot be considered in isolation from economics, and vise versa. In other words economic growth begets power and power can beget economic growth.

Power in International Politics

Power manifests itself in the ability of one actor to persuade another to do what it otherwise would not do. Power is the exercise of influence over another; it is the ability to coerce or to obtain what one wants through manipulation. Indeed, to say that nations pursue power is to say that they seek the ability to control others.[18]

When power is viewed in this way, the following question arises, What enables states to achieve their goals? That is, what kinds of capabilities or resources are necessary to attain influence over others? According to Yamout, many factors simultaneously enhance a state's ability to achieve its goals vis-à-vis others, and these multiple factors, or some combination of them, provide a composite measure of states' relative power potential (pp. 331–45).

Of all resources that make for national power, economic resources and military force are usually regarded as the most important, with the former providing the basis for the acquisition of the latter.[19] The reviewed works assert that economic resources enable the development of military capabilities with which states can project their power; they enhance a state's political leverage in its dealings with others and provide the means to the end of military power. The assumption that the capacity to inflict military defeat is crucial to calculating power ratios derives from the conviction that it leads to the capacity to influence. The conviction rests in turn on the corollary that to make others act according to one's will, the ability to inflict punishment is greatly important, more so than the ability to offer rewards.[20]

In addition to military capability, Yamout stresses other factors or combinations of them that presumably contribute to national power. Power differentials are thought to spring also from relative differences in state's population and territorial size, geographic location, raw materials, degree of dependence on foreign supplies of materials, technological capacity, efficiency of governmental decision making, industrial productivity, volume of trade, savings and investment, and educational level (pp. 345–63).[21] Clearly, our authors believe that suppression of power potentials of Israel necessitates exerting efforts by the Arab states at limiting economic growth of their foe. Market closure in the face of this potential enemy's products is a route that they advocate that policymakers should consider.

The Arms Race in the Middle East and Regional Security

This essay has investigated Arab authors' positions on the possibility of normal economic relations emerging under grave security concerns. In the Arab-Israeli case, economic relations would be far-fetched under the current political and security environment, especially when we know that Arab intellectuals believe that

> [e]fforts are being exerted to advance economic considerations and establish new realities and institutional and organizational structures that will gradually contribute to the restructuring of the Arab world's map. . . . [T]he main objective of these efforts is to integrate Israel into the fabric of the Arab world and guarantee its security even though it refuses to honor the peace process dogmas, embraces expansionist and racist policies, and continues to shelter a nuclear arsenal. (Kaylani, p. 51)

The reviewed works suggest that national security can be enhanced by weakening the economies of rivals or potential rivals as well as by fortifying and organizing its own and those of its allies. Economic warfare (e.g., imposing trade sanctions) is waged by nations to increase their economic strength or to weaken or disrupt the ability of enemies or potential enemies to provide economic support for their national policies. All of the strategies adopted by nations require economic resources in some form or another for their preparation and execution. Limitations of resource availability will exclude certain strategies completely from consideration. Apparently, one of the major objectives of public policy is to assure that these economic limitations on possible courses of action afforded by a potential rival are increased to a sufficient level.

The opening of Arab markets to Israel's exports enhances the latter's economic capabilities which, in turn, account for growth in military spending in Israel. However, higher levels of military spending account for lower levels of economic growth. Applied research revealed that the combined effect of military expenditure on the output growth rate in Israel is significantly negative; increased military spending retards economic growth in Israel.[22] The implications of the latter part of the investigation are substantial and have deep policy implications for economic cooperation between Israel and the Arab world. Since relatively high military expenditure in Israel cannot be used to generate economic growth in the country, policymakers in Israel are clearly making military spending decisions for security purposes only. Surely, the Arab states are principal targets of Israeli security planning. Consequently, the Arab states perceive economic cooperation with Israel as precarious to their national security and are expected to restrain the evolvement of any significant economic interaction. Apparently, comprehensive political settlements to the conflict in the region are indispensable for an Arab-Israeli peace that can be followed by an arms control agreement, leading to a balance of power at lower armament levels. According to Jordin Cohen et al.,

> The peace race stage [in the Middle East] requires a protective environment to flourish. No peace dividend, regardless of its original stimulus, can survive without continued regional disarmament and de-escalation. The peace dividend requires very specific conditions to thrive, and takes a long time to develop, often appearing suddenly and by surprise. Just the same, the peace race can be permanently and irreparably damaged.[23]

Israel's perceptions of its relations with the Arab world explain why Israel's defense budget has not been reduced significantly since the commencement of the peace process in 1991. A substantial reallocation of resources toward nonmilitary sectors is subject to the strategic plans of Israel.

The ongoing exchange among Arab and Israeli security experts is not encouraging. For example, Ariel Levité of Tel Aviv University's Jaffee Center for Strategic Studies, pronounces that

> in the course of the evolutionary transition [peace] process Israel should be consciously allowed to retain certain assets and to cultivate its qualitative edge [over the Arabs] in certain key areas that are vital for its security and the confidence of its public. Some may wish to call this special treatment accorded to Israel "favorable discrimination." My personal viewpoint is that it ought to be looked upon as an act of political realism, whereby Israel is allowed to retain certain assets and capabilities as a hedge against setbacks or reversal of the peace process until such time that the gains made in the process appear sufficiently far reaching and secure, so as to obviate the need for such a hedge.[24]

Shai Feldman, also of Tel Aviv University's Jaffee Center for Strategic Studies, maintains that "[a]lthough unaware of the concepts and discourse of international relations theory, by instinct most Israelis are disciples of Kenneth Waltz . . . they regard their regional and international environment as a self-help anarchic system."[25] Feldman also maintains that

> Without Israel's cumulative deterrence remaining intact, it would be impossible to ensure that current trends in the region favoring accommodation with Israel were not reversed. Yet Israel's deterrence posture may have to be restructured, making it complementary to the efforts to implement arms control in the region . . . while the trends toward moderation and accommodation in the Arab world are unmistakable, other regional developments signal increasing extremism, hostility, and potential violence. . . . Clearly, a less certain environment will result in greater reluctance to make unilateral concessions or to adopt regional initiatives which might advance efforts to control the flow of arms to the region.[26]

Both Levité and Feldman unequivocally imply that the security dilemma has to haunt the Middle East for some time to come. Arab security experts, on the other hand, sound their somber concerns and suggest contrasting arrangements to uphold regional security. Taha Abdel Halim, a retired general in Egypt's armed forces and a senior associate at the National Center for Middle East Studies in Cairo, argues that regional security and arms limitation arrangements in the region should be based upon "[a] quantitative and qualitative symmetry in the military capabilities of the region's states, including the indigenous military industrial capabilities since the prevailing dangerous asymmetry cannot continue. . . . [Moreover,] security should be achieved through agreed-upon political arrangements, excluding military superiority."[27] Ahmed Hashim, a research fellow at the International Institute for Strategic Studies in London, suggests that

> [i]n operational terms the threat posed by this hi-tech crusader state . . . means the tendency of this state to succumb to hubris and an arrogant display of its military and technological superiority. . . . While Israel has always been concerned that the quantitative balance is permanently tipped against it, the Arabs have increasingly begun to view the qualitative balance—based on Israeli scientific, technological, and educational superiority—as being more important. . . . [A]lmost all the major components of Israeli military strategy, doctrine, and capabilities are viewed with deep apprehension by the Arabs.[28]

Eliot Cohen et al. maintain that Israel

> will undoubtedly maintain and even increase the gap in conventional military capabilities that currently exists between it and potential Arab opponents. Drawing on a more literate and technically sophisticated population and equipped with military hardware comparable, at its best, to that fielded by the United States, the IDF will dominate the armies and air forces of its neighbors. . . . Israel's ability to manufacture and maintain advanced arms is much more solid than that of its potential opponents who lack sophisticated defense industries, and whose economies lag well behind that of the Jewish state.[29]

Conclusion

The works reviewed here consider whether an expanding web of economic relations between Israel and the Arab states should materialize under the current levels of military expenditures and threats to national securities. They also look into whether the expanding web of economic ties in the Middle East between Israel and the Arab states will mute conflicts in the region, creating a more stable security environment, or whether those ties will define new lines of conflict, reinforcing or exacerbating regional security problems.

The authors suggest that the emerging distribution of economic capabilities indicate regional rivalry, where each nation's drive for security would lead it to accumulate state power at the expense of the others. Kayali correctly argues that security in the Middle East would be a very different game from what we have been accustomed to during the Arab-Israeli military conflict (pp. 111–18). It is feared that "security threats" in the Middle East will no longer refer just to missiles and tanks but also to the control of markets, investment, and technology. Economic rivalry can beget political and possibly military confrontations. Governments concerned about the growing economic and technological resources of a rival or the risks of dependency may fixate on the possibility of a loss of position and power.

In the Arab world the perception is that expanding investment and trade will create an Israel-dominated market hierarchy. Israeli preeminence in advanced technologies, its free trade agreements with the United States and the European Union, and its marketing infrastructure all will give Israel increasing economic influence within the region. Economic dependence on Israel could set the lines of conflict as its Arab rivals in the region seek to build autonomous industrial and technological positions from which they could challenge Israel and break loose from their position of dependency. Efforts to break out could pit Israel against the Arab countries. Since Israel enjoys a military edge over the Arab states, the latter will have extremely limited foreign policy options. This, of course, also applies to noneconomic issues.

Kaylani argues that movement toward a final settlement of the Arab-Israeli conflict should be accompanied by serious efforts to mitigate hovering security concerns. Foremost among these efforts is a significant curb on military spending within the context of a practical security regime (pp. 58–69).

Military expenditures have extensive social and economic consequences. Economic effects are most pronounced in leading military spenders. The negative long-term consequences of military expenditures overshadow any positive short-term effects. Therefore, military expenditures, contributing to economic stagnation and structural dislocation, influence the economic and political future of high spenders and their mutual relations, shaped by competition for control over modern technologies. In the Middle East, there exists a choice between the urgent need to stimulate economic development, on the one hand, and military spending on the other hand. The social and cultural consequences of the arms race are visible in every country involved in it, affecting both the allocation of resources and the political atmosphere in their societies. There is a genuine trade-off between the allocation of national resources to military purposes and the ability to solve regional social problems. Yamout regards trade specifically, and economic interactions generally, as the dynamic foundations of distribution and levels of national power. National power rests on economic productivity and on the ability of the state to apply it as force. Yamout identified the interests of producers with the national interest, and the economic wealth and growth of industry with the political-military power of the state. He asserted that it is the responsibility of Arab industry to generate wealth through efficient production, and of Arab commerce to increase it through advantageous trade (p. 351). Trading relations are the dynamic basis of political relationships, distribution of power, and absolute levels of national power, the issues that most often lead to conflict.[30] Higher levels of trade confer higher, disproportionate, economic gains on potential national adversaries, and render states vulnerable to international economic fluctuations or economic manipulation by trading partners.

The dialogue among Middle Eastern security experts indicates that the region will have to live with a fervent arms race for the foreseeable future. This, of course, implies that broad trade relations between Israel and the Arab states will not materialize as long as the fears have not vanished.

The arms race between Israel and the Arab states has a multidimensional character in that it contains political, economic, technological and, most important, security elements. The cause-and-effect nature of the security element is reflected in the connection between the arms race and interstate rivalries. This means that regional tensions, disputes, and conflicts provide reasons for acquiring new and more weapons, while the acquisition of weapons in turn exacerbates difficult relationships and conflicts. Even more important, the arms race involves the risk of war.

Political and military tensions are not only always the overriding factor in accounting for the changes in military budgets. Economic constraints can bring about a decrease in military spending in spite of serious and continuing confrontation between the states in the area. However, the resolution of military conflicts and political instabilities remains essential for any reliable and long-lasting arrangement for reducing significantly the military burden of countries in the Middle East.

Notes

1. See Klaus Knorr, *The Power of Nations: The Political Economy of International Relations* (New York: Basic, 1975); Knorr, "Economic Interdependence and National Security," in *Economic Issues and National Security,* eds. Knorr and Frank Trager (Lawrence: Regents Press of Kansas, 1977), 1–18; Knorr,"International Economic Leverage and its Uses," in *Economic Issues and National Security,* 99–126; Kenneth Waltz, *Theory of International Politics* (Reading, MA: Addison-Wesley, 1979); Richard Bissell, "The Importance of the Economic Base to National Security," in *Strategic Dimensions of Economic Behavior,* eds. Gordon McCromick and Richard Bissell (New York: Praeger Publishers, 1984), 87-103; David Deese, "The Vulnerabilities of Modern Economies," in *Strategic Dimensions of Economic*

Behavior, 148–80; Robert Gilpin, "Structural Constraints on Economic Leverage: Market-Type Systems," in *Strategic Dimensions of Economic Behavior,* 105–28; Joseph Grieco, "Anarchy and the Limits of Cooperation: A Realist Critique of the Newest Liberal Institutionalism," *International Organization* 42 (August 1988): 485–507; Raymond Vernon and Ethan Kapstein, "National Needs, Global Resources," *Daedalus* 120:4 (Fall 1991): 1–22.

2. Klaus Knorr, *Power and Wealth: The Political Economy of International Wealth* (New York: Basic, 1973),133.

3. See John Herz, *Political Realism and Political Idealism* (Chicago: University of Chicago Press, 1951).

4. Glenn Snyder, "The Security Dilemma in Alliance Politics," *World Politics* 36 (July 1984): 461.

5. See Robert Baldwin and David Kay, "International Trade and International Relations," *International Organization* 29:1 (Winter 1975): 99–131.

6. Economic warfare may be defined as "all actions, other than military, taken to weaken or disrupt the ability of an enemy or potential enemy to provide economic support for its national policy." George Lincoln, *Economics of National Security: Managing America's Resources for Defense* (Englewood Cliffs, NJ: Prentice-Hall, 1957), 522.

7. See Michael Malecki, *Technology and Economic Development* (Essex, England: Longman Scientific and Technical, 1991).

8. See Joseph Grieco, *Cooperation among Nations: Europe, America, and Non-Tariff Barriers to Trade* (Ithaca, NY: Cornell University Press, 1990).

9. See Robert Bowker, *Beyond Peace: The Search for Security in the Middle East* (Boulder, CO: Lynne Rienner Publishers, 1995), 87–108.

10. Simon Kuznets, *Modern Economic Growth* (New Haven, CT: Yale University Press, 1966), 344.

11. See Simon Kuznets, "Characteristics of Modern Economic Growth," in *Postwar Economic Growth: Four Lectures* (Cambridge: Belknap Press of Harvard University Press, 1964).

12. See Knorr, *Power and Wealth.*

13. Kenneth Waltz, "The Emerging Structure of International Politics," *International Security* 18:2 (Fall 1993): 44-79, especially pp. 50, 63.

14. Robert Keohane and Joseph Nye. *Transnational Relations and World Politics* (Cambridge: Harvard University Press, 1972), 374–75.

15. See Aaron Sarna, *Boycott and Blacklist: A History of Arab Economic Warfare Against Israel* (Totowa, NJ.: Rowan and Littlefield, 1986). The Council of the Arab League adopted on 11 December 1954 the Unified Law in Boycott of Israel—Resolution No. 849. Andreas Lowenfeld paraphrased the text of said resolution as follows:

- All persons within the enacting country are forbidden to conclude any agreement or transaction, directly or indirectly, with any person or organization situated in Israel, affiliated with Israel through nationality, or working for or on behalf of Israel, regardless of place of business or residence.
- Importation into the enacting country is forbidden for all Israeli goods, including goods manufactured elsewhere containing ingredients or components of Israeli origin or manufacture.
- Foreign companies with offices, branches, or general agencies in Israel shall be considered prohibited corporations for purposes of the prohibition on agreements or transactions.
- All goods destined for Israel, directly or indirectly or for persons prohibited by the proceeding paragraphs, are considered Israeli goods and therefore subject to the ban on exports as well as transit.
- The Central Boycott Office shall maintain blacklists of firms that license their trademarks or patents in Israel, banks that finance Israeli projects, and ships that call at an Arab and Israeli port on the same voyage. Prohibition against dealing with blacklisted firms is enforced by a self-certification process by firms doing business in the Arab League countries.

Lowenfeld, "'. . . Sauce for the Gander:' The Arab Boycott and United States Political Trade Controls," *Texas International Law Journal* 12 (1977): 26–27.

16. See Albert Hirschman, *National Power and the Structure of Foreign Trade* (Berkeley and Los Angeles: University of California Press, 1980).

17. For example, in 1994, Egypt's and Syria's military spending was 5.9 and 8.6 percent of their GDP, respectively. During the same year the countries' imports of conventional weapons were $1.37 billion for Egypt and $194 million for Syria. See UNDP, *Human Development Report 1996* (New York: United Nations Development Programme, 1996).

18. David Baldwin, "Power Analysis and World Politics: New Trends versus Old Tendencies," in *Power, Strategy, and Security*, ed. Knorr (Princeton, NJ: Princeton University Press, 1983), 17–22.

19. John Rothgeb, *Defining Power: Influence and Force in the Contemporary International System* (New York: St. Martin's, 1993), 173–75.

20. Ibid., 138, 152–61.

21. See also ibid., 168–69.

22. See Jordin Cohen, Alex Mintz, Randolph Stevenson, and Michael Ward, "Defense Expenditures and Economic Growth in Israel: The Indirect Link," *Journal of Peace Research* 33:3 (1996): 341–52; Maen Nsour, *Economic Relations and the Threats of Domination: Israel and the Arab World* (Cairo: Al-Ahram Center for Strategic Studies, 2003) (in Arabic).

23. Cohen et al., "Defense Expenditures and Economic Growth in Israel," 350.

24. Ariel Levité, "Israel's Security Concerns: Characteristics and Implications," in *Confidence Building and Verification: Prospects in the Middle East* ed. Shai Feldman (Boulder, CO: Westview Press, 1994), 192–93.

25. Feldman, "Israel's Changing Environment Implications for Arms Control," in Feldman, *Confidence Building and Verification,* 195.

26. Ibid., 201–2.

27. Taha Abdel Halim, "Regionalism on the Likud Agenda," *Al-Ahram Weekly,* 21–27 November 1996.

28. Ahmed Hashim, "Arms Control and the Arabs' Strategic Environment," in Feldman, *Confidence Building and Verification,* 171, 173.

29. Eliot A. Cohen, Michael J. Eisenstadt, and Andrew J. Bacevich, *Knives, Tanks and Missiles: Israel's Security Revolution* (Washington, D.C.: Washington Institute for Near East Policy, 1998), 131–32.

30. See Hirschman, *National Power and the Structure of Foreign Trade.*

Part 6

Israel Studies Around the World

13. Changing Italian Perspectives on Israel

Antonio Donno,
University of Lecce, Italy

This analysis of Italian scholarship illustrates shifts in Italian attitudes toward Israel and the Arab-Israel conflict from a hollow enthusiasm for the birth of Israel, through a long period of Communist- and Catholic-inspired condemnation and distortions directed against the Jewish State, to a post-Oslo improvement of the Italian attitude toward Israel. While concluding that the field of Israel Studies remains tremendously underdeveloped in Italian universities, this essay highlights the work of individual Italian scholars whose research and publications will serve as the basis for future serious study of Israel in Italy.

Bisera, Olga, *The Middle East: A Bitter Peace,* Milan: Mursia, 1994 (in Italian: *Medio Oriente: una pace amara*).

Codovini, Giovanni, *A History of the Arab-Israeli-Palestinian Conflict,* Milan: Bruno Mondadori, 1999 (in Italian: *Storia del conflitto arabo-israeliano-palestinese*).

Coen, Fausto, *Israel: 50 Years of Hope*, Genova: Marietti, 1998 (in Italian: *Israele: 50 anni di speranza*).

De Luca, Daniele, *Fires Over the Canal: The Suez Crisis, the United States and the Search for a New Policy in the Middle East, 1955–1958,* Milan: M&B Publishing, 1999 (in Italian: *Fuochi sul Canale. La crisi di Suez, gli Stati Uniti e la ricerca di una nuova politica in Medio Oriente, 1955–1958*).

Levi, Arrigo, *Report on the Middle East,* Bologna: Il Mulino, 1998 (in Italian: *Rapporto sul Medio Oriente*).

Nirenstein, Fiamma, *Israel: A Peace in War,* Bologna: Il Mulino, 1996 (in Italian: *Israele: una pace in guerra*).

Segre, Dan Vittorio, *The Middle Eastern Rifle Range: The End of the Arab-Israeli Problem?*, Bologna: Il Mulino, 1994 (in Italian: *Il poligono mediorientale. Fine della questione arabo-israeliana?*).

Segre, Dan Vittorio, ed., *Society and Peace Process in the Middle East*, Milan: Angeli, 1996 (in Italian: *Società civile e processo di pace in Medio Oriente*).

Tappero Merlo, Germana, *The Middle East and the Forces of Peace: 50 Years of Wars and Multinational Intervention in Israel, Lebanon and the Persian Gulf*, Milan: Angeli, 1997 (in Italian: *Medio Oriente e forze di pace. Cinquant'anni di guerre e interventi multinazionali in Israele, Libano e Golfo Persico*).

Tonini, Alberto, *An Equation of Too Many Unknowns: The Western Countries and the Arab-Israeli Conflict, 1950–1967*, Milan: Angeli, 1999 (in Italian: *Un'equazione a troppe incognite. I paesi occidentali e il conflitto arabo-israeliano, 1950–1967*).

I

The birth of the Israeli State on 14 May 1948 did not change the foreign policy of the Italian Republic, itself born in the wake of German occupation and the defeat of Fascism. Italy's new moderate leaders made a definite choice in favor of the West, defying Italy's Communist party, which was molded on the Soviet model and was the strongest Communist party in the Western world. Virtually destroyed in the Second World War, Italy supported the establishment of an economically and politically united Europe to serve as a Western bastion against the Soviet bloc. The Cold War enhanced Italy's alliances with the strongest countries of Western Europe and strengthened its partnership with the United States, which controlled the Mediterranean area—first alongside Great Britain and eventually replacing it as the external power broker in this large strategically vital and politically unstable region.

The creation of Israel in a region which was at that time beyond Italian interests did not cause any particular political agitation in Italy. Political differences notwithstanding, most Italians sympathized with the extreme pain suffered by Europe's Jews during the Holocaust and generally accepted the justice of the establishment of the Jewish State. Since both Washington and Moscow had voted—for very different, even opposite, reasons—for the United Nations Partition Plan on 29 November 1947 and then promptly recognized Israel after its establishment on 14 May 1948, both pro-Western and pro-Soviet Italian political forces welcomed Israel's creation, also for their own reasons. Catholic and moderate-left forces welcomed the opportunity to support a Jewish State in the Middle East allied with the West as a bulwark against Soviet penetration. For their part, Italian Communists went along with Soviet assessments that considered the creation of Israel a blow to British leadership in the Middle East and a potential boon to Soviet interests there. At the end of the 1940s, Moscow's global foreign policy perspective overlooked the possibility of continued regional conflict between Arabs and Jews. But when Israel finally put itself firmly in the pro-Western camp, Italian Communists immediately followed Moscow's lead in embracing the Arab cause. This happened in the first half of the 1950s, and not after the 1967 Arab-Israeli Six-Day War, as is often suggested. Italian Communists did not defect to the Arab side out of any sympathy for the Palestinian cause, but simply followed the Soviet Union's new line in the early 1950s, when Moscow started supporting the Arabs as its proxies against the Israeli "proxy" of the United States. It was the Cold War, and not the Palestinian cause, which made the Italian Communists end the pretense of affection for the Jewish people and Israel.

There was, however, the question of antifascism. In Europe, the massive spread of Communist ideology in the aftermath of World War II by the Red Army, which had "freed" all of Eastern Europe from Nazism, associated antifascism with Communism. One would think that Jews, in particular, should have been grateful to the Soviet Union, champion of antifascism and liberator of the Jews from the Nazi menace. International Communism, and therefore its Italian manifestation, considered Israel's eventual embrace of the West tantamount to treason. This aspect goes a long way toward explaining the negative attitudes of the Italian Communist Party and its various newspapers toward Israel in the 1960s and 1970s, and their sympathy for Palestinian terrorism of that era. To all this, it is necessary to add the strong reservations of the Vatican concerning Israeli control of the holy places and the presence of a Jewish State in the Holy Land. From an emotional point of view, Italian Catholics considered the birth of Israel the right reparation for what the Jewish people had suffered, and the chance to clear their consciences after the Vatican's silence during the Holocaust and the fateful results of centuries of Catholic anti-Semitism. But from a political-theological point of view, strong opposition persisted toward the establishment of a Jewish State in the land where Jesus once walked. Therefore, as far as Italian Catholics and Communists were concerned, the Palestinian problem was "added" to the original reasons that caused opposition to Israel among Italian Catholics and Communists: theological reasons for the former and political ones (the Cold War) for the latter.

For Italian Socialists, the course was partially different. Notwithstanding its relationship with the Soviet Union until the end of the 1950s, Italian socialism accepted with real enthusiasm the birth of Israel and publicly defended the Jewish State during the 1948–1949 war, all through the 1950s and the 1960s, and up to the 1967 war. Socialists considered Egyptian President Gamal Abdel-Nasser a Fascist and an anti-Semite, along with almost all the Arab states' leaders hostile to Israel.[1] It was the Six-Day War and the international prominence of the Palestinian problem that changed, little by little, the Socialists' political leanings. When the Italian Socialist Party split from the Soviet Communist Party in the late 1950s, rejecting most of international communism's experience in favor of a Western-style democratic socialism, it (or part of it) also condemned Israel because of Palestinian suffering, even questioning "Israel's historical legitimacy."[2] The new position of a faction of Italian Socialists—siding with the Palestinians against Israel—can be explained by two factors, namely: the general policy of the Socialist International which, in the 1970s, embraced the Palestinian cause; and the rise to power in 1977 of the Likud party in Israel. The new right-wing Israeli government became the favorite whipping boy of the European Left.

The 1970s were difficult years for Israel's image in Europe and abroad. Many among those who had endorsed the establishment of a Jewish State now showed how their approval had been hypocritical. Israel's overwhelming victory in the war of 1967 gave most of the Italian moderate or left-wing political camps the opportunity to reverse their earlier pro-Israel stance. It was inconceivable to them that the Israelis could shamelessly conquer so much Arab territory. American support for Israel was also a factor in Italy's changing attitude toward Israel. Italians perceived Washington's military and political support as having enabled Jerusalem to win the war, at a time when the Vietnam War—that had caused world public indignation and consequently a wave of anti-Americanism—was at its climax, placing Israel in an even more unfavorable light. For some, Vietnam played a fundamental role in discrediting the Israeli victory in 1967. Public opinion on the left, both Socialist and Communist, did not give up the idea that Israel served as American imperialism's *longa manus* (long arm) in the Middle East. Anti-Americanism, fueled by American involvement in Vietnam's "dirty war," implicated Israel in a general dispute raging among most Italian political parties: the more traditionalist Italian Catholics saw in Israel's victory the triumph of evil; Socialists distanced themselves from Israel; and Communists, following Moscow's directives, actually embraced the Arab countries' position and their most extreme aims. Each party accused and isolated Israel for its own reasons. The Arab states, and unfortunately Palestinian terrorism as well, benefited from the anti-Israeli climate in Italy in those years.

The attitudes of Italy's political parties toward Palestinian terrorism were ambiguous. While various radical-left groups supported the Palestinian struggle even by means of terrorism, parliamentary political forces, also hostile to Israel, condemned terrorist actions even while justifying them as the understandable expression of Palestinian despair. In this atmosphere, Italian public opinion demonstrated a reserved reaction to, or at most a mild disapproval of, violence against Israeli or Jewish civilians. The accusation of unilateral Israeli responsibility for the Palestinians' condition flew in the face of any historic consideration about the origins of the problem, but successfully prevailed over the open disapproval of terrorism and its bloody consequences. Many Italian scholars quickly redefined terrorism as "armed struggle,"[3] while others completely ignored it.[4]

The anti-Israel atmosphere throughout the 1970s and the 1980s discredited Israel for most of the Italian public. The lack of information, biased judgments, and news falsification—together with the reemergence of real anti-Semitism on both the right and left—seriously damaged the Italian view of Israel. Across the political spectrum and with few exceptions, Italian Catholics, Socialists, and Communists of various shades supported the Palestinians and consequently the Arab world in pillorying Israel. Italian public opinion forgot the Holocaust and Italian history books reduced it to a marginal or negligible event in twentieth-century European history, making room to cover the Arab-Israeli and Israeli-Palestinian conflicts, with particular attention to, and sympathy for, the Palestinian cause. Marxist historiography excelled in this cultural operation, which presented Zionist history as the story of a few influential men controlling international power centers, looking for political legitimization in order to dispossess the Palestinians of their property and to establish a Jewish State there. While most of the Western world celebrated the Camp David Accords (1978) and the Egypt-Israel Peace Treaty (1979) as the first peace agreements between Israel and an Arab state, Italian Marxists considered them an Egyptian surrender to Israel.[5] By the late 1970s, a mixture of Marxist rhetoric and Third Worldism, with a touch of anti-Semitism, had come to dominate Italian historiography on the subject of the Arab-Israeli peace process, negatively influencing public opinion and Italian academia.

II

The fall of the Berlin Wall in 1989 marked a turning point. The end of East European communism and the collapse of the Soviet Union dealt a lethal blow to the cultural legitimacy of Marxist historiography. In Italy in the 1990s, ex-Communists (or post-Communists) rose to power, together with some Catholic fringe groups. The demise of Marxist ideology, the legitimization of the power newly acquired by ex-Communists, and the opening of the Arab-Israeli Peace Conference in Madrid in 1991 caused a sudden, somewhat opportunistic change in the Italian attitude toward the Middle Eastern crisis, Israel's position, and the Palestinian question. Although many Italians still considered the Israeli-PLO Oslo Agreements as Yasir Arafat's surrender, Palestinian acceptance of a two-state solution put an end to Italy's most uncompromising anti-Israeli positions and gave birth to a more scholarly, rather than ideological, Italian approach to the Middle Eastern crisis.

A rapid succession of events at the end of the 1980s and at the beginning of the 1990s affected Italian views on Israel. First, the demise of communism deeply influenced the revival of the Arab-Israeli peace process in Madrid. In fact, it is hard to imagine that the peace process would have begun if the Soviet Union and communism had not crumbled. The cultural effects were considerable. In Italy, Marxist historiography suffered a strong backlash, and today, as far as the Middle Eastern question is concerned, a breath of fresh air blows through the world of journalists, historians, and other academics. Opportunism, of course, cannot be excluded. Nevertheless, since 1994 many Italian books have been published whose approach to the Middle Eastern question and to Israeli history is more open and objective, driven more by historical data than by ideology. Some of these recent works adopt a journalistic or geopolitical approach, while others are historical works.

The first group of works includes Olga Bisera's *Middle East: A Bitter Peace,* an interesting collection of interviews of the leading Middle East players, among them Arafat, Muammar Qadaffi, King Hassan II of Morocco, the late King Hussein of Jordan, Egyptian President Hosni Mubarak, Turkish Prime Minister Turgut Ozal, and Israel's former prime ministers Shimon Peres and Yitzhak Shamir. The second part of the book is comprised of analyses of the Middle Eastern question by Italy's leading journalists. Both the interviews and the journalists' contributions paint a picture in which hope and skepticism are mixed. When the book was first published in 1994, the peace process was just beginning, so for journalists and interviewees caution was natural. But one of Shamir's observations regarding the PLO remained relevant to the relationship between Arafat and his people for quite some time after Oslo: "Neither Arafat nor [Jerusalem leader Faisal] Husseini are the legitimate representatives of the Palestinian people. They have never been elected. Nobody has voted for them.[6] Arafat has tried to exercise his power and control which often take the form of terrorism over the local population" (p.132).

The terrorism question is crucial for the future of the peace process, as Peres was well aware: "Terrorism is strong to the extent that anti-terrorism is weak. If we are weak, terrorism grows stronger, because terrorism is a product of weakness, not of power" (p.127). This is one of the reasons for the subtitle, *A Bitter Peace,* meaning one that has only barely overcome some of the merely political disagreements and must still conquer the even deeper cultural divide between Jews and Arabs.

As for Israel, it is a question of "a peace in war." Fiamma Nirenstein's book of that title analyzes Israel's myriad reactions to the peace process, alternating between hope and fear, overtures and hostilities, and confidence and skepticism toward a process that gambles on the future security of the Jewish State and demolishes the old certainties based on the constant need to be on guard against external enemies. Once besieged, in the 1990s Israel looked for long-denied normalcy. Post-Zionists claimed that past discipline and Zionist values, which molded the "new Jew," allow for a peaceful, affluent, "normal" society along the lines of those in the West. But this aspiration clashes with Israel's uniquely difficult and hostile geopolitical situation. Nirenstein subtly demonstrates that, in their pursuit of normalcy, Israelis are actually adopting a political course of action that threatens to create a dangerous gap between reality and desire. The apparent failure of the Oslo peace process and the descent to violence in the second Intifada, beginning in September 2000, seem to confirm Nirenstein's argument.

Dan Vittorio Segre thoroughly analyzes the peace process in his book, *Society and Peace Process in the Middle East*. In his view, distrust and unrest in the Middle East today reflect not only the Arab-Israeli conflict ignited by the "breakdown" caused by the Jews' return to Palestine to establish their own state—but above all by the problems of power and legitimacy prevailing in the five states produced by the Anglo-French mandates (Syria, Lebanon, Iraq, Jordan, and Israel) for whom "the lack of state traditions . . . has interfered with the establishment of strong national identities, turning their foreign and military policy into means of integration and national legitimation" (p. 77). For this reason, the Middle East's main problem—as in the Balkans, the lands of the former Soviet empire and other ex-colonial regions—is not the containment of old conflicts, but the emergence of new tensions and radicalism caused by economic frustration and, at the same time, by collateral issues such as water scarcity, demographic pressures, and the nuclear question. Segre argues that the geocultural obstruction to peace is even more complex than the geopolitical one. In the former, the obstacles to the peace process are rooted in a deep mutual mistrust:

> The most absurd, precarious and paradoxical effect of this mixture of mutual mistrust, violence, anti-democratic radicalism, and political-religious fanaticism, is that, in the end, the Arab-Israeli peace process could be taken hostage by little terrorist factions supported by wide political movements influenced, on both sides, by a deep identity crisis. (p. 87)

Other considerable obstacles are also represented by the social and military gaps between Israel and the Arab countries, and by the advantage conferred upon Israel by its advanced modernization and Westernization (as is also the case with Turkey). Finally, uncertainty as to Syrian policies and stability in the wake of President Hafiz al-Asad's death contributes heavily to regional doubts and fears.

Another important question that emanates from the book edited by Segre is whether Islamic radicalism is the offspring of authoritarian Arab regimes born from nationalist revolutions in the 1950s (Azmi Bishara, "Thought and Reality in the Civilized Society: A Middle Eastern Debate"), or a phenomenon due to Arab disappointment with the failures of the same nationalist regimes (Emmanuel Sivan, "Islamic Radicalism and Middle Eastern Stability," in Segre). This is also one of the main questions dealt with in Arrigo Levi's book, *Report on the Middle East*. This work is based on Levi's report, *State and Prospects of the Israeli-Palestinian Peace Process,* drawn up for the Trilateral Commission.[7] The book draws on the author's journey to Cairo, Amman, Damascus, Beirut, Jerusalem, and Ramallah, during which he runs up against very different realities of today's Middle East peace process. In his analysis of the mixture of peace and war that characterizes the situation, Levi states that peace between Israel and the Arab world could be, as far as the meeting of the two cultures is concerned, the beginning of peace and cooperation between the West and the Islamic world.

The authors of this first group of books put special emphasis on Israel's role in the peace process. Notwithstanding the deep mistrust on both sides, the enormous difficulties of finding a mutually acceptable settlement and the need for reciprocal recognition between the two cultures and civilizations, these books all focus on how unilateral gestures and concessions by Israel can advance the peace process. Previously, Western intellectuals hoped (and expected) that Israel would be more moderate, accommodating, and self-controlled, in order to show, by means of democratic example, a political flexibility not demanded (or expected) of the Arab countries. Today Israeli democracy is similarly asked for a tangible show of commitment stronger than what is expected of the Arabs. This suggests that the authors are applying a double-standard in assessing the peace process—one that puts Israel at a disadvantage.

III.

Since 1994, several historiographical studies have been published in Italy, representing a turning point in the treatment of Israeli and Middle Eastern questions. In the 1970s and 1980s, ideological opposition to Israel dominated Italian scholarship on the Middle East. But since the early 1990s, with the fall of communism and the beginning of the Madrid peace process, Italian historiography seems to have cast off that heavy ideological influence. All the works reviewed in the following section strive for objectivity and accurate analyses of events, and have the merit of consulting primary sources and a wide range of American and English publications.

While all of the books under review deal with the Middle East conflict and the role played by Israel since the end of World War II, each author emphasizes different aspects of the story. In *The Middle Eastern Rifle Range: The End of the Arab-Israeli Problem?*, Segre analyzes the last fifty years of Middle Eastern history in light of the conflict between Arab and Jewish nationalisms. In contrasting the two, the author argues that, while Zionism had a consistent history of forward development and (despite domestic divisions and struggles) succeeded in reaching its goal of establishing a Jewish State in Palestine, Arab nationalism went through much rockier stages and internal conflicts, which retarded its progress. If in the 1950s Arab nationalism aspired to the modernization and development of Arab societies, Segre considers the years between 1956 and 1967 a decade of "wars of a failed revolution" (p. 127). The Arab nationalist movement failed to separate the state from Islam, a standard requirement for the modernization of any society's social structure. From the political point of view, that failure constituted a substantial weakness in Arab civil society, and the Arab states succeeded in establishing only authoritarian regimes which—notwithstanding demagogic statements—were unable to advance modernization or redistribute wealth. Plans for Israel's destruction became those regimes' diversionary tactic, creating a mythology which, for a long time, stimulated Arab nationalism but worsened the social and economic situation in Arab countries. Now, however, most have come to realize that Israel cannot be destroyed, while the social and economic problems of many Arab societies (including Egypt and Syria) become more acute. Arab nationalist regimes are facing deep crises, threatened by domestic radical protests that aim to overthrow them.

Zionism, as Jewish nationalism of secular European origins, was successful in modernizing Jewish life and in bringing to Palestine a set of values, behaviors, mentality, and worldly knowledge of the modern, European variety. The activity of religious Zionists notwithstanding, Judaism as a religion played an important but not fundamental role in the state's establishment. Segre states, "Jewish nationalism . . . had a strong revolutionary vocation and a nearly morbid desire to change, modernize, break with the past. Most of Israel's achievements, energy, and social, military, and economic creativity spring from this frantic need for action" (p. 103).

Though written in a journalistic tone, Fausto Coen's *Israel: 50 Years of Hope* follows a traditional approach from both the methodological and historiographical points of view. His book is a work of political history that analyzes diplomatic and political events in the Jewish State's history, particularly its relationship with the international community and, above all, within its hostile Middle East neighborhood. Interestingly, Coen does not address the recent work of Israel's "new historians," probably because he is after a "classic" interpretation of Israel's history. Although methodologically problematic, this decision probably reflects a strong rejection of decades of Marxist history's falsifications of Israeli history. Perhaps as a corrective, Coen's work offers a more complete and objective presentation of Israel and the Middle East. "But," as Ernesto Galli della Loggia asks in his preface to Coen's book, "can the efforts made to ascertain the truthfulness of facts ever succeed in defeating prejudice? . . . The problem exists of a 20th-century mass enlightenment, triumphing in the West's common thought, which fails to understand features of Jewish history, features which radically clash with its tenets" (p. XII). Despite these caveats, Coen's book, which is in its fourth edition, is a useful and sympathetic account of Israel's history.

The history of Israel is one of a modern and complex country, which has achieved a high standard of living and remarkable social, economic, and institutional organization. But it is impossible to separate Israeli history from the Middle Eastern wars of its first fifty years. Drawing on a rich bibliography, Giovanni Codovini's *History of the Arab-Israeli-Palestinian Conflict* emphasizes that this conflict must be considered both a bilateral and a trilateral one, and that the Palestinian national movement has, over time, modified the original points of contention: "During these last fifty years, the term anti-Zionism has acquired further meanings with respect to the original debate, becoming a catch-all concept covering many subjects and attitudes which conceal forms of anti-Semitism" (p. 80). Over the years, the effect of Arab nationalism has become clearer, gradually assuming an identity and an ideological cohesion based on opposition to Zionism and Israel and trying—through its most extremist factions—to reconcile "the political aim of the destruction of the Zionist enemy with the religious plan of the Koranic Law. . . . To free the Earth of Jews is a religious must. Anti-Zionism becomes anti-Judaism and anti-Semitism" (p. 81). In those factions less bound to religious tenets, Marxist ideology pronounced a similar judgment on Israel: "a fifth column of American imperialism, ... demagogically associated with a reactionary ideology which opposes legitimate human aspirations" (p. 82).

In his book, Codovini weaves together the history of the conflict and a set of fundamental historical judgments on its main cruxes. He also includes a wide documentation of primary sources. This makes the book an excellent starting point for readers who want to embark on a study of one of the most ticklish questions of contemporary history in a relatively unbiased manner.

Germana Tappero Merlo's *The Middle East and the Forces of Peace: 50 Years of Wars and Multinational Intervention in Israel, Lebanon and the Persian Gulf* deals with the role played by the United Nations in the Middle East in the aftermath of World War II. This is an original point of view, concerning not only the conflict between Israel and the Arab world, but also regional crises that had a direct and indirect impact on it. The author's estimation of UN intervention in the Middle East since 1948 is negative. The book deals with international involvement in the Arab-Israeli conflict up to 1979, when the Camp David agreements seemed to usher in a new period of moderation. But this was not to be; in fact, in the following years, the UN became even less effective, unable to accomplish even the task of separating the combatants, an operation that it had accomplished between 1957 and 1967, a period that the author defines as the "Arab Cold War" (p. 95), recalling Malcolm Kerr's classic work on the subject. The book also analyzes the role of multinational forces in Lebanon between 1958 and 1996. What began as a domestic crisis became a regional crisis with increasing Israeli involvement. In the aftermath of Israel's 1982 invasion of Lebanon, the UN sent a multinational force to impose an end to the fighting. Most recently, a "Pax Syriana" has postponed sine die the solution of the Lebanese question. Tappero Merlo's work also deals with the two Gulf wars (Iran-Iraq, 1980–1989, and Iraq vs. the U.S.-led-coalition, 1990-1991) and the UN's role, especially after the emergence of the United States as the only superpower. The leading role played by the United States in the Middle East since 1945, together with the UN's inability to solve the Arab-Israeli and Palestinian-Israeli conflicts, leads the author to conclude that only Washington can nurture moderation and peace in the Middle East.

Alberto Tonini's *An Equation of Too Many Unknowns: The Western Countries and the Arab-Israeli Conflict, 1950–1967* focuses on the role of the Western powers in the Middle East from 1950 to 1967. The book introduces two important innovations in Italian historiography of the Middle East: the inclusion of a thorough English and American bibliography and the use of sound historical sources. Since Tonini's book is based on primary sources, it suggests a scientific approach to the problem. Nevertheless, his personal viewpoint is clearly expressed. The bibliographic selection reveals a critical attitude toward Israel and underestimates Arab responsibilities for the conflict and its resolution—an attitude faintly recalling the ideological biases against Israel of the Italian works of the 1970s and 1980s. Yet, on the whole, this study can be counted among those contributions which, in the 1990s, have returned some academic credibility to the field of Italian historiography of the Middle East.

The analysis of the role of the Western powers following the 1950 Tripartite Declaration focuses on the conflicting attitudes between Washington and London toward Israel, the Arab states, and the Palestinian refugees at the time of the 1956 Suez crisis, in the light of Great Britain's withdrawal from the region and the constant Western concern to minimize Soviet influence there. Tonini argues that an exaggerated preoccupation with possible Soviet penetration into the Middle East proved to be a handicap for the Western countries: "In fact, for many years, Arab and Israeli leaders, aware of the importance their countries had in the opinions of European and American strategists, enjoyed many advantages for their regimes' survival in exchange for only a presumed loyalty to the Western allies" (p. 232). This last statement by Tonini raises again the objectivity criticism. Until the end of the 1950s, Western countries scarcely acknowledged Israel's requests, whereas Britain, in particular, supplied the Arab states with a considerable quantity of arms. Israel did purchase French arms, but the Jewish State was under heavy Euro-American pressure to accommodate the Arab countries. Israel became a strategic asset for the Americans only at the end of the 1960s, whereas the Arab states manipulated their openness to possible Soviet penetration in the region in order to command deep U.S. political and military consideration from the onset of the Cold War. Furthermore, it is historically unacceptable to lump together Israeli democracy and Arab dictatorships, the latter having been rejuvenated by the Soviet Union, especially after every battlefield defeat. Israel's loyalty to the Western powers was not "presumed," but rather founded upon the deep sharing of democratic principles that were foreign to the Arab dictatorships.

Daniele De Luca's *Fires Over the Canal: The Suez Canal, the United States and the Search for a New Policy in the Middle East, 1955–1958* focuses on a watershed in post-World War II international relations: the Suez conflict. This book is the first Italian-language analysis of the 1956 crisis based on primary sources, and as such has the advantage of filling a serious gap in Italian Middle East historiography. Using American, Israeli, British, and other international sources, the author analyzes how the United States gradually assumed Britain's role as the Western power broker in the Middle East, and the resulting tensions in U.S.-Arab and U.S.-Israel relations. The main chapter of De Luca's book deals with a detailed reconstruction of the Sèvres collusion. At Suez, the United States actually sided with Egypt against the Israeli, British, and French invaders, and the end of the crisis—a forced withdrawal of all three from the Sinai Peninsula—served to confirm U.S. hegemony in the region, although without actually preventing Moscow's entry into the area.[8]

IV

The 1990s witnessed a substantial change in the attitude of Italian historiography on Israel and the Middle Eastern question. As if by magic, the fall of communism and the beginning of the Madrid peace process pulled the ideological rug out from under those mainstream Italian historians whose work habitually cut Israel to the quick. With the Italian government actively working toward European unity and the European Union (EU) involved in supporting the Middle East peace process, Italy began paying more attention to the Middle East than in the past, and adopted a more balanced perspective on Israel and the Arab countries than it did in the 1980s.

Two traditionally anti-Israel political forces are no longer playing an influential role. Italian communism, which used to regularly present Israel as the enemy, has become a small party lacking the propaganda and influence with which to condemn Israel as it used to. Most Italian Communists, now part of the governing party with a new name ("Democrats of the Left"), are more interested in participating in the Social-Democrat group in the EU Parliament devoted to strengthening the European Union. This explains why Italian Communists have given up their anti-Israeli position. Whether this new position is sincere is a totally different question. As for the Italian Catholics, they are divided among many different little parties and therefore do not have the political influence to direct the Vatican's Middle East policy as they did in the past.

Despite the outbreak of the second Intifada, the new outline of Italian politics in the 1990s continues to have a deep influence on universities and in the field of history. The time of left-wing (or right-wing) student demonstrations against Israel is only a bad memory. University professors who had been despised and marginalized for their commitment to teaching Middle East history without ideological prejudice are now valued members of Italy's scholarly community. The consequences are important. Although Italy does not have a grand tradition of Middle East academic programs and the few Middle Eastern study centers are of limited scope, important changes have taken place in Italian historiography of the Middle East. This review has highlighted noteworthy new publications in Italian and in the more balanced articles that are appearing with greater frequency in Italian scholarly journals.[9]

Also relevant are the Italian translations of important works concerning Israel.[10] Overall, Italian scholarship in the 1990s demonstrated a more friendly approach to Israel. The "new historians," while causing a considerable stir among scholars of Israel elsewhere, have had little impact in Italy. Israeli scholars highly critical of cherished Israeli national myths, these revisionist historians echo the anti-Israel themes of earlier Marxian analyses, now largely discarded among Italian intellectuals and academics. Their work has been an important catalyst for vigorous academic debate, but only two of their major publications have appeared, to date, in Italian translation.[11] The accessibility of these controversial books to Italian scholars is a necessary step toward the advancement of Israel Studies in Italy, a field that has made impressive strides in the 1990s. But given the demagogic bombast against Israel in past

Italian historiography, Italian scholars newly sympathetic to Israel are understandably not inclined to wrestle with even Israeli self-criticism at this time.

Notes

1. Nasser was considered a "little Hitler" or "a ridiculous little Hitler." Moreover, "the liberation of countries with a colonial form of government . . . cannot pass through fascism." Even the Italian Communists' attack is very harsh: "What we cannot accept is that our own Communists should claim that Soviet support for Nasser springs from the 'Socialist' tenet of peoples' self-determination, liberation from colonialism and semi-colonialism." Piero Caleffi, "Nazi Nasser," *Il Ponte* 8–9 (August-September 1956):1324–25 (in Italian).

2. Giampaolo Calchi Novati, "Middle East: Goodbye to Sharm-el-Sheik," *Il Ponte* 3 (March 1971): 307 (in Italian).

3. Livia Rokach, "The Palestinian Question," in *A History of Africa,* ed. A. Triulzi, (Firenze: La Nuova Italia, 1979), 406 (in Italian).

4. This is the case of Michele Achilli's work, *Socialists between Israel and Palestine: From 1892 to Our Days* (Milan: Marzorati, 1989) (in Italian).

5. Rokach, "Palestinian Question," 414.

6. January 1996 elections made Yasir Arafat president of the Palestine National Authority.

7. Arrigo Levi, *State and Prospects of the Israeli-Palestinian Peace Process,* a report prepared in 1997 for the Trilateral Commission, a private organization founded in 1973 and devoted to the discussion of the main issues of international policy. Levi's report was discussed at the Twenty-first European Conference of the Commission in Aja, Italy, 24–26 October 1997. The proceedings of the conference are entitled *Near East Checkpoints: Facilitating Israeli-Palestinian Peace,* Winter 1997–1998.

8. See also the recent works on U.S.-Israel relations by the author of this essay: *The United States, Zionism, and Israel: 1938–1956* (Roma: Bonacci, 1992); *The United States and the Middle East, 1945–1960)* (Manduria: Lacaita, 1992); *The United States, the Shoah, and the First Years of Israel, 1938–1957* (Firenze: La Giuntina, 1995); *In the Shadow of the Cold War: The United States in the Middle East during the Eisenhower Administration, 1953–1961* (Napoli, Italy: Edizioni Scientifiche Italiane, 1998). (All works cited in Italian.)

9. See, especially, Sergio Minerbi, ed., *Israel, Half a Century,* special issue of *Nuova Storia Contemporanea,* May 1998.

10. Among the most important are Shmuel N. Eisenstadt, *Jewish Civilization: The Jewish Historical Experience in a Comparative Perspective* (Roma: Donzelli, 1993); Eli Barnavi, *The History of Israel from the Birth of the State to Rabin's Assassination* (Milan: Bompiani, 1996); *Israel: From Moses to the Oslo Agreements* (Bari, Italy: Dedalo, 1999). (All works cited in Italian.)

11. At the time of writing, only Zeev Sternhell, *The Birth of Israel: Myths, History, Contradictions* (Milan: Baldini & Castoldi, 1999) and Benny Morris, *Righteous Victims* (Milan: Rizzoli, 2001) [both reviewed by Deborah Wheeler in this volume in chapter 7], have been translated into Italian. Among the more prominent new historians' works awaiting Italian translation are those of Avi Shlaim and Ilan Pappé.

14. Israel Turns Fifty: New Books Published in Germany

Angelika Timm,
Free University of Berlin

Many Israel-focused publications appeared in Germany, in German, on the occasion of Israel's fiftieth anniversary in 1998. Along with translations of Hebrew and English books, young German scholars and journalists produced several original contributions to the field of Israel Studies. This essay holds that while previous German books adopted either a pro- or anti-Israeli stance, this new generation of German scholarship strives for a more balanced portrayal of Israeli society, taking into account its many divisive elements. Among the authors one finds both Jewish and non-Jewish German historians, political scientists, and journalists. To varying degrees among them, however, the burden of the German-Jewish relationship still plays a role more than five decades after the Holocaust.

Bernstein, Reiner, *A History of the State of Israel from its Founding in 1948 to the Present: Religion and Modernity,* Schwalbach: Wochenschau-Verlag, 1998 (in German: *Geschichte des Staates Israel—Von der Gründung 1948 bis heute: Religion und Moderne).*

Bremer, Jörg, and Florian Adler, *Israel—Promised Land and Land of Broken Promises,* Karlsruhe: G. Braun, 1997 (in German: *Israel. Land der Verheißungen und der gebrochenen Versprechen).*

Broder, Henryk M., *The Crazy People of Zion,* Hamburg: Hoffman & Campe, 1998 (in German: *Die Irren von Zion).*

Dachs, Gisela, *Divided Worlds: Israeli and Palestinian Life Stories*, Basel, Switzerland: Lenos Verlag, 1998 (in German: *Getrennte Welten. Israelische und palästinensische Lebensgeschichten*).

Nocke, Alexandra, *Israel Today—A Self-portrait in Transformation*, Bodenheim: Philo Verlagsgesellschaft, 1998 (in German: *Israel heute—Ein Selbstporträt im Wandel*).

Schneider, Richard Chaim, *Israel at the Crossroads: From Democracy to Fundamentalism?* Munich: Kindler Verlag, 1998 (in German: *Israel am Wendepunkt. Von der Demokratie zum Fundamentalismus?)*

Schreiber, Friedrich, *Shalom Israel: News from a Peace-less Country*, Munich: C. H. Beck, 1998 (in German: *Schalom Israel. Nachrichten aus einem friedlosen Land*).

Watzal, Ludwig, *Enemies of Peace*, Berlin: Aufbau Taschenbücher, 1998 (in German: *Friedensfeinde*).

Wolffsohn, Michael, *The Unpopular Jews: Israel—Legends and History*, Munich/Zürich: Diana, 1998 (in German: *Die ungeliebten Juden. Israel—Legenden und Geschichte*).

The State of Israel celebrated the fiftieth anniversary of its founding in the year 1998—an occasion for authors and publishers throughout the world to launch new works on the development of the Jewish State, its history and politics, as well as current problems facing Israeli society. In Germany as well, the anniversary inspired several publishers to significantly expand their offerings on Israel. New editions of translations of Israeli authors such as Amos Oz, Amos Kenan, A. B. Yehoshua, and Sami Mikhael were issued; an anthology of stories and poems, edited by Patricia Reimann, endeavored to illustrate the development of Israeli literature with expressive examples.[1] In addition to fiction and poetry, many nonfiction works, including an abundance of memoirs and travel literature, were translated from Hebrew, English, or French and published in large numbers. They range from Shlomo Avineri's well-known volume *The Making of Modern Zionism: The Intellectual Origins of the Jewish State*[2] in German translation for the first time, to dialogues with Shimon Peres[3] and Teddy Kollek's memoirs,[4] to satires by Ephraim Kishon.[5] Window-shopping in Berlin bookstores displaying books on Israel's anniversary, the observant passerby could discover a new edition of David Ben-Gurion's memoirs,[6] first published in 1969; Amnon Kapeliuk's study, *The Political Assassination of Rabin—Nationalism and Right-wing Violence in Israel*;[7] as well as the splendid volume, *Fifty Years of Israel in Magnum Photographs*.[8] The books featured even included crime novels—sporting the sticker "Israel Turns 50."[9] In addition to translations of works by Israeli authors, publishers also introduced a substantial number of new books written by Germans—primarily young historians, political scientists, and journalists. Compared with the 1970s and 1980s, when books containing extensive information about the Jewish State appeared only sporadically,[10] the spectrum of publications at the end of the 1990s was considerably broader. Many addressed the historical and political development of Israel since its establishment as a state.[11] Interviews provided a forum for the views of Israelis of various political colors, ethnic groups, and social classes. Several authors wrote about their own experiences in the "Holy Land"—impressions gleaned from repeated trips or longer sojourns in Israel.

In the past, books written and published in Germany about Israel could almost invariably be characterized as taking either a pro-Israeli or a pro-Palestinian/pro-Arab stance. Most of the new publications from the 1990s, in contrast, evince an earnest attempt to sketch a balanced, differentiated image that depicts a complex reality. The reasons for this change in perspective are many. To some extent, it was the result of the end of the Cold War and the acceleration of the peace process in the Middle East; but it also stemmed from the increasingly open debate within Israeli society about the future of the Jewish State. Furthermore, a new generation of social scientists and publicists with personal experience with Israel has come of age in Germany; some have studied there and are conversant in Hebrew—and often Arabic as well. Those born after the Holocaust—both Jewish and non-Jewish authors—also perceive Israel from a different point of view than that of the previous generation. Although their books in no way ignore the historical burden on German-Jewish relations, the Holocaust is no longer the dominant point of reference in portrayals of Israel.

Among the authors of new nonfiction are several German-Jewish writers, who examine present-day Israeli reality in a sober and extremely critical manner. For example, Richard Chaim Schneider, born in Munich in 1957, writes in the preface of his book

Israel at the Crossroads: From Democracy to Fundamentalism? that while it is nothing new for him, "as a Jew, to illuminate the problematic aspects of the Zionist state, it is indeed unique to do so for a German readership" (pp. 12f.). Schneider responds to the question, or rather the accusation, on the part of Israeli discussion partners, of "What kind of Jew are you? Instead of living here and doing your share to build up Israel, you write a book for Germans, and then proceed to focus on the bad aspects of the state!" Schneider explains that the primary goal of his book is "to illuminate several background aspects of Israeli politics for a German readership, and above all, to show clearly that the political debate in Israel is much more pluralistic, complex and multi-faceted than is reflected in this country"—that is, in Germany (p. 14).

The 1990s also let us hear more from historians, political scientists, social scientists, and journalists, who analyzed the "phenomenon of Israel" without having any personal relationship with Judaism. Their numbers are increasing, and their primary motivation for writing seems more academic than political. Prior to 1967, those most interested in Israeli kibbutz socialism were supporters of the German political left; this group also expressed political commitment by taking the side of the Jewish State in the Middle East conflict. That changed after the Six-Day War. When the West-German political establishment celebrated the Israel Defense Forces' (IDF's) *blitzsieg* and took the side of the Israeli victors, significant factions of the German left declared their solidarity with the Arab states and with the PLO.[12] Quite often during those years, the books published in Germany on Zionism, the Arab-Israeli conflict, and Israel contained more information about the political attitudes of the authors than about the actual situation within the Jewish State and the region. A similar situation existed in the German Democratic Republic (GDR), whose government strictly rejected all Israeli demands for reparations, took advantage of the assistance of the Arab countries in attaining international recognition of the East German state, and provided both political and military support to the Palestinian liberation movement. In the Federal Republic, differentiated portrayals of Israel were the exception to the rule; but in the GDR, they were completely nonexistent.

At the end of the 1990s, there was a broad readership in Germany with an interest in books on Israel. In addition to members of the Jewish community, which expanded in that decade with the arrival of immigrants from the former Soviet Union and now numbers ninety thousand people, large numbers of German intellectuals—primarily students, educators, journalists, and politicians—became interested in Israeli history and politics within the context of the Middle East, as well as in developments in Judaism and Islam. There were also many people with strong Christian traditions, for whom Palestine/Israel is of central religious significance and who participate actively in the Christian-Jewish dialogue—for reasons that include German responsibility for the Holocaust. Finally, the actual and/or potential circle of readers includes significant numbers of citizens of the new *länder* (states of the former East Germany), among whom there is a great demand for information due to the one-sided media policy in the former GDR; at the end of the twentieth century these people were newly discovering Israel. Given this highly differentiated circle of readers, it is no wonder that many of the new nonfiction books on Israel did not deal with the Jewish State from a scientific or academic perspective; rather, their goal was to impart a wealth of basic information about the country and its people. They focused on those problematic aspects publicized in the print and electronic media, for instance, the Israeli-Palestinian conflict; they also increasingly addressed issues such as the relationship between state and religion, the *kulturkampf,* and changing values within Israeli society. The nine books reviewed reflect this broad-based interest and run the gamut of personal experiences and specific intentions of the authors, which makes each work's substantive content, judgments, and approach unique. Despite the differences among them, however, the books contain some thematic common ground. One can ask meaningfully of each book,

- How does it identify and explain present-day Israel's reality, its intrasocietal contradictions and tensions, and the trend toward a "mosaic society"?
- What role does it give to the relationship between politics and religion, a topic of social urgency and intense debate in Israel?
- What emphasis does it accord to the reality and the legacy of the Holocaust, and within that context, German-Israeli relations?

German Perspectives on Israeli Intrasocietal Tensions

While the books published in Germany on the occasion of Israel's fiftieth anniversary initially focus on known facts in describing historical events in Palestine and Israel, they also include new insights gained by Israeli social scientists.[13] In this context, it is noteworthy that the most well-known representatives of the "new historians," Ilan Pappé and Benny Morris, who are quite controversial in Israel, are cited relatively frequently, while references to the works of "conservative historians" are largely lacking.

The German publications are also consistent with new trends in international literature on Israel: Israel is no longer portrayed as a homogeneous society united by national consensus, but rather as a multi-ethnic and multicultural state; authors no longer gloss over the many crevices that divide the nation and that grow wider every year. This basic tenor characterizes nearly all of the new publications. For example, journalist Gisela Dachs, born in 1963 and Israel correspondent for the weekly *Die Zeit* since 1994, writes in *Divided Worlds: Israeli and Palestinian Life Stories,*

> Israeli society has many facets. The tensions between the left and the right; between Jews of European origin and Jews from Islamic countries; between the descendants of the old, established pioneer generation and new immigrants; between the secular and the religious; between the poor and the rich, seem to have intensified in the past several years. In this young nation of immigrants, a major debate, aside from the still-open future of the peace process, has emerged on who is allowed to exercise political power. In their conflict with one another, however, these trends create a vitality and a mobility which may other societies have long since lost. (p. 10)

Dachs addresses both intrasocietal contradictions and Israeli-Palestinian tensions. She presents eighteen portraits of Israelis and Palestinians who, without exception, were born after the Jewish State was founded. Those portrayed include Israeli-born *sabras,* Jewish immigrants from Russia and Ethiopia, and Palestinians who have returned to the Palestinian autonomous regions following long years of exile. The author's thesis is that, transported to another place, the people she interviews would likely get along very well, and might even become friends. "But because we are dealing with Israelis and Palestinians who are now living in the Middle East, their lives take place in completely different worlds—despite their geographic proximity" (p. 9). With her writing, Dachs attempts to break down clichés abundant in Europe, and especially in Germany, regarding both Israelis and Palestinians. Therefore, she introduces us not only to prominent individuals from economics, culture, and politics—such as pop star Aviv Geffen, the first Ethiopian Knesset representative Adisso Messele, Arafat aide Ahmed Tibi, Palestinian first lady Suha Arafat, and the director of the planning and project division of the Palestinian Ministry of Culture, Hassan Khader—but also to "simple folk" she interviewed, such as a Palestinian from Gaza who works in Israel, a psychologist from Nazareth, the publisher of a Hebrew-Arabic children's newspaper, and other people who have not before been in the public spotlight.

Friedrich Schreiber, the Tel Aviv correspondent for ARD (German Public Television) for almost a decade until 1997, and who currently teaches courses in the politics and history of the Middle East at the Universities of Erlangen, Bamberg, and Munich, has chosen a similar approach to Dachs's. Schreiber's primary thesis in *Shalom Israel: News from a Peace-less Country* is this: Israel turns fifty. A state celebrates itself; but the society is coming irreconcilably apart because of the decisions to be made regarding the fundamental values of *pikuah nefesh* (saving souls) and *shlemut ha-aretz* (entirety of the land), of crucial relevance to peace policies. A people seek a peaceful future, but they are so irrevocably divided on basic issues such as their national security, relations with the Palestinians, and the malicious campaigns of radical forces, that the assassination of a democratically elected prime minister stands as a wretched symbol of their inner disunity and conflict (pp. 10f.). Even in his book's subtitle, the author describes Israel as a "peace-less country."

Alexandra Nocke in *Israel Today—A Self-portrait in Transformation* similarly characterizes Israel as a "strong, democratically-governed state" that is nonetheless "more deeply divided domestically" now than "ever before in the fifty years of its existence." She emphasizes, "Since the Six-Day War in 1967, the centrifugal forces driving Israel apart have been intensifying" (p. 11). Nocke is the youngest of the reviewed authors. She has reworked the thesis written to complete her studies in cultural education at the University of Hildesheim into this new book. In speaking of Israel, she refers to an acute and "dangerous historical crisis," and simultaneously of "a decisive turning point, where decisions affecting the nation's political and moral principles and the shaping of its future, are imminent" (pp. 11, 163).

Henryk M. Broder, who was born in 1946 and who lives in Berlin and Jerusalem, also focuses on the deep rifts in Israeli society. He quotes Israeli writer Yoram Kaniuk: "We are dealing with two conflicts here, and both are insoluble: between us and the Palestinians, and between secular Jews and Jewish fundamentalists" (p. 135). Broder's *Crazy People of Zion* is simultaneously a cynical assessment and a critical reflection of present-day Israeli society. It includes personal reminiscences and views, and describes historical events with ironic comments or biting humor; nonetheless, its casual form should not detract from the underlying seriousness of the author's assertions. On the conflict between the Orthodox and secular movements, for example, Broder quotes a Jerusalem attorney: "We built up the country, and they are paid by the state to converse with God" (p. 41). A glossary, chronological table, and several maps included as background materials amplify the author's presentation. Broder is convinced that the protagonists take perverse pleasure in making history and captivating a global audience with their "never-ending drama in the provincial Middle East." In the end, continues the book's jacket text, those affected may have to pay with their lives.

Michael Wolffsohn was born in Tel Aviv in 1947, has been living in Germany since 1954, and is professor of contemporary history at Bundeswehr University in Munich. Like Broder, his goal is to do away with "legends." His criticism of Israel in the year 1998, and of Israeli policy of the past decades, is motivated by "solidarity and concern," but is set forth, he insists, "with loyalty and a feeling of inner connection," in his book, *The Unpopular Jews: Israel—Legends and History* (p. 14). Sometimes cynical like Broder, but with a more academic approach and underscoring his points with source references, Wolffsohn analyzes Israeli history by delving into the founding myths of 1948, the development of the Jewish State during its first two decades until the fateful year of 1967, and its subsequent transformation into "Greater Israel." In his view, it took very little time for "the pioneering society . . . to gradually [change] into a totally middle class—often petty bourgeois—society whose primary goal was to enjoy life" (p. 307). The author finds particularly noteworthy the "transformation [of Israel] from an Ashkenazi to an

Ashkenazi-Oriental society," which was manifested in Menahem Begin's election victory in 1977; he characterizes this victory as passing the test of Israeli democracy (p. 319). According to his thesis, Israel's Jews are unpopular in Germany and Europe because they are too stark a reminder of the dismal chapter of twentieth-century history, characterized by anti-Semitism, persecution, and extermination. While Germans are entitled to criticize certain aspects of Israel, Wolffsohn also believes that they should simultaneously show more "understanding for Israel's existential concerns and problems" (p. 328).

Jörg Bremer, born in 1952 in Düsseldorf, has been living in Jerusalem with his family since 1991, and has reported on Israel and the Palestinian territories as a correspondent for *Frankfurter Allgemeine Zeitung*. The title of his book, coauthored with Florian Adler, *Israel—Promised Land and Land of Broken Promises,* suggests a discussion of Israeli politics rather than a volume of photographs. The book nonetheless delivers on both counts. Full-page photographs show the beautiful and varied landscape of the country, while portraits reflect the multitude of faces in Israeli society and illustrate the contradictions between Jews and Arabs as well as between Jewish Israelis of European and Oriental origin. The accompanying text does not flinch from enumerating the state's problems, addressing the disillusionment of kibbutz idealism and the conflicts between secular and ultra-Orthodox Jews. But it is questionable whether that antagonism should be termed a *religious war,* even if we agree with the author's statement that the religion of the *haredim* (the ultra-Orthodox) has developed into an ideology that "rejects its secular neighbors, and often despises Jews from the Reform or Conservative movements more than non-Jews" (p. 98). From his own experience, Bremer knows that everyday Israeli life is often overshadowed by terror. He acknowledges the trauma rooted within Jewish history, but emphasizes, "The Holocaust and Arab terror have nothing to do with one another" (p. 99). The author characterizes Israeli sensibilities as "the yearning for security, an instability stemming from vulnerability and pride, pretended gruffness to disguise frazzled nerves;" he characterizes the Palestinians as the "first victims of this Israeli contradiction" (p. 99). The book not only calls upon Germans to travel to this often romantically transfigured land of the world's three major religions; it also inspires the potential visitor to reflect on cold political realities and conflicts concealed behind pastoral scenes of the "Holy Land."

In contrast to the other authors reviewed here, Ludwig Watzal, born in 1950 and a freelance editor and journalist living in Bonn, concentrates less on the situation of the Israelis and more on that of the Palestinians. Watzal, who made a name for himself by publicizing human rights violations in the territories occupied by Israel in 1967, again pleads the case of the Palestinians living in the West Bank and Gaza Strip in *Enemies of Peace*. "A hundred and one years after the proclamation of the Zionist claim to Palestine, and fifty years after the founding of the state of Israel, the Palestinians are farther away than ever before from their own country within the borders of 1967. The same fact that, for Jews, represents the fulfillment of their desires, has burrowed itself into the collective Palestinian consciousness as a catastrophe" (p. 7). However, the author does not limit himself to discussing the effects of Israeli occupation policies. With an equally critical approach, he describes Palestinian human rights violations in areas under the Palestinian Authority (pp.189f.). He also discusses the alliance between the New Right and religious fanatics, the contrasts between Ashkenazim and Sephardim, and the Israeli "historians' debate" of the 1990s.

Religion and State

The complicated relationship between state and religion in Israel, dealt with as a separate issue in recent German books, has sometimes led to confusion. For example, the German press commemorated the occasion of Israel's fiftieth anniversary with comprehensive special sections and series of articles that endeavored to reflect the varied nature of Israeli reality. However, the accompanying photographs very often portrayed a completely one-sided picture to the viewer, confirming clichés instead of working against them. For example, those depicted most often are members of the ultra-Orthodox movement, men with earlocks, black hats, and black coats who seem to have emerged from a previous century. The *haredim* were thus stylized into the optical prototype of present-day Israel. The authors discussed here avoid this inaccurate image, but even their efforts at differentiation demonstrate the relative lack of objective and scientific study of Israeli pluralism in German writing.

Reiner Bernstein, director of studies of the Melanchthon Academy in Cologne, subtitles his book *A History of the State of Israel from Its Founding in 1948 to the Present* with *Religion and Modernity*. He begins his remarks with the following assertion: "A deep cleft runs through the society of Israel. Religion and modernity have become involved in an irreconcilable fight, and the outcome is open" (p. 9). A few sentences later, he states that religious orthodoxy is far from being a closed formation, but that in the State of Israel, "those who put the case for a return to atavism have the upper hand." Unfortunately, this provocative claim is not sufficiently documented in the almost 80 pages of text that follows.

As shown by the Knesset election in 1999, the influence of the *haredim* on political events in Israel is in fact increasing. Secular Israelis fear that the proponents of a *Halakhic* (religiously ruled) state will continue to gain even more influence, which they perceive as a threat to the very foundations of Israeli society. Nonetheless, statistically, the ultra-Orthodox do not represent present-day Israeli society. Similarly, the statement that all religious people are opponents of the peace process also falls short of reality. There are definitely differences of opinion within the religious camp, even among the *haredim*, as both Wolffsohn (pp. 55f.) and Schneider (pp. 50f., 104f.) point out. In contrast, while Bremer does differentiate in his text among the many subgroups in both the Jewish and Palestinian communities, he perpetuates stereotypes by virtue of the gap between prose and image. Misleadingly, the book's photos support the perception of Israel as an Oriental country in which Jews and Palestinian Muslims and Christians all wear traditional dress and dedicate themselves to prayer for most of the day. What we would recognize as "modern" Israel is almost completely absent from the photographs.

Nocke advocates an original view of the state-religion issue. She not only attempts to transpose Samuel P. Huntington's theory from the "Clash of Civilizations" to the Jewish-Arab confrontation; she also characterizes "the cultural struggle between Ashkenazim and Sephardim, between 'hawks' and 'doves,' between the secular and the religious, and between "*sabras*" and the new immigrants, as a clash of cultures" (p. 155). This categorization supports the perception that Israeli society is irreconcilably split into the dyads mentioned above. It ignores the fact that a significant portion of Israel's citizens cannot be classified as clearly belonging to either the secular or the religious poles, but rather describe themselves as "traditional," that is, they observe religious tradition with varying degrees of intensity and consistency and above all feel committed to a Jewish national identity. With respect to the peace process as well, more than a few Israelis hold positions that defy classification as either pure "doves" or unabashed "hawks."

The connection between religion and violence inspires both reflection and discussion. Several authors deal in detail with the activists of the religious right who launched the settlement movement following the Six-Day War, relentlessly opposing any ideas advocating compromise and steadfastly rejecting the peace processes of Madrid and Oslo (Schreiber, pp. 147f.; Schneider, pp. 21f.). However, statements like Schneider's that "[t]here is no basis for discussions between the settlers and liberal-democratic forces" (p. 54) foster the general stereotype—seen in the German media as well—that all settlers are right-wing extremists. The reader is not made aware that some settlers reside in the West Bank not primarily due to religious motives or extremist ideologies, but rather because of economic considerations, and would definitely consider relocating to Israel proper if they were appropriately compensated. Likewise, there is no reference to the fact that some of these nonreligious Jews in the occupied territories often espouse decidedly anti-Arab sentiments. Similarly, religious peace groups such as *Oz ve-Shalom* (Strength and Peace) are barely mentioned, and/or are not considered as an alternative to religion-based extremism.

The Holocaust and the Burden of History

The subject of the Holocaust—the German shadow over the Jewish State—is present in all of the publications under review, either subliminally or directly. According to Reiner Bernstein, the debate about whether Zionism or the Holocaust represents the justification for the Jewish State has still not been resolved; however, he finds the whole discussion irrelevant in the end, "because Zionism was also not able to leave the dark shadows of anti-Semitism" (p. 19). In the section on Israel's foreign policy, the author examines German-Israeli relations and recalls the difficult beginnings in the post-World War II period, the signing of the Luxembourg [Reparations] Agreement in 1952, large-scale weapons sales from 1958 to 1962, and the initiation of diplomatic relations in 1965. He characterizes the relations between the two countries in subsequent years, however, as more of a "business relationship." At times racist and antiforeigner eruptions in Germany cause friction between the two countries, but for the most part, according to Bernstein, Israeli politicians discount these as "a German domestic matter" not targeting Israel (p. 79). That assessment initially seems correct, since German-Israeli relations are in fact guided by political realism and pragmatic premises.

Nonetheless, there is no doubt that, even in the 1990s, the legacy of national socialism in Germany continued to burden relations; the unique relationship between the two states and their peoples is still discernible. The Jewish dimension of German history is evident in the ongoing debates over a Holocaust memorial in Berlin and in the negotiations on compensation for slave labor. It influences German-Israeli relations and shapes the image of Israel in the political culture of Germany. The formal reunification of the two Germanies in October 1990 presented a major challenge for German-Israeli relations. Liberal-democratic circles in both Germany and Israel feared that nationalism, xenophobia, and anti-Semitism would be strengthened and endanger German democracy. Nonetheless, Israel and most Israelis supported German unification despite lingering misgivings. But concern soon reappeared following an upsurge of neo-Nazi violence in the early 1990s: brutal "skinhead" attacks on asylum seekers and refugee housing in East German cities (1991, 1992); the burning of Turkish homes in the West German towns of Mölln and Solingen (1992, 1993); the torching of a synagogue in Lübeck (1994); and the desecration of a number of Jewish cemeteries. The loud public outcry in Israel against these acts of anti-Semitism and xenophobia influenced the political debate and the political culture in Germany. While Holocaust controversies before 1990 had been more or less elite affairs, in the 1990s the broad German public reached a new level of awareness of anti-Semitism and xenophobia. Scholarly controversies about the Holocaust entered a wider public arena than ever before.

Alexandra Nocke addresses the Holocaust issue head-on, and goes into a detailed discussion of the "ever-present past." She seeks to answer the question of the extent to which, in addition to the "ever-present threat" within the region, the Holocaust continues to comprise a fundamental aspect of Israeli national identity. According to Nocke, not only the common historical trauma—persecution, expulsion, and genocide—but also the traditional roots of Judaism are exploited in today's conflicted Israeli society "to compensate for the painful loss of unity and the resulting spiritual vacuum" (p. 45).

While religious people who live according to the provisions of *Halakha* might feel obliged to erect Jewish settlements on biblical sites in Judea and Samaria (the West Bank), an increasing tendency has been observable since the 1980s among secular Israelis to increase Holocaust awareness and "to honor the legacy of the Holocaust as a demonstration of their Jewish heritage" (p. 46). To prove her point, the author quotes Israeli historians and authors, but also interviews some forty Israelis from various social and ethnic groups, generations, and of differing political worldviews.

Nocke points to the critical view of Israeli history undertaken by the "new historians" and/or "post-Zionists." While these same scholars lament the exploitation of the Holocaust for present-day politics, their own accusatory accounts of Israeli history promote a "trend toward losing identity-promoting concepts" (p. 89). There may be some truth in Nocke's observation. Nonetheless, the *Shoah* continues to be a fundamental aspect of Israel's collective consciousness and the Israeli view of history. The claim that it is the *primary* influence on present-day Israeli identity, as made by several Israeli historians,[14] is worthy of further discussion. In contrast, Watzal's theory (p. 282) that Israel's unwillingness to achieve lasting peace is rooted in the fact that the Holocaust still represents a collective trauma for the population of Israel is fundamentally questionable. Watzal fails to provide convincing proof for this theory, which similarly fails to acknowledge differentiated approaches within Israeli society, in particular among the elites.

The often critical discussion among Israelis regarding the purpose of having visiting dignitaries take part in wreath-laying ceremonies at the Yad Vashem Holocaust Memorial, dictated by protocol and highly ritualized, is an indicator of the lengths to which Israeli intellectuals are going in analyzing this sensitive aspect of their history. In this context, Bremer quotes Avner Shalev, Yad Vashem's first director who does not belong to the generation of Nazi victims, as expressing his opposition to the "automatism of the past," while simultaneously calling upon the Memorial to remain a center of remembrance for both Israel and the entire world (pp. 101f.). The Holocaust is also no longer the exclusive point of reference in terms of Israel's relationship with Germany. More and more young Israelis are showing an interest in present-day, post-Holocaust, Germany; the universities in Jerusalem, Tel Aviv, and Beersheva have thriving institutes for the study of German history and culture, and the Goethe Institutes in Tel Aviv and Jerusalem report increased numbers of students and visitors.

More than the other authors, Broder examines new avenues in studying the Israeli-German relationship in the light of the *Shoah*. Some of his highly informative interviews bring fresh perspectives to light—for instance, Broder's interview with Elyakim Haetzni, one of the founding fathers of the Israeli settlers' movement. Ironically, Jewish insecurity in Germany echoes in Haetzni's life journey: he was born in Kiel, emigrated to Palestine with his parents in 1938 to escape the Nazis, and moved to Kiryat Arba near Hebron on 5 September 1972, the day of the terrorist attack on the Israeli Olympic team in Munich (pp. 73f.).

Gisela Dachs's account of Palestinian Nabila Espagnoli's experiences with German attitudes gives cause for further reflection. When the Nazareth-born Espagnoli was studying psychology in Bamberg in the 1980s, many Germans were surprised that she was not Jewish, although she was an Israeli citizen; they also expected a Palestinian to support anti-Semitic attitudes that they themselves held. As Dachs explains, Espagnoli "had trouble with the expectations she experienced so often: that she, as a Palestinian, would automatically have anti-Jewish attitudes. She still hears the voices of Germans saying things like, "Hitler wasn't so bad, and if he had been able to complete his work, you wouldn't be having problems today" (p. 87). While Espagnoli also got to know Germans with other opinions, as a whole she came away convinced that many Germans had not examined the Nazi era from a sufficiently critical perspective, and that the German people had not finished coming to terms with their National Socialist past.

Transitions in German Scholarship on Israel

The nine books reviewed here are similar in that their authors decline to provide conclusive answers to the complicated questions associated with the development of Israeli society. This sets them apart from German publications of past decades, which often attempted to provide simplistic answers. German authors in the 1990s agree that history is an open question both in terms of the Middle East conflict and in the future shaping of Israeli society (see Wolffsohn, p. 328; Schreiber, p. 345; Nocke, p. 165; Bernstein, p. 14). Not only the Palestinians, and not only Israel's Arab neighbors, but also the Israelis are feeling pressure to achieve peace. The future of Israeli society will depend upon whether domestic protagonists can bridge the gaps between them, whether Israel, the Arab states, and the Palestinians can come to mutually acceptable compromises, and whether the parties can move toward genuine regional cooperation. German Middle East specialists are following the current search for final-status agreements in Israeli-Palestinian, Israeli-Syrian, and Israeli-Lebanese relations with much attention and increasing sophistication. Their interest in the subject and their responsible scholarly intentions are important, but are not the only prerequisites for serious research.

Because of the Holocaust, Germans are closely watching Middle East affairs in general and developments in Israel in particular. They search for both general and detailed information on the history and the present situation in the region. Some of them are surely motivated by the feeling that once Israel is at peace in the region and enjoys greater security, Germany can finally relieve itself of some of its Holocaust burden. But there are many others who are genuinely dedicated to Israel and want to bridge the remaining gaps between Germans and Israelis.

The books reviewed here do an important job in presenting Israeli reality, but they represent only a transitional stage in the process of drawing a complete and balanced picture. The next round of books should include results of research done by German scholars in Israel and in cooperation with Israeli institutions. In order to do serious research on Israel, German universities and research institutions must pay more attention to the Middle East and Israel, teach specific courses on Israeli domestic and foreign politics, and provide young German scholars interested in these subjects with the necessary facilities. Unfortunately, academic and political decisions made during the last few years in Germany do not take this necessity into consideration, but show the opposite tendency. Consider the situation at Humboldt University in Berlin. For a time, it was the only German institution that offered an M.A. in Israel Studies, with more than a hundred students enrolled in the program. Its Institute of Israel Studies was closed in 1998. At the Free University of Berlin, the Middle Eastern Studies Section of the Department of Political Science is to be closed when the head of the section retires in 2003. It should be noted that departments of political studies at German universities deal mostly with German and European politics, and partly with American affairs, but rarely with Israel and the Middle East. On the other hand, departments of Jewish Studies continue to do an important job in teaching classical and modern Hebrew, Jewish literature, religion, and history, but they do not deal with the modern State of Israel. While there are several institutes at the universities of Jerusalem, Tel Aviv, and Beersheva where Israeli scholars teach German language, culture, history, and politics and do research on past and present Germany, there is no chair in Germany exclusively dedicated to Israel Studies. If the situation does not change, the only way for German audiences to receive a multifaceted picture of Israel as a modern country in the Middle East will be via the translation of books written by Israeli, American, British, and other non-German scholars. Without any doubt, these translations into German should also be done, but they will not answer the important question of how German scholars approach the Jewish State more than five decades after the Holocaust.

Notes

1. Patricia Reimann, *Israel. Ein Lesebuch* (Israel: A reader) (Munich: Deutscher Taschenbuchverlag, 1998).

2. Shlomo Avineri, *Profile des Zionismus*, Gütersloh: Gütersloher Verlagshaus, 1998 (translation of *The Making of Modern Zionism: The Intellectual Origins of the Jewish State,* New York: Basic, 1981).

3. Robert Litell, *Arbeit für den Frieden. Fünf Gespräche mit Shimon Peres* (Frankfurt am Main, Germany: S. Fischer, 1998) (originally published in French as *Conversations avec Shimon Peres* [Paris: Éditions Denoël, 1997]).

4. Teddy Kollek, *Jerusalem und ich* (translation of *Yerushalayim shel Teddy* [Tel Aviv: Maariv, 1994], (Frankfurt am Main, Germany: Fischer Taschenbücher, 1998).

5. Ephraim Kishon, *. . . und was machen wir am Nachmittag? Satirisches über ein kleines Land* (. . . and what shall we do in the afternoon? Satiric remarks on a small country) (Munich: Langen/Müller, 1998).

6. David Ben Gurion, *Israel. Der Staatsgründer erinnert sich* (Israel: Memoirs of David Ben Gurion) (Frankfurt am Main, Germany: Fischer Taschenbücher, 1998).

7. Amnon Kapeliuk, *Rabin—Ein politischer Mord. Nationalismus und rechte Gewalt in Israel.* (Heidelberg, Germany: Palmyra, 1997) (originally published in French as *Rabin—Un assassinat politique* [Paris: Le Monde Éditions, 1996]).

8. *Fünfzig Jahre Israel in Magnum Photographien* (Fifty years of Israel in Magnum photographs) (Reinbek: Rowohlt, 1998).

9. Ora Schem-Ur, *Mord in der Knesset* (Murder in the Knesset) (Frankfurt am Main, Germany: Fischer Taschenbuch Verlag, 1996); Batya Gur, *Du sollst nicht begehren* (Thou shalt not covet) (Berlin: Goldmann, 1997); Batya Gur, *So habe ich es mir nicht vorgestellt* (This was not at all what I Had Imagined) (Berlin: Goldmann, 1998).

10. Hermann Meier-Cronemeyer, *Kibbutzim-Geschichte, Geist und Gestalt* (The Kibbutzim: History, Ideology and Structure) (Hannover, Germany: Verlag für Literatur und Zeitgeschehen, 1969); Franz Ansprenger, *Juden und Araber in Einem Land. Die politischen Beziehungen der beiden Völker im Mandatsgebiet Palästina und im Staat Israel* (Jews and Arabs in One Country: The Political Relations between Both Peoples in Mandatory Palestine and in the State of Israel) (Munich: Kaiser/Grünewald 1978); Michael Wolffsohn, *Politik in Israel* (Politics in Israel) (Opladen: Leske und Budrich, 1983); Hajo Funke and Christian Sterzing, *Geschichte und Arbeit israelischer Friedensgruppen* (History and Activities of the Israeli Peace Movement) (Frankfurt am Main, germany: Haag und Herchen, 1989).

11. See also Angelika Timm, *Israel. Geschichte des Staates seit seiner Gründung* (Israel: History of the State since its Founding, 3rd ed.) (Bonn: Bouvier, 1998).

12. See Martin Kloke, *Israel und die deutsche Linke. Zur Geschichte eines schwierigen Verhältnisses* (Israel and the German Left: History of a Difficult Relationship) (Frankfurt am Main, Germany: Haag und Herchen, 1994).

13. Reiner Bernstein, Freidrich Schreiber, Ludwig Watzal, and Michael Wolffsohn wrote substantial chapters on the history of Palestine and the political development of Israel during the first decades of statehood.

14. See Shmuel N. Eisenstadt, *The Transformation of Israeli Society* (London: Weidenfeld & Nicolson, 1985), 164; Moshe Zimmermann, "Israels Umgang mit dem Holocaust" (Israel's Approach to the Holocaust), in Rolf Steininger, ed., *Der Umgang mit dem Holocaust. Europa—USA—Israel* (The Approach to the Holocaust: Europe, United States, Israel) (Wien/Köln/Weimar, Germany: Böhlau 1994), 387.

15. Israel in Chinese Scholarship

Xu Xin,
Nanjing University

This essay examines recent Chinese scholarship on Israel as it both reflects and shapes Chinese perceptions of Jews, Judaism, and the State of Israel. As a field of its own, Israel Studies is a new subject in Chinese academic circles. Much of the early Chinese scholarship was written in the context of Communist criticism of Israel, but contemporary Chinese scholars achieve greater balance in their examination of Israeli history. An analysis of the new scholarship suggests a gradual attitudinal change, in government, academia, and among the people, from ignorance and hostility towards curiosity and admiration for the Jewish State.

Pan Guan, Yu Jianhua, and Wang Jian, *The Revitalization of the Jewish People*, Shanghai: Press of the Shanghai Academy of Social Sciences, 1998 (in Chinese: *Youtai Minzu Fuxing Zhilu).*

Sun Zhengda, Zhang Xuan, and Jiang Jiaming, *The State of Israel*, Beijing: Contemporary World Publishing House, 1998 (in Chinese: *Yiselie Guo).*

Xu Xiangqun, and Yu Congjian, eds., *The Third Temple: The Rise of Israel*, Shanghai: Far East Publishing House, 1994 (funded by the National Foundation for Social Sciences) (in Chinese: *Disan Shengdian: Yiselie De Jueqi).*

Zhao Weiming, *The Israeli Economy*, Shanghai: Shanghai Foreign Language Education Press, 1998 (funded by the Department of Education of China) (in Chinese: *Yiselie Jingji*)

Both the Chinese and Jewish cultures are great, rich civilizations. Each of them has had a significant impact upon world history, although the two cultures seldom met. As a result, little was known about Jews, Jewish culture, and Israel in China until recently. During my first visit to Israel and to The Hebrew University of Jerusalem in 1988, I made the sweeping statement that "Chinese find Israel a country even more alien and mysterious than those in the Western Hemisphere." To understand why, one must begin with Chinese knowledge of and attitudes toward Jews, historically, before the 1948 founding of the State of Israel.

The Jewish presence in China can be traced back to at least the seventh century. The Kaifeng Jewish community is believed to have arrived in China in the eleventh century and has resided in Kaifeng ever since, practicing as an observant Jewish community continually for at least seven hundred years. But the fact that Jews resided in China does not mean that the Chinese had any great awareness of their presence. In fact, until the middle of the eighteenth century, Jews were simply called *Blue Hat Hui Hui,* "people who came from the West to China," or *Tiao-jin-jiao,* the "Sect that Plucks Out the Sinews." Both names are based on some customs of the Kaifeng Jews. But not even the most knowledgeable scholars in China had a glimmer of suspicion that the Jews in Kaifeng might represent a larger religious population who were scattered in many countries, held common beliefs, and shared similar lifestyles.[1]

Historically, Chinese society has been quite ethnocentric. China considered herself the Middle Kingdom, which mediated between heaven and earth and was thus superior to all other civilizations. Traditional Chinese education, therefore, did not cover the Western world, let alone a small minority like the Jews. Despite periodic encounters between China and the Western world, academic work on Occidental subjects remained unknown in China for a very long time. The situation began to change around 1840, when China was defeated by European gunships in the Opium Wars and was forced to open her doors to the West. At the end of the nineteenth century and the beginning of the twentieth, Western scholarship became very popular among Chinese academics, especially after they saw the increasing power of Japan due to her open-door policy to the West. For a time, science and democracy became "teachers"—there was even an inspirational movement called the Movement of "Mr. Science" and "Mr. Democracy" in China in the 1910s and 1920s.

Early Judaic Studies in China

Judaic Studies first appeared in China as a result of the deepening of Occidental Studies there, since Judaism is an important source of Western civilization. Information about Jews and Judaism was disseminated through two main sources: foreigners who now were permitted to enter China for missionary, commercial, trade, or diplomatic ventures, and Chinese who had been sent to study or work abroad and who returned to China with new information gleaned from their exposure to the Western world.

Publications in Judaic Studies by Chinese scholars before the 1930s encompass a surprisingly large number of subjects, such as the Jewish Diaspora in China, Yiddish literature, Judaism, Zionism, and Jewish history. However, early writings about Jews in the Chinese language were brief, vague, and often heavily biased. One 1918 article begins: "Jewish people are a mystery. For a long time the Jew has been a symbol of greediness, meanness and shame in our world."[2]

The attitudes of Chinese intellectuals toward Zionism, the Jewish national movement, prior to 1948 were largely favorable. The most important positive statement by a Chinese politician comes from a letter written by Dr. Sun Yat-Sen, the founding father of the Chinese democratic movement and of modern China, to N. E. B. Ezra, the editor in chief of *Israel's Messenger,* an English magazine published in Shanghai, on 20 April 1920:

> I wish to assure you of my sympathy for this movement, which is one of the greatest movements of the present time. All lovers of democracy cannot help but support wholeheartedly and welcome with enthusiasm the movement to restore your wonderful and historic nation, which has contributed so much to the world and which rightfully deserve an honorable place in the family of nations.[3]

Despite the limited knowledge among a small number of Chinese intellectuals, the vast Chinese majority still knew almost nothing about Jews and Israel-related matters. The movement to learn from the West was cut short by foreign interference, Japan's invasion in China in the 1930s, and civil wars between the Communists and the Nationalists.

When the two countries, the State of Israel and the People's Republic of China, were founded in 1948 and 1949, respectively, there were many valid reasons for them to have normal and close relations. Both newly established societies were basically socialist; both faced hostility from the Arab world.[4] Israel recognized Red China on 9 January 1950, making it the first country in the Middle East to do so. All this should have augured well for the promotion of Israel Studies among the Chinese.

But China-Israel talks on establishing formal relations were delayed until after the Korean War. In January 1955, an Israeli Trade and Good Will delegation visited China and signed a five-point protocol, demonstrating China's interest in establishing full and mutual relations with Israel. However, the Israeli government slowed the process to avoid complicating relations with the United States. In April 1955, Chinese Premier Zhou Enlai met Egyptian President Nasser and other Arab leaders at the Bandung Conference of nonaligned nations. Zhou was greatly influenced by the Arab version of the Arab-Israeli conflict, and soon afterward established diplomatic relations with Egypt, Syria, and Yemen. During the 1956 Suez War, China stood firmly on the Arab side, where it remained for the next thirty years.

New China was (and is) a highly politicized country, and political ideology plays a decisive role in all fields, including academia and education. The ultra-leftist policies adopted in Chinese social and academic circles since 1949 made it almost impossible for Chinese scholars to conduct serious academic research in the field of Judaica, especially after China condemned Israel as the aggressor of the Suez War. Because Chinese reports of the Mideast conflict always assigned blame to Israel, the Chinese people imagined Israelis as bellicose, aggressive, and full of martial spirit. It followed that the Zionists' only purpose was to steal land from its rightful (Arab) owners. Israel was habitually defined as "a running dog of the Western imperialist powers."

A major consequence of these abnormal relations between the two countries is that Israel Studies became a suspended subject in China. Direct contact between Chinese and Israelis became impossible. Very few, if any, Chinese publications dealt with Israeli or Jewish culture, society, and life. The limited Chinese knowledge of Israel never went beyond the abstract and superficial, always more negative than positive. Chinese attitudes swung from support for Israel in the early 1950s to a long period of condemnations, distortions, and falsifications directed against the Jewish State—both trends largely a reflection of China's subservience to the line espoused by Moscow.

In 1976 the death of Chinese Communist leader, Mao Zedong, marked the end of China's ultra-leftist political policies. Major policy shifts occurred in almost every field, including the government's attitude toward academia and its foreign policy toward Israel. The open-door policy and reforms adopted by Chinese leaders in 1978 created a more liberal environment for academic studies. Direct contacts with foreign scholars and the availability of their publications stimulated many Chinese scholars to revive previously banned research.

The study of Israeli subjects[5] by Chinese scholars started in the 1980s and accelerated following the normalization of diplomatic relations between China and Israel in 1992. This came in the wake of many contacts, both open and secret, between the two countries since 1979. Recognition of Israel was one of a number of steps that the Chinese leadership felt would improve China's image after the 4 June 1989 massacre in Tiananmen Square in Beijing. In so doing, China was able to play a bigger role in international affairs and avoided the embarrassment of being the only permanent member of the United Nations Security Council to be excluded from the 1991 international Middle East conference in Madrid. After 1992, a large number of books and articles on various Jewish and Israeli subjects appeared in Chinese. The four volumes under review here are the most prominent.[6] Because there are so few books dealing with the subject in Chinese, these books try to cover almost every aspect of Jewish and Israeli life, from the people, their history, politics, geography, economy, and culture to foreign relations and military achievements. Since Israel Studies is a new subject in Chinese academic circles, both scholars and the general public are more in need of basic information than of highly nuanced academic insights. The books reviewed here constitute the early foundations for the development of a critical and scholarly tradition of Chinese scholarship in Israel Studies. This essay focuses on the political and historical context within which these books were written and assesses not only how current scholarly publications may reflect typical Chinese perceptions of Jews, Judaism, and the State of Israel, but also how these scholars contribute to the shaping of popular perceptions of Israel in China.

Trends in Chinese Scholarship on Israel

There are a few characteristics shared by those books under review. First of all, except for *The Israeli Economy* by Zhao Weiming, each of them is a result of a collective, rather than an individual, effort. Secondly, most of the authors are amateurs in the field of Israel Studies, meaning that they lack formal training in the subjects on which they have written, although many are professionally trained in other fields of research. They have jumped into Israel Studies and Judaica largely because of personal interest. For instance, Xu Xiangqun graduated from the Arabic Language Department of Peking University and was involved in the translation of Arabic-language materials for the Chinese army for many years. He eventually realized that the Jewish side of the Arab-Israeli conflict interested him even more, and shifted his research emphasis from Arab to Israel Studies. Yu Congjian was trained as a language specialist in the Western Languages Department of Peking University. Pan Guan graduated from the Department of International Political Studies of China's People's University. His interest in the Jews of Shanghai grew out of his personal contacts, as a youth, with Jewish refugees there during World War II. Sun Zhengda graduated in Economics from Peking University in 1952. His coauthors are similarly "green-horns" in the field of Israel Studies in China, although they have published books or articles on other subjects. Zhao Weiming was a history major who became interested in Israeli affairs after meeting with the first group of Israeli students on a China-Israel academic exchange program who studied at his college in 1992.

Secondly, the phenomenon of books on Israel being written by such "amateur" authors may seem strange in other countries, but it is absolutely "normal" in China. Since Israel Studies is very new in China, no one should expect that China would have trained her own experts overnight. However, the phenomenon tells us two things: Israel Studies is indeed a new field in Chinese academic circles, and there are still only a few Chinese specialists with any formal training in this field in China today. This situation is not ideal, but it is an important start. Thirdly, all Chinese books on Israel start with ancient Jewish history, even when their declared intent is to deal with the modern state. The authors no doubt understand that this deep historical background lays a necessary foundation for the general Chinese reader, although it is redundant to scholars in the field.

Fourthly, all these books aspire "to make foreign things [in this case, Israel Studies] serve China." Xu and Yu's *Third Temple: The Rise of Israel* hopes that Israeli Studies will "benefit us in deepening our reform and promoting our four modernizations" (Pan, p.1). Yu Jianhua, and Wang Jian's *Revitalization of the Jewish People* wants to "draw useful lessons . . . for revitalizing China" (p. 2). Sun Zhengda, Zhang Xuan, and Jiang Jiaming's *State of Israel* aims "to meet the needs of China's reform and opening to the outside world as well as the promotion of China's cultural and economic exchanges with other countries ("Editor's Note").

Those who are familiar with the earlier Chinese scholarship written largely to criticize Israeli policies toward the Arabs will see changes in the attitude of Chinese scholars toward Israel now. Chinese scholars today strive for greater balance and reflect a gradual change in attitudes, both in the government and among the people, from ignorance and hostility toward objectivity and even admiration and sympathy. The dramatic reassessment of Zionism by Chinese scholars is an indicator of changes in their political views toward Israel-related issues. *The Third Temple* is the first Chinese book ever to provide a detailed, balanced description of Zionism. It provides the historical, religious, and political background of the rise of the Zionist movement and its developments and accomplishments at various stages. For the first time, Chinese readers as well as Chinese academics can understand the historical link between Jews and the Land of Israel, and the role played by modern anti-Semitism in the founding of the Zionist movement. Describing Zionism as a national movement of the Jewish people, the book even declares that "China was an active supporter of the Balfour Declaration" (p. 66).[7] The change of viewpoint is even more stunning if we take into consideration the attitude of the same author[8] toward the Balfour Declaration ten years earlier. In his article, "From the Rise of Zionism to the Founding of the State of Israel," Yu Congjian wrote that the British government had issued the Balfour Declaration because it wanted "to use Zionism as a tool to suppress the national liberation movement of the Arabs."[9] Yu argued that Balfour had "defied the national rights of the Arabs and disregarded the fundamental interests of Arabs in order to give the Jews the land on which the Arabs were the majority."[10] Ten years later, although retaining the "tool" metaphor, Yu and his coauthor of *The Third Temple* restate it in more neutral terms, namely, that "great powers made use of Zionism for their aggressive expansion, which was one of the important factors that promoted the rise and development of Zionism" (p. 25).

The issue of Zionism is further addressed in *The Revitalization of the Jewish People,* which is the most comprehensive work to date dealing with the Zionist movement in Chinese. The title of the book reveals the authors' priority. According to them, the "revitalization" means the revival of the Jewish people with a focus on the rebirth of a Jewish State in Palestine. For that reason, the book deals with the Zionist movement within the broader perspective of Jewish revitalization. It reflects the latest thinking of Chinese scholars on the issue. For instance, the authors criticize the "tool theory" after giving detailed background on the issue of the Balfour Declaration, arguing that "the Zionist movement was not at all a tool of the British in that political game. There existed a partnership between the two sides. Each of the two looked after its own needs. . . . Both were winners, if we have to choose" (p. 85). The book makes it clear that the Balfour Declaration reflected Jewish tactical pressure on the British government during World War I.

Another new fact for Chinese readers concerns the role played by the Soviet Union in voting for the partition of Palestine in the United Nations in 1947. Chinese readers used to be told that it was American imperialism that supported the Partition Resolution of 29 November 1947, thus "creating" the Mideast conflict. The new scholarship contradicts this earlier Chinese assessment. Thanks to these studies of the Zionist movement by Chinese scholars, plus Chinese translations of *A History of Zionism* by Walter Laqueur,[11] and *A Hundred Years of Settlement* by Chaim Givati,[12] Chinese academics and the public now have the opportunity for a deeper understanding of Zionism in Eretz-Israel. Nobody would say anymore that Zionism's only purpose was to steal Palestine from its rightful owners.

Another dramatic change is in the Chinese attitude toward the Israeli-Arab conflict. Through the media, Chinese born after the founding of the People's Republic of China grew up learning that Israel was the aggressor. Now, Chinese books hold the Arabs responsible for starting the 1948 war. *The Revitalization of the Jewish People* describes the beginning of the war: "As soon as the State of Israel was declared, five countries of the Arab League—Egypt, Transjordan, Iraq, Syria, and Lebanon, the states surrounding Palestine—began to take their long-planned 'decisive measures' to send their armies into Palestine. Thus began an all-out war between Jews and Arabs" (pp. 201–2). *The Third Temple* emphasizes that the first four Israeli-Arab wars were all "defensive wars" (p. 315) for Israel because the Jewish State was forced to remove the

Arab threat to its very survival. The book further points out that "it does not matter whether it was an offensive war to anticipate the enemy, or a counterattack war to answer the enemy's strike" (p. 315). Though the Chinese government's attitude is still more sympathetic to the Arab countries than to Israel, the political stance of the government has little impact on scholarly studies now.

Israel's political structure interests Chinese scholars greatly. All of the books under review have a separate section covering the election of the president and his duties, the composition of the Knesset and its functions, the working and decision-making procedures of the executive authority of the state, and the judiciary system. The analyses in *The Third Temple* are unique in many ways and reflect original scholarship and the special perspective of Chinese scholars, particularly if we compare it with the bland approach of *Israeli Politics,*[13] a book edited by Yan Ruisong, a professor from Northwest University in Xi'an and the translator of the Chinese version of *My People, My Country*, by Abba Eban.[14] *Israeli Politics* provides a comprehensive overview of Israel's politics, power structure, political parties, history, Arab minority, and future prospects, but seldom with any particularly incisive analysis.

In *The Third Temple*, Xu Xiangqun, the author of the domestic politics section, points out approvingly that "Israel is the only country in the Middle East region that carries out a stable parliamentary democracy successfully" (p. 154). The authors of *The Revitalization of the Jewish People* similarly call Israel a "democratic fortress" (p. 288) in the Middle East. Such comments are unusual for Chinese scholars, since their own country does not endorse this sort of democratic system.

Xu often compares the Israeli political system with that of Arab countries, highly favoring the former. He twice uses the adjective "genuine" to describe Israeli democracy—to distinguish it, I believe, from the rubber-stamp parliaments and single-candidate elections common in the Arab world. He points out, for instance, that "the multi-party system not only means that multiple parties exist, but also that the system allows for these many parties to share in the power of the state" (p. 154). It is possible that Xu means to compare it to the Chinese multiparty system, in which multiple parties exist in name only, while the Communist Party monopolizes state power. Xu also emphasizes the importance of the Israeli democratic system in the establishment of the "special relationship" between Israel and the United States: "Among many reasons that the United States regards Israel as her strategic partner in the Middle East, the most fundamental one is that Israel's values and political system are very close to those of the United States in the eyes of the Americans" (p. 154). Such comments on the importance of common values have never been heard before in Chinese academia, and could make Chinese rethink their country's relations with the United States.

The strategy and accomplishments of the Israeli military since the establishment of the state have also greatly interested the Chinese, military and civilian alike. In the early 1980s, long before China had any formal relations with Israel, a Chinese writer wrote a story describing, from a reporter's perspective, how the Israeli army won its wars against the Arab countries. Millions of copies of that story were read widely in China.[15] Due to Israel's victories in its successive wars, most Chinese know that Israel is very strong; few, however, understand why. *The Third Temple* offers the best military analysis yet by Chinese scholars, perhaps because one of the authors, Xu Xiangqun, served in the Intelligence Branch of the Chinese People's Liberation Army for over thirty years. He is also one of the few Chinese who has studied Israel consistently since the 1960s, although his major at college was Arabic studies. Many of his remarks differ substantially from standard Chinese government comments in the past. For instance, instead of denouncing Israel for an aggressive policy, he notes that Israel's strategy for maximizing its security is to compel the Arab countries to recognize its existence by constantly strengthening its military power, thereby disabusing the Arabs of the hope that they can destroy the Jewish State and forcing them to accept peaceful coexistence with it (p. 280). Contradicting the old picture of an aggressive Israel, Xu portrays the first four Israel-Arab wars—1948, 1956, 1967, and 1973—as "defensive wars" (p. 315). He also believes that the most fundamental factor in repeated Israeli victories has not been sophisticated weapons, but rather the high caliber of Israeli soldiers (p. 315). These views are new in Chinese academic circles, and reflect the increasingly independent thinking of Chinese scholars on highly political issues.

The study of Israel's foreign relations in *The Third Temple* offers a new explanation for the fact that the United States usually sides with Israel in international forums, staving off attempts to push through anti-Israel resolutions. The traditional ultra-left explanation in the Chinese media was that "Israel is a running dog of the United States." In the chapter "Israeli Policy towards the United States," Yu Congjian presents an historical perspective on

Israeli policy toward the United States: its origins, adjustments, and developments. Since seeking great power support was a basic strategy of the Zionist movement, the bond with the U.S. has naturally been one of the basic principles of Israel's effort to secure its existence. His analysis offers readers a logical explanation for how the Israeli-U.S. "special relationship" developed, ranging from the preservation of Israel as a "basic tenet" of American foreign policy, to Israel as a "strategic asset," to a "major non-NATO ally" for various American administrations. The common values and similar political systems emerge as the solid foundation for the "strategic partnership" between the two countries, putting to rest at last the old characterization of Israel as an American "running-dog." The book also cites the positive role played by American Jewry in promoting the "special relationship" between the Jewish State and America. The authors believe that the outstanding status of Jews in American political life is one of the most important factors in getting much-needed support for Israel. *The Revitalization of the Jewish People* believes that U.S.-Israel friendship is bolstered by a supportive Jewish community as well as by a generally supportive wide segment of American society.

All four books under review address the subject of Israel's foreign policy toward China. *The Third Temple* examines that policy from a historical viewpoint, noting that Israel was the first country in the Middle East and one of the few non-Communist nations in the world to recognize Communist China (p. 473). Israel's move was very valuable to China, then struggling for recognition from the international community. The Israeli initiative also brought the two countries, both hated by the Arab/Muslim world, closer at that time. (In the early 1950s, Arab fears of "godless" communism extended to China as well as to the Soviet Union.) In addition, Israel did not have the major obstacle faced by many other countries in establishing diplomatic ties with China, since Israel had never tried to develop political relations with Taiwan (although there were trade and business relations between the two.) *The Third Temple* also examines objectively the two opinions regarding Israeli policy toward China in the 1950s. Prime Minister David Ben-Gurion advocated establishing diplomatic relations with China as soon as possible, whereas Foreign Minister Moshe Sharett favored a more cautious approach, so as not to harm Israel-U.S. relations. The author notes sympathetically that, with Israel's security at stake, it was understandable that Israel's leaders were of two minds (p. 474).

The Revitalization of the Jewish People includes a well-researched, documented survey on the evolution of Israel-China relations. The best part deals with the post-Korean War period, in which the author describes the circumstances that interfered with efforts on both sides to establish normal relations in the wake of Israel's recognition of China. A chronology of official Chinese government statements allows readers to follow China's changing attitudes toward relations with Israel, and shows that, while Israel acted more independently in determining policy toward China, the latter was restricted in developing relations with Israel by virtue of being locked into a pro-Arab posture since Suez. In a remarkable criticism of China's rigid ultra-left foreign policy, the authors explain that it became increasingly difficult for China to respond to various Israeli initiatives during the 1960s and 1970s (p. 317). Chinese scholars praised the establishment of full diplomatic relations between the two countries in 1992. Pan's book hails that event for opening "a complete new page in relations between the two countries: China and Israel, and two peoples: Chinese and Jewish" (p. 320). *The Third Temple* declares that "the establishment of normal relations between China and Israel ushers in a broad prospect for exchanges in the fields of science and technology, economy and trade, and culture" (p. 476).

The achievements of the Israeli economy since independence impress the Chinese a great deal. As economic development and activities play an increasing role in Chinese society, Chinese scholars pay close attention to the Israeli economy in their books. Xu and Yu have a separate section devoted to the subject. Pan, Yu, and Wang have a chapter entitled "Economic Miracle in the Desert." Sun, Zhang and Jiang also devote a chapter to the Israeli economy, covering trade and economic relations between China and Israel; the book even offers a number of "rules" and "anecdotes" for doing business with Israelis.

By far best treatment of this issue is Zhao Weiming's *Israeli Economy*. This book deals with no other subject but Israel's economy. Zhao uses updated data from authoritative sources (Israeli Central Bureau of Statistics, March 1998), and offers a concise analysis based on concrete data. The value of the discussion lies in its focus not only on the achievements of Israeli economic policy but also on its problems over 50 years of statehood. This method makes the study more valuable to Chinese academics. The purpose of the book, as the author puts it, is as follows: "Stones from other hills may serve to polish the jade from this one. We hope that the study of the achievements and problems of the Israeli economy and a discussion of the success and failures of Israeli economic policies will provide useful advice and lessons for our socialist economy" (preface). The discussion of economic cooperation between China and Israel in Chapter 12 describes the close economic relations between the two countries since the establishment of bilateral political ties and shows bright prospects for the twenty-first century. Zhao's book is no doubt the most comprehensive single book on the Israeli economy ever written by a Chinese scholar.

Religion is not discussed extensively by the books under review here, although all mention briefly Judaism's role in daily life in Israeli society. *The Third Temple* treats it as part of Israeli politics. *The Revitalization of the Jewish People* mentions the religious impact on domestic affairs, as in the determination of who is a Jew, the assimilation of Jewish rituals into national daily life, and the organization of Jewish education. The best single study of Jewish religion by a Chinese scholar is *Cactus in the Desert: A Sketch of the Jews* by Xu Xiangqun.[16] Xu, who is also one of the editors of *The Third Temple* reviewed here, devotes several pages of *Cactus in the Desert* to the question, "What is Judaism?"[17]

Cultural life in Israel has not been forgotten by Chinese scholars. *The Third Temple* has a separate section on Jewish culture. In addition to summaries of the literary achievements of Jews through the ages, it gives extensive coverage to all fields of Israeli culture, including literature, fine arts, music, dance, theater, cinema, museums, and media. The importance of this broad treatment becomes clear when we remember that, except for the Chinese version of the *Encyclopedia Judaica,* few books written by Chinese deal with Hebrew literature or artistic expression.

Aware of the recent increasing popular Chinese curiosity about Jews and Israel, Chinese publishers are now interested in publishing relevant books. Aside from many translations of Hebrew and English books written by Jewish authors,[18] there are a few by Chinese authors. *The State of Israel* is one such book. Books of this type are written for the general public rather than for those in academia. Sun, Zhang and Jiang's volume is part of the thirty-volume "Nations of the World" series, published by The Contemporary World Publishing House, one country per volume. Senior editor Sun Zhengda, a well-known Chinese scholar with many national prize-winning books to his credit, now serves as editor in chief of this series. Each title is designed to serve as "a comprehensive survey of an individual country, integrating geography, history, nationality, economy, society, culture, customs and traditions in one volume" ("Editor's Note"). The purpose is to help Chinese become familiar with the condition of the country under survey. Although the self-declared aim of *The State of Israel* is "to satisfy intellectual, recreational, practical and academic interests" and it is "written in prose which lends itself to smooth reading" ("Editor's Note"), its tone suggests that its primary goal is to satisfy recreational interest first and foremost.

None of three authors of *The State of Israel* has previously published in the field of Israel Studies in China, and, not surprisingly, they have borrowed heavily from other books. They rely, for instance, on both the Chinese version of the *Encyclopedia Judaica* and *The Third Temple,* thereby signaling the important contributions of scholars such as the author of this essay[19] and Xu Xiangqun to the shaping of popular perceptions of Israel in China. The book functions well as a popular reader for a general audience because it provides detailed information about daily life and customs in Israel in a single volume. While it lacks academic value from a scholarly point of view, lay readers who want more sophisticated treatment will find its list of sources fair and useful. It covers a wide range of topics, including entertaining anecdotes.

Ora Namir, then Israel's ambassador to China, contributed the preface to *The State of Israel*, affirming that the book "offers a comprehensive look at various aspects and characteristics of Israel: history, politics, geography, economy and culture" (p. 4). Besides Israeli customs and etiquette, the most interesting new information provided by the book is the description of Israel's historical sites for tourists, relying on guidebooks published by Israel's Ministry of Tourism. This may attract potential Chinese tourists to Israel, which *The State of Israel* depicts as a normal, safe country with its own distinctive customs and traditions.

Newfound Chinese Interest in Israel

Although the state of books on Israel published in Chinese in the last ten years leaves much to be desired, the books under review here do serve several important purposes. To varying degrees, they address new developments in Israel and provide a more balanced picture of Israeli society today. Moreover, they have laid a solid foundation for a better understanding of Israel and Israeli culture, which is extremely important for the future of friendly relations between Israel and China. They are also the cornerstones of serious scholarly attention to Israel Studies in China, an academic field now only in its infancy.

What has brought about this newfound Chinese interest in Israel? Among the many plausible reasons, the following three are most important.

China's New Willingness to Meet the West

Only in the late 1970s, after the death of Communist chief Mao Zedong, did China begin to realize that her backwardness and poverty were largely caused by her self-isolation. "Go to the World" became a slogan for modernization. It was understood that China has first to understand the West if she wants to meet the West. Great efforts have been made to learn about the West. As a result, Occidental Studies have become a popular subject once again in China. Confucius, the great Chinese sage of the sixth century B.C.E., once said, "Do not worry about people not understanding you, but worry about not understanding people" (Analects 1:16).[20] Jewish and Israel Studies have benefited as subsets of such learning, since Jewish culture is one of the major sources of western civilization. The slogan "Not to understand Jewish culture is not to understand the world" is actually the informal motto of the Judaic Studies circle in China.[21]

The Awakening of Chinese Intellectuals

Intellectuals are beginning to appreciate the value of independent thought. The first group of Chinese scholars who visited Israel before 1992 believed it was important to see Israel and to make their own assessments. To some extent, they risked their careers by doing so, but none of them hesitated when the opportunity to go to Israel arose. These and other visits brought back firsthand knowledge and information about Israel, which, in due course, is replacing dated and stereotypical perceptions of Israel and its people. Those who pursued Israel Studies in the 1980s should similarly be regarded as courageous pioneers. Their awakening made it possible for the authors under review here to air their own views on Israeli topics.

Appreciation of the Value of Jewish Culture

Chinese scholars and the Chinese public have developed a positive appreciation for the value of Jewish culture. Chinese who had early contacts with Jews realized that Jewish culture is like a rich mine of human society, whose contents contain much valuable inspiration and wisdom for the Chinese. For instance, Dr. Sun Yat-sen made references to Jews several times in his famous lecture series "On the Three People's Principles." Chinese nationalism, he declared,

> disappeared because the Chinese nation was subjugated and the country was conquered by foreigners [referring to the Manchus who had ruled China since 1644, when they defeated and replaced the Ming Dynasty]. But China was not the only nation which had been conquered. The Jewish people also lost their country. . . . Though their country was destroyed, the Jewish nation exists to this day. . . . What is the answer that other nations, such as the Jews, lost their country two thousand years ago, but their nationalism still exists; while our China was conquered only three hundred years ago, but Chinese nationalism has entirely disappeared?[22]

The same issue was addressed by the well-known Chinese intellectual in the 1930s, Yu Songhua, who also hoped to draw inspiration from the Jewish experience. "What can we," he asked, "looking at Jews, question about ourselves?"

> From ancient time to the present, prominent figures have come forth in large numbers among the Jews, while we have only some great figures in our history but have no outstanding personage in modern times. We should feel ashamed, compared with the Jews, as well as facing our own ancestors. . . .
>
> The Jews are a people without country and a people who have been despised everywhere, but they are still struggling very hard, never discouraged by difficulties and setbacks, to carry on the restoration movement. So those peoples who have their own countries should strive even harder and resolve to make their countries strong. . . . If our Chinese fellow-countrymen could have the same enthusiasm and determination that the Jews displayed in their resurgent movement, to exploit our natural resources and to

> promote our national culture, I believe our achievements would be much greater than those of the Jews.[23]

Those were forerunners in the first half of the twentieth century who took a very positive attitude toward Jews and Jewish culture. Since the 1980s, a new generation of Chinese scholars has had a similar experience. In 1993, I myself wrote in the preface to the Chinese version of the *Encyclopedia Judaica,*

> As we enter the 21st century, the Chinese are facing a challenge to move towards a more active world role. To understand Jewish culture is an essential step in preparation for the challenge before us, because the whole world has been stirred by Jewish thought. Virtually no civilization has been untouched, no history of western civilization can be recounted, without considering the Jewish component: what Jews have thought, felt, written and achieved. Not to understand the Jewish culture is not to understand the world. Not to understand our fellow man is ultimately not to understand ourselves.[24]

Gu Jun, the author of *Jewish Wisdom,* believes that "Chinese people could find in Jewish wisdom some important substance to make up for their deficiency, to improve themselves, and to perfect themselves."[25] Liu Hongyi, author of *The Jewish Spirit*, writes,

> In the past several thousand years, the Jewish people have been migrating from the regions of the Middle East and dispersing throughout the world. They have developed a great many complicated and unintelligible [*sic,* in orig.] cultural facts. Struggling between cultures of alien nations, the Jews have not only preserved completely their age-old traditions but also accomplished the rebirth of the national culture within the conflict and fusion with other cultures. With their extraordinary success in the social and cultural fields, the Jews have made outstanding contributions to human civilization, which have exerted a profound influence on the whole world.
>
> The Jewish people have cultivated and promoted the unique Jewish spirit in the tortuous historical process of the cultural development. And Jewish culture has compressed many universal rules of cultural development.[26]

Gu Xiaoming, editor in chief of the *Series on Jewish Culture,* underscores the significance and importance for Chinese to study Jewish culture, arguing that Jewish culture, which started some four thousand years ago, has not only developed fully through its contacts and integration with various cultures worldwide, but also retains its continuity and many characteristics of the original culture. It is perhaps the only culture that can be compared academically with Chinese culture.[27]

With scholars asserting such strong ideas, it is no wonder that Israel Studies—which is inseparable from Jewish Studies—in China has picked up speed. The post-1992 development of Chinese-Israeli relations has brought the two nations closer than ever before. Political contacts, cultural exchanges, and economic cooperation have reached new heights. In contrast to ten years ago, when only a few books were available (and, even then, provided largely distorted information on Israeli society and politics), the interested Chinese reader can now find a broad spectrum of respectable publications about Israel. With the establishment of diplomatic relations between China and Israel, the Chinese media, and especially Chinese scholars, have taken a more "benevolent" position toward Israel. Chinese knowledge of Israel and her history and culture has already broadened beyond the abstract and superficial. The advancement of Israel Studies in China has been great and the impact on Chinese academia has been strong. But there is still a long way to go and much to be done. Chinese scholars need to deepen their study of, and research in, Israel. It is imperative for Chinese scholars to upgrade their studies to meet international standards. How to continue to improve their scholarship in general, and how to make unique contributions to the scholarly study of Israeli subjects in particular, are the challenges currently faced by Chinese scholars. I believe that Chinese scholars will not only meet these challenges with customary courage, but will also produce fruitful results of value to their colleagues in Israel Studies the world over.

Notes

Sources in Chinese unless otherwise noted.

1. Hong Jun, a well-known Chinese historian, an envoy of the Qing Dynasty to Europe in the late nineteenth century, and the author of the

first scholarly essay about the Jews of Kaifeng a hundred years ago, wrote, "I learned from the Westerners that are now in Kaifeng of Henan, China, that there are still Jews [there]." See his "A Study of the Names of Religions in Yuan Period," *Annotations to the Chinese Translation of the Yuan Annuals* 29 (1897): 1.

2. Jun Shi, "The Future of Jewish People," *Oriental Magazine* 15:10 (1918): 45.

3. Sun Yat-Sen, "To N.E.B. Ezra," *The Collected Works of Sun Yat-Sen* (Beijing: Zhonghua Shujiu Publishing House, 1985), 5:256–57.

4. On the basis of their UN votes on the China issue and their refusal to recognize Communist China, the Arab regimes impressed the Chinese government as subservient to Western imperialism and hostile toward Communism and the New China.

5. So far there is no distinction between Israel Studies and Jewish Studies in China.

6. Two earlier books about Israel are Da Zhou et al., *Israel in the Eyes of Chinese People* (Beijing: Xinhua Publishing House, 1990), and Yang Mansu, ed., *Israel: A Mysterious Country* (Beijing: World Knowledge Publishing House, 1992).

7. Evidence for this claim is a December 1918 letter from the Chinese foreign ministry to Lord Kadoorie endorsing the Balfour Declaration, and the letter of Dr. Sun Yat-Sen, cited in *Collected Works of Sun Yat-Sen.*

8. The section on Zionism was written by Yu Congjian.

9. Yu Congjian, "From the Rise of Zionism to the Founding of the State of Israel," *Materials about West Asia and North Africa* 18 (1984): 12.

10. Ibid.

11. Walter Laqueur, *A History of Zionism,* trans. Xu Fang and Yan Ruisong (Shanghai: Sanlian Publishing House, 1992).

12. Chaim Givati, *A Hundred Years of Settlement,* trans. He Daming (Beijing: Publishing House of the Chinese Social Sciences, 1996).

13. *Israeli Politics,* ed. Yan Ruisong (Xi'an, China: Northwest University Press, 1995).

14. *History of the Jews* (*Youtai Shi*), trans. Yan Ruisong (Beijing: China Social Sciences Publishing House, 1986). This is the Chinese translation of Abba Eban's *My People, My Country.*

15. See Liu Yazhou, *Middle East Wars,* a pamphlet issued by the Military Publishing House in Beijing, 1982.

16. Xu Xiangqun, *Cactus in the Desert: A Sketch of the Jews* (Beijing: Xinhua Press, 1998).

17. Ibid., 111–24.

18. Books about Yitzhak Rabin published by different Chinese publishers in last three years include Yang Mansu, *Yitzhak Rabin* (Chendu: Sichuan People's Publishing House, 1997); Li Guangbing, *Rabin: Sacrifice of the Peace Process* (Changchun, China: Changchun Publishing House, 1997); Lei Yu, *A Biography of Yitzhak Rabin* (Beijing: Oriental Press, 1998).

19. The Chinese version of the *Encyclopedia Judaica,* eds. Xu Xin and Lin Jiyiao (Shanghai: Shanghai People's Publishing House, 1993) is the major Chinese-language reference book on Jewish culture by Chinese.

20. *The Confucian Bible Book 1. Analects,* English and Modern Chinese versions authored, compiled, and edited by John B. Khu, Vicente B. K. Khu, William B. S. Khu, and Jose B. K. Khu (Beijing: World Affairs Press, 1997).

21. The China Judaic Studies Association was founded in 1989 to promote the study of Jewish subjects among Chinese. The author of this essay, Xu Xin, is its founder and current president. Its Website is *http://servercc.oakton.edu/~friend/chinajews.html.* There are many other organizations such as the Shanghai Judaic Studies Association, the Shanghai Center for Judaic and Israeli Studies, and the Beijing Center for Jewish Studies.

22. Sun Yat-Sen, "On the Three People's Principles," Lecture Three, *Selected Works of Sun Yat-Sen* (Beijing: People's Publishing House,1956), 620–21.

23. Yu Songhua, "Jews and Jewish Resurgent Movement," *Oriental Magazine* 24: 17 (1924): 25.

24. Xu Xin, *Encyclopedia Judaica,* ii-iii.

25. Gu Jun, *Jewish Wisdom* (Hangzhou: Zhejiang People's Publishing House, 1995), 6.

26. Liu Hongyi, "Abstract," *The Jewish Spirit* (Nanjing, China: Nanjing University Press, 1995).

27. Gu Xiaoming, "Preface for a Series on Jewish Culture," appearing in each book of the series (Shanghai: Sanlian Shudian, 1991), 1.

Notes on the Contributors and the Editors

The Contributors

Khawla Abu Baker is a Lecturer in the Women's Studies and Behavioral Sciences Departments at Emek Yezreel College, Israel, and Director of the "Mar'ah" Institute for Middle East Women's Studies. Email: khawlaa@yvc.ac.il

Ruth Amir is a Lecturer in the Department of Political Science at Emek Yezreel College, Israel. Email: rutha@yvc.ac.il

Mordechai Bar-On is a Research Fellow at Yad Ben-Zvi in Jerusalem. Email: YBenZvi@h2.hum.huji.ac.il

Rachel Feldhay Brenner is a Professor of Hebrew Literature in the Department of Hebrew and Semitic Studies at the University of Wisconsin-Madison. Email: brenner@wisc.edu

Antonio Donno is a Professor of North American History at the University of Lecce, Italy. Email: andonno@ilenic.unile.it

Motti Golani is a Senior Lecturer in, and Chair of, the Department of Israel Studies at the University of Haifa. Email: golani@research.haifa.ac.il

Amal A. Jamal is a Lecturer in the Political Science Department of Tel Aviv University. Email: ajamal@post.tau.ac.il

Benny Morris is a Professor in the History Department of Ben-Gurion University of the Negev. Email: Bennymo@bgumail.bgu.ac.il

Ilham Nasser is an Assistant Professor of Early Childhood/Elementary Education, School of Education, Trinity College, Washington D.C. Email: nasseri@trinitydc.edu

David Newman is a Professor of Political Geography and is Chair of the Department of Politics and Government at Ben-Gurion University of the Negev, Israel. Email: newman@bgumail.bgu.ac.il

Maen F. Nsour is Regional Programme Adviser, Regional Bureau for Arab States, United Nations Development Programme. Email: maen.nsour@undp.org

Leah Rosen is a Lecturer in the Department of Political Science at Emek Yezreel College, Israel. Email: leahr@yvc.ac.il

Stephen Schecter is a writer and Professor of Sociology at the Université du Québec à Montréal. Email: schecter.stephen@uqam.ca

Mira Sucharov is an Assistant Professor of Political Science at Carleton University in Ottawa, Canada. Email: Mira_Sucharov@carleton.ca

Ephraim Tabory is Deputy Chair and Director of the Graduate Studies Program of the Department of Sociology at Bar Ilan University, Israel. Email: tabore@mail.biu.ac.il

Angelika Timm teaches in the Department of Political Science at the Free University, Berlin. Email: Angtimm@zedat.fu-berlin.de

Deborah L. Wheeler is a Lecturer at the University of Washington. Email: wheelerd@u.washington.edu

Xu Xin is a Professor of the History of Jewish Culture and Director of the Center for Jewish Studies at Nanjing University. Email: xuxin49@jlonline.com

The Editors

Mohammed Abu-Nimer is an Assistant Professor at the School of International Service at American University in Washington DC. Email: abunim@american.edu

Neil Caplan teaches in the Humanities Department, Vanier College, and holds an adjunct position in the History Department, Concordia University, Montréal, Canada. Email: caplann@vaniercollege.qc.ca

Laura Zittrain Eisenberg is a Visiting Associate Professor in the History Department at Carnegie Mellon University. Email: le3a@andrew.cmu.edu

Naomi B. Sokoloff is a Professor at the University of Washington, where she teaches Hebrew language and literature and Israeli culture. Email: naosok@u.washington.edu